PATROL INSPECTOR

THE COMPLETE STUDY GUIDE FOR SCORING HIGH

PATROL INSPECTOR

By

DAVID R. TURNER, M.S. in Ed.

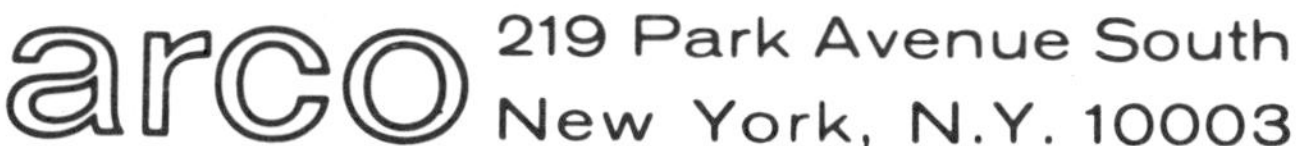

219 Park Avenue South
New York, N.Y. 10003

Fourth Edition (B-940)
First Printing, 1977

Published by Arco Publishing Company, Inc.
219 Park Avenue South, New York, N. Y. 10003

Library of Congress Catalog Card Number 72-1775
ISBN 0-668-04301-6

Printed in the United States of America

CONTENTS

HOW TO USE THIS INDEX
Slightly bend the right-hand edge of the book. This will expose the corresponding Parts which match the index, below.

PART

WHAT THIS BOOK WILL DO FOR YOU 9

How this book was prepared; what went into these pages to make them worth your while. How to use them profitably for yourself in preparing for your test. The essentials of successful study.

1

2

3

PART ONE

APPLYING AND STUDYING FOR YOUR JOB

AN OFFICIAL ANNOUNCEMENT 13

Facts that foreshadow your test and help you do your best.

EXAMINATION FORECAST 19

Samples of each type of question slated for the test. Forewarned is forearmed with this priceless preview. Plan your study time accordingly.

DUTIES OF THE JOB 24

Information and explanations limited to what you may expect to be asked on the test.

APPLYING FOR FEDERAL JOBS 29

Job openings . . . the job announcement . . . United States Civil Service regions . . . The application form . . . The government tests you.

THE FEDERAL JOB ANNOUNCEMENT 31

What you do with it. What it tells you. Meeting the requirements. Facts that foreshadow your test.

THE GOVERNMENT TESTS YOU 33

The kinds of examinations given, and how you are rated.

WORKING FOR THE U.S. 35

Salary and working conditions: pay rates, hours, advancement, transfers, efficiency incentive awards, vacation and sick leave, injury compensation, group life insurance, health benefits, retirement, layoffs, unemployment compensation, severance pay, employee organizations, additional information.

STUDYING AND USING THIS BOOK 41

How to study with maximum efficiency. Five basic steps in attacking each assignment. The techniques of learning . . . concentrating . . . taking notes . . . testing yourself . . . developing careful reading habits . . . analyzing your weaknesses—and correcting them.

HOW TO BE A MASTER TEST TAKER 47

Master each of these methods—they apply to question types you may meet on your exam. Practice them when testing yourself in this book to insure a top performance on your actual exam.

...continued on next page

CONTENTS continued

PART TWO

BACKGROUND AND STUDY MATERIAL FOR THE EXAM

PART

1 CRIMINAL INVESTIGATION 55

Introduction to scientific criminology .... Sources of information .... Undercover investigations .... Arrests and searches of the person .

SIGN CUTTING 63

2 *An important investigative technique. Historical background. The education of a signcutter. How to look for and follow sign. Noting peculiarities of tracks. Backtracking. Tracking smugglers, illegal aliens, fugitives, and other criminals.*

3 TRACING THE SUSPECT 69

To help you score high on your test, here is a concise review of the key techniques of investigation. Disguises . . . leads . . . clues. Traits . . . telephoning . . . trailing . . . co-operation. Description of persons, property and scenes of crime.

EVIDENCE IN LAW ENFORCEMENT 79

A review of evidence plus previous exam questions and answers. What evidence is admissible? Kinds of evidence. How to mark evidence . . . presenting evidence in court. Constitutional rights of the defendant . . . 24 previous exam questions ..... Answers.

READINGS IN LAW ENFORCEMENT 87

Questions to test your understanding, as a law enforcement officer, of a sentence or paragraph ..... Answers.

READING QUESTIONS ON ROUTINES 101

JUDGMENT AND REASONING QUESTIONS 109

46 multiple choice questions test your reasoning ability Answers.

JUDGMENT FOR LAW ENFORCEMENT OFFICERS 117

Exercise your judgment on these 41 questions. Answers.

JUDGMENT ON THE JOB 122

PREDICTIVE PRACTICE EXAMINATION 127

An examination specially constructed to give you a comprehensive and authoritative view of the actual test. An opportunity to employ all you've learned. A situation that closely simulates the real thing.

CONTENTS continued

PART 1 2 3

PART THREE

PRACTICE AND PREPARATION FOR THE GENERAL TEST SUBJECTS OF THE EXAMINATION

ARRANGING PARAGRAPHS IN LOGICAL ORDER 143

For further practice towards your high-scoring success, here are 18 paragraphs for you to unscramble. Answers.

READING COMPREHENSION AND INTERPRETATION.................. 147

Fifteen pages of pointers and practice questions to help you read faster and more accurately. Don't be discouraged . . . How to read better and faster. The reading interpretation test . . . A sample question analyzed. Seventy-one questions on reading interpretation and comprehension. Answers.

LANGUAGE PRACTICE...163

TOP SCORES ON VOCABULARY TESTS......................................174

Six valuable steps in building your word power. Also, two charts of prefixes and suffixes, with sample words, show how a knowledge of etymology can help increase your vocabulary.

VOCABULARY TEST QUESTIONS FOR PRACTICE..........................178

A sample question analyzed, followed by a series of short quizzes in the often-met forms and variations you may find on your test: synonyms tests. Each test is followed by the correct answers for your ease in correcting and scoring yourself.

VERBAL ANALOGIES.. 189

An intensive analysis of this difficult kind of question. The many different forms and types of analogy questions . . . and how to answer each one correctly. In a very real sense this chapter is an introduction to right thinking.

SPELLING...197

Sixteen pages contain rules, words frequently misspelled, and four hundred forty questions and answers of the type usually asked on examinations. Some general rules of spelling. Words frequently misspelled. Sample test questions. Key answers.

TEST-TAKING MADE SIMPLE.. 213

Test-taking strategy for successful exam performance. How to prepare yourself emotionally, factually, physically. During the exam . . . budgeting your time . . . following directions. "Musts" for the master test-taker.

ARCO BOOKS...221

You'll want to consult this list of Arco publications to order other invaluable career books related to your field. The list also suggests job opportunities and promotions that you might want to go after with an Arco self-tutor.

ARCO
BUILDS
CAREERS

WHAT THIS BOOK WILL DO FOR YOU

To get the greatest help from this book, please understand that it has been carefully organized. You must, therefore, plan to use it accordingly. Study this concise, readable book earnestly and your way will be clear. You will progress directly to your goal. You will not be led off into blind alleys and useless fields of study.

Arco Publishing Company has followed testing trends and methods ever since the firm was founded in 1937. We have specialized in books that prepare people for tests. Based on this experience it is our modest boast that you probably have in your hands the best book that could be prepared to help *you* score high. Now, if you'll take a little advice on using it properly, we can assure you that you will do well.

To write this book we carefully analyzed every detail surrounding the forthcoming examination . . .

* the job itself
* official and unofficial announcements concerning the examination
* all the available previous examinations
* many related examinations
* technical literature that explains and forecasts the examination.

As a result of all this (which you, happily, have not had to do) we've been able to create the "climate" of your test, and to give you a fairly accurate picture of what's involved. Some of this material, digested and simplified, actually appears in print here, if it was deemed useful and suitable in helping you score high.

But more important than any other benefit derived from this research is our certainty that the study material, the text and the practice questions are right for you.

The practice questions you will study have been judiciously selected from hundreds of thousands of previous test questions on file here at Arco. But they haven't just been thrown at you pell mell. They've been organized into the subjects that you can expect to find on your test. As you answer the questions, these subjects will take on greater meaning for you. At the same time you will be getting valuable practice in answering test questions. You will proceed with a sure step toward a worthwhile goal: high test marks.

Studying in this manner, you will get the feel of the entire examination. You will learn by "insight," by seeing through a problem as a result of experiencing *previous similar situations*. This is true learning according to many psychologists.

In short, what you get from this book will help you operate at top efficiency . . . make you give the best possible account of yourself on the actual examination.

CAN YOU PREPARE YOURSELF FOR YOUR TEST?

We believe, most certainly, that you *can* with the aid of this "self-tutor"!

It's not a "pony". It's not a complete college education. It's not a "crib sheet", and it's no HOW TO SUCCEED ON TESTS WITHOUT REALLY TRYING. There's nothing in it that will give you a higher score than you really deserve.

It's just a top quality course which you can readily review in less than twenty hours . . . a digest of material which you might easily have written yourself after about five thousand hours of laborious digging.

To really prepare for your test you must motivate yourself . . . get into the right frame of mind for learning from your "self-tutor". You'll have to urge *yourself* to learn and that's the only way people ever learn. Your efforts to score high on the test will be greatly aided by the fact that you will have to do this job on your own . . . perhaps without a teacher. Psychologists have demonstrated that studies undertaken for a clear goal . . . which you initiate yourself and actively pursue . . . are the most successful. You, yourself, want to pass this test. That's why you bought this book and embarked on this program. Nobody forced you to do it, and there may be nobody to lead you through the course. Your self-activity is going to be the key to your success in the forthcoming weeks.

Used correctly, your "self-tutor" will show you what to expect and will give you a speedy brush-up on the subjects peculiar to your exam. Some of these are subjects not taught in schools at all. Even if your study time is very limited, you should:

- Become familiar with the type of examination you will meet.
- Improve your general examination taking skill.
- Improve your skill in analyzing and answering questions involving reasoning, judgment, comparison, and evaluation.
- Improve your speed and skill in reading and understanding what you read—an important part of your ability to learn and an important part of most tests.
- Prepare yourself in the particular fields which measure your learning—

  Vocabulary
  Problem solving
  Mathematics

This book will tell you exactly what to study by presenting in full every type of question you will get on the actual test. You'll do better merely by familiarizing yourself with them.

This book will help you find your weaknesses and find them fast. Once you know where you're weak you can get right to work (before the test) and concentrate your efforts on those soft spots. This is the kind of selective study which yields maximum test results for every hour spent.

This book will give you the *feel* of the exam. Almost all our sample and practice questions are taken from actual previous exams. Since previous exams are not always available for inspection by the public, these sample test questions are quite important for you. The day you take your exam you'll see how closely this book follows the format of the real test.

This book will give you confidence *now*, while you are preparing for the test. It will build your self-confidence as you proceed. It will beat those dreaded before-test jitters that have hurt so many other test-takers.

This book stresses the modern, multiple-choice type of question because that's the kind you'll undoubtedly get on your test. In answering these questions you will add to your knowledge by learning the correct answers, naturally. However, you will not be satisfied with merely the correct choice for each question. You will want to find out why the other choices are incorrect. This will jog your memory . . . help you remember much you thought you had forgotten. You'll be preparing and enriching yourself for the exam to come.

Of course, the great advantage in all this lies in narrowing your study to just those fields in which you're most likely to be quizzed. Answer enough questions in those fields and the chances are very good that you'll meet a few of them again on the actual test. After all, the number of questions an examiner can draw upon in these fields is rather limited. Examiners frequently employ the same questions on different tests for this very reason.

Probably the most important element of tests which you can learn is vocabulary. Most testers consider your vocabulary range an important indication of what you have learned in your life, and therefore, an important measuring rod of your learning ability. With some concentration and systematic study, you can increase your vocabulary substantially and thus increase your score on most tests.

After testing yourself, you may find that your reading ability is poor. It may be wise to take the proper remedial measures now.

If you find that your reasoning ability or your ability to handle mathematical problems is weak, there are ways of improving your skill in these fields.

There are other things which you should know and which various sections of this book will help you learn. Most important, not only for this examination but for all the examinations to come in your life, is learning how to take a test and how to prepare for it.

PART ONE

Applying and Studying For Your Job

Practice Using Answer Sheets

Alter numbers to match the practice and drill questions in each part of the book. Make only ONE mark for each answer. Additional and stray marks may be counted as mistakes. In making corrections, erase errors COMPLETELY. Make glossy black marks.

1 A B C D E	1 A B C D E	1 A B C D E	1 A B C D E	1 A B C D E
2 A B C D E	2 A B C D E	2 A B C D E	2 A B C D E	2 A B C D E
3 A B C D E	3 A B C D E	3 A B C D E	3 A B C D E	3 A B C D E
4 A B C D E	4 A B C D E	4 A B C D E	4 A B C D E	4 A B C D E
5 A B C D E	5 A B C D E	5 A B C D E	5 A B C D E	5 A B C D E
6 A B C D E	6 A B C D E	6 A B C D E	6 A B C D E	6 A B C D E
7 A B C D E	7 A B C D E	7 A B C D E	7 A B C D E	7 A B C D E
8 A B C D E	8 A B C D E	8 A B C D E	8 A B C D E	8 A B C D E
9 A B C D E	9 A B C D E	9 A B C D E	9 A B C D E	9 A B C D E
0 A B C D E	0 A B C D E	0 A B C D E	0 A B C D E	0 A B C D E

1 A B C D E	1 A B C D E	1 A B C D E	1 A B C D E	1 A B C D E
2 A B C D E	2 A B C D E	2 A B C D E	2 A B C D E	2 A B C D E
3 A B C D E	3 A B C D E	3 A B C D E	3 A B C D E	3 A B C D E
4 A B C D E	4 A B C D E	4 A B C D E	4 A B C D E	4 A B C D E
5 A B C D E	5 A B C D E	5 A B C D E	5 A B C D E	5 A B C D E
6 A B C D E	6 A B C D E	6 A B C D E	6 A B C D E	6 A B C D E
7 A B C D E	7 A B C D E	7 A B C D E	7 A B C D E	7 A B C D E
8 A B C D E	8 A B C D E	8 A B C D E	8 A B C D E	8 A B C D E
9 A B C D E	9 A B C D E	9 A B C D E	9 A B C D E	9 A B C D E
0 A B C D E	0 A B C D E	0 A B C D E	0 A B C D E	0 A B C D E

1 A B C D E	7 A B C D E	13 A B C D E	19 A B C D E	25 A B C D E
2 A B C D E	8 A B C D E	14 A B C D E	20 A B C D E	26 A B C D E
3 A B C D E	9 A B C D E	15 A B C D E	21 A B C D E	27 A B C D E
4 A B C D E	10 A B C D E	16 A B C D E	22 A B C D E	28 A B C D E
5 A B C D E	11 A B C D E	17 A B C D E	23 A B C D E	29 A B C D E
6 A B C D E	12 A B C D E	18 A B C D E	24 A B C D E	30 A B C D E

TEAR OUT ALONG THIS LINE AND MARK YOUR ANSWERS AS INSTRUCTED IN THE TEXT

AN OFFICIAL ANNOUNCEMENT

Here's a fairly good example of the kind of official statements issued to describe your test and your job. Read it all rather carefully because there are clues here as to the kind of test you'll be taking and how you have to prepare yourself. In writing this book we have examined quite a number of these announcements and have guided ourselves accordingly. We urge that you read and understand all such statements that are issued to you, personally. They will undoubtedly contain facts that foreshadow your test.

A CAREER SERVICE

The Immigration and Naturalization Service offers splendid opportunities to intelligent and energetic young men interested in immigration law enforcement who want to prepare themselves for positions of greater responsibilities through on-the-job and Service-offered training.

The Immigration and Naturalization Service is the agency of the U.S. Department of Justice that is responsible for administering the immigration and nationality laws of the United States. Its officers are on duty throughout the United States and at stations in Europe, Bermuda, Nassau, Puerto Rico, Canada, Mexico, and the Philippines. They perform a great variety of duties. In the performance of these duties officers are required to conduct investigations, detect violations of the law, and determine whether aliens may enter or remain in the United States; they collect and evaluate evidence, adjudicate applications for benefits such as petitions for visas, and preside over and present the Government's case at hearings; they prevent illegal entrance of aliens into the United States and make recommendations to the courts in such matters as petitions for citizenship.

These duties present new challenges, new and different problems to solve. To meet these challenges and to solve these problems requires an energetic and dedicated group of officers who are able to develop and keep pace with an ever changing variety of situations with which they are confronted in the performance of their duties.

The Service has an employee development program designed to assist employees in the performance of their work and to enable them to prepare for advancement. "Know how" is furnished to employees through organized training. This includes training on the job, attendance at Service schools and correspondence lessons. It is accompanied by changes in work assignments and posts of duty to enable officers to gain new and varied experience and to use their "know how" to advantage.

The Immigration and Naturalization Service is a career service in which advancement is based upon merit. Vacancies from the "journeyman" level up to executive levels are filled by the promotion of officers who have demonstrated their capacity for advancement. The Service has developed an officer selection board system to insure that each vacancy, throughout the Service, is filled by the best qualified officer available. As an integral part of this system all officers are kept currently informed about the requirements for supervisory, management, and executive positions so that they may know the opportunities for advancement and the experience they must gain in order to prepare for promotion.

BEGIN AS AN OFFICER

One way for new officers to enter the Service is through appointment to the position of Border

Patrol Agent (formerly known as Immigration Patrol Inspector) in the Service's Border Patrol. This is a mobile uniformed enforcement organization. Its principal purpose is to prevent the smuggling and illegal entry of aliens into the United States, and to detect, apprehend, and initiate departure of aliens illegally in this country. Border Patrol Agents are assigned along international boundaries and coastal areas. They may also be assigned to areas within the country. A variety of law enforcement functions are covered in the work of a Border Patrol Agent. These include patrolling areas to apprehend persons seen crossing the border; stopping vehicles on highways and inquiring about the citizenship of the occupants; inspecting and searching trains, buses, airplanes, ships and terminals to detect aliens entering illegally; checking the citizenship and immigration status of farm and ranch workers; apprehending and interrogating persons suspected of violating immigration laws; and many other duties to enforce the immigration law. The work is hazardous when dealing with dangerous criminals and other persons who exhibit violent and unpredictable behavior. Many of the posts are located of necessity, in small, isolated communities.

Soon after entry on duty, persons selected for appointment as Border Patrol Agent, GS–7, report to the Border Patrol Academy for approximately 3 months of intensive training. While in attendance at the training school, appointees are required to devote full time to their studies. They are taught the history and responsibilities of the Service and instructed in immigration and nationality laws, Spanish, physical training, marksmanship, and other courses pertinent to the work of the patrol. During the balance of the probationary year, their intensive training program is continued under the direction of a sector training officer and in the company of a senior officer. The new employees are given further written and oral examinations at the conclusion of 5½ and 10 months' service. Those candidates who do not succeed during the course of the probationary period are separated.

SALARY AND WORKWEEK

Salaries are based on the standard Federal workweek of 40 hours. Additional compensation is provided for authorized overtime worked in excess of the 40-hour week. As they gain additional experience, officers become qualified for promotion to supervisory positions in the Border Patrol and other positions in other activities of the Service even up to executive levels.

For current salary information, refer to Civil Service Commission Salary Supplement AN 2500, which may be obtained at most places where Civil Service Forms are available.

MINIMUM REQUIREMENTS

Competitors must pass ALL of the following requirements to be considered finally eligible in this examination. There are no experience requirements.

Written Test

All competitors for the position of Border Patrol Agent are required to take a written examination designed to measure verbal abilities, and judgment. The written examination requires about 2 hours. Applicants should indicate on their application cards where they wish to take the test.

Competitors are rated on the basis of the written examination on a scale of 100. To pass the written examination, competitors must attain a rating of at least 70 on the examination as a whole.

Oral Interview

Competitors who qualify in the written test are required to appear for an oral interview in the order of their standing on the register and only in such numbers as the needs of the Service may require. The oral interview is designed to determine if applicants possess the personal qualities necessary for successful performance of the duties of the position.

Automobile Driving Experience

Applicants must possess a valid automobile driver's license and must have had at least one year of licensed automobile driving experience. After entry on duty, appointees will be required to pass a road test before being issued a U.S. Government Motor Vehicle Operator's Identification Card.

Citizenship

Applicants must be citizens of or owe permanent allegiance to the United States.

Age Limits

Applicants must have reached or passed their 21st birthday on the date of appointment. However, persons between 20 and 21 years of age may apply for this examination. Such persons will be examined and if qualified in all other respects may be tentatively selected but may not enter on duty prior to attaining the age of 21 years. There is no maximum age limit.

Physical Requirements

Since the duties of these positions involve physical exertion under rigorous environmental conditions, irregular as well as protracted hours of work, patrol duties on foot, motor vehicle, and/or aircraft, and participation in physical training, applicants must be in sound physical condition and be of good muscular development.

Applicants must measure at least 67 inches in height, barefoot, and must be of proportional weight. They must weigh at least 140 pounds, without clothes, at time of appointment.

Eyes.—Vision in each eye without glasses must test at least 20/40 snellen and binocular vision without glasses must test at least 20/30 snellen. Uncorrected vision must be tested without artificial aids of any kind, including contact lenses. Applicants must be able to distinguish shades of colors (color plate test only). The following conditions will disqualify an applicant for appointment: Chronic eye disease or any functional abnormality of either eye.

Ears.—Applicants must be able to hear the whispered voice at 15 feet each ear. The use of a hearing aid is not permitted.

Teeth.—Applicants must have 14 serviceable molar or bicuspid teeth properly entering into serviceable occlusion. These teeth may be either sound teeth, filled teeth, well fitting crowns, bridge work, dentures, or any combination thereof. An applicant with any of the following remediable conditions must have them corrected before he can be accepted: Unsightly absence of front teeth, caries, pyorrhea, pus pockets around roots, other foci of infection, or unsatisfactory prosthetic appliances. The following will disqualify an applicant for appointment: Advanced pyorrhea, multiple cavities, abscessed roots or gross irregularities which interfere with serviceable occlusion.

Nose, mouth, and throat.—Applicants must be free from conditions which interfere with distinct speech (as lisping or stuttering) or with free breathing. The following conditions will disqualify an applicant for appointment: Disfiguring scars or blemishes; diseased tonsils; or chronic disease or condition affecting function.

Extremities.—The following conditions will disqualify an applicant for appointment: Noticeable deformities or conditions which are disfiguring or which interfere with functions; amputation of arm, hand, finger (other than little finger), thumb, leg, foot, great toe, or any two toes on same foot; or severe varicose veins.

Identifying body marks, scars, tattoos.—The following conditions will disqualify an applicant: Extensive or thin scars or offensive disfigurations, including conspicuous tattoos, on portions of the body subject to public notice. (Border Patrol Agents wear short-sleeved shirts in the summer.)

Lungs.—A history of pulmonary tuberculosis arrested or healed less than 2 years and greater than minimal involvement, or chronic disease or abnormal condition of the lungs, will disqualify an applicant for appointment.

Heart and blood vessels.—A history or presence of organic heart disease, compensated or not; hypertension above 150 systolic or 90 diastolic; hypotension below 100 systolic or 60 diastolic; or a pulse rate of 110 or over, or of 50 or under, when persistent in the recumbent position, will disqualify an applicant for appointment.

Genito-urinary.—The following conditions will disqualify an applicant for appointment: Acute or chronic genito-urinary disease; presence of albumen, sugar, pus, casts, or blood in the urine; incontinence; large or painful varicocele or hydrocele; or acute or chronic venereal disease.

Nervous system.—Applicants must be free from emotional instability and have no history of mental disease or nervous condition.

Other defects.—Applicants must be free from hernia; diabetes mellitus or insipidus; chronic disease of the stomach or intestines; or a history of gastric or duodenal ulcer.

Any serious deviation from a sound physical condition will be grounds for rejection of an applicant for appointment regardless of whether or not the condition is mentioned above.

Remediable defects or curable disease will not exclude a person from examination but proof that such defects have been remedied, or the disease cured, must be received during the life of the eligible register before persons otherwise qualified may be considered for appointment under Civil Service rules.

Physical requirements will not be waived in any case.

Prior to completion of the 1-year probationary period following appointment, each incumbent may be required to undergo a physical examination and meet the same physical requirements as those required for appointment. Subsequent medical examinations may also be required.

FRINGE BENEFITS

Appointees enjoy many "fringe benefits" such as vacation leave each year, sick leave with pay, low-cost life insurance and health insurance for which the Government shares in the cost. Employees who have rendered at least 20 years of service as Border Patrol Agents may, after attaining the age of 50, apply for retirement. These same benefits are available to those who have been promoted from Border Patrol Agent positions to many supervisory and executive positions. Such applications are subject to the final approval of the U.S. Civil Service Commission.

GENERAL INFORMATION

Examinations conducted only within the United States and Puerto Rico.—The written tests, oral interviews, and physical examinations will be conducted only within the United States and Puerto Rico.

Travel expenses.—Travel to written, oral, and physical examination points, and if appointed, to the first duty station, will be at the expense of the applicant.

Uniforms.—New appointees are required to buy a rough duty and an official uniform. The former costs about $125 and must be purchased immediately. A basic official uniform must be purchased within three months after entry on duty at a minimum cost of $150. Additional uniform items costing a minimum of $150 must be purchased before completion of the probationary year. An annual allowance of $125, payable shortly after appointment, is provided by law for those officers of the Service who are required to wear uniforms in the performance of their official duty.

Living quarters.—While at the Border Patrol Academy, new appointees are required to live in dormitories provided by the Government. Three meals are served each day at the Academy at a nominal cost payable 2 weeks in advance.

Nature of appointments.—Appointments to these positions will be career-conditional unless otherwise limited. The first year of a career-conditional appointment will be a probationary period. Upon satisfactory completion of the probationary period, employees acquire a competitive civil service status. Career-conditional appointments become career appointments when employees have completed 3 years of substantially continuous service.

Investigation of fitness.—All appointments will be made subject to a thorough investigation. Persons appointed will be investigated in order to obtain evidence of their qualifications, loyalty to the Government of the United States, honesty, integrity, and general character. Evidence of habitual use of intoxicants to excess, disloyalty, moral turpitude, disrespect for law, unethical dealings, or material misstatement of fact on the application for employment and related documents will be considered sufficient reasons for separation.

Such other investigation will be conducted as may be necessary under the Security Regulations for Government Employment.

Sex.—Because of the nature of the duties, the Immigration and Naturalization Service will employ only men for these positions.

Period of employment consideration.—The term of eligibility for employment consideration as a result of qualifying in this examination is 15 months, beginning with the date of the notice of rating. Persons who are not appointed during their 15-month term must reapply by filing a SF-171 if they are still interested in being considered for appointment.

Persons who attained eligibility under the previous announcement for Immigration Patrol Inspector and who have had less than 12 months of employment consideration will be carried over to the eligible list from this announcement for the remaining portion of their term.

Note.—Additional information about Federal employment, including veterans preference and other matters not included in this announcement, may be found in Pamphlet 4, *Working for the U.S.A.* This pamphlet may be obtained at most places where Civil Service forms are available.

ARCO
BUILDS
CAREERS

PATROL INSPECTOR

EXAMINATION FORECAST

Sample Questions That Forecast the Test

If you want a preview of your exam, look these questions over carefully. We did . . . as we compiled them from official announcements and various other sources. A good part of this book is based on these prophetic questions. Practice and study material is geared closely to them. The time and effort you devote to the different parts of this book should be determined by the facility with which you answer the following questions.

A look at the following questions is the easiest, quickest, most important help you can get from this book. These predictive questions give you foresight by providing an "overview" with which to direct your study. They are actual samples of the question types you may expect on your test.

Before you're finished with this book you'll get plenty of practice with the best methods of answering each of these question types. However, you're going to do a little work yourself. You're going to plan your study to make sure that each available hour is used most effectively. You're going to concentrate where it will do you the most good. And you'll take it easy where you have no trouble.

In other words, discover what you're going to face on the test and make plans to pace yourself accordingly.

TESTS OF VERBAL ABILITIES

Tests of verbal abilities (often referred to in Civil Service usage as "general tests") are designed to test a wide range of abilities, including the ability to understand words, interpret the meaning of sentences and paragraphs, and recognize and apply the rules of grammar and spelling.

Vocabulary

These words are not limited only to words actually used on the job. Vocabulary questions are a good measure of a competitor's general ability, as well as his aptitude for work requiring skill with words.

There is no printed list of all words whose meanings are tested in civil service examinations. Study of a selected list of words is likely to help in preparing for an examination. The general improvement of your vocabulary will help and you will find that this improvement will make other kinds of questions more understandable also.

Directions: In each of the following questions you are to find which one of five words or phrases offered as choices has most nearly the same meaning as the word or phrase in CAPITAL LETTERS or *italics*. On the answer sheet mark the letter of the suggested answer which you think is the best.

1. If a report is VERIFIED it is
   A) changed
   B) confirmed
   C) replaced
   D) discarded
   E) corrected

Since "confirmed," lettered B, means most nearly the same as "verified," the space under B is marked on the answer sheet for question 1.

2. A clerk who shows FORBEARANCE TOWARD THE OPINION OF OTHERS shows
   A) severity
   B) hypercriticism
   C) tolerance
   D) quietness
   E) thankfulness

3. *A controversy* between two persons is
   A) an agreement
   B) a dispute
   C) a partnership
   D) a plot
   E) an understanding

4. To say that a condition is *generally or extensively existing* means that it is
   A) artificial D) timely
   B) prevalent E) transient
   C) recurrent

5. *Authentic* means most nearly
   A) detailed D) technical
   B) reliable E) practical
   C) valuable

6. *The two farms lie close to each other, but are not in actual contact.* This sentence means most nearly that the two farms are
   A) adjoining
   B) abutting
   C) touching
   D) adjacent
   E) united

The space under D is marked for this question because "adjacent" best describes the meaning of the sentence in italics. The other choices all indicate that the farms are in contact in some degree or are touching each other.

Word Relations

In each of the following questions the first two words in capital letters go together in some way. Find how they are related. Then select from the last five words the one that goes with the third word in capital letters in the same way that the second word in capital letters goes with the first. The answer sheet is marked to show the correct choice of answers for these two questions.

7. FOOD is to HUNGER as SLEEP is to
   A) night D) health
   B) dream E) rest
   C) weariness

Food relieves hunger and sleep relieves weariness. Therefore, C, the letter before "weariness," is marked on the answer sheet for this question.

8. SPEEDOMETER is related to POINTER as WATCH is related to
   A) case D) spring
   B) hands E) numerals
   C) dial

On the answer sheet the space under B has been blackened to show that *watch* and *hands* are related in most nearly the same way as *speedometer* and *pointer.*

	A	B	C	D	E
1		▌			
2			▌		
3		▌			
4		▌			
5		▌			
6				▌	
7			▌		
8		▌			

Spelling

1. Select the one misspelled word.
   A) reliable B) detailed C) different D) accurrate E) sanctioned

In questions like the following, find the correct spelling of the word and blacken the proper space on your answer sheet. If none of the suggested spellings is correct, blacken space D on your answer sheet.

2. A) occassion C) ocassion
   B) occasion D) none of these

The correct spelling of the word is *occasion*. Since the B spelling is correct, the space under B is marked for this question.

Look at each word in the following list and decide whether the spelling is *all right* or *bad*. On the answer sheet blacken space
A if the spelling is ALL RIGHT
B if the spelling is BAD

3. running
4. indien
5. skool

Correct Answers for Sample Questions

	A	B	C	D	E
1				▌	
2		▌			
3	▌				
4		▌			
5		▌			
6			▌		

In questions like 6, a sentence is given in which one word, which is underlined, is spelled as it is pronounced. Write the correct spelling of the word in the blank. Then decide which one of the suggested answers, A, B, C, or D, is the correct answer to the question. (Sometimes the question will refer to one letter in the word, sometimes to a combination of letters.)

6. The new treasurer uses the same system that his pred-eh-sess'-urr did.
   In the correct spelling, ..., what is the tenth letter?
   A) s
   B) e
   C) o
   D) none of these

The correct spelling of the underlined word is *predecessor*. Since the tenth letter is "o," which is given as answer C, the space under C has been blackened.

(For practice with previous test questions of this type, see page 197.)

VERBAL ABILITIES

Interpretation of Paragraphs

Each question consists of a quotation followed by a series of five statements. Among the five statements there is only one that *must* be true if the quotation is true. Other statements among the five may or may not be true, but they are not necessary conclusions from the quotation. You are to select the *one* statement which is *best supported* by the quotation.

1. (*Reading*) "The application of the steam engine to the sawmill changed the whole lumber industry. Formerly the mills remained near the streams; now they follow the timber. Formerly the logs were floated downstream to their destination; now they are carried by the railroads."

   What besides the method of transportation does the quotation indicate has changed in the lumber industry?

   A) speed of cutting timber
   B) location of market
   C) type of timber sold
   D) route of railroads
   E) source of power

The quotation says nothing about the speed of steam-powered sawmills, location of the market for lumber, the type of timber sold, or the route of railroads. It does, however, mention "the application of the steam engine to the sawmill"—which gave a new source of power for sawmill operations. E is therefore the answer, and the space under E is blackened for question 1.

2. (*Reading*) "More patents have been issued for inventions relating to transportation than for those in any other line of human activity. These inventions have resulted in a great financial saving to the people and have made possible a civilization that could not have existed without them."

   Select the alternative that is best supported by the quotation. Transportation

   A) would be impossible without inventions
   B) is an important factor in our civilization
   C) is still to be much improved
   D) is more important than any other activity
   E) is carried on through the Patent Office

The space on the Answer Sheet under B is marked for question 2 because the statemen lettered B is implied in the quotation. A is not strictly true, since manpower without inventions could supply transportation of a sort; C is probably true but is not in the quotation; D is exaggerated; E is not implied in the information given.

3. (*Reading*) "There exists a false but popular idea that a clue is some mysterious fact which most people overlook, but which some very keen investigator easily discovers and recognizes as having, in itself, a remarkable meaning. The clue is most often an ordinary fact which an observant person picks up—something which gains its significance when, after a long series of careful investigations, it is connected with a network of other clues."

   According to the quotation, to be of value, clues must be

   A) discovered by skilled investigators
   B) found under mysterious circumstances
   C) discovered soon after the crime
   D) observed many times
   E) connected with other facts

The quotation does not say that the clue must be (A) discovered by an investigator in order to make it of value; it does not mention (B) the circumstances under which a clue must be found; nothing in the paragraph implies that the value of a clue depends upon the (C) time of its discovery, nor upon the (D) number of times it is observed. E is the answer, because the quotation does say that a clue gains its significance, or value, when *connected with other clues or facts.*

4. (*Reading*) "Just as the procedure of a collection department must be clear-cut and definite, the steps being taken with the sureness of a skilled chess player, so the various paragraphs of a collection letter must show clear organization, giving evidence of a mind that, from the beginning, has had a specific end in view."

   The quotation best supports the statement that a collection letter should always

   A) show a spirit of sportsmanship
   B) be divided into several paragraphs
   C) express confidence in the debtor
   D) be brief, but courteous
   E) be carefully planned

Sample Answer Sheet

	A	B	C	D	E
1	⁞	⁞	⁞	⁞	⁞
2	⁞	⁞	⁞	⁞	⁞
3	⁞	⁞	⁞	⁞	⁞
4	⁞	⁞	⁞	⁞	⁞

Correct Answers for Sample Questions

	A	B	C	D	E
1	⁞	⁞	⁞	⁞	▌
2	⁞	▌	⁞	⁞	⁞
3	⁞	⁞	⁞	⁞	▌
4	⁞	⁞	⁞	⁞	▌

Judgment and Reasoning

These questions are based on a variety of facts, sometimes on facts with which the candidate would be expected to be familiar, sometimes on facts explained in the question itself. The questions are of various degrees of difficulty. In some cases judgment items may pertain to a particular field of subject-matter, knowledge of which is necessary for the job.

1. Hospital beds are usually higher than beds in private homes. Which of the following is the BEST reason for this fact?
   A) Hospital beds are in use all day, instead of at night only.
   B) Many hospital patients are children.
   C) Private homes seldom have space enough for high beds.
   D) The care of patients is less difficult when the beds are high.
   E) The danger of falling out of bed is greater where there are no nurses.

The suggestion lettered D is the answer and is marked on the answer sheet. Of all the suggestions given as possible reasons why hospital beds are higher than other kinds, the one lettered D is clearly the most reasonable and best.

2. Objects are visible because
   A) they are opaque
   B) they are partially in shadow
   C) they absorb light from the sun
   D) light falls on them and is reflected to the eye
   E) light rays penetrate their surfaces

On the section of the answer sheet at the right, the space under D is marked for question 2 because the statement lettered D is the only one that explains why objects are visible. The other statements may be true, but they do not account for the visibility of objects.

	A	B	C	D	E
1				■	
2				■	
3			■		
4				■	

3. In starting a load, a horse has to pull harder than he does to keep it moving, because
   A) the load weighs less when it is moving
   B) there is no friction after the load is moving
   C) the horse has to overcome the tendency of the wagon to remain at rest
   D) the wheels stick to the axles
   E) the horse becomes accustomed to pulling the load

4. Which of the following would be the *surest* indication that a druggist may have violated the legal requirement that narcotic drugs be dispensed only on a physician's prescription?
   A) A number of people known to have purchased other drugs from him are believed to possess narcotics, but no prescriptions issued to these persons are in the druggist's file.
   B) He is himself an addict.
   C) His wholesaler refuses to sell him narcotics.
   D) The total of his present narcotics stock and the amount legally accounted for is much less than his purchases.
   E) The supply of narcotics in stock is less than the amount which he recently reported.

The facts related in A do not indicate that these customers have secured their narcotics from this druggist—the narcotics may have been obtained from some other druggist on a proper prescription; B is no indication that prescriptions did not cover all the narcotics he has dispensed, either for his own use or for other people; C might be true for many reasons—for example, his credit may be bad; and E could be explained by legal sales made since his last report. The answer is D, because violation of the requirement mentioned is a likely explanation of the large difference; therefore D is marked on the answer sheet.

(For additional practice with this question type, see page 109.)

Order of Sentences

1. Select the one of the four suggested orders in which the following three events most probably happened.
   1. The officer arrested the man as he attempted to enter the house through the window.
   2. About midnight he saw the stranger break a window.
   3. The officer became suspicious when he noticed a stranger loitering near the house.

   (A) 3–1–2 (B) 2–1–3 (C) 3–2–1 (D) 1–3–2.

Before he could arrest the stranger, the officer must have seen the man breaking the window. Therefore, event 1 must have happened after event 2. Since event 3 states that the officer became suspicious of the stranger, the officer must have noticed him before the man actually broke the window. Therefore, event 3 must have happened before event 2. This means that the order in which the events most likely happened is 3–2–1, so the space under C is marked for question 2.

In the following question there are four sentences, numbered (1), (2), (3), and (4). Four sequences, or arrangements, lettered (A), (B), (C), and (D), are suggested for these sentences. Read the sentences in these various sequences and decide which is the most logical arrangement of the ideas. Then blacken the space under the corresponding letter on the answer sheet.

2. (1) The year 1850 was an outstanding one for Tennyson, for, besides the success of *In Memoriam*, it brought him his appointment as poet laureate of England.
   (2) In 1842 he published two volumes of verse which met with instant and extraordinary success.
   (3) Tennyson, poet laureate of England for 42 years, was born in Somersby, Lincolnshire.
   (4) He died in 1892 and was buried in Westminster Abbey.
   (A) 1–2–3–4
   (B) 3–2–1–4
   (C) 3–4–1–2
   (D) 3–2–4–1

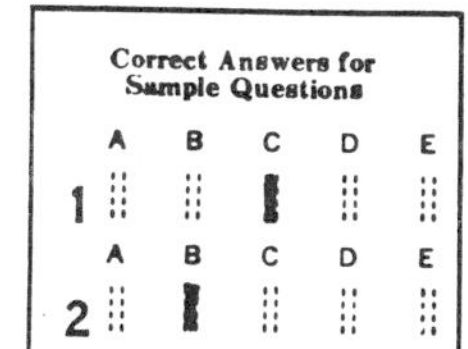

It would be most logical to put these sentences in chronological order, that is, to start with the poet's birth and have the other events in the order in which they occurred. The chronological sequence is represented by (B) 3–2–1–4; hence, the space under B is marked for question 3.

(If you feel the need to brush up on this kind of question, see page 143.)

PATROL INSPECTOR

THE U.S. BORDER PATROL

The Federal Government, the largest employer in the United States, had about three million civilian workers early this year. Federal employees are engaged in occupations representing nearly every kind of job.

To understand the problems daily faced by the Border Patrol, it is necessary to know something about the nature and tactics of the opposition. The individual alien without other unlawful objectives than to get across the border represents the situation in its simplest aspect. Unassisted it is difficult for him to enter at points remote from civilization, and in attempting to cross the line along established routes he is very apt to find himself outwitted by Patrol inspectors and immigration officials. If it were not for the activities of smugglers, guarding of the border would be far easier than it is.

Like any lucrative field--lawful or unlawful--the business of smuggling aliens into the United States has attracted many promoters, some of whom are persons of unusual cunning and daring. Since the days of the first oriental invasion, smugglers have applied themselves steadily to the problem of keeping open avenues of illegal entry across the border. Their ingenuity, at times, is startling if not admirable.

In the course of time, every known means of conveyance has been used, from covered wagons, row boats, and freight cars to airplanes.

Reference has already been made to the use of airplanes by smugglers. As early as 1927 it was reported that at least 15 planes were being operated by smugglers in the Los Angeles district.

Faced by organized opposition of such ruthless and resourceful characters, accurate information concerning the movements of the smugglers is of first importance. In this respect, Patrol inspectors have a double job. First, they must conceal their own movements, and, second, they must find out as much as possible concerning the plans of their opponents.

The first is a matter of moving quickly and unexpectedly. Were inspectors to patrol their sectors on a regular schedule smugglers would soon know exactly what the schedule was, and, therefore, when it was safe for them to operate. For this reason, inspectors pursue a devious course, doubling and redoubling on their tracks, departing from whatever plans they may have announced beforehand and, in general, using all possible devices to conceal their movements.

In getting information, inspectors are called upon to play the part of secret-service operatives. It is essential to their success that they have a wide acquaintance. Almost anyone in border communities may be a potential source of information concerning smuggling operations.

A district director gives the following account of the work of a Patrol inspector:

The assignments of a patrol inspector are many and varied. One shift may find him watching the international boundary. Another will send him through the country away from the boundary line checking roads and trails for contraband aliens who may have evaded the watch on the border. Another will keep him on the move between railroad and bus stations examining arriving and departing passengers. His assignment may then shift to checking highways for a suspected car; or to watching a landing field for a suspicious airplane; or perhaps he will be found with ragged clothes, hob-nobbing with the habitues of a hobo camp or hangouts of the underworld. Or he may be making an official call upon neighboring peace officers or ranchmen or farmers or garage men or bus drivers or railroad men or tourist camp operators; for every citizen is a potential immigration officer, but only after he has been properly coached; and even then this citizen "immigration officer" must be constantly reminded of his status as such or he will grow lax in his part of the law enforcement.

There is one angle to the work of the Border Patrol which links it with the Indian fighters of the early days. The science of tracking is constantly called into use by inspectors. Broken reeds on a river bank may tell the plain story of the landing of a smuggler's boat. Automobile tracks in the mud of a lonely trail may give all the information necessary for the capture of the quarry.

One of the great difficulties facing the Border Patrol is that its warfare against alien smugglers must be carried on in the midst of "noncombatants" whose rights and sensibilities must be respected.

Suppose that an inspector has definite information that two aliens are to be smuggled into the United States by automobile at a certain place and time. He cannot get to the designated spot and stop every car that comes along until the right one appears. The resentment of the innocent victims of his search would tend to arouse public indignation to the detriment of the Service and the hampering of the Patrol's future efforts. Instead, the inspector must station himself on the highway and determine by alert observation and quick deduction which car is the one that he is after.

The object of the Service, in this respect, goes beyond mere deference to the feelings of legitimate travelers. For success in our work we must have the good will, respect, and active support of the public. Courtesy and tact under all circumstances must be a cardinal rule of the organization.

There was a period when pressure from the Department for arrests and deportations inculcated a competitive spirit in the force and led to grave abuses and invasions of the rights of both citizens and aliens. That policy and the practices that grew up under it have ended. Patrol inspectors are required to strictly enforce the law--but by legal means. Invasions of the rights of citizen or alien, unnecessary detentions, and anything approaching third-degree methods are absolutely prohibited and when found to exist are punished with immediate dismissal from the force.

To the credit of the force it must be said that such abuses have never been other than the rare exception to the general rule. When the Border Patrol was first established, consideration for the suspected alien led to the naming of qualified immigration inspectors as chief inspectors, thus eliminating the hardship and inconvenience incident to transporting suspects long distance to regularly established immigration officers for examination. Cases are on record in which Patrol inspectors have taken it upon themselves to assist deportees by helping them to collect wages due them, and by moving them, their families, and belongings to the border.

To those not intimately acquainted with the relation of the Border Patrol to the regular Immigration Service, it is necessary to explain that there is no real distinction between them except in the nature of their respective duties. They are both part of the same organization; they both exist for the same purpose--the administration and enforcement of immigration laws and regulations.

In addition to the other special difficulties surrounding the work of the Border Patrol, there has existed an interesting, and sometimes harassing, legal puzzle. The question: What are the exact legal powers of a Border Patrol inspector? During the first year of its history the Patrol operated without any specific definition of its authority. On February 27, 1925, Congress approved the following provision, included in an appropriation act:

That hereafter any employee of the Bureau of Immigration authorized so to do under regulations prescribed by the Commissioner General of Immigration, with the approval of the Secretary of Labor, shall have power without warrant (1) to arrest any alien who in his presence or view is entering or attempting to enter the United States in violation of any law or regulation made in pursuance of law regulating the admission of aliens and to take such aliens immediately for examination before an immigrant inspector or other official having authority to examine aliens as to their right to admission to the United States, and (2) to board and search for aliens any vessel within the territorial waters of the United States, railway car, conveyance, or vehicle, in which he believes aliens are being brought into the United States; and such employee shall have power to execute any warrant or other process issued by any officer under any law regulating the admission, exclusion, or expulsion, of aliens.

That was definite enough--almost too definite, in fact. A literal interpretation of the clause granting inspectors power to arrest, without warrant, "any alien who in his presence or view is entering or attempting to enter the United States" in violation of law, would have rendered the Patrol impotent as a dog enjoined from following a rabbit through a fence. As a matter of fact, some of the most effective work of the Patrol is in pursuing and capturing illegally entered aliens after they have crossed the border.

This point was clarified by the decision in a Chinese smuggling case. The Court held that the act of entering the country was a progressive operation lasting until the arrival of the alien at his final destination in the United States.

The service which the Patrol has rendered in the prevention of crimes and the apprehension of criminals has won for it the respect and admiration of the communities in which it operates. Many isolated border towns have come to depend on the Patrol for protection.

It has been said that the Border Patrol is the ounce of prevention that is worth a pound of cure. The truth of that statement is amply apparent to all those who are familiar with the deportation activities of the Immigration Service. Aliens, like any other group of human beings are made up of both good and bad. The exclusion of criminal aliens is an essential part of our effort to control crime and vice in this country. The exclusion of aliens of good character who do not have the legal right to enter may avert such heartaches and hardships as the alien himself would flee from, if he knew they lay ahead of him.

ORGANIZATION OF THE IMMIGRATION AND NATURALIZATION SERVICE

Pursuant to Reorganization Plan V, approved June 4, 1940, and effective June 14, 1940, the Immigration and Naturalization Service was transferred from the Department of Labor to the Department of Justice.

The Immigration and Naturalization Service, created by the act of March 3, 1891 (26 Stat. 1085), administers the immigration and naturalization laws relating to the admission, exclusion, and deportation of aliens, and the naturalization of aliens lawfully resident in the United States. It investigates alleged violations of those laws and makes recommendations for prosecutions when deemed advisable. It patrols the borders of the United States to prevent the surreptitious entry of aliens into the United States in violation of law.

It is responsible for the detention of civilian alien enemy internees and for the control of foreign travel.

It supervises naturalization work in the specific courts designated by section 301 of the Nationality Act of 1940 (54 Stat. 1140; 8 U. S. C. 701), to have jurisdiction in such matters. This includes requirement of accountings from the clerks of such courts for naturalization fees collected, investigations -- through field officers -- of the qualifications of citizenship applicants, and representation of the Government at all court hearings. It cooperates with the public schools in providing citizenship textbooks and other facilities and services for the preparation of candidates for naturalization.

The Immigration and Naturalization Service also registers and fingerprints aliens in the United States, as required by the Alien Registration Act, approved June 28, 1940 (54 Stat. 670; 8 U. S. C. 137, 155, 156a, 451-60; 18 U. S. C. 9-13).

The Board of Immigration Appeals. -- The Board is a quasi-judicial body established in the Office of the Attorney General. The Board has jurisdiction to review on appeal the orders entered by, or under the general direction of, the Commissioner of Immigration and Naturalization in cases of, or relating to, applications for admission, in deportation cases, and in cases of fines and penalties imposed on steamship companies or other carriers for violation of the immigration laws. It also has jurisdiction to consider and determine such cases which are not appealed but which the Commissioner certifies to it for final decision.

APPLYING FOR FEDERAL JOBS

Since so many jobs must be filled, the Government cannot accept applications for all kinds of jobs all the time. Opportunities to apply for specific types of positions are announced when there is a need to fill such positions. The "announcement" tells about the jobs—what experience or education you must have before your application will be accepted, whether a written test is required, where the jobs are located, what the pay is, and so on. The "announcement" foreshadows your test. You have to know something about it in order to read and understand it.

KEEPING POSTED

Your Federal Job Information Center provides information about:

– All current job opportunities in any part of the United States.

– Specific vacancies in shortage categories

– Opportunities for overseas employment

– Employment advisory service

These centers are specially equipped to answer all inquiries about Federal employment opportunities. If you have any questions, write, visit, or phone your local Job Information Center.

To assist the Federal Job Information Center, many post offices also furnish information about current job opportunities and given out application forms. Your local post office can give you information about job opportunities or tell you the location of the nearest post office where this information can be obtained.

The following also have civil service information: State Employment Service Offices, national and State headquarters of veterans' organizations, placement officials at colleges, and personnel officers in Government agencies.

Such newspapers as the *Civil Service Leader* and the *Chief* (both published in New York City) run extensive listings of government job openings, including those abroad. The government itself uses newspapers and sometimes the radio for recruitment.

As a special service to disabled veterans, the Civil Service Commission maintains a file of those who are interested in specific kinds of jobs. A ten-point veteran may write to the Commission in Washington, D.C., and ask that his name be placed in this file.

FEDERAL JOB INFORMATION CENTERS

The Interagency Board system, operated by the Civil Service Commission, consists of 65 boards of civil service examiners located in centers of Federal population throughout the country.

These boards announce and conduct examinations. They evaluate applicants' work experience, training, and aptitude. They refer the names of people who meet the requirements to Federal agencies who are seeking new employees. Each board also provides, through its **Federal Job Information Center,** a complete one-stop information service about Federal job opportunities in the area as well as in other locations.

Address Executive Officer, Interagency Board of U.S. Civil Service Examiners, at the location that serves your area. Telephone numbers may be found under the U.S. Government listing in the telephone director in cities where Federal Job Information Centers are located.

UNITED STATES CIVIL SERVICE REGIONS

YOUR APPLICATION FOR THE EXAMINATION SHOULD BE FILED WITH THE OFFICE HAVING JURISDICTION OVER THE PLACE WHERE YOU WISH TO TAKE THE WRITTEN TEST.

ADDRESSES OF CIVIL SERVICE OFFICES		AREAS OF JURISDICTION
REGION	HEADQUARTERS	AREA SERVED
Atlanta.............	Atlanta Merchandise Mart, 240 Peachtree Street NW., Atlanta, Ga., 30303	Alabama, Florida, Georgia, Mississippi, North Carolina, South Carolina, Tennessee.
Boston	Post Office and Courthouse Building, Boston, Mass., 02109	Connecticut, Maine, Massachusetts, New Hampshire, Rhode Island, and Vermont.
Chicago.............	Main Post Office Building, 433 W. Van Buren Street, Chicago, Ill., 60607	Illinois, Indiana, Kentucky, Michigan, Ohio, and Wisconsin.
Dallas	1114 Commerce Street, Dallas, Tex., 75202	Arkansas, Louisiana, Oklahoma, and Texas.
Denver..............	Building 20, Denver Federal Center, Denver, Colo., 80225	Arizona, Colorado, New Mexico, Utah, and Wyoming.
New York	New Federal Bldg., 26 Federal Plaza, NYNY. 10007	New Jersey and New York, Puerto Rico, and Virgin Islands.
Philadelphia	Customhouse, Second and Chestnut Streets, Philadelphia, Pa., 19106	Delaware, Maryland, Pennsylvania, Virginia, and West Virginia.
St. Louis...........	1256 Federal Building, 1520 Market Street, St. Louis, Mo., 63103	Iowa, Kansas, Minnesota, Missouri, Nebraska, North Dakota, and South Dakota.
San Francisco.....	Federal Building, Box 36010, 450 Golden Gate Avenue, San Francisco, Calif., 94102	California, Hawaii, Nevada, and the Pacific Overseas Area.
Seattle..............	3004 Federal Office Building, First Avenue and Madison Street, Seattle, Wash., 98104	Alaska, Idaho, Montana, Oregon, and Washington.
Main Office........	WASHINGTON, D.C. 20415 Civil Service Commission Bldg. 1900 E. St. NW.	District of Columbia; Charles, Montgomery, and Prince Georges counties, Md.; Arlington, Fairfax, Prince William, King George, Stafford, and Loudoun counties, Va.; Alexandria, Falls Church, and Fairfax, Va.; and overseas areas except Western Pacific area

THE FEDERAL JOB ANNOUNCEMENT

When a position is open and a civil service examination is to be given for it, a job announcement is drawn up. This is generally from two to six printed pages in length and contains just about everything an applicant should know. The announcement begins with the job title and salary. A typical announcement then describes the work, the location of the position, the education and experience requirements, the kind of examination to be given, the system of rating. It may also have something to say about veteran preference and the age limit. It tells which application form is to be filled out, where to get the form, and where and when to file it. Study the job announcement carefully. It will answer many of your questions and help you decide whether you like the position and are qualified for it.

MEETING THE REQUIREMENTS

Before you apply, read the announcement carefully. It gives information about the jobs to be filled and what qualifications you must have to fill one of them.

If the announcement says that only persons who have 1 year of experience along certain lines will qualify and you don't have that experience, don't apply. If the announcement says that the jobs to be filled are all in a certain locality and you don't want to work in that locality, don't file. Many disappointed applicants would have been saved time and trouble if they had only read the announcement carefully.

Credit will be given for unpaid experience or volunteer work such as in community, cultural, social service and professional association activities, on the same basis as for paid experience, that is, it must be of the type and level acceptable under the announcement. Therefore, you may, if you wish, report such experience in one or more of the experience blocks at the end of your personal qualifications statement, if you feel that it represents qualifying experience for the positions for which you are applying. To receive proper credit, you must show the actual time, such as the number of hours a week, spent in such activities.

QUALITY OF EXPERIENCE

For most positions, in order to qualify *on experience* for any grade above the entrance level, an applicant must have either 6 months or 1 year of experience at a level comparable in difficulty and responsibility to that of the next lower grade level in the Federal Service. In some instances for positions at GS–11 and below, experience may have been obtained at two levels below that of the job to be filled.

Depending on the type of position, the next lower level may be either one or two grades lower. If you were applying for a position as a Stenographer (single grade interval position), at grade GS–5, you should have at least 1 year of experience doing work equivalent to that done by a Stenographer at the GS–4 level. If you were applying for a two-grade interval position, however, such as Computer Specialist GS–7, you would need at least 1 year of experience equivalent to that of a GS–5 Computer Specialist in Federal Service, or 6 months equivalent to the GS–6 level. Where necessary, the announcement will provide more specific information about the level of experience needed to qualify.

THE DUTIES

The words *Optional Fields* – sometimes just the word *Options* – may appear on the front page of the announcement. You then have a choice to apply for that particular position in which you are especially interested. This is because the duties of various positions are quite different even though they bear the same broad title. A public relations *clerk*, for example, does different work from a payroll *clerk*, although they are considered broadly in the same general area.

Not every announcement has options. But whether or not it has them, the precise duties are described in detail, usually under the heading: *Description of Work*. Make sure that these duties come within the range of your experience and ability.

SOME THINGS TO WATCH FOR

In addition to educational and experience requirements, there will be some general requirements you will have to meet.

Age. "How old are you?" There is no maximum age limit. The usual minimum age limit is 18, but for most jobs high school graduates may apply at 16.

If you are 16 or 17 and are out of school but not a high school graduate, you may be hired only (1) if you have successfully completed a formal training program preparing you for work (for example, training provided under the Manpower Development and Training Act, in the Job Corps, in the Neighborhood Youth Corps, and in similar Government or private programs), or (2) if you have been out of school for at least 3 months, not counting the summer vacation, and if school authorities sign a form agreeing with your preference for work instead of additional schooling. The form will be given you by the agency that wants to hire you.

REMEMBER, JOB OPPORTUNITIES ARE BEST FOR THOSE WHO GRADUATE. IF YOU CAN, YOU SHOULD COMPLETE YOUR EDUCATION BEFORE YOU APPLY FOR FULL-TIME WORK.

If you are in high school, you may be hired for work during vacation periods if you are 16. (For jobs filled under the Summer Employment Examination, however, you must be 18 if still in high school.) You may also be hired for part-time work during the school year if you are 16 and meet all the following conditions:

(1) Your work schedule is set up through agreement with your school,
(2) Your school certifies that you can maintain good standing while working, and
(3) You remain enrolled in high school.

Some announcements may set a different minimum age limit. Be sure to check the announcement carefully before applying.

Citizenship. Are you an American citizen? Only citizens and people who owe permanent allegiance to the United States can receive competitive appointments.

Physical requirements. What is your physical condition? You must be physically able to perform the duties of the position, and must be emotionally and mentally stable. This does not mean that a handicap will disqualify an applicant so long as he can do the work efficiently without being a hazard to himself or to others.

For most positions, appointees must have good distant vision in one eye and be able to read without strain printed material the size of typewritten characters. They may use glasses to meet these requirements.

Persons appointed are usually required to be able to hear the conversational voice. They may use a hearing aid to meet this requirement. Blind persons and deaf persons may apply and be examined for positions with duties they can perform.

An amputation of an arm, hand, leg, or foot does not in itself bar a person from Federal employment. Here again the test is whether the person can do the duties of the position satisfactorily and without hazard to himself or others.

The Federal Government is the world's largest employer of handicapped people and has a strong program aimed at their employment. It recognizes that, in almost every kind of work, there are some positions suitable for the blind, the deaf, and others with serious impairments. If reading is necessary to perform duties, the blind person is permitted to provide a reader at no expense to the Government.

Of course, there are some positions – such as border patrolman, firefighter, and criminal investigator – that can be filled only by people in topnotch physical condition. Whenever this is the case, the physical requirements are described in detail in the announcements.

THE GOVERNMENT TESTS YOU

Most applicants for civil service jobs are worried by that awesome instrument called **the test.** *Haunted by schoolday memories, applicants often approach the examination with fear, imagining that someone is going to give them a big list of trick questions, to trap them; or that they will have to sit down and laboriously work out the answers to difficult problems. The only factor that helps many people face the test is the knowledge that they aren't alone, that everybody else competing with them faces the same problems. Those who have any dealings with civil service applicants never cease to wonder how widespread this attitude is. If you are one of those who has this concept of a government test, change your opinion. It's all wrong!*

You have found the position you'd like, filled out the application form, and sent it off to the Civil Service Commission.

What now?

KINDS OF TESTS

The announcement describes the kind of test given for the particular position. Please pay special attention to this section. It tells what areas are to be covered in the written test and lists the specific subjects on which questions will be asked. Sometimes sample questions are given.

The test and review material in this Arco book are based on the requirements as given in this section as well as on actual tests.

If the announcement said that a written test would be given, you will receive a notice through the mail telling you when and where to report for the test.

Special arrangements will be made for applicants who are blind, deaf, or otherwise handicapped who indicate the nature of their disability when they apply for the test.

The written test will be practical. It will test your ability to do the job that you applied for, or it will test your ability to learn how to do it.

If you fail a written test, you can usually take it again as long as applications are being accepted for it. If you pass it but want to try to improve your score, you can take it again after a year has passed provided it is still open.

Usually the announcement states whether the examination is to be assembled or unassembled. In an *assembled* examination applicants *assemble* in the same place at the same time to take a written or performance test. The *unassembled* examination is one where an applicant does not take a test; instead he is rated on his education and experience and whatever records of past achievement he is asked to provide.

If you apply for a position that does not involve a written test, your rating will be assigned on the basis of the experience and training you describe in your statement and any additional evidence secured by the board of examiners. Your qualifications may also be verified with your former employers and supervisors.

If your examination is of the *unassembled* variety, the Commission may ask you to submit further evidence of your ability, in the form of work accomplished. In the meantime, the statements on your application form are being checked. When all this information is gathered, you are "rated" and the Commission will write to you, telling you how your qualifications look to the examiners. That's all there is to it, until you are called to the job.

In announcements that cover several grades or salary levels, you will be rated for those you qualify for, but you will not be rated for any grade if the pay for that grade is less than the minimum pay you state you will accept.

You will be notified whether you passed or failed the examination by the office that announced it. Be sure to notify that office of changes in essential information, such as address, name, availability, etc. When writing, give your full name, the title of the announcement, the rating you received, and your date of birth.

There are two main types of tests—competitive and non-competitive.

In a *competitive* examination all applicants for a position compete with each other; the better the mark, the better the chance of being appointed. In a *non-competitive* examination the applicant is tested solely to determine his qualification for a given position; he need only pass to become eligible for appointment.

The method of rating on all civil service written tests is on a scale of 100, with 70 as the passing mark.

RATING EXAMINATIONS

The rating of the examination is usually done by the office which has issued the announcement—sometimes the central office of the Civil Service Commission in Washington, sometimes a regional office.

Written tests are most frequently rated by machine. In some written examinations, and for rating experience and training, two examiners work independently. In case of a protest about the rating a third examiner will be assigned to rate the exam again. Thus the chances of error, arbitrary grading, or bias are almost completely eliminated.

Evaluating Education. In evaluating the candidate's background, credit may be given for appropriate training received in the armed forces. A certificate of completion from an education instiution for a correspondence course is often counted as good background. Courses offered through the Armed Forces Institute are granted credit, too, in rating examinations. The announcement always tells the kind of education needed for the specific job, and the examiners give careful consideration to the entire educational background of the candidate as listed in the application form. Often courses which the candidate may not consider relevant are found by the examiners to be helpful for the post. They raise the total rating.

Evaluating Experience. When experience is a factor the examiners give credit for all kinds of valuable background, including experience gained in religious, civic, welfare, service, and organizational activities. Whether the experience was paid or unpaid makes no difference, but its length and quality do.

Veterans obtain special experience credit in one of the following ways, whichever would benefit the candidate more.

1. Military service may be considered an extension of the employment in which the applicant was engaged just before his entrance into the armed forces.

2. Duties performed while in military service may be considered on the basis of their value to the job for which the veteran is applying.

"Suitability." Investigations to determine an applicant's "suitability qualifications" with respect to character and loyalty are considered a part of the entire examining process, regardless of whether such investigations are conducted before or after appointment.

When all the parts of an examination have been rated the applicant is notified of his *numerical rating,* or mark.

If he has passed, he is now an *eligible,* that is, his name is placed on a list and is ready to be submitted, in due course, to a government department for appointment.

This is the crucial period . . . the time for which this book was made. Now that you know you're going to take the test and have some idea of the subjects to be tested, it behooves you to bend every effort toward thorough preparation.

Later on we will give you guidance on methods of scheduling your available study time, and how to make the most of the brief time at your disposal. Even though the text of your book has been carefully edited to provide you with every possible short-cut, it does require that you absorb a great deal of material. So, if you want to get that job you mustn't regard this book as another homework assignment to be put off till Sunday night. Get cracking! Start right now. Every hour counts.

WORKING FOR THE U.S.

Working for the government is different from working in private industry. You can't always give orders and expect them to be carried out pronto; you're likely to bump into a regulation. You can't be too active politically; if you are, you'll be slapped down. There is a complicated system of judging and reporting on your work—a system that may affect your earning power. It's pretty easy to get fired. And with what seems sickening frequency, some Congressman sounds off against "inefficient bureaucrats"—meaning you. On the other hand, if you work authorized overtime, you get paid for it, your vacation and sick-leave time is generous, chances for promotions and pay increases are frequent, and the government often gives valuable training on the job. If you make government service a career, you'll retire with a substantial annuity.

SALARY AND WORKING CONDITIONS

After selecting its employees on the basis of merit, the Government pays them, and promotes them, on the same basis.

Employees are paid according to the principle of "equal pay for equal work." When jobs in the higher grades become vacant, or new ones are set up, the general practice is to fill them by promoting employees in lower grades who are qualified to perform the more difficult duties.

You will want to know more about these matters, and about other features of Federal employment. As you learn about them, you will find that the Government, the largest employer in the United States, is also a progressive employer.

PAY

In general, the Government pays good salaries. Its policy is that salaries of Government employees should be comparable to those paid by private employers for work of the same level of difficulty and responsibility.

Government salaries are reviewed frequently and changes made, or recommended to Congress, as needed. This means that persons choosing careers in Government may expect, over the years, pay realistically geared to the economy.

The Government has several pay plans. For most trades positions, wages are set from time to time to bring them into line with prevailing wages paid in the same locality by private industry.

Postal employees have a pay system of their own, which is fixed by law.

A few Federal agencies and a few classes of employees have still other pay plans. The Tennessee Valley Authority, the Foreign Service (Department of State), and physicians, dentists, and nurses, in the Department of Medicine and Surgery of the Veterans Administration are in this group.

Other employees (45 percent) are paid under the General Schedule (GS), which applies to most white-collar employees and to protective and custodial employees such as guards and messengers. Positions are graded by number according to how difficult the work is, starting with grade GS-1 and going up to grade GS-18.

Each grade has a set salary range; thus the grade of a position sets the pay. Hard-to-fill positions frequently have a higher salary range than other positions in the same grade. In all cases, salaries are listed in the announcement or in a separate supplement.

PAY RATES OF THE GENERAL SCHEDULE (5 U.S.C 5332), AS ADJUSTED BY EXECUTIVE ORDER 11576, JANUARY 8, 1971

(The top line opposite each grade number shows the rates which became effective beginning with the first pay period on or after January 1, 1971. The second line shows the rates which were formerly in effect beginning with the first pay period on or after December 27, 1969.)

GENERAL SCHEDULE - BASIC PER ANNUM RATES

GRADE	1	2	3	4	5	6	7	8	9	10	AMT. OF WITHIN-GRADE INCREASE
1	**$4,326** $4,125	**$4,470** $4,262	**$4,614** $4,399	**$4,758** $4,536	**$4,902** $4,673	**$5,046** $4,810	**$5,190** $4,947	**$5,334** $5,084	**$5,478** $5,221	**$5,622** $5,358	**$ 144** $ 137
2	**4,897** 4,621	**5,060** 4,775	**5,223** 4,929	**5,386** 5,083	**5,549** 5,237	**5,712** 5,391	**5,875** 5,545	**6,038** 5,699	**6,201** 5,853	**6,364** 6,007	**163** 154
3	**5,524** 5,212	**5,708** 5,386	**5,892** 5,560	**6,076** 5,734	**6,260** 5,908	**6,444** 6,082	**6,628** 6,256	**6,812** 6,430	**6,996** 6,604	**7,180** 6,778	**184** 174
4	**6,202** 5,853	**6,409** 6,048	**6,616** 6,243	**6,823** 6,438	**7,030** 6,633	**7,237** 6,828	**7,444** 7,023	**7,651** 7,218	**7,858** 7,413	**8,065** 7,608	**207** 195
5	**6,938** 6,548	**7,169** 6,766	**7,400** 6,984	**7,631** 7,202	**7,862** 7,420	**8,093** 7,638	**8,324** 7,856	**8,555** 8,074	**8,786** 8,292	**9,017** 8,510	**231** 218
6	**7,727** 7,294	**7,985** 7,537	**8,243** 7,780	**8,501** 8,023	**8,759** 8,266	**9,017** 8,509	**9,275** 8,752	**9,533** 8,995	**9,791** 9,238	**10,049** 9,481	**258** 243
7	**8,582** 8,098	**8,868** 8,368	**9,154** 8,638	**9,440** 8,908	**9,726** 9,178	**10,012** 9,448	**10,298** 9,718	**10,584** 9,988	**10,870** 10,258	**11,156** 10,528	**286** 270
8	**9,493** 8,956	**9,809** 9,255	**10,125** 9,554	**10,441** 9,853	**10,757** 10,152	**11,073** 10,451	**11,389** 10,750	**11,705** 11,049	**12,021** 11,348	**12,337** 11,647	**316** 299
9	**10,470** 9,881	**10,819** 10,210	**11,168** 10,539	**11,517** 10,868	**11,866** 11,197	**12,215** 11,526	**12,564** 11,855	**12,913** 12,184	**13,262** 12,513	**13,611** 12,842	**349** 329
10	**11,517** 10,869	**11,901** 11,231	**12,285** 11,593	**12,669** 11,955	**13,053** 12,317	**13,437** 12,679	**13,821** 13,041	**14,205** 13,403	**14,589** 13,765	**14,973** 14,127	**384** 362
11	**12,615** 11,905	**13,036** 12,302	**13,457** 12,699	**13,878** 13,096	**14,299** 13,493	**14,720** 13,890	**15,141** 14,287	**15,562** 14,684	**15,983** 15,081	**16,404** 15,478	**421** 397
12	**15,040** 14,192	**15,541** 14,665	**16,042** 15,138	**16,543** 15,611	**17,044** 16,084	**17,545** 16,557	**18,046** 17,030	**18,547** 17,503	**19,048** 17,976	**19,549** 18,449	**501** 473
13	**17,761** 16,760	**18,353** 17,319	**18,945** 17,878	**19,537** 18,437	**20,129** 18,996	**20,721** 19,555	**21,313** 20,114	**21,905** 20,673	**22,497** 21,232	**23,089** 21,791	**592** 559
14	**20,815** 19,643	**21,509** 20,298	**22,203** 20,953	**22,897** 21,608	**23,591** 22,263	**24,285** 22,918	**24,979** 23,573	**25,673** 24,228	**26,367** 24,883	**27,061** 25,538	**694** 655
15	**24,251** 22,885	**25,059** 23,648	**25,867** 24,411	**26,675** 25,174	**27,483** 25,937	**28,291** 26,700	**29,099** 27,463	**29,907** 28,226	**30,715** 28,989	**31,523** 29,752	**808** 763
16	**28,129** 26,547	**29,067** 27,432	**30,005** 28,317	**30,943** 29,202	**31,881** 30,087	**32,819** 30,972	**33,757** 31,857	**34,695** 32,742	**35,633** 33,627		**938** 885
17	**32,546** 30,714	**33,631** 31,738	**34,716** 32,762	**35,801** 33,786	**36,886*** 34,810						**1,085** 1,024
18	**37,624*** 35,505										

*The rate of basic pay for employees at these rates is limited by section 5308 of title 5 of the United States Code, as added by the Federal Pay Comparability Act of 1970, to the rate for level V of the Executive Schedule (as of the effective date of this salary adjustment, $36,000).

JANUARY 1971

Hiring usually is done at the first rate of a grade. Employees who perform their work at an acceptable level of competence receive within-grade increases at intervals. They may qualify for these increases every year for 3 years; then the increases occur less frequently until the top rate of the grade is reached. Employees may be awarded additional within-grade increases for exceptionally meritorious work, but not above the top of the grade.

You will be interested in knowing how jobs get to be in one grade or another. Position classifiers study the duties of the jobs. They find out how difficult the duties are, how much responsibility the person holding the job has, and what knowledge or experience or skill goes into performing the duties. Then they put the jobs in appropriate grades under standards set by the Civil Service Commission.

HOURS OF WORK

The usual Government workweek is 40 hours. Most Government employees work 8 hours, 5 days a week, Monday through Friday, but in some cases the nature of the work may call for a different workweek.

As in any other business, employees sometimes have to work overtime. If you are required to work overtime while a Government employee, you will either be paid for overtime or given time off to make up for the extra time you worked.

ADVANCEMENT

Many of the men and women in top jobs in the Government began their careers "at the bottom of the ladder." They did their jobs well, and prepared for the job ahead. They learned more and more about the work of their agencies. As they became more useful on the job, they were promoted to one more important position after another.

Most agencies fill vacancies, whenever possible, by promoting their own employees. Promotion programs in every agency are designed to make sure that promotions go to the employees who are among the best qualified to fill higher positions. How fast employees are promoted depends upon openings in the higher grades, and upon their ability and industry.

Federal employees receive on-the-job training. They may also participate in individualized career development programs and receive job-related training in their own agency, in other agencies, or outside the Government (for example, in industrial plants and universities).

It is not always necessary to move to a new job in order to advance in grade. Sometimes an employee's work assignments change a great deal in the ordinary course of business. His job "grows." When that happens it is time for a position classifier to study the job again. If he finds that the job should be put in a higher grade because of the increased difficulty or responsibility of the duties, the change is made.

TRANSFERS

Transferring to other civil service jobs for which an employee is qualified is another way of getting a better job.

Agencies consider the qualifications of an employee for promotion as higher grade positions become vacant. However, for transfer to positions in other agencies, an employee would have to "find his own job," by such means as interviews with officials in those agencies. If he can find a vacant position in another agency, and if the hiring officer is impressed with his qualifications, arrangements may be made to transfer him.

Occasionally, the Job Information Center may be able to assist Federal employees in locating vacancies.

EFFICIENCY COUNTS

At intervals, employees are rated on their job performance. In most agencies, the ratings are "Outstanding," "Satisfactory," and "Unsatisfactory."

Employees with "Outstanding" ratings receive extra credit for retention in layoffs.

An employee whose rating is "Unsatisfactory" must be dismissed or assigned to another position with duties which he can be expected to learn to do satisfactorily.

INCENTIVE AWARDS

Government agencies encourage their employees to suggest better ways, or simpler ways, or more economical ways, of doing their jobs. They may give a cash award to an employee for a suggestion or invention that results in money savings or improved service. They may also reward outstanding job performance or other acts that are particularly meritorious and deserving of recognition.

VACATION AND SICK LEAVE

Most Federal employees earn annual leave, for vacation and other purposes, according to the number of years (civilian plus creditable military service) they have been in the Federal service. They earn it at the rate of 13 days a year for the first 3 years and 20 days a year for the next 12 years. After 15 years, they earn 26 days of annual leave each year.

Sick leave is earned at the rate of 13 days a year. You can use this leave for illnesses serious enough to keep you away from your work, and for appointments with a doctor, dentists, or optician. Sick leave that is not used can be saved for future use. It is one of the best forms of insurance an employee and his family can have in case of extended periods of illness.

New Year's Day, Washington's Birthday, Memorial Day, the Fourth of July, Labor Day, Veterans Day, Thanksgiving, and Christmas are holidays for Federal employees.

INJURY COMPENSATION

The Government provides liberal compensation benefits including medical care, for employees who suffer injuries in the performance of official duty. Death benefits are also provided if an employee dies as a result of such injuries.

GROUP LIFE INSURANCE

As a Federal employee, you may have low-cost term life insurance without taking a physical examination. Two kinds of insurance are provided—life insurance and accidental death and dismemberment insurance.

As a Federal employee, you may have low-cost term life insurance—plus equal accidental death and dismemberment insurance—in an amount which usually is at least $2,000 more than your annual base pay. The Government pays one-third of the premium cost and the employee pays the emainder. The minimum amount of each kind of protection is $10,000. In addition, an employee may purchase an extra $10,000 of optional insurance for which he pays full premium, also through payroll deductions.

HEALTH BENEFITS

The Government sponsors a voluntary health insurance program for Federal employees. The program offers a variety of plans to meet individual needs, including basic coverage and major medical protection against costly illnesses. The Government contributes part of the cost of premiums and the employee pays the balance through payroll deductions.

RETIREMENT

Six and a half percent of a career or career-conditional employee's salary goes into a retirement fund. This 6½ percent comes out of every paycheck. This money is withheld as the employee's share of the cost of providing him or his survivors with an income after he has completed his working career.

If you leave the Government before you complete 5 years of service, the money you put into the retirement fund can be returned to you. If you leave after completing 5 years of service, you have a choice of having your money returned or leaving it in the fund. If you leave it in the fund, you will get an annuity starting when you are age 62.

The Government has a liberal retirement system. For example, if you work for the Government for 30 years, and if your average salary durng any 5 consecutive years was $8,000, you can retire at 55 and get $4,500 a year for the rest of your life. Also, an employee who becomes disabled after at least 5 years of Government service may retire on an annuity at any age.

LAYOFFS

In Government, layoffs are called *reductions in force,* and may be caused by a cut in appropriations, a decrease in work, or some similar reason.

In a reduction in force, the four things which determine whether an employee goes or stays are: Type of appointment (career, career-conditional, temporary); whether he has veteran preference for this purpose (20-year retired veterans generally do not); seniority (how long an employee has worked for the Government); and job performance.

UNEMPLOYMENT COMPENSATION

Federal employees who are separated in lay-offs or whose appointments are terminated are entitled to unemployment compensation similar to that provided for employees in private industry. They are covered by the unemployment insurance system under conditions set by the State in which they worked.

SEVERANCE PAY

Federal employees who are involuntarily separated without cause, and who are not entitled to an immediate retirement annuity, may be eligible for severance pay. This pay is based on years of service and years of age over 40, and may not exceed 1 year's basic compensation.

EMPLOYEE ORGANIZATIONS

There are a number of unions and other employee organizations in the Federal Government. Some of them are for special groups, such as postal employees. Others have general membership among Government employees. Their main objective is to improve the working conditions of Federal employees.

Federal employees are free to join or to refrain from joining such organizations. But, as mentioned before, they may not join an organization which asserts the right to strike against the Government of the United States.

GETTING ADDITIONAL INFORMATION

Information about Federal civil service job announcements can be obtained from any Federal Job Information Center and at many post offices.

Practice Using Answer Sheets

DIRECTIONS: Read each question and its lettered answers. When you have decided which answer is correct, blacken the corresponding space on this sheet with a No. 2 pencil. Make your mark as long as the pair of lines, and completely fill the area between the pair of lines. If you change your mind, erase your first mark COMPLETELY. Make no stray marks; they may count against you.

SAMPLE

1. CHICAGO is
1-A a country 1-D a city
1-B a mountain 1-E a state
1-C an island

1 A B C D E

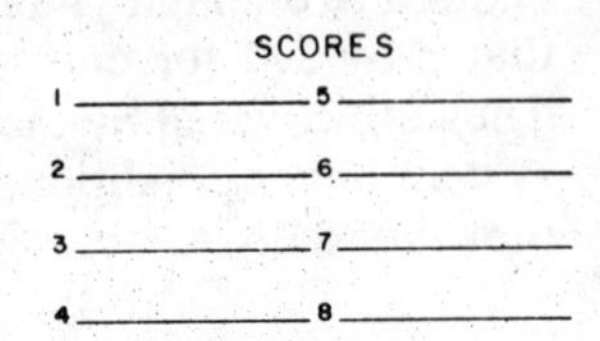
SCORES

1 ____	5 ____
2 ____	6 ____
3 ____	7 ____
4 ____	8 ____

1 A B C D E	2 A B C D E	3 A B C D E	4 A B C D E
5 A B C D E	6 A B C D E	7 A B C D E	8 A B C D E
9 A B C D E	10 A B C D E	11 A B C D E	12 A B C D E
13 A B C D E	14 A B C D E	15 A B C D E	16 A B C D E
17 A B C D E	18 A B C D E	19 A B C D E	20 A B C D E
21 A B C D E	22 A B C D E	23 A B C D E	24 A B C D E
25 A B C D E	26 A B C D E	27 A B C D E	28 A B C D E
29 A B C D E	30 A B C D E	31 A B C D E	32 A B C D E
33 A B C D E	34 A B C D E	35 A B C D E	36 A B C D E
37 A B C D E	38 A B C D E	39 A B C D E	40 A B C D E
41 A B C D E	42 A B C D E	43 A B C D E	44 A B C D E
45 A B C D E	46 A B C D E	47 A B C D E	48 A B C D E
49 A B C D E	50 A B C D E	51 A B C D E	52 A B C D E
53 A B C D E	54 A B C D E	55 A B C D E	56 A B C D E
57 A B C D E	58 A B C D E	59 A B C D E	60 A B C D E
61 A B C D E	62 A B C D E	63 A B C D E	64 A B C D E
65 A B C D E	66 A B C D E	67 A B C D E	68 A B C D E
69 A B C D E	70 A B C D E	71 A B C D E	72 A B C D E
73 A B C D E	74 A B C D E	75 A B C D E	76 A B C D E
77 A B C D E	78 A B C D E	79 A B C D E	80 A B C D E
81 A B C D E	82 A B C D E	83 A B C D E	84 A B C D E
85 A B C D E	86 A B C D E	87 A B C D E	88 A B C D E
89 A B C D E	90 A B C D E	91 A B C D E	92 A B C D E
93 A B C D E	94 A B C D E	95 A B C D E	96 A B C D E
97 A B C D E	98 A B C D E	99 A B C D E	100 A B C D E
101 A B C D E	102 A B C D E	103 A B C D E	104 A B C D E
105 A B C D E	106 A B C D E	107 A B C D E	108 A B C D E
109 A B C D E	110 A B C D E	111 A B C D E	112 A B C D E
113 A B C D E	114 A B C D E	115 A B C D E	116 A B C D E
117 A B C D E	118 A B C D E	119 A B C D E	120 A B C D E
121 A B C D E	122 A B C D E	123 A B C D E	124 A B C D E
125 A B C D E	126 A B C D E	127 A B C D E	128 A B C D E
129 A B C D E	130 A B C D E	131 A B C D E	132 A B C D E
133 A B C D E	134 A B C D E	135 A B C D E	136 A B C D E
137 A B C D E	138 A B C D E	139 A B C D E	140 A B C D E
141 A B C D E	142 A B C D E	143 A B C D E	144 A B C D E
145 A B C D E	146 A B C D E	147 A B C D E	148 A B C D E
149 A B C D E	150 A B C D E		

TEAR OUT ALONG THIS LINE AND MARK YOUR ANSWERS AS INSTRUCTED IN THE TEXT

STUDYING AND USING THIS BOOK

Even though this course of study has been carefully planned to help you get in shape by the day your test comes, you'll have to do a little planning on your own to be successful. And you'll also need a few pointers proven effective for many other good students.

SURVEY AND SCHEDULE YOUR WORK

Regular mental workouts are as important as regular physical workouts in achieving maximum personal efficiency. They are absolutely essential in getting top test scores, so you'll want to plan a test-preparing schedule that fits in with your usual program. Use the Schedule on the next page. Make it out for yourself so that it really works with the actual time you have at your disposal.

There are five basic steps in scheduling this book for yourself and in studying each assignment that you schedule:

1. SCAN - the entire job at hand.
2. QUESTION - before reading.
3. READ - to find the answers to the questions you have formulated.
4. RECITE - to see how well you have learned the answers to your questions.
5. REVIEW - to check up on how well you have learned, to learn it again, and to fix it firmly in your mind.

Scan

Make a survey of this whole book before scheduling. Do this by reading our introductory statements and the table of contents. Then leaf through the entire book, paying attention to main headings, sub-headings, summaries, and topic sentences. When you have this bird's eye view of the whole, the parts take on added meaning, and you'll see how they hang together.

Question

As you scan, questions will come to your mind. Write them into the book. Later on you'll be finding the answers. For example, in scanning this book you would naturally change the headline STUDYING AND USING THIS BOOK into *What don't I know about studying? What are my good study habits? How can I improve them? How should I go about reading and using this book?* Practice the habit of formulating and writing such questions into the text.

Read

Now, by reviewing your questions you should be able to work out your schedule easily. Stick to it. And apply these five steps to each assignment you give yourself in the schedule. Your reading of each assignment should be directed to finding answers to the questions you have formulated and will continue to formulate. You'll discover that reading with a purpose will make it easier to *remember* the answers to your questions.

Recite

After you have read your assignment and found the answers to your questions, close the book and recite to yourself. For example, if your question here was "What are the five basic steps in attacking an assignment?" then your answer to yourself would be scan, question, read, recite, and review. Thus, you check up on yourself and "fix" the information in your mind. You have now seen it, read it, said it, and heard it. The more senses you use, the more you learn.

Review

Even if you recall your answers well, review them in order to "overlearn". "Overlearning" gives you a big advantage by reducing the chances of forgetting. Definitely provide time in your schedule for review. It's the clincher in getting ahead of the crowd. You'll find that "overlearning" won't take much time with this book because the text portions have been written as concisely and briefly as possible. You may be tempted to stop work when you have once gone over the work before you. This is wrong because of the ease with which memory impressions are bound to fade. Decide for yourself what is important and plan to review and overlearn those portions. Overlearning rather than last minute cramming is the best way to study.

Your Time is Limited—Schedule Your Study

Plan your program. When you start your Course, look first at the table of contents to give yourself a preliminary idea of the material in the book. If you know the date of your examination, figure out how many half-hour sessions you can set aside for test-preparation, and once you have made up a schedule, stick to it.

STUDY TIMETABLE

Mon.									
Tues.									
Wed.									
Thur.									
Fri.									
Sat.									
Sun.									

HOW TO USE THE STUDY TIMETABLE

At right is a sample timetable filled in for a whole week to show you how a typical schedule might be arranged. The letters *A*, *B*, *C*, etc., are keyed to your study subjects so that, for example, *A* might stand for Vocabulary, *B* for Numerical Relations, and so forth. You will note that each day is divided into nine possible study hours and each hour, in turn, is divided into four 15-minute periods.

	7AM	12 PM		7PM	8PM	9PM			
Mon.	BB	AA	B	BCC	CCEE	EGG			
		12 PM		7PM	8PM	9PM			
Tues.		FF	A	AABB	DDD	DGG			
	7AM	12PM		7PM					
Wed.	CC	BB	BB	BB					
		12PM		7PM	8PM	9PM	10PM		
Thur.		A	A	A	BBEE	EFF	HH		
	7AM		7PM	8PM					
Fri.	AA	FF	FEE	CC					
	10AM	11AM	12PM	3PM	4PM				
Sat.	DDD	AAAA		BBB	FF				
	1PM	2PM	3PM	4PM	8PM				
Sun.	DDD	CCC	CAA	HHH	BB				

Plan to study difficult subjects when you can give them your greatest energy. Some people find that they can do their best work in the early morning hours. On the other hand, it has been found that forgetting is less when study is followed by sleep or recreation. Plan other study periods for those free times which might otherwise be wasted . . . for example lunch or when traveling to and from work.

Plan your schedule so that not more than 1½ or 2 hours are spent in the study of any subject at one sitting. Allow at least a half-hour for each session with your book. It takes a few minutes before you settle down to work.

You will find that there is enough time for your study and other activities if you follow a well-planned schedule. You will not only be able to find enough time for your other activities, but you will also accomplish more in the way of study and learning. A definite plan for study increases concentration. If you establish the habit of studying a subject at the same time each day, you will find that less effort is required in focusing your attention on it.

Where To Study

SELECT A ROOM THAT WILL BE AVAILABLE EACH DAY AT THE SAME TIME. THIS WILL HELP YOU CONCENTRATE.

USE A DESK OR TABLE WHICH WILL NOT BE SHARED SO THAT YOU CAN "LEAVE THINGS OUT". IT SHOULD BE BIG ENOUGH TO ACCOMMODATE ALL YOUR EQUIPMENT WITHOUT CRAMPING YOU. ELIMINATE ORNAMENTS AND OTHER DISTRACTIONS.

SELECT A ROOM WHICH HAS NO DISTRACTIONS. KEEP IT THAT WAY.

PROVIDE FOR GOOD AIR CIRCULATION IN YOUR STUDY ROOM.

KEEP THE TEMPERATURE AROUND 68°.

PROVIDE ADEQUATE LIGHTING . . . USE A DESK LAMP IN ADDITION TO OVERHEAD LIGHTS.

NOISE DISTRACTS SO KEEP RADIO AND TV TURNED OFF.

ARRANGE TO HAVE A PERMANENT KIT OF NECESSARY STUDY EQUIPMENT . . . PEN, PENCIL, RULER, SHEARS, ERASER, NOTEBOOK, CLIPS, DICTIONARY, ETC.

Study On Your Own

As a general rule you will find it more beneficial to study with this book in your room, alone. There are times, however, when two or more individuals can profit from team study. For example, if you can't figure something out for yourself, you might get help from a friend who is also studying for this test. Review situations sometimes lend themselves to team study if everyone concerned has already been over the ground by himself. Sometimes you can gain greater understanding of underlying principles as you volley ideas back and forth with other people. Watch out, though, that you don't come to lean on the others so much that you can't work things out for yourself.

PROVEN STUDY SUGGESTIONS

1. Do some work every day in preparation for the exam.
2. Budget your time—set aside a definite study period for each day during the week.
3. Study with a friend or a group occasionally—the exchange of ideas will help all of you. It's also more pleasant getting together.
4. Answer as many of the questions in this book as you can. Some of the questions that you will get on your actual test will be very much like some of the questions in this book.
5. Be physically fit. Eat the proper food—get enough sleep. You learn better and faster when you are in good health.
6. Take notes.
7. Be an active learner. Participate. Try harder.

TECHNIQUES OF EFFICIENT STUDY

DO NOT ATTEMPT SERIOUS STUDY WHILE IN TOO RELAXED A POSITION.

AVOID SERIOUS STUDY AFTER A HEAVY MEAL.

DO SOMETHING WHILE STUDYING . . . MAKE NOTES, UNDERLINE, FORMULATE QUESTIONS.

BEGIN CONCENTRATING AS SOON AS YOU SIT DOWN TO STUDY. DON'T FOOL AROUND.

MAKE TIME FOR STUDY BY ELIMINATING NEEDLESS ACTIVITIES AND OTHER DRAINS ON YOUR PRECIOUS TIME.

MAKE UP YOUR OWN ILLUSTRATIONS AND EXAMPLES TO CHECK ON YOUR UNDERSTANDING OF A TOPIC.

FIND SOME PRACTICAL APPLICATION OF YOUR NEWLY ACQUIRED KNOWLEDGE.

RELATE NEWLY ACQUIRED KNOWLEDGE TO WHAT YOU KNEW BEFORE.

CONSCIOUSLY TRY TO LEARN, TO CONCENTRATE, TO PAY ATTENTION.

LOOK UP NEW WORDS IN YOUR DICTIONARY.

Concentrating

Most students who complain that they don't know how to concentrate deserve no sympathy. Concentration is merely habit and ought to be as readily acquired as any other habit. The way to begin to study is simply to begin.

Don't wait for inspiration or for the mood to strike you, nor should you permit yourself to indulge in thoughts like, "This chapter is too long" or "I guess I could really let that go until some other time."

Such an attitude throws an extra load on your mental machinery, and by making you work against a handicap, makes it harder for you to begin.

Reading aloud is a good device for those whose minds wander while studying. Articulating "subvocally" for a few moments is another tonic for drifting thoughts. If this doesn't work, write down the point you happen to be dealing with when your mind "goes off track."

Do your studying alone, and you'll find it much easier to concentrate. If you are certain you need help on doubtful or difficult points, check these points and list them; you can go back or ask about them later. In the meantime, proceed to the next point.

A "little tenseness" is a good thing because it helps you keep alert while studying. Do without smoking, or newspapers, or magazines, or novels which may lead you into temptation. Studying in one place all the time also helps.

Boiling it all down, the greatest asset for effective studying is plain, garden variety "common sense" and will power.

Grasshoppers Never Learn

Don't be a "skipper." Jumping around from one part of your course to another may be more interesting, but it won't help you as much as steady progress from page one right through the book.

Studying and learning takes more than just reading. The "text" part of your course can be a valuable tool in test-preparation if you use it correctly. Introductions to the various sections of your book must be "studied." Re-read the paragraph that gives you trouble. Be certain that you understand it before you pass on to the next one. Many persons who have been away from school for a long time, and those people who have a habit of reading rapidly, find that it helps if they hold a piece of white paper under the paragraph they are reading, covering the rest of the page. That helps you concentrate on the facts you are absorbing. Keep a pen or pencil in your hand while reading, and underline important facts. Put a question mark after anything that isn't quite clear to you, so that you can get back to it. Summarize ideas in the margins of your book. You'll be surprised how much easier it is to remember something once you have written it down, and expressed it in your own words.

Taking Notes

Although your "self-tutor" has done a great deal for you in summarizing the information that is essential to success on the test, it's still worth your while to do some notetaking. Your notes, which can be made either in a separate notebook or in the margins of this book, will help you concentrate; are a form of self-recitation; will provide you with concise outlines for review before the test; will help you identify basic and essential materials; will help you retain what you learn, with greater accuracy for a longer period of time; and will help you learn better because they require thinking and active participation on your part.

The following suggestions will help you take the kind of notes that will be of greatest use to you on the test:

RECORD ESSENTIAL FACTS AND AVOID TOO MUCH DETAIL. JOT DOWN CLUES.

ADOPT AN ACTIVE MEANING-SEEKING ATTITUDE. STICK TO BASIC SIGNIFICANCE.

USE YOUR OWN WORDS. BUT BE BRIEF.

DON'T HURRY. WRITE READABLY AND ACCURATELY. YOU'LL BE READING THEM AGAIN.

BE NEAT. WRITE TITLES AND LABELS. DON'T BE SPARING OF PAPER.

USE A SINGLE LOOSELEAF NOTEBOOK SO THAT YOU CAN RE-ORGANIZE AND COMBINE NOTES.

TAKE NOTES IN ALL LEARNING SITUATIONS RELATING TO THIS TEST.

DON'T COPY VERBATIM.

REVIEW YOUR NOTES OF THE PREVIOUS DAY BEFORE STARTING THE CURRENT ASSIGNMENT.

USE QUESTION MARKS IN THE MARGINS OF THE BOOK FOR VAGUE OR DIFFICULT PASSAGES WHICH MAY BE CLARIFIED AS YOU READ ON. YOU MAY WANT TO COME BACK TO THEM TO BE SURE YOU UNDERSTAND THEM.

TRY TO DO SOME FOLLOW UP WORK ON UNDERLINED SECTIONS.

SOME SUGGESTED SYMBOLS FOR MAKING NOTES IN THIS BOOK.

| , ( ), [ ] A vertical line in the margin, or a bracket, or parenthesis around a sentence or group of sentences is used to indicate an important idea or ideas.

— Underlining is used to indicate especially important materials, specific points to be consulted during reviews.

O A circle around a word may be used to indicate that you are not familiar with the word, and that you will come back later to look it up in the dictionary.

√ E The letter "E" or a check mark (√) in the margin may be used to mark materials that are important and likely to be used in the examination.

1 , 2 , 3 , 4 Arabic numerals, circled or uncircled may be placed before a word or at the beginning of a sentence to indicate a series of facts, ideas, important dates, etc.

D The letter "D" may be used to indicate your disagreement with a passage or a statement.

Keep in mind that effective notetaking is vital to learning. If your notes are effective, your learning is likely to be effective.

Test Yourself Frequently

The major part of your course consists of study questions and answers prepared by experts. Try to answer every question in the book as you reach it. Each study session should end with a self-test.

Develop Careful Reading Habits

While present-day examinations seldom have "trick" questions, the men who make up examinations often frame questions so that careful reading is necessary to understand the question fully and to give the proper answer. Use this book as a personal reading-improver. Rephrase every question in your own words before you answer, to be sure that you really understand what is being asked.

Don't Try to Memorize

It is true that the same questions often reappear on examinations of the same kind, but it would not be worthwhile to try to memorize the hundreds of questions in your book. After all, the *scope* of any examination is fairly limited. Using your book as a self-tester will show you the fields in which you may be weak or strong. The questions and answers will help put you into the important examination-taking frame of mind, and give you an excellent idea of the different types of information about which you will be questioned on your test.

Be Tough With Yourself

One error made by many persons who are preparing for examinations is to give themselves too much of a break. They will peek at the book answer to a question and excuse themselves on the grounds that if they had "really" been taking a test, they would have been more careful and would have given the correct answer. Don't let yourself get away with that!

You have to be a stern teacher to get the most out of any program of self-study. When you test yourself, be as tough as if the test-taker were someone you didn't know. Don't let yourself get away with an "almost right" answer. Today there is keen competition on most tests, and the habits you develop while preparing for your test will show up on the examination in the form of earned or lost percentage points. Mark yourself rigidly. Be honest in appraising your weaknesses, and try to correct them before you sit down to take the real test.

And don't take anything for granted. Even if you find yourself scoring 100% in some area of your test, don't relax too much. When you find that you have answered a question correctly, use that as a lever for self-improvement. Ask yourself *why* your answer was correct. Try to think of other forms in which the same question could have been asked. Try to frame your own questions that are "harder" or more demanding than the ones you can answer easily.

You may find that some sections of this book are difficult, just as some portions of the test will be more difficult than others. Don't worry about it. Don't panic. Remember that the test is a competitive one . . . that your score is relative to the scores of all the oher competitors. What's hard for you will be just as hard (or harder) for them.

When the going gets rough you're on notice to study more carefully. You've discovered one of your weaknesses. You're ahead of the game because you have the opportunity of strengthening yourself. Concentrate on your weak spots and you won't be caught off balance by the test questions.

On the other hand don't permit yourself to be lulled into a false sense of security when you discover material which is very easy for you. Don't quit studying—just give the easy portions less time. Adjust your schedule and use the time you pick up in this way to work where it is most needed.

This technique of devoting as much time and thought as is required by each job (and no more) should be applied to the actual test, with one caution. The easy questions should be answered as rapidly as you can, as you come to them. But if a question appears very difficult and likely to take a lot of time to answer, defer spending too much time on it. Continue on, giving the quick, easy answers. Then go back and use the time remaining to answer the slow, hard ones.

Scissors and Glue for Review

One helpful form of review, as your examination date approaches, is this: Cut out individual questions from your book. Paste them on slips of paper, and mark the correct answers on the back of each question.

Then, whenever you have a few minutes to spare, you can shuffle the questions around and find out whether you have the correct answers in your mind. This is especially helpful in dealing with questions of the "information" type which are basically tests of how well you remember important information and facts.

Another good learning technique is to have someone read the questions and suggested answers to you. "Hearing" will serve as a memory aid after you have read and studied the material.

Analyze Your Weaknesses—And Correct Them

One purpose of this course is to familiarize you with the types of questions you will face and to prepare you for them. Perhaps its more important purpose is to help you find your own weaknesses and to correct them before the examination.

Every time you give the incorrect answer to a practice question you should ask yourself, "Why?" Be honest with yourself and you'll soon discover the subjects in which you're weak. Devote extra time to these subjects and you will have taken giant steps to test success.

We have analyzed test failures and have found time after time that many persons who are perfectly able to pass a test fail it simply because of their weakness in such basic subjects as arithmetic or vocabulary.

If you find that you have such a problem, be brave. Put in the extra effort each day.

HOW TO BE A MASTER TEST TAKER

It's really quite simple. Do things right . . . right from the beginning. Make successful methods a habit by practicing them on all the exercises in this book. Before you're finished you will have invested a good deal of time. Make sure you get the largest dividends from this investment.

SCORING PAPERS BY MACHINE

A typical machine-scored answer sheet is shown below, reduced from the actual size of 8¼ x 11 inches. Since it's the only one that reaches the office where papers are scored, it's important that the blanks at the top be filled in completely and correctly.

The chances are very good that you'll have to mark your answers on one of these sheets. Consequently, we've made it possible for you to practice with them throughout this book.

ANSWER SHEET

SERIES No ______ YOUR IDENTIFICATION NUMBER ______

TEST No ______ PART ______ TITLE OF POSITION ______ (AS GIVEN IN EXAMINATION ANNOUNCEMENT - INCLUDE OPTION, IF ANY)

PLACE OF EXAMINATION ______ (CITY OR TOWN) ______ (STATE) DATE ______

RATING

IF YOU CLAIM VETERAN PREFERENCE, PUT AN "X" IN THE APPROPRIATE BOX

☐ VETERAN ☐ DISABLED VETERAN ☐ DISABLED VET'S WIFE ☐ VET'S WIDOW ☐ VET'S MOTHER

USE THE SPECIAL PENCIL. MAKE GLOSSY BLACK MARKS.

1 A B C D E	26 A B C D E	51 A B C D E	76 A B C D E	101 A B C D E
2 A B C D E	27 A B C D E	52 A B C D E	77 A B C D E	102 A B C D E
3 A B C D E	28 A B C D E	53 A B C D E	78 A B C D E	103 A B C D E
4 A B C D E	29 A B C D E	54 A B C D E	79 A B C D E	104 A B C D E
5 A B C D E	30 A B C D E	55 A B C D E	80 A B C D E	105 A B C D E
6 A B C D E	31 A B C D E	56 A B C D E	81 A B C D E	106 A B C D E
7 A B C D E	32 A B C D E	57 A B C D E	82 A B C D E	107 A B C D E
8 A B C D E	33 A B C D E	58 A B C D E	83 A B C D E	108 A B C D E
9 A B C D E	34 A B C D E	59 A B C D E	84 A B C D E	109 A B C D E
10 A B C D E	35 A B C D E	60 A B C D E	85 A B C D E	110 A B C D E

Make only ONE mark to answer any one item. Additional and stray marks may be counted as mistakes. In making corrections, erase errors COMPLETELY.

11 A B C D E	36 A B C D E	61 A B C D E	86 A B C D E	111 A B C D E
12 A B C D E	37 A B C D E	62 A B C D E	87 A B C D E	112 A B C D E
13 A B C D E	38 A B C D E	63 A B C D E	88 A B C D E	113 A B C D E
14 A B C D E	39 A B C D E	64 A B C D E	89 A B C D E	114 A B C D E
15 A B C D E	40 A B C D E	65 A B C D E	90 A B C D E	115 A B C D E
16 A B C D E	41 A B C D E	66 A B C D E	91 A B C D E	116 A B C D E
17 A B C D E	42 A B C D E	67 A B C D E	92 A B C D E	117 A B C D E
18 A B C D E	43 A B C D E	68 A B C D E	93 A B C D E	118 A B C D E
19 A B C D E	44 A B C D E	69 A B C D E	94 A B C D E	119 A B C D E
20 A B C D E	45 A B C D E	70 A B C D E	95 A B C D E	120 A B C D E
21 A B C D E	46 A B C D E	71 A B C D E	96 A B C D E	121 A B C D E
22 A B C D E	47 A B C D E	72 A B C D E	97 A B C D E	122 A B C D E
23 A B C D E	48 A B C D E	73 A B C D E	98 A B C D E	123 A B C D E
24 A B C D E	49 A B C D E	74 A B C D E	99 A B C D E	124 A B C D E
25 A B C D E	50 A B C D E	75 A B C D E	100 A B C D E	125 A B C D E

C. S. C. FORM 3636, DECEMBER 1950 **UNITED STATES CIVIL SERVICE COMMISSION** IBM FORM I.T.S. 1000A 2145

FOLLOW DIRECTIONS CAREFULLY

It's an obvious rule, but more people fail for breaching it than for any other cause. By actual count there are over a hundred types of directions given on tests. You'll familiarize yourself with all of them in the course of this book. And you'll also learn not to let your guard down in reading them, listening to them, and following them. Right now, before you plunge in, we want to be sure that you have nothing to fear from the answer sheet and the way in which you must mark it; from the most important question forms and the ways in which they are to be answered.

HERE'S HOW TO MARK YOUR ANSWERS ON MACHINE-SCORED ANSWER SHEETS:

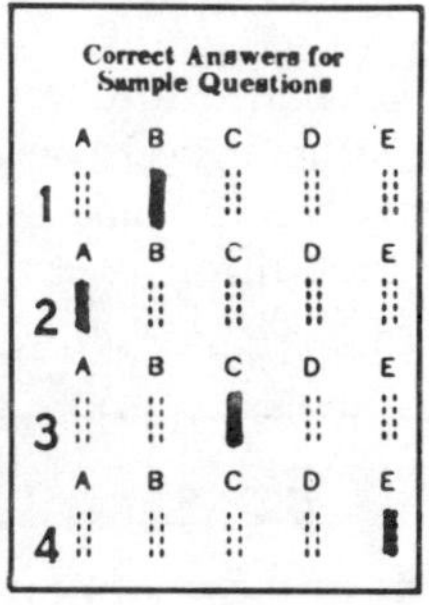

Make only ONE mark for each answer. Additional and stray marks may be counted as mistakes. In making corrections, erase errors COMPLETELY. Make glossy black marks.

(a) Each pencil mark must be heavy and black. Light marks should be retraced with the special pencil.

(b) Each mark must be in the space between the pair of dotted lines and entirely fill this space.

(c) All stray pencil marks on the paper, clearly not intended as answers, must be completely erased.

(d) Each question must have only one answer indicated. If multiple answers occur, all extraneous marks should be thoroughly erased. Otherwise, the machine will give you *no* credit for your correct answer.

MULTIPLE CHOICE METHODS

Multiple choice questions are very popular these days with examiners. The chances are good that you'll get this kind on your test. So we've arranged that you practice with them in the following pages. But first we want to give you a little help by explaining the best methods for handling this question form.

You know, of course, that these questions offer you four or five possible answers, that your job is to select *only* the *best* answer, and that even the incorrect answers are frequently *partly* correct. These partly-true choices are inserted to force you to think . . . and prove that you know the right answer.

USE THESE METHODS TO ANSWER MULTIPLE CHOICE QUESTIONS CORRECTLY:

1. Read the item closely to see what the examiner is after. Re-read it if necessary.
2. Mentally reject answers that are clearly wrong.
3. Suspect as being wrong any of the choices which contain broad statements hinging on "cue" words like

absolute
absolutely
all
always
axiomatic
categorical
completely
doubtless
entirely
extravagantly
forever
immeasurably
inalienable
incontestable
incontrovertible
indefinitely
indisputable
indubitable
inevitable
inexorable
infallible
infinite
inflexible
inordinately
irrefutable
inviolable
never
only
peculiarly
positive
quite
self-evident
sole
totally
unchallenged
unchangeable
undeniable
undoubtedly
unequivocal
unexceptionable
unimpeachable
unqualified
unquestionable
wholly
without exception

If you're unsure of the meanings of any of these words, look them up in your dictionary.

4. A well-constructed multiple choice item will avoid obviously incorrect choices. The good examiner will try to write a cluster of answers, all of which are plausible. Use the clue words to help yourself pick the *most* correct answer.
5. In the case of items where you are doubtful of the answer, you might be able to bring to bear the information you have gained from previous study. This knowledge might be sufficient to indicate that some of the suggested answers are not so plausible. Eliminate such answers from further consideration.
6. Then concentrate on the remaining suggested answers. The more you eliminate in this way, the better your chances of getting the item right.
7. If the item is in the form of an incomplete statement, it sometimes helps to try to complete the statement before you look at the suggested answers. Then see if the way you have completed the statement corresponds with any of the answers provided. If one is found, it is likely to be the correct one.
8. Use your head! Make shrewd inferences. Sometimes with a little thought, and the information that you have, you can reason out the answer. We're suggesting a method of intelligence guessing in which you can become quite expert with a little practice. It's a useful method that may help you with some debatable answers.

NOW, LET'S TRY THESE METHODS OUT ON A SAMPLE MULTIPLE-CHOICE QUESTION.

1. Leather is considered the best material for shoes chiefly because
   (A) it is waterproof
   (B) it is quite durable
   (C) it is easily procurable
   (D) it is flexible and durable
   (E) it can be easily manufactured in various styles.

Here we see that every one of the answer statements is plausible: leather is waterproof if treated properly; it is relatively durable; it is relatively easily procurable; it bends and is shaped easily, and is, again, durable; it constantly appears in various styles of shoes and boots.

However, we must examine the question with an eye toward identifying the key phrase which is: *best* for shoes *chiefly*.

Now we can see that (A) is incorrect because leather is probably not the *best* material for shoes, simply because it is waterproof. There are far better waterproof materials available, such as plastics and rubber. In fact, leather must be treated to make it waterproof. So by analyzing the key phrase of the question we can eliminate (A).

(B) seems plausible. Leather is durable, and durability is a good quality in shoes. But the word *quite* makes it a broad statement. And we become suspicious. The original meaning of *quite* is completely, wholly, entirely. Since such is the case we must reject this choice because leather is *not completely* durable. It does wear out.

(C) Leather is comparatively easy to procure; but would that make it *best* for shoes? And would that be the *chief* reason why it is used for making shoes? Although the statement in itself is quite true, it does not fit the key phrase of the question and we must, reluctantly, eliminate it.

(D) is a double-barreled statement. One part, the durability, has been suggested in (B) above. Leather is also quite flexible, so both parts of the statement would seem to fit the question.

(E) It is true that leather can be manufactured in various styles, but so can many other materials. Again, going back to the key phrase, this could be considered one, but not the *chief* reason why it is *best* for shoes.

So, by carefully analyzing the *key* phrase of the question we have narrowed our choices down to (D). Although we rejected (B) we did recognize that durability is a good quality in shoes, but only one of several. Since flexibility is also a good quality, we have no hesitation in choosing (D) as the correct answer.

The same question, by slightly altering the answer choices, can also call for a *negative* response. Here, even more so, the identification of the key phrase becomes vital in finding the correct answer. Suppose the question and its responses were worded thus:

2. Leather is considered the best material for shoes chiefly because
   (A) it is waterproof
   (B) it is easily colored
   (C) it is easily procurable
   (D) it can easily be manufactured in various styles
   (E) none of these.

We can see that the prior partially correct answer (B) has now been changed, and the doubly-correct answer eliminated. Instead we have a new response possibility (E), "none of these."

We have analyzed three of the choices previously and have seen the reason why none of them are the *chief* reason why leather is considered the *best* material for shoes. The two new elements are (B) "easily colored," and (E) "none of these."

If you think about it, leather *can* be easily colored and often is, but this would not be the chief reason why it is considered *best*. Many other materials are just as easily dyed. So we must come to the conclusion that *none* of the choices are *completely* correct—none fit the key phrase. Therefore, the question calls for a negative response (E).

We have now seen how important it is to identify the key phrase. Equally, or perhaps even more important, is the identifying and analyzing of the key *word*—the qualifying word—in a question. This is usually, though not always, an adjective or adverb. Some of the key words to watch for are: *most, best, least, highest, lowest, always, never, sometimes, most likely, greatest, smallest, tallest, average, easiest, most nearly, maximum, minimum, chiefly, mainly, only, but* and *or*. Identifying these key words is usually half the battle in understanding and, consequently, answering all types of exam questions.

Rephrasing the Question

It is obvious, then, that by carefully analyzing a question, by identifying the key phrase and its key words, you can usually find the correct answer by logical deduction and, often, by elimination. One other way of examining, or "dissecting," a question is to restate or rephrase it with each of the suggested answer choices integrated into the question.

For example, we can take the same question and rephrase it.

(A) The chief reason why leather is considered the best material for shoes is because it is waterproof.

or

(A) Because it is waterproof, leather is considered the best material for shoes.

or

(A) Chiefly because it is waterproof, leather is considered the best material for shoes.

It will be seen from the above three new versions of the original statement and answer that the question has become less obscure because it has been, so to speak, illuminated from different angles. It becomes quite obvious also in this rephrasing that the statement (A) is incorrect, although the *original* phrasing of the question left some doubt.

The rules for understanding and analyzing the key phrase and key words in a question, and the way to identify the *one* correct answer by means of intelligent analysis of the important question-answer elements, are basic to the solution of all the problems you will face on your test.

In fact, perhaps the *main* reason for failing an examination is failure to *understand the question*. In many cases, examinees *do* know the answer to a particular problem, but they cannot answer correctly because they do not understand it.

METHODS FOR MATCHING QUESTIONS

In this question form you are actually faced with multiple questions that require multiple answers. It's a difficult form in which you are asked to pair up one set of facts with another. It can be used with any type of material . . . vocabulary, spatial relations, numbers, facts, etc.

A typical matching question might appear in this form:

Directions: Below is a set of words containing ten words numbered 3 to 12, and twenty other words divided into five groups labeled Group A to Group E. For each of the numbered words select the word in one of the five groups which is most nearly the same in meaning. The letter of that group is the answer for that numbered item.

Although this arrangement is a relatively simple one for a "matching" question, the general principle is the same for all levels of difficulty. Basically, this type of question consists of two columns. The elements of one of the columns must be matched with some or all of the elements of the second column.

3. fiscal
4. deletion
5. equivocal
6. corroboration
7. tortuous
8. predilection
9. sallow
10. virtuosity
11. scion
12. tenuous

Group A
indication ambiguous
excruciating thin

Group B
confirmation financial
phobia erasure

Group C
fiduciary similar
yellowish skill

Group D
theft winding
receive procrastination

Group E
franchise heir
hardy preference

Correct Answers

3. B	6. B	9. C	10. C
4. B	7. D	8. E	11. E
5. A			12. A

There are numerous ways in which these questions may be composed, from the simple one shown above to the most difficult type of arrangement. In many cases the arrangement of the question may be so complicated that more time may be spent upon the comprehension of the instructions than on the actual question. This again, points up the importance of fully and quickly understanding the instructions before attempting to solve any problem or answer any question.

Several general principles apply, however, when solving a matching question. Work with one column at a time and match each item of that column against all the items in the second column, skipping around that second column looking for a proper match. Put a thin pencil line through items that are matched so they won't interfere with your later selections. (This is particularly important in a test that tells you to choose any item only once. The test gets real tricky, however, when you are asked to choose an item more than once.)

Match each item very carefully—don't mark it unless you are certain—because if you have to change any one, it may mean changing three or four or more, and that may get you hopelessly confused. After you have marked all your *certain* choices, go over the unmarked items again and make a *good* guess at the remaining items, if you have time.

USE CONTROLLED ASSOCIATION when you come to an item which you are not able to match. Attempt to recall any and all facts you might have concerning this item. Through the process of association, a fact recalled might provide a clue to the answer.

TRUE-FALSE TACTICS

True-false questions may appear on your test. Because they are easier to answer they are used less frequently than multiple-choice questions. However, because examiners find that they are easier to prepare, here are some suggestions to help you answer them correctly.

1. Suspect the truth of broad statements hinging on those *all or nothing* "cue" words we listed for you in discussing multiple-choice questions.
2. Watch out for "spoilers" . . . the word or phrase which negates an otherwise true statement.

Vegetation is sparse on the Sahara desert where the climate is hot and humid. T F

3. Statements containing such modifiers as *generally, usually, most,* and similar words are usually true.
4. If the scoring formula is "Rights minus Wrongs", don't guess. If you know it's true, mark it T. If you don't know it's true, ask yourself "What have I learned that would make it false?" If you can think of nothing on either side, omit the answer. Of course, if the R-W formula is not being used it is advisable to guess if you're not sure of an answer.
5. Your first hunch is usually best. Unless you have very good reason to do so, don't change your first answer to true-false questions about which you are doubtful.

Single-Statement Question

The basic form of true-false question is the "single-statement" question; i.e., a sentence that contains a single thought, such as:

13. The Statue of Liberty is in New York T F

The same statement becomes slightly more difficult by including a negative element

14. The Statue of Liberty is not in New York T F

or, more subtly:

15. The Statue of Liberty is not in Chicago T F

or, by adding other modifiers:

16. The Statue of Liberty is sometimes in New York T F
17. The Statue of Liberty is always in New York T F

Even from these very simple and basic examples of a "single-statement" true-false question it can be seen that a *complete understanding* of the subject area as well as of the phrasing of the question is essential before you attempt to answer it. Careless or hasty reading of the statment will often make you miss the *key* word, especially if the question appears to be a very simple one.

An important point to remember when answering this type of question is that the statement must be *entirely true* to be answered as "true"; if even just a *part* of it is false, the answer must be marked "false."

Composite-Statement Question

Sometimes a true-false question will be in the form of a "composite statement," a statement that contains more than one thought, such as:

18. The Statue of Liberty is in New York, and Chicago is in Illinois T F

Some basic variations of this type of composite-statement question are these:

19. The Statue of Liberty is in New York, and Chicago is in Michigan T F
20. The Statue of Liberty is not in New York and Chicago is in Illinois T F
21. The Statue of Liberty is not in New York and Chicago is in Michigan T F

Of the four questions above, only question 18 is true. Each of the other statements (19, 20, 21), is false because each contains at least *one* element that is false.

It can be seen from the above that in a composite statement *both* elements, or "substatements," must be true in order for the answer to be "true." Otherwise, the answer must be "false."

This principle goes for all composite statements that are, or can be, connected by the word "and," even if the various "thoughts" of the statement seem to be entirely unrelated.

We have seen how to handle a composite statement that consists of *unrelated* substatements. Finally, we will examine a composite true-false statement which consists of *related* elements:

22. The Golden Gate Bridge is in San Francisco, which is not the capital of California. T F
23. The Golden Gate Bridge is in San Francisco, the capital of California. T F
24. The Golden Gate Bridge is not in San Francisco, the capital of California. T F
25. The Golden Gate Bridge is not in San Francisco, which is not the capital of California. T F

Again, only the first composite statement (22) is true. All the rest are false because they contain at least one false substatement.

PART TWO

Background and Study Material for the Exam

Practice Using Answer Sheets

DIRECTIONS:

Read each question and its lettered answers. When you have decided which answer is correct, blacken the corresponding space on this sheet with a No. 2 pencil. Make your mark as long as the pair of lines, and completely fill the area between the pair of lines. If you change your mind, erase your first mark COMPLETELY. Make no stray marks; they may count against you.

SAMPLE

I. CHICAGO is
I-1 a country
I-2 a mountain
I-3 an island
I-4 a city
I-5 a state

I ::::: 1 ::::: 2 ::::: 3 ▬ 4 ::::: 5

SCORES

1______ 5______
2______ 6______
3______ 7______
4______ 8______

	T	F					T	F					T	F					T	F			
1	a	b	c	d	e	2	a	b	c	d	e	3	a	b	c	d	e	4	a	b	c	d	e
5	a	b	c	d	e	6	a	b	c	d	e	7	a	b	c	d	e	8	a	b	c	d	e
9	a	b	c	d	e	10	a	b	c	d	e	11	a	b	c	d	e	12	a	b	c	d	e
13	a	b	c	d	e	14	a	b	c	d	e	15	a	b	c	d	e	16	a	b	c	d	e
17	a	b	c	d	e	18	a	b	c	d	e	19	a	b	c	d	e	20	a	b	c	d	e
21	a	b	c	d	e	22	a	b	c	d	e	23	a	b	c	d	e	24	a	b	c	d	e
25	a	b	c	d	e	26	a	b	c	d	e	27	a	b	c	d	e	28	a	b	c	d	e
29	a	b	c	d	e	30	a	b	c	d	e	31	a	b	c	d	e	32	a	b	c	d	e
33	a	b	c	d	e	34	a	b	c	d	e	35	a	b	c	d	e	36	a	b	c	d	e
37	a	b	c	d	e	38	a	b	c	d	e	39	a	b	c	d	e	40	a	b	c	d	e
41	a	b	c	d	e	42	a	b	c	d	e	43	a	b	c	d	e	44	a	b	c	d	e
45	a	b	c	d	e	46	a	b	c	d	e	47	a	b	c	d	e	48	a	b	c	d	e
49	a	b	c	d	e	50	a	b	c	d	e	51	a	b	c	d	e	52	a	b	c	d	e
53	a	b	c	d	e	54	a	b	c	d	e	55	a	b	c	d	e	56	a	b	c	d	e
57	a	b	c	d	e	58	a	b	c	d	e	59	a	b	c	d	e	60	a	b	c	d	e
61	a	b	c	d	e	62	a	b	c	d	e	63	a	b	c	d	e	64	a	b	c	d	e
65	a	b	c	d	e	66	a	b	c	d	e	67	a	b	c	d	e	68	a	b	c	d	e
69	a	b	c	d	e	70	a	b	c	d	e	71	a	b	c	d	e	72	a	b	c	d	e
73	a	b	c	d	e	74	a	b	c	d	e	75	a	b	c	d	e	76	a	b	c	d	e
77	a	b	c	d	e	78	a	b	c	d	e	79	a	b	c	d	e	80	a	b	c	d	e
81	a	b	c	d	e	82	a	b	c	d	e	83	a	b	c	d	e	84	a	b	c	d	e
85	a	b	c	d	e	86	a	b	c	d	e	87	a	b	c	d	e	88	a	b	c	d	e
89	a	b	c	d	e	90	a	b	c	d	e	91	a	b	c	d	e	92	a	b	c	d	e
93	a	b	c	d	e	94	a	b	c	d	e	95	a	b	c	d	e	96	a	b	c	d	e
97	a	b	c	d	e	98	a	b	c	d	e	99	a	b	c	d	e	100	a	b	c	d	e
101	a	b	c	d	e	102	a	b	c	d	e	103	a	b	c	d	e	104	a	b	c	d	e
105	a	b	c	d	e	106	a	b	c	d	e	107	a	b	c	d	e	108	a	b	c	d	e
109	a	b	c	d	e	110	a	b	c	d	e	111	a	b	c	d	e	112	a	b	c	d	e
113	a	b	c	d	e	114	a	b	c	d	e	115	a	b	c	d	e	116	a	b	c	d	e
117	a	b	c	d	e	118	a	b	c	d	e	119	a	b	c	d	e	120	a	b	c	d	e
121	a	b	c	d	e	122	a	b	c	d	e	123	a	b	c	d	e	124	a	b	c	d	e
125	a	b	c	d	e	126	a	b	c	d	e	127	a	b	c	d	e	128	a	b	c	d	e
129	a	b	c	d	e	130	a	b	c	d	e	131	a	b	c	d	e	132	a	b	c	d	e
133	a	b	c	d	e	134	a	b	c	d	e	135	a	b	c	d	e	136	a	b	c	d	e
137	a	b	c	d	e	138	a	b	c	d	e	139	a	b	c	d	e	140	a	b	c	d	e
141	a	b	c	d	e	142	a	b	c	d	e	143	a	b	c	d	e	144	a	b	c	d	e
145	a	b	c	d	e	146	a	b	c	d	e	147	a	b	c	d	e	148	a	b	c	d	e
149	a	b	c	d	e	150	a	b	c	d	e												

CRIMINAL INVESTIGATION

Properly conducted criminal investigation deals not only with those matters familiar to the older officer, but calls to its aid all of the newer sciences, trades and arts. It may well be said that the sum total of human knowledge should be at the disposal of the criminal investigator.

GENERAL. a. Science in many cases has been found essential in the solution of crime. The investigator should know the facilities of a scientific laboratory and some of the techniques used by the laboratory technician in order that the utmost assistance can be obtained in the solution of cases. It is not expected, nor desired, that the investigator should become an expert in all scientific subjects, but he is expected to know what the laboratory can do and how he should submit physical evidence in such condition that a maximum amount of information can be obtained from it. The investigator should have sufficient knowledge of the facilities of the laboratory to tell the technician what sort of examination he wants and to give relevant facts to assist in the examination. For example, in a poisoning case, a description of the appearance and actions of the deceased prior to death is helpful to the technician.

b. The laboratory can furnish leads for the investigator as well as testimony for use in court. For instance, in a case involving a typewritten letter the laboratory frequently can give appreciable assistance in determining the make of the machine, kind of type used, probable age of the machine, and certain characteristics in its style of type. These are invaluable investigative leads. When the time comes for the presentation of evidence before a court, the good laboratory criminologist can prove by enlarged pictures and other data exactly how and why he reached his conclusions. Such evidence is very graphic and difficult to refute. Full use should be made of the laboratory even though the investigator may be uncertain of what can be accomplished.

TYPES OF EXAMINATIONS. Some of the types of examinations that can be accomplished by a laboratory are:

a. Toxicological examinations. Toxicology is the science of poisons and the examinations which are conducted in connection with poison cases.

b. Fingerprint developments. More extensive fingerprint developments are made in the laboratory through the use of chemical processes than are possible in the field by the use of developing powders.

c. Microscopic examination. Very minute particles of evidence may be examined by using such laboratory equipment as research microscopes, high power comparison microscopes, optical micrometers, precision rotary microtomes, and low power binocular microscopes. Coal dust, hair, soil particles, rope, twine, glass, and other small bits of evidence may be examined to determine their constituency. One field of microscopy, known as petrography or the examination of minerals and soils, is particularly valuable in certain cases. For example, if a subject in the course of a burglary drilled through a brick wall and upon his arrest particles of brick material were found on his clothing and the petrographer found the constituency of this material to be identical with that of the material used in the brick wall of the building, such circumstantial evidence in conjunction with other factors, might be sufficient to effect a conviction.

d. Spectography. Spectography is the science of measuring the wave length of a substance. Every substance has a characteristic wave length, which, to a laboratory technician, is the equivalent of a fingerprint of that substance. The advantage and importance of spectography is that it can be used effectively on the most minute specimen. For example, spectographic examination of the metal clinging to a chisel blade, might reveal the particles on the chisel to be of identical composition with the metal of a safe or box which had been burglarized, thus providing the investigator with valuable information. The importance of spectography cannot be overemphasized in the identification of materials.

e. Metallurgical examinations. Metallurgy is the science of the manufacture and treatment of metals and alloys. The metallurgical examination of metallic substances by quantitative, gravimetric, and volumetric analyses is frequently helpful in comparing two or more samples of evidence. Small but not minute samples are suitable for this type of examination. For example, wire trip cord on an explosive device may be found by metallurgical examination to be identical with a short piece of wire found on the person of a suspect, thereby constituting an important link in a chain of circumstantial evidence.

f. Firearms identification. Every gun has certain characteristic marks which appear on every bullet and cartridge fired from the gun.

g. Tool marks. Like a gun, every tool leaves a characteristic mark on material with which it comes in contact. The mark of a pair of pliers on a pipe or of a jimmy on a metal, or even a wood, surface may be compared and the tool identified.

h. Number restoration. Especially important to the investigator is the fact that serial numbers on motor blocks, weapons, tools, and other metal objects can be restored even though obliterated. For number restoration, articles should be sent to the laboratory.

i. Unusual photography. The uses for microphotography of small particles, and infrared and ultraviolet ray photography.

j. Powder patterns. When a gun is fired, fine portions of powder are discharged from the barrel. The patterns made by this powder on an object differ depending upon the make of the gun, the distance from which the gun was fired, and other factors. The laboratory, by conducting various tests, can determine many characteristics peculiar to the shot fired which may be helpful in solving a homicide or other case in which firearms are involved.

k. Bloodstains. The laboratory can be of great assistance in the determination of whether a substance or stain found at the scene of a crime or on the clothing or person of a suspect or victim is blood, and if so whether it is human or animal blood and its type.

l. Polygraph. The polygraph, more commonly known as "lie detector," is a combination of several different machines; namely, the pneumograph which records respiration, the sphygmograph which records blood pressure, the cardiograph which records heart movement through the pulse, and the galvanograph which records the activity of sweat glands. Hence the name "polygraph," the word "poly" meaning *many* and the word "graph" meaning *writing*. In the hands of an expert this machine is highly accurate and is helpful in furnishing investigative leads, although not yet accepted by the courts as proper evidence.

HAIRS AND FIBERS. a. General. In many crimes the origin and texture of hairs and fibers found on the crime scene or upon the body, clothing, or headgear of a suspect or victim may be exceedingly important. This is particularly true in homicide cases and in sex crimes.

b. Hair. (1) Each hair is made up of three parts: the medulla or inner section, the cortex or middle section, and the cuticle or outer surface. The size and texture of these parts of the hair vary not only between animals and humans, but also between the human races and between sexes of the same race. This fact combined with an analysis by the laboratory of the length, diameter, pigmentation and general anatomy of the hair will provide important circumstantial evidence of value to the investigator. Some of the conclusions which the laboratory may reach are:

(*a*) Whether the hair sample is that of a human being or an animal.

(*b*) Whether the hair was cut, broken, or torn from the body.

(*c*) Probable race of the owner.

(*d*) Probable sex of the owner.

(*e*) Approximate age of the owner.

(*f*) Part of the body from which the hair came.

(*g*) Whether the hair was bleached or dyed.

(2) Hair, unlike fingerprints, is not absolutely different in each individual. A determination that two hair samples are definitely from the body of the same person is not possible based upon a laboratory examination alone. The laboratory report may state that it is possible that two samples could have come from the same person, if they are identical. A laboratory can, however, give a negative report from a comparison of two hair samples and show definitely that they are not from the same person.

(3) Much can be learned from the study of hair and it should not be overlooked by the investigator. Gross in his work on Criminal Investigation reports a case in which a homicide was committed and the murderer while fleeing dropped his hat. The hat had no identifying marks, but within the hat were two hairs. The hairs were sent to a scientist who found some of the pigmentation in the medulla of the hairs was jet black though the hairs were gray. It was concluded that the hairs were from the head of a dark man, fairly young but beginning to grow gray. There was also evidence that the hair had been recently cut. The roots of the hair were wasted which indicated a loss of the hair and there were certain indications of excessive perspiration. From these two hairs the scientist gave the following description of the murderer: "a man of middle age, of robust constitution, inclined to obesity, black hair intermingled with gray hair, recently cut; commencing to grow bald." The value of this description is self-evident.

c. Fibers. Fibers, bits of rope, and similar evidence found at a crime scene should be forwarded to the laboratory. The laboratory can distinguish between natural fibers such as silk, cotton, and hemp, and the artificial fibers such as rayon, and nylon. Also a comparison can be made between a known cloth and samples of an unknown cloth. Threads, twine, and rope are made up of varying numbers of strands according to the manufacturer. A count of these strands compared with known standards will enable the technician to identify the material. A comparison of the dye and constituency of two samples of fiber to determine whether they are both from the same original piece can be of material assistance to the investigator.

SOURCES OF INFORMATION

RECORD SOURCES. The following is a list and brief description of some frequently consulted sources of recorded information:

a. Federal records. (1) *War Department.* (*a*) *Office of The Adjutant General.* The Adjutant General maintains records of all organizations, officers, and enlisted personnel that are or have been in the military service of the United States and also maintains such other records as authorized.

(*b*) *Service commands.* The Security and Intelligence Divisions of the various service command headquarters maintain records which may be of assistance to the investigator.

(*c*) *Provost marshals.* Provost marshals at posts, camps, or stations, and at oversea establishments, maintain records which the investigator may consult.

(2) *Navy Department. The Office of Naval Intelligence* and the several Naval District Intelligence Officers have information on the movements of travelers and ships, and on persons investigated by Naval Intelligence.

(3) *Department of Justice.* (*a*) *The Federal Bureau of Investigation* has on file fingerprint cards on many classes of persons, card indices on all persons whose names have come to the attention of the FBI, and a complete scientific laboratory for analyzing and identifying criminal evidence.

(*b*) *The Immigration and Naturalization Service* has photographs, fingerprints, and brief biographies of aliens and immigrants, their residence and employment addresses, and the status of their naturalization. To aid in identifying the subject, the investigator should provide the Immigration and Naturalization Service with the name of the vessel, the date and the port of entry if this information can be obtained.

(4) *Treasury Department Agencies* have information relative to their respective functions, some of which are mentioned below.

(*a*) *The United States Secret Service* suppresses counterfeiting and protects the person of the President.

(*b*) *The Bureau of Narcotics* investigates violations of the narcotic laws.

(*c*) *The Intelligence Unit Bureau of Internal Revenue* investigates violations of federal income tax laws.

(*d*) *The Alcohol Tax Unit Bureau of Internal Revenue* investigates violation of the laws relating to manufacture, storage, and sale of alcoholic beverages.

(*e*) *The Bureau of Customs* enforces the customs laws, supervises the importation of articles into the Unites States, patrols the borders of the United States, and apprehends smugglers.

(5) *The Post Office Department* will provide the investigator with all the information which appears on the outside of envelopes in the United States mail addressed to a particular individual. This service is known as a "mail cover" and will be continued for a specific period agreed upon by the investigator and the postal authorities. Mail may not be read except by censorship authorities or when seized pursuant to a search warrant. In securing a search warrant for mail the investigator should confer with the local postal inspector. At military establishments, the postal officer should be consulted for assistance.

(6) Other Federal agencies which have investigation units:

(*a*) Division of Investigations, Interior Department.

(*b*) Wages and Hours Division, Labor Department.

(*c*) Division of Investigation, U. S. Civil Service Commission.

(7) *The Veteran's Administration* has information relating to former members of military and naval forces.

(8) *The United States Maritime Commission* has records relating to the activities of the Merchant Marine and its officers and crews.

(9) *The Department of State* has information relating to passports and visas.

10) *The Federal Communications Commission* investigates and reports on all organizations engaged in interstate radio or wire communication, and licenses and monitors all radio stations.

b. State, county, and municipal records. Among the various records which may have information of value to the investigator are those of the following:

(1) State police and highway patrols.
(2) Local police departments.
(3) State Attorney's office.
(4) Sheriff's office.
(5) Fish and game wardens.
(6) County agent's office.
(7) Coroners or medical examiners.
(8) Fire marshals.
(9) City Attorney or City Prosecutor.
(10) Health, sanitation, building and license inspectors.
(11) Truant officers.
(12) Public welfare and social service agencies.
(13) Penal and probationary agencies.
(14) Courts.
(15) Tax assessors.
(16) Public and private schools, colleges, and universities.
(17) County clerks, city clerks.
(18) Marriage license bureaus.
(19) Workmen's compensation boards.

c. Private agencies. (1) *American Red Cross.*

(2) *Commercial credit bureaus* maintain extensive files on persons who have made use of personal credit, and these include addresses, bank accounts, charge accounts, records of judgment, assets, and financial standing.

(3) *Banks and loan and finance companies* may have information relative to the financial transactions of the subject.

(4) *Insurance Company Clearing House.* The National Association of Life Underwriters, 11 West 42nd Street, New York City, and various civilian credit agencies, have records on all persons who have or have had an interest in life insurance policies. The National Board of Fire Underwriters, 85 John Street, New York City, has the same information with regard to fire insurance.

(5) *Railroad companies* and their investigators are cooperative in furnishing information relative to the place of departure and destination of individuals and shipments.

(6) *Bus lines* maintain bills of lading at points of shipment and transfer points.

(7) *Steamship companies and air lines* usually have records of the names and addresses of passengers, the dates of travel, the point of disembarkation for each passanger, and the reservations made for land transportation or hotel accommodations.

(8) *Telephone companies'* records of long distance calls show the number calling and the city and number called. On certain calls, the name of the caller and the name and address of the person called are recorded.

(9) *Telegraph companies* have records and copies of telegrams and money orders.

(10) *Water, electric, and gas companies* are often the first agencies to obtain the addresses of persons newly arrived in a city.

(11) *Newspaper files,* commonly called "morgues," disclose the extent and type of publicity which an individual has received.

(12) *Real estate agencies,* have information concerning their tenants.

(13) *Automobile associations* can furnish information regarding the registration and ownership of members' automobiles.

(14) *Hospitals* keep records of wounds, injuries, illnesses, scars, births, and deaths.

(15) *Hotel associations* maintain files on criminals, such as bad check passers, card sharks, and confidence men. By inquiring at the association's office the investigator may learn about any guest of a member hotel.

d. Miscellaneous. (1) *Telephone directories* ordinarily are arranged according to the names of the subscribers or according to the business of the subscriber. Special telephone directories are compiled for large business and other agencies, arranged according to street addresses.

(2) *City directories* furnish addresses, occupations, names, and members of families living in the city at the time the information for the directory was collected. Early editions will reveal the year a person moved into the locality, former addresses, and occupations.

UNDERCOVER INVESTIGATIONS

GENERAL. An investigator is operating "undercover" when he abandons his official identity and adopts a completely different character which will enable him to associate with and get information from criminals without disclosing his real identity. He accomplishes his mission by gaining the confidence of the subjects, talking with them, listening to their conversations, and observing their actions. This is a highly specialized type of investigation, particularly useful in investigating espionage, frauds, the illegal sale of narcotics, the operations of gangs dealing in stolen Government property, contraband, or black market operations, and other similar crimes.

PRETEXTS. The investigator on an undercover mission must assume an identity which will enable him to associate with the subjects without arousing suspicion. Regardless of the pretext, the investigator must have at least a fundamental knowledge of the actual part to be played and must tell a story which cannot be discredited except by an intensive investigation, which the subjects are rarely able to make.

QUALIFICATIONS OF UNDERCOVER INVESTIGATOR. Although all of the qualifications listed below may not be necessary for a particular assignment, investigators who have the following characteristics usually make the best undercover men: actor-type personality; complete self-confidence in ability to play the part assumed; good judgment, resourcefulness, and wit; will power sufficent to avoid intoxication, drugs, and women on the assignment; language qualifications, such as knowledge of appropriate accents, colloquialisms, trade and underworld slang, and foreign tongues; wide experience in trades and criminology. The man who is not absolutely confident of his ability to accomplish an undercover mission properly should not be given such an assignment. Hesitation or bungling may result in failure of the mission or in danger to the life of the investigator.

PREPARATION FOR ASSIGNMENT. Investigators will undertake undercover assignments only upon express authorization of their commanding officer. After the type of character to be used has been determined, the following preparations are recommended:

a. Prepare a fictitious background and history for the character, including the names, addresses, and descriptions of the assumed places of education, employment, associates, neighborhoods, trades, and travels. The investigator's background story should seldom, if ever, be wholly fictitious. It is usally advisable for the investigator to choose a city in which he has lived and with which he is well acquainted. If it can be avoided, the home town of one of the subjects, unless it be a very large city, should not be selected as the origin of the investigator. Arrangements should be made to have principals in the fictitious history ready to corroborate the assertions of the undercover investigator, as the subjects may investigate his claims. It is good practice to select, where possible, corroborating personnel from among persons who are engaged in occupations which will not cause suspicion or arouse too much interest on the part of the subjects, as for example, bartenders, night club operators, waiters, and waitresses.

b. Obtain personal possessions which are appropriate to the character assumed in quality, price, age, fit, degree of cleanliness, laundry marks, and manufacturer's design. Personal possessions may include clothes, pocketbook, ring, watch, money, tokens, a suitcase, stubs of tickets from amusement places and transportation agencies, matches, photographs, letters, and certificates. Complete new sets of tools of a trade or profession assumed by the undercover man arouse suspicion which may be avoided by securing worn or used instruments. The undercover investigator must not possess any articles which will suggest his true identity. Badges or credentials showing the investigator's true identity must NEVER be found on the person of an undercover agent; and a firearm or other weapon may be carried only when consistent with the investigator's background story.

c. Memorize all details in connection with the assumed role and the fictitious portion of the biography.

d. Arrange secret methods of communication with headquarters.

e. Arrange for a check by supervising investigators on the welfare of the undercover investigator when he fails to report within a specified period of time.

CONDUCT OF ASSIGNMENT. a. The undercover man must in every respect live the part which he plays. His apperance, language, attitude, opinions, interests, and recreations must support the assumed past and trade, as he may be called upon to demonstrate his knowledge. Bragging, showing too much knowledge, and spending money out of character are likely to invite unwanted attention.

b. Normally, the first hurdle for the undercover investigator is to become acquainted with the subject or subjects. As a general rule, the undercover man should create a situation where the subject or subjects become interested in him and approach him in his assumed identity. In many investigations, a subject has become interested in an undercover man who lived in the same rooming house, or whom he encountered frequently in the neighborhood or at a club or business house, or one who supposedly was vacationing, hunting a job, or claimed to be an expert in a matter which was a hobby of the subject.

c. It is against public policy for an officer of the law to incite or participate in the commission of a crime; the undercover man must therefore be careful to avoid involvement as an accessory to a crime. He may pretend to fall in with the criminals' plans, but he should never render any active assistance in the preparation of crime. The term in law for improper activity on the part of an officer as outlined above is "entrapment."

d. Women associates of criminals are usually emotional and jealous; it is best, therefore, to treat them with consideration, but avoid close association. The women or one of the criminals may become jealous and precipitate investigation leading to detection of the investigator.

TAKING NOTES. Notes should be made by an investigator only when they are of unusual importance and when they cannot otherwise be remembered. Notes should be written in such a manner as to be unintelligible to anyone else. Numbers may be written as parts of a mathematical problem or as a telephone number. They may be written on inconspicuous materials such as chewing gum or cigarette wrappers, toilet paper, paper napkins, match boxes and covers, magazines, or on the wall paper in certain types of dwellings.

COMMUNICATION WITH HEADQUARTERS. a. Communication between headquarters and the undercover investigator must be accomplished by secret methods. In calling headquarters by telephone it is best to use a dial telephone in a public booth not connected with a local switchboard operator. To lessen the possibility of wire tapping, the investigator should use a different telephone for each call. Sometimes it is well to forward reports by telephoning a headquarters employee at his residence.

b. Written reports may be addressed to a fictitious name or organization at a prearranged general delivery address which is under the control of headquarters. Return addresses should appear on the communication only when required by circumstances. Since criminals usually have little correspondence, the investigator must not become conspicuous by posting numerous letters. To preclude the possibility of the reports falling into improper hands before mailing, they may sometimes be written in the post office and mailed there.

c. Representatives from headquarters may be met at secret, prearranged, rendezvous but such meetings are dangerous, as the investigator may be followed to the rendezvous. If an investigator is on his way to a rendezvous and discovers that he is being followed, he should elude his follower in a seemingly innocent manner, forego the rendezvous and pursue a course which appears natural.

d. The possibility of making telephonic reports to superiors while in the presence of the subjects should not be overlooked when it is imperative that headquarters be notified of the latest developments. This report may be accomplished by calling an unlisted number at headquarters or at the home of an associate investigator, under the pretext of calling a friend or business person on some routine matter. It is imperative that the investigator be sure that the person telephoned knows the alias the investigator is using, understands the situation, and will cooperate.

ARREST OF UNDERCOVER INVESTIGATOR.

a. If the investigator is arrested by the police he will act in accordance with his orders.

b. If he has not received orders regarding the disclosure of his identity in case of arrest by civil authorities, he must act according to his judgment. In such a situation, if retaining the assumed character does not serve a useful purpose, the investigator should refuse to make a statement until taken into custody, after which he can disclose in private his identity and ask to speak with military authorities.

ARRESTS AND SEARCHES OF THE PERSON

DEFINITIONS. To arrest a person is to deprive him of his liberty. There are several different types of arrest:

a. Temporary restraint while questioning (no accusation or charge being made).

b. Taking into custody (which generally includes the charge "You are under arrest.")

c. Officially charging with an offense.

GENERAL PRINCIPLES. The following general principles should be observed in making arrests:

a. Two or more investigators should be used to effect an arrest. Assistant should cover the arresting agent and watch for associates of the criminal. Investigators should, whenever possible, obtain assistance of military police in making arrests.

b. When practicable, the arrest should be made in an inconspicuous manner at a place offering few avenues of escape and a minimum of congestion and outside interference. Unless absolutely necessary, arrests should not be made in crowded streets or other public places where pursuit is difficult, and where if the criminal attempted to escape, the use of firearms might endanger innocent persons. Arrests made at places frequented by associates of the criminal or persons sympathetic with him may give him an opportunity to come to the criminal's assistance; arrests effected at a street intersection afford the criminal several avenues of escape.

c. The arresting investigator should be certain that the individual arrested is the person wanted. If he does not know the criminal by sight, he should have him pointed out or he should know his description well enough to preclude the possibility of a mistaken identity. An arrest should not be attempted by shooting at persons fleeing in an automobile unless there is justification for killing them.

d. The investigator should next identify himself to the criminal. The display of a badge or credentials, depending upon the circumstances, is an effective means of identification. He should then inform the criminal that he is under arrest. The arrest is complete when the criminal acknowledges the fact by words or actions or when the arresting investigator touches the person of the criminal.

e. The arresting investigator should be firm but courteous. In the event of resistance, only as much force as is necessary to accomplish the arrest should be used.

f. The prisoner should be given a preliminary search at the scene of the arrest.

g. *No request of the criminal should be granted until the* *complete search of his person has been conducted at the place of detention.* The criminal should be carefully guarded and given no opportunity for escape while being escorted to the place of detention.

h. Before leaving the place of arrest the premises should be searched in the presence of the prisoner for any article which may have been discarded by the prisoner or for evidence of the prisoner's criminal activity.

i. If the arrested criminal has a vehicle it should be driven by another investigator or military policeman to the place of detention or disposition, where it is carefully searched. The person arrested should not be transported from the place of arrest in his own vehicle.

j. The precautions described above should be observed whenever practicable, but they do not limit the conditions under which an arrest may be made. Whenever an immediate arrest is imperative it is made without delay, regardless of the location.

k. The five main points in any arrest are:

(1) Manpower—have plenty of help.

(2) Firearms superiority.

(3) Movement—don't delay. Arrange to cut off all avenues of escape. Know where your assistants are.

(4) Simplicity of operation.

(5) Surprise.

DON'TS. a. Don't be unnecessarily rough. Be firm and give the impression that you are in command of the situation.

b. DON'T let the prisoner make excuses or delay. Insist on immediate response to your orders.

c. DON'T grant requests.

d. DON'T underestimate any man you are placing under arrest. Remember that the unresisting, apparently harmless person may cause trouble when your guard is down.

e. DON'T get too close to the prisoner with firearms.

f. DON'T talk too much. Be brief and clear in issuing orders.

g. DON'T allow other people to come between you and the prisoner. On crowded streets, keep away from pedestrians. Keep the prisoner between yourself and building. Get into a doorway, if necessary, until help arrives.

h. DON'T allow prisoners to separate. Keep them all together. Keep your assistants well separated, however.

i. DON'T create a scene. Be quiet and cool. Effect the arrest in an orderly efficient manner.

j. DON'T face the prisoner. Turn his back to you after you have made the arrest. DON'T rest your gun on his back, he may take it away from you.

PRELIMINARY SEARCH. a. When a person subject to military law is placed in arrest or confinement for a crime, he should be given a preliminary search at the scene of the arrest to recover concealed weapons. A more complete search is conducted when the prisoner has been transported to the place of detention. The preliminary search of the prisoner should be made *immediately* upon arrest, and preferably in the presence of a witness.

b. The "wall search" is usually the most effective and safe method of conducting a preliminary search.

In this method the prisoner is placed in an awkward and off-balance position from which it would be difficult for him to attack the searcher, and is particularly useful when one or two men must handle several prisoners. The prisoner is required to face a wall and to lean against it with his hands over his head on the wall, the arms spread apart. His body is inclined at an angle with the wall and his feet are well apart and as far back as he can get them without falling on his face. His head must be kept down. The searching agent does not touch the prisoner in any way until the prisoner is in the proper position for searching. If there is no wall, vehicle, embankment, or either upright surface available, the prisoner should be made to kneel on the ground with his hands in the air.

c. The persons conducting the search should search carefully for concealed weapons.

d. During the course of the preliminary search the prisoner should not be allowed to move toward the searcher, or be permitted to dispose of or destroy any property in his possession.

e. When there is more than one prisoner, all the prisoners should be made to take the wall-search position and the prisoners searched while another investigator covers them. One investigator should not try to search more than two prisoners by himself but should send for assistance. When searching a group of prisoners the prisoners should all be lined up as described and the searching investigator should first search the last man in the line against the wall. Upon completion of that search, the prisoner is moved to the head of the line so that the searching investigator can then proceed to the next prisoner and will not get between the prisoners or between a prisoner and the line of fire of the covering investigator. The searching investigator stands back while the prisoner makes the shift. During the shift the prisoner keeps his hands high in the air. The other prisoners do not move. The searching investigator should begin the search on the right-hand side of the line, while the covering investigator stands away from the line and well to the left of the searcher so that the searcher will not be in the line of fire. While searching the right side of the prisoner, the investigator places his right leg in front of the prisoner's right leg. While searching the left side, the investigator's left leg is placed in front of the prisoner's left leg. By so placing his legs, the searcher can easily trip the prisoner if he attempts to resist. The searching investigator's firearm should be held in his left hand, close to the hip, while the search is conducted with the right hand on the right side of the prisoner. When moving to the left of the prisoner, the position of the firearm is changed to the right hand and the search is conducted with the left hand.

f. In conducting the wall search, the following procedure is recommended.

(1) Remove the prisoner's headgear and examine for concealed weapons.

(2) Feel between the shoulder blades, down to the waist, and up the right side to the armpit.

(3) Feel the right arm to the wrist, outside and inside the clothing.

(4) Feel the throat, breast, and waist.

(5) Empty the small watch pocket.

(6) Search all coat pockets, emptying them.

(7) Watch for false pockets or bulges.

(8) Feel the necktie and the lapels of the coat.

(9) Empty the right trousers pockets, side and hip.

(10) Search carefully in the vicinity of the groin.

(11) Search down the inside of the right leg to the ankle. Check bottom of trousers, stockings, and feel inside the top of the shoes.

(12) Then search up the outside of right leg.

(13) Follow the same procedure on left side.

g. *Do not pat* when searching. Thin flat objects will be missed if this is done. The hand is *run* over the prisoner's entire body. It must be borne in mind that a weapon may be concealed anywhere.

COMPLETE SEARCH. a. When the prisoner arrives at the place of dentention, a more complete search should be made. The complete search should be conducted in a closed room, with only the prisoner, another investigator to assist in the search, and a guard present. Only one prisoner should be searched at a time. The subject should be required to remove all his clothing and place it on a table. The prisoner's body should then be searched carefully. When necessary, all body crevices should be examined for concealed objects. After the search of the prisoner's body, he should be provided with a set of coveralls and a pair of slippers.

b. The prisoners clothing and personal effects are then carefully searched. Particular attention should be paid to the following:

(1) Articles that might be used against the investigator or to effect an escape (firearms, knives, blackjacks, knucklers, explosives, hacksaw blades, lockpicks, keys of all sorts, and any unusual or odd device.

(2) Articles that might be used by the prisoner to commit suicide (poisons, narcotics, razor blades, glasses).

(3) Articles that constitute the fruit of the crime (stolen property or suspected stolen property of any type).

(4) Articles used in the commission of the crime.

(5) Articles of evidence that may be used to support charges against the prisoner (papers, maps, sketches, documents, names and addresses, baggage, checks, etc.).

(6) Articles relating to any other criminal activity of the prisoner.

c. The prisoner's clothing should be examined as follows:

Hat: Outer band, sweat band, and lining.

Cap: Peak and lining.

Topcoat: Collar, lapels, false pockets, pocket flaps, seams, lining, large buttons, and any ornaments.

Coat: Collar, lapels, pocket flaps, false pockets, seams, buttons, and lining.

Vest: Lining, seams, strap and buttons.

Belt: Inside false pocket, buckle.

Shirt: Collar band, cuffs, pocket, or false pocket.

Tie: Lining and the knot, if tied.

Trousers: Seams, false pockets, and cuffs.

Shoes: Under the sole, hollow heel, inside of counter, lining of tongue.

d. All miscellaneous items should be searched thoroughly. Billfolds, tobacco cans, match boxes, and packages of cigarettes should be opened and emptied. Pens, pencils, cigars, rings, and watches should also be examined.

IDENTIFICATION OF ARTICLES FOUND ON SUBJECT. At the conclusion of the search, a written inventory is made of the articles found. All objects pertinent to the investigation are marked for identification.

Each pertinent article of evidence is placed in a separate container which then is sealed and labeled. All articles retained by the arresting authority as evidence are kept in a secure place pending proper disposition. All evidence should be listed in the report of investigation.

SIGN CUTTING

Most people who take exams are busy people. They cannot afford to waste time searching in libraries and elsewhere for the precise study material required. If you're such a person, this chapter should help. It presents a workable plan for broadening your background and strengthening your ability in this probable test subject.

HISTORICAL BACKGROUND OF SIGN CUTTING

The art (and it is an art) of finding and interpreting marks left by something that has passed was perhaps used more extensively by American Indians prior to the arrival of the Pilgrim Fathers than at any time since, although early (and present) hunters and plainsmen, trappers, pioneers generally, and all others who have had occasion to leave the beaten trails, have resorted to *sign cutting* to determine what has happened during their absence, to locate game, to determine whether the enemy has been in the vicinity. With the development of our country and with the natural increase in the number of criminals, *sign cutting* was found to be a most satisfactory method of running down cattle rustlers, train robbers, murderers, and other fugitives. This method of determining how the crime was committed, and by whom, gradually developed until today it is not unusual to see tracks of vehicles, animals, and human beings brought into the courts in the form of plaster-of-paris casts, and to see important convictions secured when such evidence is explained by expert witnesses—trained *sign cutters*.

It is noteworthy that when our modern criminal leaves the centers of population for the open country, where he must leave evidence of his presence, he is usually apprehended if a good *sign cutter* is available.

There is perhaps no branch of law enforcement today wherein the reading of *sign* plays a more important part or produces more accurate and timely information than in the patrolling of our land and water boundaries. Unless aircraft is employed, tracks must be left by those who enter surreptitiously at points where surfaced highways are not available, and where docks are not provided for the landing of watercraft.

It can be said that there is no form of intelligence information which is more reliable and timely when interpreted by a competent officer than *sign*. In the Border Patrol we receive information from a great many sources: informers, grudge, paid and voluntary; friends; brother officers in other services, and others. Some of such information is usually accurate, at least in some particulars, but it is only the physical evidence—the tracks of the alien who entered—properly interpreted by a competent officer, that can at all times be fully relied upon to determine:

1. where illegal crossing is done, in order that assignments may be made accordingly, and
2. to determine where the illegal crossers are going in order that they may be apprehended.

SIGN CUTTING IN GENERAL

It should be constantly borne in mind that the law-enforcement officers are not the only ones who *cut sign* in order to aid them in their work. We find that smugglers quite generally have doubled back on their trail to determine whether the officers have cut their *sign* with a view to changing the route of travel if it appears that their former trail has been found and will be guarded. Realizing this, the officers often recut the *sign* before making assignments requiring heavy expenditure of man power and definitely determine whether the smugglers have learned that their former trail has been located. This practice makes it necessary at times for the officers to brush out their tracks. The brushing out of tracks is also advisable when considerable crossing is taking place in a more or less congested area, in order that the officers will not lose so much time in determining those recently made and those made upon prior occasions.

TRAINING OF SIGN CUTTERS

It goes without saying that the officers who take most readily to *sign cutting* are those who have lived in the open: cattlemen, hunters, trappers, and so forth. These men, even though at first they know little or nothing about the habits and methods of smugglers, and find it difficult to determine just what took place from the tracks viewed, have a big jump on the officer who has had no training in this work. They have cultivated the habit of looking for tracks and they know from what angles to look for them in various types of country. These are two of the most important qualifications in a *sign cutter* and they apply with equal force to all classes of *sign cutting*.

An officer might be able to read and interpret *sign* with fair accuracy, and he might be able to follow a track in dust, sand, rocks, grass, and so forth, but he may not have cultivated the habit of subconsciously looking for *sign*, and therefore he would be of little value to his service. The most important thing is to cultivate the habit of looking for *sign*. When on vacation, picnics, working anywhere, force yourself to look for tracks and significant marks or unusual signs and it will not be long until you will be doing so unconsciously. The technique of interpreting correctly what you have seen will gradually follow.

HOW TO LOOK FOR AND FOLLOW SIGN

It will be found that tracks can best be seen when the sun is low and not too glaring, and that tracks on hard, smooth ground can only be seen at an angle unless made by a heavy vehicle or shod animal. Having located tracks near or crossing the international line, the first thing is to determine what made the tracks, and whether it would be worthwhile to follow them.

First, it is always well, if possible, to determine the general direction of the tracks, so in case the trail is lost it can be *cut* and relocated with the least possible loss of time. At times, in certain sections, it is understood that aliens and smugglers of aliens, who cross afoot and mounted, guide on some prominent landmark. In other sections such methods are not employed. However, it is usually possible to determine quickly the general direction in which the vehicle, animal or human was headed, providing the tracks merit further investigation. Having determined this, they are followed by focusing the eyes much the same as when *sign cutting*—that is, somewhat in advance of the vehicle or animal used as a means of transportation. In loose sand and dust little difficulty should be encountered, but occasionally loose rock and hard smooth ground is encountered, and here the trail might be very difficult to follow or might be temporarily lost. At such times it is well to dismount, or if the difficult section is short, to ride rapidly forward and *cut* the trail in more favorable ground and proceed. Here is where a knowledge of the general direction of the trail becomes of definite assistance to the *sign cutter*. On the other hand, should the difficult stretch be long and give the person, vehicle, or animal trailed an opportunity to double back, it can be followed by watching closely for misplaced rocks or bent grass through the use of field glasses.

It goes without saying that the more experience a smuggler of aliens has had, the more difficult it will be for a novice *sign-cutter* to follow his trail. Having determined that a group of aliens crossed the international line, headed north or south, it is always well to suspect that trickery might have been employed. For example, such groups will often walk backwards across the international line to leave the impression that they are proceeding south instead of north. Close scrutiny will show that the stride will be short, the heel prints will be deeper, and the "drag" of the heel will be at the back of the imprint with a very slight imprint made with the toe of the shoe. Another popular method of endeavoring to evade *sign cutters* who make the mistake of *cutting sign* along the same trail each day is for a group of aliens to step in each other's tracks; to walk on weeds or rocks while passing the *sign-cutter's* trail; to walk on their heels; and to brush out their tracks as they proceed through the area where sign is usually *cut*. It therefore becomes necessary not only for the *sign-cutter* to look for trampled grass, rocks which have been turned out of place, but also dents which might be made by heels.

The importance of closely studying tracks to be

followed, as soon as a plain set is encountered, will be realized when, after following a trail for some distance, the trail leads into a section where it merges with other tracks of approximately the same age. Tracks, like fingerprint records, have their own peculiarities; and if the proper study has been given them, they can usually be identified, and followed even though merged with others on the same trail.

Where the destination of the thing trailed can be more or less determined—at least the general direction is known—and where dangerous smugglers are liable to be encountered, *sign-cutters* at times ride back and forth across the trail at varying intervals to determine that they are still on the trail and at other times ride a safe distance from and parallel to the trail. This practice prevents riding into an ambush, as was done in Arizona some years back by a former Patrol Inspector.

WHAT TO LOOK FOR WHEN CUTTING SIGN

Obviously, all tracks crossing the international boundary are not followed by *sign cutters*, for many are made by cattlemen, miners, hunters, fishermen, trappers, and others. Loose stock also cross the international line in some sections, and to attempt to track down all conveyances, animals, and human beings who leave their tracks at the international line would indeed be a stupendous task. So the first thing the *sign-cutter* must do is to determine whether such tracks merit further investigation. He can usually eliminate the hunter because he will wander into sections that a smuggler would never enter unless to conceal contraband. A fisherman will usually leave evidence of his activity on the banks of the river. The trapper will shortly disclose the location of his trap-line. The prospector will be stopping to pick up rock and to knock corners off stones which might carry metal values. Stray stock, too, unless they be stolen stock homeward bound, will usually disclose their purpose in crossing by wandering from grazing spot to grazing spot or to water. In these and many other ways the trained *sign-cutter* determines whether or not he should follow a trail.

Here again we find trickery is at times employed. Five woodchoppers from Mexico have been known to cross in one group and leave ample evidence of their purpose in crossing. Four tracks only will be seen to cross the international line and return. In *cutting sign* around the area in which they have "dug" mesquite roots, however, it has been found that one of the number headed afoot into the interior. Again we have the proposition of an alien stepping in the tracks of another with the hope that the trail will not be followed because four aliens checked in and four checked out.

Range animals are seldom shod, whereas animals used to any extent over rocky country by smugglers are always shod and appear to have a definite objective or to be heading in a definite direction. While it cannot always be determined that a horse is carrying a rider, a deeper track will usually be found when he trots, and he will appear to have a more even gait. He will, unless going to water, proceed more directly.

DEDUCTIONS FROM TRACKS

Considerable has been said about determining when a track was made. It is very important usually to determine this, for upon this element rests the decision of whether pursuit should be attempted and if so, the means of transportation to be employed. It is extremely difficult at times in the desert regions of the Southwest to make any accurate estimate as to when a track was made, unless due to the action of the elements the track has been somewhat altered. At times such action does not take place for days, and the track will continue to appear fresh. On the other hand, during certain seasons of the year when the wind kicks up the sand and when some moisture is in the air, some very accurate deductions as to when the track was formed can be made. Knowing the habits of the rats and lizards, when the dew (if any) falls, when it rained during the preceding night, when the wind came up, when the frost hit and when it froze, all contribute to making it possible for an intelligent *sign-cutter* to determine when a track was made.

Rats in sandy sections, in warm weather, travel as long as the moon shines, while during cold weather or when there is no moon, they travel only during the fore part of the night. The little desert lizard, on the other hand, apparently gets up with the crack of dawn and is busily engaged in making *sign* all day. If *sign* is cut daily in a section it is only necessary for the *sign-cutter* to determine whether the track was made before or after midnight, depending upon the distance which he has in which to run down the aliens before they reach some congested area where it may take a search warrant to find them. The *sign-cutter* therefore, at times when convenient, asks the officers on duty at night as to when the wind blew the night before, whether it rained, when the dew fell, and so forth—or observes these matters himself—and is guided accordingly when he finds tracks.

Sign in loose rock soon changes, and that part of the rock which was moved from its protected position will soon acquire the appearance of the rest of the rock. Grass which has been stepped on will soon begin to straighten up; and tracks on very hard ground fade rapidly. If tracks in such sections appear to be fresh, it can be reasonably concluded that they were made a short time before—say within several hours at the most.

NOTING PECULIARITIES OF TRACKS

Noting peculiarities of tracks is very important, as was pointed out. Each officer should familiarize himself with the various patterns of tire treads, in order that he may determine the make of a tire that makes a track which he sees under suspicious circumstances. In this way he is at times able positively to identify the vehicle when overtaken or when seen at a later date. He should note whether the tires are new, worn, smooth, or badly worn, and the wheel on which an easily identified tire is used. A horse track can easily be distinguished from a mule track, for the latter is longer and narrower. A *sign-cutter* should immediately decide whether the animal is a horse, mule, colt, or burro, and then scrutinize the tracks to determine whether the animal was shod, and if so, which feet carry shoes. He should also note any peculiarities in the shape of the tracks and the feet which make them.

Human tracks often furnish considerable information. It is important to make careful note of the length and width of the shoe tracks; whether rubber composition or leather soles; whether soles were worn to such an extent as to be easily identified; and the foot on which the easily identified shoe was worn; whether heels are run over; or the track was distinctive in other respects. The size of a person making a track can be very accurately determined by the size of his shoe and the length of his stride; and the shape of the shoe at times furnishes the officer with an accurate idea of the type of person who made the track—cowpuncher, laborer, or other calling.

Airplane tracks should always be studied carefully. More and more we find it necessary to combat this form of smuggling. The make of the tires, the type of tail-skid employed, and so forth, should be noted. Bearing in mind that airplanes with modern equipment can land in very small clearings it is well to be constantly on the lookout for airplane *sign* wherever an officer may be operating. A good way to become familiar with tracks left by airplanes on different types of ground is to go to a landing field and look over such tracks.

When following a trail, look for anything that might have been dropped; inspect places where the crossers have come to rest. Look for prints of loads or packages. Note on which side of bushes crossers rest, for this will help in determining the age of the track because of the shade. Note how they walk, for if it is dark they will walk right into a bush before turning around it, and also, when the light is good, they will select the firmest ground on which to walk.

BACK-TRACKING

It is always well to back-track an apprehended alien or smuggler to the international line in order that he cannot months later change his story and deny illegal crossing. Furthermore, corroborative evidence of an alien having crossed, apart from his confession, is often necessary.

TEAR OUT ALONG THIS LINE AND MARK YOUR ANSWERS AS INSTRUCTED IN THE TEXT

DIRECTIONS FOR ANSWERING QUESTIONS

DIRECTIONS: For each question read all the choices carefully. Then select that answer which you consider correct or most nearly correct. Write the letter preceding your best choice next to the question. Should you want to answer on the kind of answer sheet used on machine-scored examinations, we have provided several such facsimiles. On some machine-scored exams you are instructed to "place no marks whatever on the test booklet." In other examinations you may be instructed to mark your answers in the test booklet. In such cases you should be careful that no other marks interfere with the legibility of your answers. It is always best NOT to mark your booklet unless you are sure that it is permitted. It is most important that you learn to mark your answers clearly and in the right place.

FOR THE SAMPLE QUESTION that follows, select the appropriate letter preceding the word which is most nearly the same in meaning as the capitalized word:

1. DISSENT: (A) approve (B) depart (C) disagree (D) enjoy

DISSENT is most nearly the same as (C), disagree, so that the acceptable answer is shown thus on your answer sheet:

A	B	C	D
⁞	⁞	▮	⁞

Practice Using Answer Sheets

Alter numbers to match the practice and drill questions in each part of the book.
Make only ONE mark for each answer. Additional and stray marks may be counted as mistakes.
In making corrections, erase errors COMPLETELY. Make glossy black marks.

	A	B	C	D	E		A	B	C	D	E		A	B	C	D	E		A	B	C	D	E		A	B	C	D	E
1	⁞	⁞	⁞	⁞	⁞	1	⁞	⁞	⁞	⁞	⁞	1	⁞	⁞	⁞	⁞	⁞	1	⁞	⁞	⁞	⁞	⁞	1	⁞	⁞	⁞	⁞	⁞
2	⁞	⁞	⁞	⁞	⁞	2	⁞	⁞	⁞	⁞	⁞	2	⁞	⁞	⁞	⁞	⁞	2	⁞	⁞	⁞	⁞	⁞	2	⁞	⁞	⁞	⁞	⁞
3	⁞	⁞	⁞	⁞	⁞	3	⁞	⁞	⁞	⁞	⁞	3	⁞	⁞	⁞	⁞	⁞	3	⁞	⁞	⁞	⁞	⁞	3	⁞	⁞	⁞	⁞	⁞
4	⁞	⁞	⁞	⁞	⁞	4	⁞	⁞	⁞	⁞	⁞	4	⁞	⁞	⁞	⁞	⁞	4	⁞	⁞	⁞	⁞	⁞	4	⁞	⁞	⁞	⁞	⁞
5	⁞	⁞	⁞	⁞	⁞	5	⁞	⁞	⁞	⁞	⁞	5	⁞	⁞	⁞	⁞	⁞	5	⁞	⁞	⁞	⁞	⁞	5	⁞	⁞	⁞	⁞	⁞
6	⁞	⁞	⁞	⁞	⁞	6	⁞	⁞	⁞	⁞	⁞	6	⁞	⁞	⁞	⁞	⁞	6	⁞	⁞	⁞	⁞	⁞	6	⁞	⁞	⁞	⁞	⁞
7	⁞	⁞	⁞	⁞	⁞	7	⁞	⁞	⁞	⁞	⁞	7	⁞	⁞	⁞	⁞	⁞	7	⁞	⁞	⁞	⁞	⁞	7	⁞	⁞	⁞	⁞	⁞
8	⁞	⁞	⁞	⁞	⁞	8	⁞	⁞	⁞	⁞	⁞	8	⁞	⁞	⁞	⁞	⁞	8	⁞	⁞	⁞	⁞	⁞	8	⁞	⁞	⁞	⁞	⁞
9	⁞	⁞	⁞	⁞	⁞	9	⁞	⁞	⁞	⁞	⁞	9	⁞	⁞	⁞	⁞	⁞	9	⁞	⁞	⁞	⁞	⁞	9	⁞	⁞	⁞	⁞	⁞
0	⁞	⁞	⁞	⁞	⁞	0	⁞	⁞	⁞	⁞	⁞	0	⁞	⁞	⁞	⁞	⁞	0	⁞	⁞	⁞	⁞	⁞	0	⁞	⁞	⁞	⁞	⁞

KEEPING SCORE FOR SCORING HIGH

Recording your score on the exams, quizzes and practice questions in this book is important to your success. It allows you to find, and not forget, those areas where further work is needed if you are to achieve your goal. When you find these areas, you should devote additional study time to them. Then, take those tests and quizzes again. Use the score boxes below to record these scores, and then compare them with your original scores. Follow this procedure until you are satisfied with your score.

SCORE 1	SCORE 2	SCORE 3	SCORE 4	SCORE 5
.... %	.... %	.... %	.... %	.... %
NO. CORRECT	NO. CORRECT	NO. CORRECT	NO. CORRECT	NO. CORRECT
NO. OF QUESTIONS	NO. OF QUESTIONS	NO. OF QUESTIONS	NO. OF QUESTIONS	NO. OF QUESTIONS

SCORE 1	SCORE 2	SCORE 3	SCORE 4
.... %	.... %	.... %	.... %
NO. CORRECT ÷	NO. CORRECT ÷	NO. CORRECT ÷	NO. CORRECT ÷
NO. OF QUESTIONS	NO. OF QUESTIONS	NO. OF QUESTIONS	NO. OF QUESTIONS

SCORE 1	SCORE 2	SCORE 3	SCORE 4
.... %	.... %	.... %	.... %
NO. CORRECT	NO. CORRECT	NO. CORRECT	NO. CORRECT
NO. OF QUESTIONS	NO. OF QUESTIONS	NO. OF QUESTIONS	NO. OF QUESTIONS

SCORE	SCORE	SCORE	SCORE	SCORE
.... %	.... %	.... %	.... %	.... %
NO. CORRECT	NO. CORRECT	NO. CORRECT	NO. CORRECT	NO. CORRECT
NO. OF QUESTIONS	NO. OF QUESTIONS	NO. OF QUESTIONS	NO. OF QUESTIONS	NO. OF QUESTIONS

SCORE 1	SCORE 2
.... %	.... %
NO. CORRECT ÷	NO. CORRECT ÷
NO. OF QUESTIONS	NO. OF QUESTIONS

SCORE .... %

NO. CORRECT ÷ NO. OF QUESTIONS

SCORE .... %

NO. CORRECT ÷ NO. OF QUESTIONS

PATROL INSPECTOR

TRACING THE SUSPECT

The first procedure in tracing a suspect is to assemble all possible information about the wanted person. Such relevant information includes physical appearance, carriage, habits, gestures, interests, peculiarities of speech and voice, his criminal record and modus operandi, his former place of employment, relatives, friends, places frequented, etc. If possible a photograph, fingerprint and signature of the suspect should be on hand in the process of tracing him. He may register in a hotel and a copy of his handwriting should be immediately available for comparison. In making inquiries in former places of residence, work, or play, showing a photograph to trustworthy persons will help identify the suspect.

DISGUISES

Disguise by a criminal is frequently practiced. There are numerous ways of changing appearance to allay suspicion and elude arrest. The hair can be dyed or shaved, or cut in a different style, or growing a beard or mustache may be resorted to as a disguise. Teeth may be altered by changing gold fillings in front teeth or by extracting certain shaped teeth. Distinctive marks can be removed or changed by plastic surgery so as to make it hard to recognize scars, moles, thick lips, certain tattoo designs. Surgery may be used to change the appearance of the eyes by alterations of the eyelids or the nose, or ears. An entirely different pattern of clothes may be worn, or the guilty person may resort to a disguise by wearing clothing of the opposite sex.

LEADS

Help can be received in tracing a suspect by making inquiries at general sources of information. The taxi that the suspect used or the express company which moved his belongings may furnish a clue to the suspect's movements. The electric light and gas company, telephone company, election registry (if he was a voter), schools (if he has children of school age), or some other source of information. Canceled checks and banks may supply information. If a deposit box can be located, a court order will facilitate an examination of its contents. Credit associations, and insurance companies may be helpful in supplying data. Passport offices, steamship and railroad companies and other means of transportation should be consulted. If a railroad ticket for any distant place is purchased, along with a Pullman berth, the agent may issue a sales ticket giving the number of the ticket, car and berth. The collected tickets are returned to the office of the railroad company. The conductor, trainman, or pullman porter may help in the identification of the fugitive suspect. A travel insurance ticket is an additional means of identification when transportation is used. All known data in local police departments, in Central Bureaus of Criminal Information operated by states, and the Federal Bureau of Investigation in Washington, should be gathered in tracing the suspect. Motor vehicle bureaus, garages, reports of accident cases and hospital records, tax assessment bureau, mailing lists and directories, fraternal, veteran or labor organizations, laundry and dry-cleaning establishments, social welfare agencies, and auto rental offices may add valuable information in tracing the suspect.

CLUES

Various circumstances should be held in mind in the quest of the suspect. The telephone operator of a hotel switchboard can furnish phone numbers left for the suspect at various times, or numbers called by the suspect. The places and persons represented by such phone numbers should be contacted for knowledge of the fugitive. Empty match boxes left on the premises may lead to restaurants, night clubs or resorts frequented by the person wanted Criminal narcotic addicts can be traced through their addiction, inasmuch as they often frequent the place where they can obtain their supply of narcotics, or to associate with other drug addicts in that place. Sometimes a psychopathic criminal feels a sense of self-importance because the authorities are searching for him, and he may talk to casual acquaintances boasting about his importance.

TRAITS

Escaping criminals are likely to shun main traffic highways, if less travelled roads are available. Criminals of the "hobo" type are likely to go to cheap lodging houses and hobo camps. On the other hand, a criminal in possession of large sums of money, or who wants to circulate counterfeit currency, may indulge in lavish spending and so attract attention to himself. They may be noticed by persons who are willing, if asked, to give information. From a study of the habits of the suspect, it is possible to trace him to places where the fugitive can satisfy his desire for special foods or drinks. A waiter or bartender may recall him through catering to peculiar whims. A suspect may leave a clue in various places he frequents by his use of some special expression or slang.

If the suspect has a prison record he might visit the residence of a former fellow inmate or the home of a friend or relative of such inmate. Special techniques have been used in obtaining a fugitive's address by writing or wiring. A registered letter is brought to the home of a friend or relative which bears the address of the suspect. The message is not actually delivered, but the mail carrier or messenger boy is instructed to inform the friend that it will be held in the office until it is called for. The friend may give the address of the fugitive or inform him that an important message is waiting for him. The post office authorities are asked to co-operate in controlling the mail of a suspect and that of his friends.

The fugitive may be of alien extraction or he may be able to read newspapers in foreign languages. If that fact is established, newsdealers who handle foreign language newspapers should be approached for information. It is possible the suspect buys such newspapers to find out what is being said of him. There are relatively few such newspapers in a city, and patronizing them may be considered by the fugitive a safe activity. Information about an alien fugitive may also be sought from the Immigration authorities or registration office if the alien is required to register, or in the office of a social service agency which specializes in giving informaton, advice or aid to immigrants. The personal history, destination and friends of an alien can be disclosed by such an organization. In addition, it is advisable to consult the port of entry and steamships from foreign ports which file with the Immigration Department lists of passengers and crews. The names of witnesses who have known the alien for a number of years and who appear when an alien applies for his naturalization papers, are on file with the government. It is possible to locate an alien fugitive or one who has become a citizen through such sources.

TELEPHONING

The fugitive may from time to time telephone a person but not disclose his whereabouts. The person receiving the call may be willing to give information in tracing the suspect. If possible, a temporary telephone should be installed on the premises. When the fugitive calls up he should be kept on the wire as long as possible. In the meantime, the investigator at the special telephone should notify the telephone company to trace the call immediately. An alarm should be issued to the radio patrol giving the information to help apprehend the fugitive.

TRAILING

When the suspect has been traced to a given vicinity it may be necessary to trail him for a time before apprehending him. If the person wanted is suspicious of being followed, he will of course try to escape and lose himself. The suspect may use any one of numerous methods. He may suddenly get on a street-car or bus and watch if anyone else got on who might be looking for him. He may get into a taxi, and suddenly leave it to lose himself in the crowd. Sometimes he goes up and down in an elevator in an office building or leaves the building by a different exit. In is therefore important in trailing the suspect to ward off suspicion.

In general, the suspect should be kept under observation in various types of situations. First, when the suspect is at home or on other premises the person trailing him should be inconspicuous, perhaps behind a window on the opposite side of the street, or he should pretend to read while sitting on some stoop, or inside a parked automobile. If it is feasible, a dictograph might be installed when the occupants are out with the co-operation of the landlord or manager of the building. The sound is increased at the listener's end of the line. The wires should be so arranged as to escape observation.

CO-OPERATION

Whether the perpetrator is known and can be seized, whether he is known and has escaped, or whether the perpetrator has escaped without being identified, great skill and ingenuity are required in apprehending him. Ability to secure information from the numerous possible sources is a great asset. It presupposes resourcefulness in law enforcement, and certain personal traits of tact and adaptability. For instance, being on friendly terms with proprietors of licensed places, taxi drivers, clerks, and other types of people helps in securing information about a suspect and facilitates tracing, trailing and apprehending him. This ability to secure the co-operation of others must be supplemented by scrupulous attention to details.

Descriptions of Persons, Property, Scenes of Crime

A high degree of accuracy in recording the minutest details cannot be too much stressed in describing a person or article under investigation. Everything which can be observed should be included in the description. Ambiguity or indefiniteness may help nullify much of the work in law enforcement.

IDENTIFICATION by witnesses will depend on their faculty of observation and the circumstances attending the transaction. In cases of forgery where the action is slow, there is more opportunity to observe the perpetrator and a better description by the witness is to be expected. In a crime involving violence or any sudden and rapid action, excitement, fear, and nervousness may inhibit accurate observation. The intelligence, education and training of the witness are factors to consider in receiving a description of a person or article. Similarity to others, bad light, suggestion, and the lapse of time are other circumstances that may mar a description. Obviously all statements or identification by witnesses should be checked for reliability.

In addition to a word picture, the witness may identify the perpetrator through a photograph. Even though the desired photograph may not be in the collection shown the witness, it is possible that some of the photographs will bear a resemblance to the person wanted. Thus some idea of his appearance can be obtained. The search is narrowed.

If the suspect is under arrest, he is confronted by the witness for identification. The usual practice is to have the witness brought into a room where there are several persons lined up, including the suspect. The witness is asked to identify the person desired. The persons in the room should not differ greatly in size or build. If the witness has described the perpetrator as a small person, he will immediately eliminate very tall persons before him for identification. The witness should be instructed not to announce his conclusion while in the presence of the group. The lighting in the room should be about the same as at the time of the crime to facilitate accurate identification. To overcome the witness' fear of identifying a suspect, the "Shadow Box" is used or some other arrangement is made so that the witness can see the suspect without being seen himself.

DESCRIPTION OF PERSONS

In addition to the information usually included in the "portrait parle" it is wise to make careful note of the following characteristics and traits in order to facilitate the conduct of investigations.

Clothes. Color and style of hat, shoes, suit, (maker's name) shirt, collar, tie, dressed neatly or carelessly, dressed well or shabbily.

Jewelry. Kind of, where worn.

Peculiarities. Twitching of features, rapid or slow gait, wearing eyeglasses, carrying a cane, stuttering, gruff or feminine voice.

Where likely to be found. Residence, former residence, places frequented or hangouts, where employed, trade or employment followed, residence of relations.

Personal associates. Friends who would be most likely to know of the movements or whereabouts of the person, or with whom he would be most likely to communicate.

Habits. Heavy drinker or smoker, gambler, frequenter of pool rooms, dance halls, night clubs, moving picture theatres, baseball games, resorts, etc., drug addicts may show certain characteristics like bright shiny eyes and air of self-confidence after taking cocaine, or appear very nervous and shaky without the "dope."

Chronic disease affliction. It is well in such cases to secure information from the family physician or neighborhood druggist, and addresses given to them by the patient during a period of years.

How he left scene of crime. Running, walking, by vehicle, direction taken.

With respect to these descriptions certain details should be kept in mind. The color of the hair is a distinctive identification. The color may be light blond, dark blond, brown, black, red, white, mixed gray, gray. The distinct colors of the iris in the eyes are blue, gray, maroon, yellow, light brown, brown. dark brown. Special peculiarities should be noted, such as different colors of the two eyes, white spots on the iris, albinos, a glossy ring around the iris, squinting, large or eccentric pupils, watery eyes, artificial eyes. The eyelids may have distinctive characteristics, e.g. skinfolds, hanging eyelids, long or short lashes, sacks under the eyes. If the color of the eyebrows is different from the hair, the fact should be noted. Peculiarities of the nose should be observed carefully. Among these peculiarities are: the root of the nose or the nose saddle may be very narrow or very wide; the bridge of the nose may be broken, wide, flat or deviating to one side. The point of the nose may be blunt or split, nostrils may be thick or thin, flat to one side or higher to the left or the right. The principal parts of the ear vary in shape, angle, adherence to the cheek, prominence, size, and the general form of ear may be oval, rectangular, triangular, round. The parts of the ear that should be observed for details are the beginning helix, upper helix, rear helix, lobule, anti-tragus, tragus, upper anti-helix, lower anti-helix. fossa digitalis, and fossa navicularis. It should be remembered in identification of a person that many distinctive marks can be removed by plastic surgery which can be used to change the shape of other features and the general appearance of a criminal.

DESCRIPTIONS OF PROPERTY

In the description of articles and property in general, materials, design and complete details for identification should be included. The following list itemizes the more general types of articles of which a description is often required:

Watches. Kind of metal, description of case, movement and numbers of each, whether a man's or woman's, use of abbreviations "h.c." for hunting case, and "o.f." for open face; initials, monograms, inscriptions, value.

Rings. Kind of metal, man's or woman's, style, setting, kind and number of stones. weight, maker's name, initials or other marks, value.

Chains. Kind of metal, male or female type, length and weight, kind of link or style, value.

Earrings or studs. Metal, syle, whether screw, coil or drop, size and number of stone, value.

Jewelry. (Miscellaneous) Name of article, kind of metal or materials, weight, kind and number of stones, design, initials, inscription, monogram, maker's name, value.

Table Silverware. Name of article, solid silver or plated, heavy or light weight, maker's name, design, such as plain, flower, beaded, animal, etc., initials, inscription, value.

Gold and Silver Goods. (Miscellaneous) Name of article, metal, plated or solid, size, design, number of pieces in set, initials, plain, chased, etched, engraved, open or solid patern, value.

Pocketbooks, Handbags, Suit Cases. Name of article, material size, color, shape, contents, initials or other marks, value.

Clothing. Name of article, material, style, color, shape, maker's name, initials or other marks, value.

Furs. Name of article, as coat, muff, collar, etc., kind, size, color, value.

Bric-a-Brac or Antiques. Name of article, materials, design, shape, carved, engraved, enameled or inlaid, age, value.

Animals. Kind, size, color or distinguishing marks age.

Trucks and Wagons. Type, shape, color of running gear, name and other distinctive marks, contents.

Bicycle. Make, color, number, kind of brake and saddle.

Typewriters. Kind, serial and model numbers.

Motorcycles. Make, year of model, number of cylinders, manufacturer's number, make of saddle, make and condition of tires, position of speedometer, horn, front and rear lights, distinctive marks.

Automobiles. License number, make, year of model, whether rebuilt and to what extent; if original lines have been changed, a full description of the appearance is necessary; kind of body, and whether rebuilt; body number, or trademark (if any), location of that number; motor number, factory number, changes or repair made on interior construction, exterior injuries, such as dents; changes made on instrument board or new instruments added; wheels, wood, wire, disk; tires, size, make, condition; precautions taken, such as having switch locked; lights, kind, where located on car, especially tail light; in escaping car, include direction going, number of passengers and description, size and color of car, radiator hood, presence of baggage rack and rear view, number of doors, hub caps, injuries e.g. dents, broken lamp, accessories, such as tires.

DESCRIPTION OF SCENE OF CRIME

To recognize evidence of crime the investigator must first know the conditions at the scene of the crime. The scene of crime may reveal clues as to the manner in which the crime was committed and the movements of the perpetrator. A diagram of the scene depicting all possible significant details should be prepared as soon as possible. Exact measurements should be taken of the room, house, or premises. The surroundings, such as yard, out-houses, garden, garage, etc. should be sketched. The drawings should be made to indicate the compass directions. The scale or dimensions used should be indicated. All notes pertinent to the description should be attached, and the date of the sketch should be given as well as the signature of the investigator.

In examining the scene, note the weather when the crime was discovered. Examine the doors, windows, furniture, etc., which may disclose the direction of entry and exit of the perpetrator. Note the position of doors and furniture—open or closed, moved from usual place. The location of bullet holes, empty shells, bloodstains, fingerprints should be indicated. Search for clues and traces, such as tools, telephone wires, cigarette ends, articles of clothing. Examine the premises in the vicinity, and note vacant lots, condition of the soil and vegetation. All findings should be recorded in a memorandum book and evidence should be preserved.

The position of various objects can help in reconstructing the situation at the time of the crime. For instance, it is found that one chair has been pulled up close to another, the inference is that two persons had seated themselves close together. An ash tray placed close to a chair near a table tends to show that the person in the chair was about to smoke, or was known to be a smoker. Having determined which are the customary objects in a room, it follows that all other objects have been placed on the scene recently and should be carefully inspected. The condition and contents of fireplaces and waste baskets may throw light on what has recently happened. Obviously, these details must fit into the picture and help account for what has occurred. A systematic general survey should be used in describing the scene of the crime.

The Techniques of Questioning

APPRAISING THE PERSON INTERVIEWED

A proper appraisal of the interviewee is indispensable in order to detect the sources of error present in the interview. The interviewer must make estimates of the intelligence, honesty and veracity of the person before him. The ability to measure significant traits of character and personality of another person is by no means an easy achievement. Coming in contact with offenders of various types, it is natural for the law enforcement agent to maintain an attitude of suspicion and skepticism and to be on the alert for a manifestation of evil traits of human nature. The personal judgment of the interviewer will play an important role in appraising the character of the individual giving information. Since the object of the interview is to determine crucial facts, objectivity on the part of the interviewer is a prime essential. His judgment of a particular trait should not be excessively influenced by a general first impression, either favorable or unfavorable. The interviewer should be on guard against the influence of preconceived notions or stereotypes in judging the interviewee. Often a person is misjudged or dealt with arbitrarily because of a preconception of the appearance of certain classes of people. In an interview for facts, the interviewer should be aware of the influence of the subtle association of prejudices in appraising the person interviewed.

It is by no means a safe guide to judge the person interviewed by his physical characteristics. The shape of the head or contour of the face are not reliable bases for judging personality. It should simplify matters if we could judge people on the shape of their jaws, the color of their hair, or the distance between their eyes, but the relationship between physical appearance and mental traits is not so simple. However, close observation of behavior should not be overlooked. The interviewer should note the posture, voice, expression of face and eyes. They are clues in estimating the value of the information that is given.

In judging the accuracy of facts elicited the investigator must check, correlate, and establish agreement of details by various methods. However, certain signs have been found in the behavior of persons during the interview which may serve as fairly reliable indications of untruthfulness. These forms of behavior are hang-dog appearance, tendency to repeat questions, talking in almost inaudible tones and acting as though he wishes the interview were quickly completed; unnatural emphasis, a defensive smile or nervous laugh unnecessarily minute accuracy, repeated assertions of desire to be truthful and frank.

METHODS OF QUESTIONING

The *free narrative* method is used in an interview in which the narrator tells his version of what happened without being subject to questions or suggestions of any sort. If the deposition is limited in scope and confined to statements of which the persons are certain, the free narrative method results in a high percentage of accuracy. It has been found that a religious oath does not guarantee accuracy, but greatly reduces error because the individual feels his responsibility.

The more prevalent method of interviewing is through questions and answers. The ability to ask questions properly will influence the success of the interview in securing facts. The question must be so phrased that it will be easily understood. Inaccurate information is sometimes given because the question is ambiguous. It is not interpreted as the interviewer expects it to be. Leading questions should be avoided. A leading question assumes a fact and by its very form suggests an answer which may not be the true one. If the interviewee wants to please the questioner, he will simply accede to the suggestion implied in the question. If he is not interested in giving the correct answer, he may still agree in order to end the interview quickly. The definite article "the" implies that there was a definite object present. For example, "Did you see the hat in the room?" implies that there was a hat in the room. On the other hand, the indefinite article "a" in the question makes no such implication, and is less likely to suggest an inaccurate answer.

If the question offers alternative answers, it should be so framed that neither one is acceptable to the person interviewed. In an interview in which the person does not respond freely there is the temptation to offer two statements in answer to a question. The person may acquiesce in one because he does not know better or because he wants to end the questioning. The interviewer should not imply what he thinks is the correct answer. Let the person interviewed originate the answer.

SUGGESTIONS ON THE TECHNIQUE OF THE INTERVIEW

Interviewing is an art which can be learned and then practiced so as to focus on essentials and obtain the truth. The interviewer must motivate the interviewee to co-operate in revealing the facts. The interview is fundamentally an interaction of two personalities. In order to give the interview direction and to control it, the interviewer must make a general plan or arrangement of the procedure; that is, he must develop a strategy. Then he must use certain tactics; he must plan what is to be said and done in the presence of the person interviewed. The planning includes a thorough knowledge of the problem, and a complete formulation of the problem for the interview. The interviewer should be quite clear in his mind as to just what information he wants. This does not mean shaping definite questions to be asked in a certain way, but the general questions should be clearly organized in his mind so that they will be asked at the right time when the opportunity arises in the conversation. A list or schedule of such questions should be prepared as a part of the plan for the interview.

It is desirable to secure information about the person interviewed before meeting him. This will help in appraising his personality and estimating the value of the facts he reveals. To reduce self-consciousness which may result in caution and inhibitions seriously limiting the frankness of statements, it is desirable to provide for privacy during the interview. Gaining the confidence of the person interviewed is the best means of establishing a relationship which will make possible a successful interview. Establish a pleasant association. An interview is difficult when the person is angry or tired or irritated. It is important to help the interviewee feel at ease. Let him become used to the surroundings and gain a litle poise. A patronizing or domineering attitude must be avoided.

The interviewer should not ask questions directly until the interviewee is ready to give information. This means that co-operation must be secured before direct questions are asked. It is well to encourage the person to talk freely and spontaneously, even though at times that talk may be irrelevant. By this method information is volunteered without resorting to direct questions which may inhibit the free and full narrative of what happened. Direct questions may be necessary, but they may also cause resentment or misunderstanding. If the interviewee rambles he should be brought back to the subject, but any hint of discourtesy should be avoided.

The interviewer should give the impression of being frank and sincere, instead of shrewd or astute. To do otherwise is to invite deceit and defeats the purpose of the interview. The person interviewed should realize his responsibility for the facts he reveals. The suggestion that the facts can be verified will help him be more careful. Tact and sound judgment rather than impertinence should be expressed if the subject becomes evasive or reserved. He should be led to talk on something more or less related to the topic, and then a question can be injected without emphasis on its special significance. The important question should be held in mind until enough information has been obtained on each one.

As the interview proceeds each statement should be scrutinized for its positive value to other questions. The interviewee should be given an opportunity to qualify his statements and he should always be required to answer "yes" or "no." In order to check the understanding of an answer, the interviewee may at times repeat it in his own words and ask whether that is what was meant. Throughout the interview attention should be concentrated on the meaning of the answers and their relation to the conclusion anticipated at the end of the interview.

The data should be recorded at the earliest possible moment. Facts must be separated from inferences. A distinction should be drawn between the observed facts and the statements made by the interviewee. It is the interviewer's responsibility to get all the facts. He must take the initiative to exhaust all the resources of data. At the close of the interview it is important to watch for additional information or new leads in casual remarks of the interviewee. Sometimes at this stage he may be more off guard and may drop a remark which he may have thought too trivial to mention during the interview. A written report of the interview should be agreed upon with the subject. This will permit later corrections or additions of data.

While the free-narrative and question and answer are two different methods used, the best results can be obtained by a combination of the two methods. The question and answer method increases the range of information but decreases the accuracy of the report. As a general proposition, it is advisable to encourage the interviewee to talk first before his questioning begins. It has been observed that free narrative is less complete but more accurate than either direct questioning or cross-examination. Success in interviewing is achieved by integrating various specific techniques required in clarifying the purpose of each interview, planning its course carefully and carrying out its successive steps with the objective of finding all the relevant facts.

WITNESSES AND THEIR STATEMENTS

1. Honest witnesses who have relevant information, and are willing to tell the enforcement agent all they know of a given situation. If they have seen the perpetrator commit the crime they are the most important.
2. Honest but incomplete witnesses who have information but owing to their mental condition distort or exaggerate the information when giving it to the investigator.
3. Honest but timid witnesses who do not want to inform the authorities because of fear of appearance at the trial and consequent vengeance by friends or accomplices of the criminal, if not by the accused himself.
4. Informers who had been confidants of the criminal but who have "peached" on him for one reason or another.
5. Accomplices of the criminal who give information to save themselves from punishment.

EVALUATING STATEMENTS OF THE WITNESSES

Witnesses may exaggerate or suffer from some illusion in observation, or they may be hostile. An excessively emotional or mentally abnormal person may be so excited by the events of the crime that he draws into his statement many imaginative ideas. The investigator should determine whether the witness is mentally competent. This may be done by making a few simple statements or framing a few questions as an intelligence test to discover the degree of his reasoning ability. If the witness is found to be mentally defective the prosecuting attorney should be informed of that fact.

The statements of witnesses who suffer from imperfect observation or who are handicapped by a defect in one or more of the senses, should be carefully scrutinized. Some people may be color blind. or have other defects of vision. Others may have defects of hearing, smell, taste, touch. It is the duty of the investigator to discover such defects, and to conduct the inquiry as tactfully as possible. The witness who suffers from such a defect may not be aware of it or may not want to admit that fact. But the facts must be sifted and analyzed for their accuracy in view of the handicap in observation. A careful inquiry should establish whether the witness is speaking of his own knowledge, or whether he is expressing an opinion, or making statements on hearsay.

The accuracy of the details given in the statement should be tested and checked. The exact time, shades of colors, quantities, amounts, speeds, distances should be examined for accuracy by comparison with statements of other witnesses and by personal inquiry. For example, if a witness says two minutes elapsed, test him for his judgment as to such length of time by the watch. If he indicates a distance of 100 feet, let him indicate an object at a similar distance and measure it. Such checking processes may involve considerable trouble and effort, but it helps assure the accuracy of the facts.

In analyzing a statement of a witness, inaccuracies arising from illusion should be taken into consideration. For instance, it has been found that people in light clothing, at a time of comparative darkness, appear taller than they are in reality; and the converse obtains for people in dark clothing. A pipe with a nickled band may be mistaken for a knife. Under conditions of poor visibility, a person wearing a tan cap may be mistaken for one without any head-covering and blond hair.

It does not necessarily follow that an improbable statement is false or that the witness is mistaken. The improbable may have happened. The witness should be carefully questioned. His statements should be taken down as he gives them. It is for the investigator after that to verify or disprove details in order to secure a proper evaluation of the statements made by witnesses.

These procedures in determining the value of a witness' statement apply also to statements of hostile witnesses or of accused persons. Witnesses who are likely to be hostile should be kept separate until their statements have been given so as to prevent possible collusion in the facts reported. A hostile witness may not want to lose time in court or he may desire to avoid publicity. Sometimes an appeal to his civic pride will persuade him to give information. If the hostile witness has a bad reputation, it is advisable to obtain details of his previous unlawful conduct and prepare questions on the basis of those facts as well as the facts that are to be learned. Such a witness must be cross-examined to get at the truth. His statement should be read to him. He should be informed of the consequences of perjury and asked if he is willing to make an affidavit to his statement.

A witness who informs after being a confidant of the perpetrator usually does so because of motives of jealousy or revenge. Such statements, when true, are of value to induce the perpetrator to confess. The truth of such statements must be investigated thoroughly because an innocent person may be accused in order to divert suspicion from the guilty one. Statements given by such persons are of little value if they are not supported by other evidence.

Interrogating the Suspect

Before the suspect is approached for a statement or questioning the preliminary investigation should be made. The scene of the crime should be visited first and as much evidence as possible should be gathered and examined. Detailed information about the suspect is a great aid in the interrogation.

The suspect should be so questioned that an admission or confession is made easier. The place where the interrogation takes place has a bearing on the results. A suspect is not likely to speak freely in the presence of members of his family, friends, employers or business associates. If the statement of the suspect includes valuable information or a partial confession, the interrogation can then be concentrated on certain parts or phases of the crime leading to a complete confession or conclusive evidence of guilt. But, if the suspect insists he is innocent, the success of the questioning will depend on the evidence assembled and the ability to plan and carry on further interrogation. The suspect should not be given any idea of the evidence on hand. He is a means of obtaining further evidence and therefore the interrogation should not accuse him of the crime. The suspect should be dealt with as a witness. It will be difficult for him to continue to lie and yet to be logical. If the interrogator knows the statements made by the suspect are not true he should not betray his disbelief. The suspect will weaken his case later if he continues to lie. If several persons are suspected of being involved in the crime they should be questioned separately but simultaneously.

INTERROGATION PROCEDURES

The suspect must be won over. Certain methods in the conduct of the interrogation have been found effective. In the first place, let the suspect do the talking. Ask questions but do not tell the suspect facts The interrogator may not like the suspect as a type but he should be fair and not let prejudice influence him in making a decision on the guilt of the person before him. There may be strong circumstantial evidence against the suspect but the interrogator must avoid jumping to conclusions. If a false conclusion is made it may result later in a great loss of time and effort in looking for the real criminal. The interrogator should realize the seriousness of the occasion and not indulge in levity or clever remarks which may give the suspect an opportunity to adopt a similar attitude.

During the interrogation of the suspect, personalities should be avoided. The interrogator should likewise avoid threatening, demanding or insulting the suspect, as well as a sneering, superior attitude. It may be advisable during the process of interrogating a suspect to asume a certain role or to "play a part." The situation may require flattering the suspect and watching the effect or assuming a naive attitude and so put the suspect less on his guard. Of course his words and actions must be convincing whatever role may be assumed. It is advisable not to let the suspect see any sign of triumph or ridicule on the part of the interrogator at the conclusion of the questioning.

The interrogator should always keep the upper hand. He should not be placed on the defensive by a lack of knowledge of the case or by not taking advantage and following up slips made by the suspect. He should control his temper though deliberate anger as a part of strategy may be at times desirable. The questioning should not be permitted to ramble aimlessly, which not only wastes time but results in a loss of control. If the interrogator is pressed for time he should not let the suspect know it because he may become dilatory and hold out or take advantage of the situation.

PROCEDURES IN OBTAINING ADMISSIONS

There may be sufficient evidence against the suspect but, nevertheless, it is important to make an effort to obtain an admission. Such a statement may include details not yet known of the crime. It may disclose accomplices who should be brought to justice or witnesses who have testimony that should be known before they come to court. The admission may be of such a nature as to contain additional evidence to assure conviction of the suspect. It is therefore important to have the suspect talk freely.

Different methods and devices have been used to realize this object. The *Direct Approach* to obtain ready admissions uses frankness and simplicity. The suspect is asked to tell the story of what happened. The simple approach may be supplemented by questioning. If the suspect responds to this approach much time is saved, and in any event, no harm has been done. It should be remembered, however, that an admission does not necessarily mean that the case is solved. Physical evidence must still be linked to the suspect. The admission must be checked and confirmed. An easy admission may be designed to divert attention from more serious crimes. It may be a false admission to protect someone else or for some other motive.

The *Emotional Approach* may be used to obtain an admission. The conscience-confessor talks freely because of his long brooding and pent-up feeling of guilt. But the interrogator must use his skill on suspects who do not talk freely. It is the task of the interrogator to discover the type of emotion to which he must appeal. The suspect may be asked what persons he likes and respects. The names given may be a key to his own feelings and emotional preferences. He may be asked to make a list of ideals and customs for which he has respect and which he violently opposes. In appealing to the suspect's emotions the interrogator must himself display emotion and play the part required by the situation. The suspect may even start crying and begin to tell his story. He suddenly breaks down because of the strong emotional appeal even though he has vehemently asserted his innocence up to this point. When this occurs the interrogator should encourage him to get it "off his chest.' He should not permit the suspect time to regain composure. The statement should be put in writing as soon as possible to forestall a subsequent denial.

In making the emotional appeal there are various reactions that should be watched to indicate that the questioning is along the right track. The appearance of perspiration with a flushed face indicates an emotion of anger, embarrassment or nervousness. Sweating with a pallid face shows great fear or shock. A blanched face may be taken as an index of guilt. A dry mouth indicates nervous tension. This may be accompanied by excessive licking of the lips. Nervous tension may also show itself by clenching of hands or twisting a handkerchief. Bringing the elbows close to the sides shows a lack of ease, is an indication of tension. When the questioning reaches a climax, breathing should be observed. A slight gasp shows a conscious effort to control breathing so that it will appear normal. Other physical reactions that should be watched are a sigh of relief after a critical question, figeting in the chair, gestures of nervousness such as rubbing the face, crossing and uncrossing the legs, clearing the throat by swallowing, biting or snapping the fingernails. Attention should not be directed to these reactions. No one of them is conclusive and the investigator should consider them only as guides. They are not necessarily proof of guilt.

Trickery has been used in interrogation. This device may be employed on suspects who are desirous of bargaining; who want to confess a lesser offense. The so-called "location trick" has many variations. The interrogator must be familiar with the whereabouts of the suspect at a particular time. A false episode is mentioned, e.g. a broken water main or fire or a collision. If the suspect were there at that time, he would deny this occurrence. On the other hand, if the episode is told convincingly, and the suspect had not been near the scene, he would agree and so betray himself. The interrogator may suggest extenuating circumstances which the suspect may plead in connection with the admission. This must be done with circumspection so that there will be no opportunity later for the suspect to say promises were made to him to get him out of trouble or mitigate the offense charged. The suspect cannot be promised anything. But if the suspect writes a statement of extenuating circumstances, he may include further details. Suggesting worrisome analogies of other cases, flattery, an appeal to pride or ego, being willing to make himself the butt of a joke, are among other devices used by the interrogator in questioning a suspect.

Whatever device is used, the "third degree" method is decried by the foremost authorities. It is physical torture in various forms which will produce a statement under duress whether the person is guilty or not. The evidence so acquired is not admissible in court. The jury are ready to believe the claim of the defense that such methods were used, with the result that conviction of the guilty party is extremely difficult.

In addition to the various approaches and methods of treating the suspect already mentioned, it might be well to add one more—a friendly appeal and kindness. Many suspects will respond to an expression of consideration. Giving the suspect a cigarette, or a meal, showing kindness to his wife and children or helping them contact social agencies, if they need help, may lead the suspect to talk. If this approach is rejected on the grounds of sentimentality, the old adage should be recalled: "Honey catches more flies than vinegar." This method has its practical value.

TESTING THE SUSPECT

In adition to the lie detector, the "Truth Serum" has been tried on some "hard-boiled" suspects. This is a drug made from henbane, and is known as scopolamine. The peculiar effect of this drug is that it releases inhibitions. The patient's memory and power of speech are not impaired. In one experiment, a criminologist under the influence of scopolamine revealed a fact regarding an episode that had occurred many years ago; when he was still boy in prep school, and which he had forgotten before the experiment. This indicates that the drug can unearth facts which had long been buried in the unconscious. Scopolamine is a dangerous drug and must be administered by a physician who understands its effects and reactions. It is unstable and may easily cause death, or violent hallucinations followed by a fatal coma. Though it requires an expert, the "truth serum" has value in testing suspects.

WORD ASSOCIATION

One of the psychological tests on suspects is based on "word-association." Although it does not reveal a lie, it indicates a consciousness of guilt which may be used in further questioning of the suspect. The test consists of requiring the suspect to answer the first word that comes to his mind when he hears a word read from a list. On this list, some of the words are linked with the crime under investigation. It has been found that the normal time to react to a word is approximately two and a half seconds. If it takes longer than that it shows there is some kind of an emotional disturbance in the suspect, or the response would come sooner. Any unusual association with a word is noted.

Another psychological test depends on the effect of color on some suspects. The accused person is placed in a room in which the walls are mirrors. As the questioning proceeds, the lights gradually change to a greenish tinge. Wherever the suspect turns he sees the "characteristic hue of guilt" on his face. He thinks his complexion betrays him and he weakens. This test has the desired effect on neurotic persons who cannot withstand the apparent expression of guilt on their faces. The ignorant type of suspect does not analyze the cause of his appearance and is ready to tell what he knows. Science and psychology have thus made valuable contributions to methods of testing a suspect of a crime.

EVIDENCE IN LAW ENFORCEMENT

"What is now proved was once only imagined."
—WILLIAM BLAKE

"For when one's proofs are aptly chosen,
Four are as valid as four dozen."
—MATTHEW PRIOR

"Some circumstantial evidence is very strong, as when you find a trout in the milk."
—H. D. THOREAU

THE LAW OF EVIDENCE is designed to bring to the minds of judges and jurors facts on the basis of which a decision must be made in a judicial investigation. The law of evidence governs the presentation of facts before a legal tribunal. It specifies *what* may be proved and *how* it may be proved.

THE "HOW" OF PRESENTING EVIDENCE is of interest to the trial judge and attorney. To the law enforcement agent "what" facts are to be proved is of greater importance. It may be said in general that any fact in issue and relevant to the case may be proved. Some evidence need not be proved, e.g. (1) admitted evidence, (2) evidence of which the court takes judicial notice, and (3) that which is presumed until refuting evidence is admitted. Evidence cannot be introduced in a trial unless it helps prove the guilt or innocence of the defendant in the very crime for which he is being tried. Whatever is logically relevant is admissible. If a fact can have no effect on the final verdict, it is excluded as immaterial.

ADMISSIBLE EVIDENCE

RES GESTAE: *Res Gestae,* meaning the things done, is a rule of evidence which states that all declarations, statements and acts involved in the transaction and which help to explain and make clear what occurred are admitted in evidence. It does not refer only to the criminal transaction itself, but is used in referring to any transaction related to the proof. For instance, circumstances attending the purchase of equipment, materials or supplies preparatory to smuggling enterprises or counterfeiting operations, may properly be included in the term *res gestae.* Such facts are admissible evidence.

ADMISSIONS & CONFESSIONS: Admissions and Confessions are declarations of the defendant which tend to prove his guilt. An admission is an acknowledgment of a fact which, together with the other facts, tends to prove the defendant guilty. On the other hand, a confession is a statement which expressly admits guilt. It may be oral or written. An admission is received in evidence whether or not it is made voluntarily, but a confession must be proved to have been made voluntarily, without force or fear in order to be accepted in evidence. A defendant who is charged with the violation of a Federal law should be informed of his rights before a confession is received from him, for a confession freely made may be used against the criminal. No promise of immunity, or a lesser sentence, or suggestion that the defendant will be benefitted in any way can be made in order to induce a confession. There must be no threat from anyone in authority. If a confession is freely made, it is admissible even if the defendant was partly under the influence of liquor at the time of the confession.

THREATS, SELF-SERVING, AND ACCUSATORY STATEMENTS: Evidence of threats is admissible to show intent or motive. Any fact which supplies a motive for an act is relevant. Statements made by the defendant subsequent to the crime in his own favor are deemed self-serving and are inadmissible when offered by the defense, for they are hearsay and incompetent. But if such statements have any tendency to prove the guilt of the defendant they may be introduced by the prosecution. If an accused has an opportunity to reply to an incriminating statement made in his presence, but is silent or makes a false statement, the accusation may be admissible in evidence against him. Any statement or conduct indicating a consciousness of guilt is admissible, including, for example, the attempt to bribe an officer or possible witness, an assault on the arresting officer or his aides, giving a false name at the time of arrest, false statements with reference to the charge against the defendant.

ACTS AND STATEMENTS OF CONSPIRATORS: Such acts are binding on all conspirators. This rule is analogous to a legal partnership in which the acts of one partner within the scope of the business in which they are engaged, are binding on his co-partner. Testimony in such cases is admissible only after proof of the existence and object of the conspiracy.

EXPERT EVIDENCE: Such evidence is admissible when presented by those who are specialists in a particular field. For instance, opinions of physicians, chemists, handwriting experts are admissible because they have expert knowledge of a special science or trade, or process. If an opinion of an expert is proved erroneous it tends to discredit his entire testimony. Experiments may be introduced, but to be admissible in evidence they must be carried out under conditions which are similar to the actual event. The conditions need not be absolutely identical, but there must be no change of conditions which could have any effect on the result of the experiment.

DOCUMENTARY EVIDENCE: Account books are admissible, if they are books of original entry, are regular and continuous and if the entries were made at or near the time of the occurrence of the transaction recorded. Proof is generally required as to the correctness of the entry by the person having personal knowledge of it. Documents kept by the public officer in the course of his duty, and coming from proper custody are admissible in evidence. Copies of public documents are regarded as equivalent to the originals if they are duly authenticated. Such records may include a register of vital statistics, stock brands, land, registers of conveyances, and judicial records. In addition, there are certain quasi-public documents which are generally considered admissible upon identification, e.g., standard mortality tables, tide tables, and astronomical calculations.

CHARACTER EVIDENCE: Witnesses may be presented by the defendant in a criminal prosecution to establish his good reputation in the community. The evidence emphasizes special traits, such as honesty, integrity, peaceable nature, implying that a person of such reputation is not likely to commit the crime charged against him. Such evidence can only be introduced in the first instance by the defendant, but after that the prosecution may introduce character witnesses to prove the bad reputation of the defendant. Either party may impugn the credibility of witnesses on the other side by proving that the witness has been guilty of a crime, or has made previous statements contrary to his testimony, or that his attitude in the case is unduly favorable or hostile. Evidence may be introduced to prove that the witness was incompetent to observe accurately. It is for the cross-examiner to test the witnesses of the other party with respect to the value of their statements, the strength of their recollection and their disposition to tell the truth.

KINDS OF EVIDENCE

CIRCUMSTANTIAL EVIDENCES This form of evidence includes facts and circumstances from which an inference may be drawn as to the existence of the fact to be established. It is evidence which tends to prove a disputed fact by proof of other facts which have a legitimate tendency because of the usual connection of things, or the ordinary transaction of business, or from the laws of nature. The judge and jury draw conclusions from circumstantial evidence and find one fact from the existence of other facts shown to them.

CORROBORATIVE EVIDENCE: This consists of additional evidence on the same point as the one already given. After an attempt to impeach the credibility of a witness has been made, he may be corroborated by explanations or denials where an attempt has been made to impeach by evidence of malice, bias, or interest. Corroboration by other evidence is always permitted in such cases.

HEARSAY EVIDENCE: Such evidence consists of statements made by some other person with respect to a past transaction, or with respect to what the witness himself has related in the past to some other person. It depends, in part, on the competency and veracity of some other person. As a general rule hearsay evidence is not admissible. The reason is that a person who knows a fact should be brought into court to state his evidence under oath. The hearsay rule applies to written as well as to oral statements. There are exceptions to this rule which are admissible, for example, dying declarations and admissions and confessions.

DIRECT EVIDENCE: This is evidence of a witness who testifies as to his actual knowledge of the facts to be proved. It tends to show the existence of a fact in question without the intervention of the proof of any other fact.

RELEVANT EVIDENCE: This is a term applied to evidence that bears some relation to the facts at issue.

MATERIAL EVIDENCE: Such evidence tends to establish some fact that is in dispute.

COMPETENT EVIDENCE: This is evidence which is proof of the fact at issue in a case.

OPINION EVIDENCE: This may be expert or nonexpert opinion. Reference has already been made to the nature and admissibility of expert opinion. Nonexpert opinion is that of an ordinary witness who has personally observed the facts on the basis of which an opinion is expressed.

EXHIBITS: These include all objects gathered to be used as evidence at the trial. Such articles to be evidence must be directly related to the facts at issue. Documents as evidence have already been mentioned. Another group of exhibits used as evidence includes "demonstrative" or "real" evidence which can be presented directly to the senses of court or jury without an intervening medium or proof. Real evidence is the object itself. It has certain observable qualities. "Representative real evidence" includes such exhibits as X-ray photographs, charts, diagrams, sketches, models, etc. Such evidence is admissible if it is duly authenticated as being correct as a representation. Experiments are included in this category of evidence.

PAROL EVIDENCE: Such evidence is presented by word of mouth, or orally as testimony of witnesses. It is not a substitute for or equivalent to a written instrument where the latter is required by law, but parol evidence is admissible to defeat a written instrument on the ground of fraud.

MARKING EVIDENCE

All articles that come into the possession of the law enforcement agent, which may be presented in a judicial proceeding, should be carefully marked. The agent should make a notation in a memorandum book of the various markings on the evidence. Merely attaching a tag on the article is not sufficient. A private mark of identification should be placed on the article.

Envelopes, boxes and containers should be used to enclose articles of evidence. These containers should be sealed in the presence of witnesses. The time, date, names of witnesses and the name of the person sealing the container should be placed on it. When the evidence is presented in court, the seal is broken in the presence of the court.

A scratch mark or initial is placed on a revolver or pistol. Note should be made of the serial number, the calibre and make. Letters or numbers appearing on empty cartridges should be noted. Cartridge shells with bullets should be similarly marked. The mark should be made sufficiently deep to prevent tampering. Any marks that may appear on the surface of bullets by discharge through the bore of the barrel should be carefully preserved. Small objects, like pieces of bones or bullets may be placed in a small clean glass vial, with a piece of cotton under and over it to prevent it from moving about. Such exhibits can be easily examined without removing them, thereby reducing the chance of losing them or confusing them with other objects. A notation or tag should be placed on such containers to indicate the nature of the exhibits.

Drugs should be placed in bottles or vessels and carefully marked as mentioned before. Clothing and documents should be marked with ink or indelible pencil. In marking paper money the name of the bank, series, kind of certificate, serial number and denomination should be noted. Exhibits which cannot be placed in a container should be wrapped in clean paper, and if necessary, should be protected by a wrapping of tissue paper or cotton. Articles which may bear fingerprints should be picked up with a clean cloth or paper and placed in a box or container free from dirt. Every effort should be made to handle exhibits with the utmost care. Preserve them in the same condition in which they were found. A record of all articles and exhibits should be kept so they may be identified when produced in court.

PRESENTING EVIDENCE IN COURT

The trial is the culmination of the investigator's work. The enforcement agent is naturally interested in having his evidence presented in the best possible manner. The case should not be prejudiced by an unconscious action on his part.

A proper personal appearance helps make a favorable impression. The agent should be neatly dressed and should act in a gentlemanly manner. Chewing gum audibly or using a toothpick do not help in creating the desired impression. The behavior of the investigator in court should not be such as to convey the thought that he is over-eager to secure a conviction. If he has done his work properly, there is no need for him to disturb the proceedings by giving the prosecutor some last bit of information or to suggest some question that should be asked of the witness on the stand. Such behavior distracts the attention of the prosecuting attorney from the testimony that is being offered at the time and from the conduct of the case. If it should be necessary to convey some information, it should be done as unobtrusively as possible by writing the information or suggestion and conveying it to the attorney. The investigator should not show any reaction of approval or displeasure when any testimony is given from the stand.

On the witness stand the agent tells frankly whether he does or not remember information that is asked for. He may be given permission to use his notes. He should be quiet, reserved, and natural. He should talk distinctly and avoid slang. Technical terms should be explained. Answers should be definite and frank. If the cross-examination is vigorous the agent should not argue wtih defendant's counsel. He should continue in a definite but courteous manner, so as to make a favorable impression on the jury.

CONSTITUTIONAL RIGHTS OF THE DEFENDANT

"In *all criminal* prosecutions, the accused shall enjoy the right to a *speedy* and public trial, by an impartial jury of the State and district wherein the crime shall have been committed . . . and to be informed of the nature and cause of the accusation; to be confronted with the witnesses against him; to have compulsory process for obtaining witnesses in his favor, and to have the assistance of Counsel for his defense."

CONSTITUTION OF THE UNITED STATES: AMENDMENT 6

* * *

1. The accused is to be presumed innocent until the contrary is shown, and if there is a reasonable doubt of his guilt, he is entitled to the benefit of the doubt, and the dismissal of the charge against him.

2. If the offense is not punishable by death, he is to be admitted to reasonable bail pending the trial of his case.

3. He is entitled to aid of counsel in his defense at a speedy and public trial.

4. To be informed of the nature of the offense charged against him, and be confronted by his accusers in open court.

5. Unless he waives the question he is entitled to be considered of good character, except when being tried as a second offender.

6. He has a right to refuse to appear on the witness stand for or against himself in an oral examination upon trial. However, the law may compel him to submit to having his fingerprints taken, to being photographed or measured, to exhibiting any marks or bruises on his body, or to being identified by a witness.

7. He has the right to compel the attendance of witnesses in his favor.

8. He has the constitutional right not to be tried for an offense which was committed prior to the enactment of a law constituting his conduct a criminal offense, i.e. an ex post facto law. If, for example, the punishment for an offense at the time committed was one year imprisonment and the punishment for that offense has been increased to five years by the time of the trial, the defendant cannot be sentenced to more than one year.

Previous exam questions on evidence

1. In making inquiries as a law enforcement officer, you should be careful not to endanger unnecessarily the reputation of any person who may be the subject of your investigation because
   (A) carelessness on the part of investigating officers might harm the reputation of an innocent individual
   (B) a reputation for making thorough investigation should be carefully built up by every officer
   (C) you may otherwise endanger your own reputation
   (D) law enforcement officers are not permitted to ask questions that reflect upon anyone's reputation.

2. An officer overhears a business man complain that his sales of tires had fallen off sharply because a new competitor has suddenly appeared in his territory and is underselling him at unbelievably low prices. He recalls that a large shipment of tires had been reported stolen a short time ago. It is advisable for him to
   (A) forget the matter as it is probably a coincidence
   (B) tell the businessman to report the new competitor to the Better Business Bureau for unfair practices
   (C) check to see if there is any connection between the two sets of circumstances
   (D) inform the businessman about the robbery and ask him if he thinks that there is a connection
   (E) arrest the owner of the new store as he is obviousy involved in the robbery.

3. Investigating the area from which you heard a shot, you find a man sitting on the steps and holding one hand to a bloody spot on his arm. It would be *least* important for you to
   (A) try to find the bullet
   (B) examine the wound
   (C) ask the man if he knows who shot at him

(D) take the names and addresses of any witnesses.

4. It has been suggested that officers should make the preliminary investigations of all crimes that are committed on their posts. The most important benefit likely to result from the adoption of this suggestion is that
   (A) important physical evidence will be more completely analyzed
   (B) his knowledge of his post conditions is thereby increased
   (C) his court testimony concerning the crime will be more carefully presented
   (D) the time and effort of the specialist is conserved for tasks that require his special skills.

5. In assembling criminal evidence, it is best to
   (A) discard the less important so as not to clutter up the record
   (B) preserve all material pertinent to the crime since an apparently insignificant item may later prove important in solving the crime
   (C) discard the trivial so that attention will not be deflected from the important considerations
   (D) preserve all objects found at the scene of the crime regardless of their nature
   (E) allow the apparent importance of the case to determine what evidence is to be preserved.

6. Of the following, the person who would normally offer the most damaging evidence in court against an individual who is being tried for a hold-up, is one who
   (A) saw the crime committed
   (B) by reason of close association with the individual, is in a position to suspect him
   (C) furnished the weapon used in the crime
   (D) saw the suspect in the vicinity in which the crime was committed
   (E) knows of a motive which would prompt the suspect to commit the crime.

7. The most important factor for you to consider in using information which you have received from a certain person as a basis for further investigation is the
   (A) availability of the person for further questioning
   (B) expense involved in finding the person
   (C) arrest record of the person
   (D) value of the information as related to the case in question.

8. When automobile tire tracks are to be used as evidence, a plaster cast is made of them. Before the cast is made, however, a photograph of the tracks is taken. Of the following, the most probable reason for taking a photograph is that
   (A) photographs can be duplicated more easily than castings
   (B) less skill is required for photographing than casting
   (C) the tracks may be damaged in the casting process
   (D) photographs are more easily transported than castings.

9. A pawnshop dealer has submitted to the police an accurate and complete description of a wrist watch which he recently purchased from a customer. The one of the following factors that would be most important in determining whether this wrist watch was stolen is the
   (A) degree of investigative perseverance demonstrated by the police
   (B) exactness of police records describing stolen property
   (C) honesty and neighborhood reputation of the pawnbroker
   (D) time interval between the purchase of the wrist watch by the pawnbroker and his report to the police.

10. You are guarding the entrance of an apartment in which a homicide occurred. While awaiting the arrival of the detectives assigned to the case, you are approached by a newspaper reporter who asks to be admitted. You refuse to admit him. Your action was
   (A) wrong; officers should cooperate with the press
   (B) right; the reporter might unintentionally destroy evidence if admitted
   (C) wrong; experienced police reporters can be trusted to act intelligently in this situation
   (D) right; this reporter should not be given an advantage over other newspaper men.

11. "An officer spots and stops a car which seems to fit the description of a blue 1960 Buick four-door sedan which had been used as a getaway car by bank robbers." The one of the following which is most likely to indicate the need for further careful investigation is that the
   (A) car has a cracked rear side window
   (B) driver does not have a registration certificate for this car
   (C) rear license plate is rusted
   (D) occupants of the car consist of three poorly dressed men.

12. The scene of a crime is the area within the immediate vicinity of the specific location of the crime in which evidence might be found. This definition serves as an acceptable working guide for the discovery of evidence by the police because
    (A) evidence found outside the crime scene can be just as valuable as evidence found nearby
    (B) it assigns the finding of evidence to those responsible for its discovery
    (C) it is likely that the most important evidence will be found within the area of the crime scene
    (D) evidence found within the area of the crime scene is more readily accepted.

13. "Whenever a crime has been committed, the criminal has disturbed the surroundings in one way or another by his presence." The *least* valid deduction for the police to make from this statement is that
    (A) clues are thus present at all crime scenes
    (B) even the slightest search at crime scenes will turn up conclusive evidence
    (C) the greater the number of criminals involved in a crime, the greater the number of clues likely to be available
    (D) the completely clueless crime is rarely encountered in police work.

14. A court order must be obtained if the Police Department wants a postmaster to
    (A) place covers on mail
    (B) furnish tracings of mail
    (C) provide forwarding addresses of persons who have moved
    (D) open a letter when a federal crime is suspected.

15. "It is important that the police officer or detective establish the fact that the crime reported is bona fide." This procedure may best be evaluated as
    (A) necessary as many crimes are reported which have not taken place
    (B) unnecessary as in only few cases are crimes simulated
    (C) unnecessary as general investigation will show the nature of the crime without any emphasis on validity
    (D) unnecessary as it may take considerable time better spent in apprehending the criminal
    (E) necessary as it gives the investigator a starting point.

16. A confession would be excluded in court as involuntary if the accused was
    (A) warned that he did not have to make the statement
    (B) promised immunity by a police sergeant for making the statement
    (C) induced to make the statement by threats to prosecute for perjury
    (D) induced by some form of deception to make the confession.

17. If a person fails to deny an accusation made in his presence, under such circumstances that he heard and fully understood what was said, and had an opportunity to reply, and would naturally have denied the accusation had he regarded it as untrue, then the fact of his silence is
    (A) admissible as evidence; this silence may be interpreted as a tacit admission of the truth of the accusation
    (B) inadmissible as evidence; this silence is not indicative of the truth or falsity of the accusation
    (C) admissible as evidence; the accused is obliged to speak in answer to accusatory statements made in his presence when he is under arrest
    (D) inadmissible as evidence; only statements made in the course of judicial procedures may constitute an admission
    (E) admissible as evidence; the accused is obliged to speak in answer to accusatory statements made in his presence when he is about to be arrested.

18. Circumstantial evidence has been so often used in a deprecating context that jurors are inclined to shy away from the true meaning of the evidence when they are told that it is "purely circumstantial". The disrepute in which such evidence is sometimes held is attributable mainly to
    (A) case histories where the circumstantial evidence was insufficient to warrant the conclusions that were drawn
    (B) the belief that testimony based on visual and other sensory experiences is often quite unreliable
    (C) the fact that circumstantial evidence is not subject to the equivalent of "cross-examination"
    (D) the fact that the increased use of scientific methods has weakened the value of circumstantial evidence

(E) the suspicion of members of the jury that such evidence is often used improperly by prosecuting authorities.

19. "Contradictory testimony from witnesses claiming to have 'seen' the same event is not infrequent. Every day in our courts of law men swear in good faith to having seen things which on cross-examination they admit they were not in a position to observe clearly." This paragraph asserts, most nearly, that eye witnesses of good faith should be expected
    (A) sometimes to be upset emotionally by hostile cross-examination
    (B) never to give contradictory testimony
    (C) sometimes to observe inaccurately
    (D) to contradict themselves
    (E) sometimes to swear to testimony which they know in advance to be false.

20. When testifying in a criminal case it is most important that an officer endeavor to
    (A) avoid technical terms which may be unfamiliar to the jury
    (B) lean over backwards in order to be fair to the defendant
    (C) assist the prosecutor even if some exaggeration is necessary
    (D) avoid contradicting other prosecution witnesses
    (E) confine his answers to the questions asked.

21. Evidence in the form of some physical object or condition is most commonly known as
    (A) substantial evidence
    (B) real evidence
    (C) intrinsic evidence
    (D) cumulative evidence.

22. Of the following, the statement concerning evidence which is *not* true is that
    (A) circumstantial evidence implies immediate experience
    (B) important bits of evidence may sometimes not be admissible in the courts
    (C) anything related to the case and experienced personally by the witness is direct evidence
    (D) a complete understanding of the fundamental rules of evidence is very useful to an officer trying to construct a case against a law violator.

23. "When a defendant claims that the presence of blood sprinkles on his clothing is due to the fact that he has touched such clothing with bloody hands, one can immediately conclude that he is lying." The fact upon which this conclusion is based is most nearly that
    (A) clothing absorbs blood
    (B) blood does not sprinkle
    (C) fingerprints would have been left by the defendant if he had touched the clothing
    (D) bloody hands will not leave the described mark
    (E) the defendant's hands were bloody.

24. The most important of the following for an officer to know when he is securing evidence concerning a person who was arrested for a crime is
    (A) what kind of reputation the suspect has
    (B) what other crimes the suspect has been accused of
    (C) what kind of evidence is admissible in court
    (D) how to classify fingerprints.

Evidence Quizzer

Correct Answers

1. A	6. A	11. B	16. C	21. B
2. C	7. D	12. C	17. A	22. A
3. A	8. C	13. B	18. A	23. D
4. D	9. B	14. D	19. C	24. C
5. B	10. B	15. A	20. E	

Practice Using Answer Sheets

Alter numbers to match the practice and drill questions in each part of the book.
Make only ONE mark for each answer. Additional and stray marks may be counted as mistakes.
In making corrections, erase errors COMPLETELY. Make glossy black marks.

1 A B C D E	1 A B C D E	1 A B C D E	1 A B C D E	1 A B C D E
2 A B C D E	2 A B C D E	2 A B C D E	2 A B C D E	2 A B C D E
3 A B C D E	3 A B C D E	3 A B C D E	3 A B C D E	3 A B C D E
4 A B C D E	4 A B C D E	4 A B C D E	4 A B C D E	4 A B C D E
5 A B C D E	5 A B C D E	5 A B C D E	5 A B C D E	5 A B C D E
6 A B C D E	6 A B C D E	6 A B C D E	6 A B C D E	6 A B C D E
7 A B C D E	7 A B C D E	7 A B C D E	7 A B C D E	7 A B C D E
8 A B C D E	8 A B C D E	8 A B C D E	8 A B C D E	8 A B C D E
9 A B C D E	9 A B C D E	9 A B C D E	9 A B C D E	9 A B C D E
0 A B C D E	0 A B C D E	0 A B C D E	0 A B C D E	0 A B C D E

1 A B C D E	1 A B C D E	1 A B C D E	1 A B C D E	1 A B C D E
2 A B C D E	2 A B C D E	2 A B C D E	2 A B C D E	2 A B C D E
3 A B C D E	3 A B C D E	3 A B C D E	3 A B C D E	3 A B C D E
4 A B C D E	4 A B C D E	4 A B C D E	4 A B C D E	4 A B C D E
5 A B C D E	5 A B C D E	5 A B C D E	5 A B C D E	5 A B C D E
6 A B C D E	6 A B C D E	6 A B C D E	6 A B C D E	6 A B C D E
7 A B C D E	7 A B C D E	7 A B C D E	7 A B C D E	7 A B C D E
8 A B C D E	8 A B C D E	8 A B C D E	8 A B C D E	8 A B C D E
9 A B C D E	9 A B C D E	9 A B C D E	9 A B C D E	9 A B C D E
0 A B C D E	0 A B C D E	0 A B C D E	0 A B C D E	0 A B C D E

1 A B C D E	7 A B C D E	13 A B C D E	19 A B C D E	25 A B C D E
2 A B C D E	8 A B C D E	14 A B C D E	20 A B C D E	26 A B C D E
3 A B C D E	9 A B C D E	15 A B C D E	21 A B C D E	27 A B C D E
4 A B C D E	10 A B C D E	16 A B C D E	22 A B C D E	28 A B C D E
5 A B C D E	11 A B C D E	17 A B C D E	23 A B C D E	29 A B C D E
6 A B C D E	12 A B C D E	18 A B C D E	24 A B C D E	30 A B C D E

TEAR OUT ALONG THIS LINE AND MARK YOUR ANSWERS AS INSTRUCTED IN THE TEXT

PATROL INSPECTOR

READINGS IN LAW ENFORCEMENT

Each of the following questions is based upon your understanding, as a law enforcement officer, of a sentence or paragraph. How well have you read the passage? Have you assimilated all the details? What conclusions can you draw? What conclusions would be illogical in the context of the reading?

1. "The force reconciling and co-ordinating all the human conflicts and directing the men in the harmonious accomplishment of their work is the supervisor. To deal with people successfully, the first one a supervisor must learn to work with is himself." According to the above paragraph, the most accurate of the following conclusions is
   (A) human conflicts are not the basic lack in harmonious accomplishment
   (B) a supervisor should attempt to reconcile all the different views his subordinates have
   (C) a supervisor who understands himself is in a good position to deal with others successfully
   (D) the reconciling force in human conflicts is the ability to deal with people successfully.

Answer questions 2 to 6 solely on the basis of the following paragraph:

"If we are to study crime in its widest social setting, we will find a variety of conduct which, although criminal in the legal sense, is not offensive to the moral conscience of a considerable number of persons. Traffic violations, for example, do not brand the offender as guilty of moral offense. In fact, the recipient of a traffic ticket is usually simply the subject of some good natured joking by his friends. Although there may be indignation among certain groups of citizens against gambling and liquor law violations, these activities are often tolerated, if not openly supported, by the more numerous residents of the community. Indeed, certain social and service clubs regularly conduct gambling games and lotteries for the purpose of raising funds. Some communities regard violations involving the sale of liquor with little concern in order to profit from increased license fees and taxes paid by dealers. The thousand and one forms of political graft and corruption which infest our urban centers only occasionally arouse public condemnation and official action."

2. According to the above paragraph, all types of illegal conduct are
   (A) condemned by all elements of the community
   (B) considered a moral offense, although some are tolerated by a few citizens
   (C) violations of the law, but some are acceptable to certain elements of the community
   (D) found in a social setting which is not punishable by law.

3. According to the above paragraph, traffic violations are generally considered by society as
   (A) crimes requiring the maximum penalty set by the law
   (B) more serious than violations of the liquor laws
   (C) offenses against the morals of the community
   (D) relatively minor offenses requiring minimum punishment.

4. According to the above paragraph, a lottery conducted for the purpose of raising funds for a church
   (A) is considered a serious violation of law
   (B) may be tolerated by a community which has laws against gambling
   (C) may be conducted under special laws demanded by the more numerous residents of a community
   (D) arouses indignation in most communities.

5. On the basis of the above paragraph, the most likely reaction in the community to a police raid on a gambling casino would be
   (A) more an attitude of indifference than interest in the raid
   (B) general approval of the raid
   (C) condemnation of the raid by most people
   (D) demand for further action, since this raid is not sufficient to end gambling activities.

6. The one of the following which best describes the central thought of this paragraph and would be most suitable as a title for it is
   (A) Crime and the Police
   (B) Public Condemnation of Graft and Corruption
   (C) Gambling Is Not Always a Vicious Business
   (D) Public Attitude toward Law Violations.

Answer questions 7 to 9 solely on the basis of the following paragraph:

"The law enforcement agency is one of the most important agencies in the field of juvenile delinquency prevention. This is so, not because of the social work connected with this problem, however, for this is not a police matter, but because the officers are usually the first to come in contact with the delinquent. The manner of arrest and detention makes a deep impression upon him and affects his life-long attitude toward society and the law. The juvenile court is perhaps the most important agency in this work. Contrary to the general opinion, however, it is not primarily concerned with putting children into correctional schools. The main purpose of the juvenile court is to save the child and to develop his emotional make-up, in order that he can grow up to be a decent and well-balanced citizen. The system of probation is the means whereby the court seeks to accomplish these goals."

7. According to this paragraph, police work is an important part of a program to prevent juvenile delinquency because
   (A) social work is no longer considered important in juvenile delinquency prevention
   (B) police officers are the first to have contact with the delinquent
   (C) police officers jail the offender in order to be able to change his attitude toward society and the law
   (D) it is the first step in placing the delinquent in jail.

8. According to this paragraph, the chief purpose of the juvenile court is to
   (A) punish the child for his offense
   (B) select a suitable correctional school for the delinquent
   (C) use available means to help the delinquent become a better person
   (D) provide psychiatric care for the delinquent.

9. According to this paragraph, the juvenile court directs the development of delinquents under its care chiefly by
   (A) placing the child under probation
   (B) sending the child to a correctional school
   (C) keeping the delinquent in prison
   (D) returning the child to his home.

10. "Crimes against the person are apt to be more spectacular than other types of crime and in consequence, space is accorded them in the public press out of proportion to their actual frequency." This means most nearly
   (A) there has been a notable increase in crimes against the person
   (B) the newspapers pay more attention to robberies than to cases of fraud
   (C) the newspapers pay no attention to crimes against property
   (D) crimes against property are not so serious as crimes against the person.

11. "Blasphemy is still a crime but you meet it at every corner." The clearest implication in this statement is
   (A) some laws are ignored
   (B) blasphemy is a serious offense
   (C) the principal purpose of any law is to catch a law-breaker
   (D) blasphemy is quite uncommon.

12. "Discipline should be education: instead it is little more than an application to adults of the theory of spanking," means most nearly
   (A) whipping is a good way to handle a man who beats his wife
   (B) a thieving banker should be imprisoned for life
   (C) those who commit crimes exhibit a marked lack of self-control
   (D) re-education is really a kind of discipline.

13. "Law must be stable and yet it cannot stand still," means most nearly
   (A) law is a fixed body of subject matter
   (B) law must adapt itself to changing conditions
   (C) law is a poor substitute for justice
   (D) the true administration of justice is the firmest pillar of good government.

14. "The treatment to be given the offender cannot alter the fact of his offenses; but we can take measures to reduce the chances of similar acts in the future. We should banish the criminal, not in order to exact revenge nor directly to encourage reform, but to deter him and others from further illegal attacks on society." According to the preceding paragraph, prisoners should be punished in order to

(A) alter the nature of their offenses
(B) banish them from society
(C) deter them and others from similar illegal attacks on society
(D) exact revenge
(E) to directly encourage reform.

15. "On the other hand, the treatment of prisoners on a basis of direct reform is foredoomed to failure. Neither honest men nor criminals will tolerate a bald proposition from anyone to alter their characters or habits, least of all if we attempt to gain such a change by a system of coercion." According to this paragraph, criminals are
(A) incorrigible
(B) incapable of being coerced
(C) absolutely different from honest men
(C) possessed of very firm characters
(E) not likely to turn into law-abiding citizens as a result of being forced to reform.

16. "A moment's reflection will show that it is never possible to determine the exact amount of blame to be attached to the criminal himself. How can we ascertain how much is due to inheritance, how much to early environment, how much to other matters over which the offender has had no control whatsoever?" According to this paragraph, criminals
(A) cannot be held to account for their crimes
(B) cannot be blamed for their crimes
(C) are variously motivated in committing crime and it is senseless to assume that we can know how much blame to attach to a particular violator of the law
(D) can blame their misdeeds on early environment
(E) none of the foregoing.

17. "While much thought has been devoted to the question of how to build walls high enough to keep men temporarily in prison, we have devoted very little attention to the treatment necessary to enable them to come out permanently cured, inclined to be friends rather than enemies of their law-abiding fellow citizens." According to this paragraph, much thought has been devoted to the problém of prisons as
(A) vengeful agencies
(B) efficient custodial agencies
(C) efficient sanatoria
(D) institutions capable of enabling prisoners to come out permanently cured
(E) places from which society's friends might issue.

18. "There has been a tragic failure on the part of the home, the school, the church, industry, and every other social agency to adjust the incompetent individual to his proper sphere and to impart to him wholesome principles of right living. The failure is finally shunted on to the prison in one last desperate effort to make him over. Theoretically the church, the school and the college have a clean page in the mind of the pupil upon which to make their impressions, but the prison school faces the tremendous task of obliterating many erroneous and corrupt notions before it can secure a clean page upon which to write." According to this paragraph, the prison has as pupils
(A) those persons with which society's educational institutions have been able to do nothing
(B) those who have failed in business and the arts
(C) those who have scoffed at God
(D) those whose minds are blanks
(E) those who have learned nothing from the outside world.

Questions 19 to 21 must be answered according to the information given in Paragraph A and not according to any other information you may have.

PARAGRAPH A

"A car will go a certain distance from the point where danger is first detected before any driver is able to apply the brakes. This is called 'reaction distance.' The distance traveled after the brakes are applied is called 'braking distance.' A car traveling at 30 miles per hour has a braking distance of 50 feet, a car traveling at 40 miles per hour has a braking distance of 88 feet, and a car traveling at 50 miles per hour has a braking distance of 138 feet. It takes a certain amount of time after an emergency arises for even the most experienced driver to see the danger and send the impulse to stop to the braking mechanism of his car. The time this requires varies with the individual driver and ranges from three-eighths of a second to a second or more."

19. According to Paragraph A
(A) a car traveling at 40 miles per hour will travel 88 feet before the brakes are applied by the driver while a car traveling at 50 miles an hour will travel 138 feet before the brakes are applied by the driver
(B) a collision will result if a driver traveling at 30 miles an hour applies the brakes at the same time as the brakes are applied

by a driver 50 feet directly behind him traveling at 50 miles per hour
(C) a driver will step on the brakes the instant he sees danger ahead
(D) reaction time is the time required to see the danger.

20. According to Paragraph A
(A) a car traveling at 20 miles per hour will have a braking distance of 44 feet
(B) an experienced driver can bring a car to a stop in less than a second while a driver with very little experience will require a second or more to bring the same car to a stop
(C) braking distance is the distance traveled from the point where the danger is detected to the point where the car is stopped minus the distance traveled before the brakes are applied
(D) reaction distance is always greater than braking distance.

21. According to Paragraph A
(A) braking distance varies with the rate of speed at which the car is traveling
(B) braking time ranges from three-eighths of a second to a second or more
(C) reaction distance is the distance the car travels before danger is detected
(D) the faster a car is traveling, the shorter the time that is required to bring it to a stop.

22. "Community organization most often includes persons whose behavior is unconventional in relation to generally accepted social definition, if such persons wield substantial influence with the residents." The inference one can most validly draw from this statement is that
(A) influential persons are often likely to be unconventional
(B) the success of a community organization depends largely on the democratic processes employed by it
(C) a gang leader may sometimes be an acceptable recruit for a community organization
(D) the unconventional behavior of a local barkeeper may often become acceptable to the community.

23. "Essential to prevention and early treatment of delinquency is discovery of potential or incipient cases. Finding them is not as difficult as making assistance available and acceptable to them and their families." On the basis of the above statement, it is most accurate to state that
(A) the families of delinquents are largely responsible for their behavior
(B) "an ounce of prevention is worth more than a pound of cure"
(C) potentiality to criminality is readily discernible
(D) the family of a delinquent may often reject a recommended plan for therapy.

24. "The safeguard of democracy is education. The education of youth during a limited period of more or less compulsory attendance at school does not suffice. The educative process is a life long one." The statement most consistent with this quotation is
(A) the school is not the only institution which can contribute to the education of the population
(B) all democratic peoples are educated
(C) the entire population should be required to go to school throughout life
(D) if compulsory education were not required, the educative process would be more effective.

25. "Another explanation of the persistence of the criminal is found in the existence of criminality or near-criminality in the general society." The statement *least* consistent with this quotation is
(A) not all criminals are apprehended and sentenced for their crimes
(B) advertisements of many commodities are often fraudulent in their claims
(C) the reformation of the offender would be much simpler if society contained more persons of the near-criminal type
(D) many business concerns are willing to purchase stolen goods.

Law Enforcement Reading Interpretation
Correct Answers

1. C	6. D	11. A	16. D	21. A
2. C	7. B	12. D	17. B	22. C
3. D	8. C	13. B	18. A	23. D
4. B	9. A	14. C	19. B	24. A
5. A	10. B	15. E	20. C	25. C

POLICE WORK READING QUIZZER

We have good reason to believe that this kind of question will appear on your test. We want you to practice now and profit later. Guide and schedule your practice.

1. "The policeman's art consists in applying and enforcing a multitude of laws and ordinances in such degree or proportion and in such manner that the greatest degree of social protection will be secured. The degree of enforcement and the method of application will vary with each neighborhood and community." According to the foregoing paragraph
   (A) each neighborhood or community must judge for itself to what extent the law is to be enforced
   (B) a policeman should only enforce those laws which are designed to give the greatest degree of social protection
   (C) the manner and intensity of law enforcement is not necessarily the same in all communities
   (D) all laws and ordinances must be enforced in a community with the same degree of intensity.

2. "Police control in the sense of regulating the details of police operations involves such matters as the technical means for so organizing the available personnel that competent police leadership, when secured, can operate effectively. It is concerned not so much with the extent to which popular controls can be trusted to guide and direct the course of police protection as with the administrative relationships which should exist between the component parts of the police organism." According to the foregoing statement, police control is
   (A) solely a matter of proper personnel assignment
   (B) the means employed to guide and direct the course of police protection
   (C) principally concerned with the administrative relationships between units of a police organization
   (D) the sum total of means employed in rendering police protection.

3. "As a rule, patrolmen, through service and experience, are familiar with the duties and the methods and means required to perform them. Yet, left to themselves, their aggregate effort would disintegrate and the vital work of preserving the peace would never be accomplished." According to the above paragraph, the most accurate of the following conclusions is
   (A) patrolmen are sufficiently familiar with their duties to need no supervision
   (B) working together for a common purpose is not efficient without supervision
   (C) patrolmen are familiar with the methods of performing their duties because of rules
   (D) preserving the peace is so vital that it can never be said to be completed.

Questions 4 through 11 are based on the following excerpt from the 1961 Annual Report of a Police Department. This material should be read first and then referred to in answering these questions, which are to be answered solely on the basis of the material herein contained.

LEGAL BUREAU

"One of the more important functions of this bureau is to analyze and furnish the department with pertinent information concerning Federal and State statutes and Local Laws which affect the department, law enforcement or crime prevention. In addition, all measures introduced in the State Legislature and the City Council, which may affect this department are carefully reviewed by members of the Legal Bureau and where necessary, opinions and recommendations thereon are prepared.

"Another important function of this office is the prosecution of cases in the Criminal Courts. This is accomplished by assignment of attorneys who are members of the Legal Bureau to appear in those cases which are deemed to raise issues of importance to the department or questions of law which require technical presentation to facilitate proper determination; and also in those cases where request is made for such appearances by a magistrate, some other official of the city, or a member of the force. Attorneys are regularly assigned to prosecute all cases in the Women's Court.

"Proposed legislation was prepared and sponsored for introduction in the State Legislature and, at this writing, one of these proposals has already been enacted into law and five others are presently on the Governor's desk awaiting executive action. The new law prohibits the sale or possession of a hypodermic syringe or needle by an unauthorized person. The bureau's proposals awaiting executive action pertain to: an amendment to the Code of Criminal Procedure prohibiting desk officers from taking bail in gambling cases or in cases mentioned in Section 552, Code of Criminal Procedure; including confidence men and swindlers as jostlers in the Penal Law; prohibiting the sale of switch-blade knives of any size to children under 16 and bills extending the licensing period of gunsmiths.

"The Legal Bureau has regularly cooperated with the Corporation Counsel and the District Attorneys in respect to matters affecting this department, and has continued to advise and represent the Police Athletic League, the Police Sports Association, the Police Relief Fund and the Police Pension Fund.

"The following is a statistical report of the activities of the bureau

	1965	1964
Memoranda of law prepared	68	83
Legal matters forwarded to Corporation Counsel	122	144
Letters requesting legal information	756	807
Letters requesting departmental records	139	111
Matters for publication	17	26
Court appearances of members of bureau	4,678	4,621
Conferences	94	103
Lectures at Police Academy	30	33
Reports on proposed legislation	194	255
Deciphering of codes	79	27
Expert testimony	31	16
Notices to court witnesses	55	81
Briefs prepared	22	18
Court papers prepared	258	258

4. One of the functions of the Legal Bureau is to
   (A) Review and make recommendations on proposed Federal laws affecting law enforcement
   (B) Prepare opinions on all measures introduced in the State Legislature and the City Council
   (C) Furnish the Police Department with pertinent information concerning all new Federal and State laws
   (D) Analyze all laws affecting the work of the Police Department.

5. The one of the following that is not a function of the Legal Bureau is
   (A) Law enforcement and crime prevention
   (B) Prosecution of all cases in Women's Court
   (C) Advise and represent the Police Sports Association
   (D) Lecturing at the Police Academy.

6. Members of the Legal Bureau frequently appear in Criminal Court for the purpose of
   (A) Defending members of the Police Force
   (B) Raising issues of importance to the Police Department
   (C) Prosecuting all offenders arrested by members of the Force
   (D) Facilitating proper determination of questions of law requiring technical presentation.

7. The Legal Bureau sponsored a bill that would
   (A) Extend the licenses of gunsmiths
   (B) Prohibit the sale of switch-blade knives to children of any size
   (C) Place confidence men and swindlers in the same category as jostlers in the Penal Law
   (D) Prohibit desk officers from admitting gamblers, confidence men and swindlers to bail.

8. From the report it is not reasonable to infer that
   (A) Fewer bills affecting the Police Department were introduced in 1965
   (B) The preparation of court papers was a new activity assumed in 1965
   (C) The Code of Criminal Procedure authorizes desk officers to accept bail in certain cases
   (D) The penalty for jostling and swindling is the same.

9. According to the statistical report, the activity showing the greatest percentage of increase in 1965 as compared with 1964 was
   (A) Matters for publication
   (B) Reports on proposed legislation
   (C) Notices to court witnesses
   (D) Memoranda of law prepared.

10. According to the statistical report, the activtiy showing the greatest percentage of increase in 1965 as compared with 1964 was
    (A) Court appearances of members of the bureau
    (B) Giving expert testimony
    (C) Deciphering of codes
    (D) Letters requesting departmental records.

11. According to the report, the percentage of bills prepared and sponsored by the Legal Bureau, which were passed by the State Legislature and sent to the Governor for approval, was
    (A) Approximately 3.1%
    (B) Approximately 2.6%

(C) Approximately .5%
(D) Not capable of determination from the data given.

12. "The number of arrests made is not always the best indication of a successful policeman." The statement most consistent with the above quotation is that
(A) a number of factors should be considered in properly evaluating the performance of a policeman
(B) there is a negative correlation between the number of arrests made and the success of a policeman
(C) policemen should avoid making arrests whenever possible
(D) the success of a policeman cannot be precisely and objectively measured.

Answer Questions 13 to 15 on the basis of the following paragraph:

"Criminal science is largely the science of identification. Progress in this field has been marked and sometimes very spectacular because new techniques, instruments and facts flow continuously from the scientists. But the crime laboratories are undermanned, trade secrets still prevail and inaccurate conclusions are often the result. However, modern gadgets cannot substitute for the skilled intelligent investigator; he must be their master."

13. According to this paragraph, criminal science
(A) excludes the field of investigation
(B) is primarily interested in establishing identity
(C) is based on the equipment used in crime laboratories
(D) uses techniques different from those used in other sciences
(E) is essentially secret in nature.

14. Advances in criminal science have been, according to the above paragraph,
(A) extremely limited
(B) slow but steady
(C) unusually reliable
(D) outstanding
(E) infrequently worthwhile.

15. A problem that has not been overcome completely in crime work is, according to the above paragraph,
(A) unskilled investigators
(B) the expense of new equipment and techniques
(C) an insufficient number of personnel in crime laboratories
(D) inaccurate equipment used in laboratories
(E) conclusions of the public about the value of this field.

Answer questions 16 through 19 solely on the basis of the following paragraph:

"Automobile tire tracks found at the scene of a crime constitute an important link in the chain of physical evidence. In many cases, these are the only clues available. In some areas, unpaved ground adjoins the highway or paved streets. A suspect will often park his car off the paved portion of the street when committing a crime, sometimes leaving excellent tire tracks. Comparison of the tire track impressions with the tires is possible only when the vehicle has been found. However, the initial problem facing the police is the task of determining what kind of car probably made the impressions found at the scene of the crime. If the make, model and year of the car which made the impressions can be determined, it is obvious that the task of elimination is greatly lessened."

16. The one of the following which is the most appropriate title for the above paragraph is
(A) The Use of Automobiles in the Commission of Crimes
(B) The Use of Tire Tracks in Police Work
(C) The Capture of Criminals by Scientific Police Work
(D) The Positive Identification of Criminals Through Their Cars.

17. When searching for clear signs left by the car used in the commision of a crime, the most likely place for the police to look would be on the
(A) highway adjoining unpaved streets
(B) highway adjacent to paved street
(C) paved street adjacent to the highway
(D) unpaved ground adjacent to a highway.

18. Automobile tire tracks found at the scene of a crime are of value as evidence in that they are
(A) generally sufficient to trap and convict a suspect
(B) the most important link in the chain of physical evidence
(C) often the only evidence at hand
(D) circumstantial rather than direct.

19. The primary reason for the police to try to find out which make, model and year of car was involved in the commission of a crime is to
(A) compare the tire tracks left at the scene of the crime with the type of tires used on cars of that make
(B) determine if the mud on the tires of the suspected car matches the mud in the unpaved road near the scene of the crime
(C) reduce to a large extent the amount of

work involved in determining the particular car used in the commission of a crime
(D) alert the police patrol forces to question the occupants of all automobiles of this type.

Answer Questions 20 through 23 solely on the basis of the following paragraph:

"When stopping vehicles on highways to check for suspects or fugitives, the police use an automobile roadblock whenever possible. This consists of three cars placed in prearranged positions. Car number one is parked across the left lane of the roadway with the front diagonally facing toward the center line. Car number two is parked across the right lane, with the front of the vehicle also toward the center line, in a position perpendicular to car number one and approximately twenty feet to the rear. Continuing another twenty feet to the rear along the highway, car number three is parked in an identical manner to car number one. The width of the highway determines the angle or position in which the autos should be placed. In addition to the regular roadblock signs, and the use of flares at night only, there is an officer located at both the entrance and exit to direct and control traffic from both directions. This type of roadblock forces all approaching autos to reduce speed and zigzag around the police cars. Officers standing behind the parked cars can most safely and carefully view all passing motorists. Once a suspect is inside the block it becomes extremely difficult to crash out."

20. Of the following, the most appropriate title for this paragraph is
(A) The Construction of an Escape-Proof Roadblock
(B) Regulation of Automobile Traffic Through a Police Roadblock
(C) Safety Precautions Necessary in Making an Automobile Roadblock
(D) Structure of a Roadblock to Detain Suspects or Fugitives.

21. When setting up a three-car roadblock, the relative positions of the cars should be such that
(A) the front of car number one is placed diagonally to the center line and faces car number three
(B) car number three is placed parallel to the center line and its front faces the right side of the road
(C) car number two is placed about 20 feet from car number one and its front faces the left side of the road
(D) car number three is parallel to and about 20 feet away from car number one.

22. Officers can observe occupants of all cars passing through the roadblock with greatest safety when
(A) warning flares are lighted to illuminate the area sufficiently at night
(B) warning signs are put up at each end of the roadblock
(C) they are stationed at both the exit and the entrance of the roadblock
(D) they take up positions behind cars in the roadblock.

23. The type of automobile roadblock described in the above paragraph is of value in police work because
(A) a suspect is unable to escape its confines by using force
(B) it is frequently used to capture suspects with no danger to the police
(C) it requires only two officers to set up and operate
(D) vehicular traffic within its confines is controlled as to speed and direction.

Answer Questions 24 through 26 solely on the basis of the following paragraph:

"A problem facing the police department in one area of the city was to try to reduce the number of bicycle thefts which had been increasing at an alarming rate in the past three or four years. A new program was adopted to get at the root of the problem. Tags were printed, reminding youngsters that bicycles left unlocked can be easily stolen. The police concentrated on such places as theaters, a municipal swimming pool, an athletic field, and the local high school, and tied tags on all bicycles which were not locked. The majority of bicycle thefts took place at the swimming pool. In 1964, during the first two weeks the pool was open, an average of 10 bicycles was stolen there daily. During the same two-week period, 30 bicycles were stolen at the athletic field, 15 at the high school, and 11 at all theaters combined. In 1965, after tagging the unlocked bicycles, it was found that 20 bicycles a week were stolen at the pool and 5 at the high school. It was felt that the police tags had helped the most, although the school officials had helped to a great extent in this program by distributing 'locking' notices to parents and children, and the use of the loudspeaker at the pool urging children to lock their bicycles had also been very helpful."

24. The one of the following which had the greatest

effect in the campaign to reduce bicycle stealing was the

(A) distribution of "locking" notices by the school officials
(B) locking of all bicycles left in public places
(C) police tagging of bicycles left unlocked by youngsters
(D) use of the loudspeaker at the swimming pool.

25. The tagging program was instituted by the police department chiefly to
(A) determine the areas where most bicycle thieves operated
(B) instill in youngsters the importance of punishing bicycle thieves
(C) lessen the rising rate of bicycle thefts
(D) recover as many as possible of the stolen bicycles.

26. The figures showing the number of bicycle thefts in the various areas surveyed indicate that in 1964
(A) almost as many thefts occurred at the swimming pool as at all theaters combined
(B) fewer thefts occurred at the athletic field than at both the high school and all theaters combined
(C) more than half the thefts occurred at the swimming pool
(D) twice as many thefts occurred at the high school as at the athletic field.

Answer Questions 27 and 28 solely on the basis of the following paragraph:

"A survey has shown that crime prevention work is most successful if the officers are assigned on rotating shifts to provide for around-the-clock coverage. An officer may work days for a time and then be switched to nights. The prime object of the night work is to enable the officer to spot conditions inviting burglars. Complete lack of, or faulty locations of, night lights and other conditions that may invite burglars, which might go unnoticed during daylight hours, can be located and corrected more readily through night work. Night work also enables the officer to check local hangouts of juveniles, such as bus and railway depots, certain cafes or pool halls, the local roller rink, and the building where a juvenile dance is held every Friday night. Detectives also join patrolmen cruising in radio patrol cars to check on juveniles loitering late at night and to spot-check local bars for juveniles."

27. The most important purpose of assigning officers to night shifts is to make it possible for them to
(A) correct conditions which may not be readily noticed during the day
(B) discover the location of, and replace, missing and faulty night lights
(C) locate criminal hangouts
(D) notice things at night which cannot be noticed during the daytime.

28. The type of shifting of officers which best prevents crime is to have
(A) day-shift officers rotated to night work
(B) rotating shifts provide sufficient officers for coverage 24 hours daily
(C) an officer work around the clock on a 24-hour basis as police needs arise
(D) rotating shifts to give the officers varied experience.

Answer Questions 29 and 30 solely on the basis of the following paragraph:

"Proper firearms training is one phase of law enforcement which cannot be ignored. No part of the training of a police officer is more important or more valuable. The officer's life and often the lives of his fellow officers depend directly upon his skill with the weapon he is carrying. Proficiency with the revolver is not attained exclusively by the volume of ammunition used and the number of hours spent on the firing line. Supervised practice and the use of training aids and techniques help make the shooter. It is essential to have a good firing range where new officers are trained and older personnel practice in scheduled firearms sessions. The fundamental points to be stressed are grip, stance, breathing, sight alinement and trigger squeeze. Coordination of thought vision and motion must be achieved before the officer gains confidence in his shooting ability. Attaining this ability will make the student a better officer and enhance his value to the force."

29. A police officer will gain confidence in his shooting ability only after he has
(A) spent the required number of hours on the firing line
(B) been given sufficient supervised practice
(C) learned the five fundamental points
(D) learned to coordinate revolver movement with his sight and thought.

30. Proper training in the use of firearms is one aspect of law enforcement which must be given serious consideration chiefly because it is the
(A) most useful and essential single factor in the training of a police officer
(B) one phase of police officer training which stresses mental and physical coordination
(C) costliest aspect of police officer training, involving considerable expense for the ammunition used in target practice
(D) most difficult part of police officer train-

ing, involving the expenditure of many hours on the firing line.

31. "The large number of fatal motor-vehicle accidents renders necessary the organization of special units in the police department to cope with the technical problems encountered in such investigations." The generalization which can be inferred most directly from this statement is that
   (A) large problems require specialists
   (B) technical problems require specialists
   (C) many police problems require special handling
   (D) many policemen are specialists
   (E) the number of motor-vehicle accidents which are fatal is large.

32. "While the safe burglar can ply his trade the year round, the loft man is more seasonal in his activities, since only at certain periods of the year is a substantial amount of valuable merchandise stored in lofts." The generalization which this statement best illustrates is that
   (A) nothing is ever completely safe from a thief
   (B) there are safe burglars and loft burglars
   (C) some types of burglary are seasonal
   (D) the safe burglar considers "safecracking" a trade
   (E) there are different kinds of thieves.

33. "The tendency for an increase in crime during the winter is most pronounced in the case of robbery, which shows a 50 percent fluctuation from minimum to maximum levels. The variation in the lengths of days and nights with the changing seasons has a direct influence here, since the winter months provide more hours of darkness during which robberies, burglaries and larcenies may be committed." Of the following, the chief implication of the above statement is that
   (A) crime is prevalent during the winter months
   (B) the influence of the seasons on crime varies from year to year
   (C) the number of robberies probably also varies from day to day
   (D) robbery is a common crime
   (E) most robberies are committed during darkness.

Answer Questions 34 to 36 solely on the basis of the following paragraph:

Pickpockets operate most effectively when there are prospective victims in either heavily congested areas or in lonely places. In heavily populated areas, the large number of people about them covers the activities of these thieves. In lonely spots, they have the advantage of working unobserved. The main factor in the pickpocket's success is the selection of the "right" victim. A pickpocket's victim must, at the time of the crime, be inattentive, distracted or unconscious. If any of these conditions exist, and if the pickpocket is skilled in his operations, the stage is set for a successful larceny. With the coming of winter, the crowds move southward—and so do most of the pickpockets. However, some pickpockets will remain in certain areas all year around. They will concentrate on theater districts, bus and railroad terminals, hotels or large shopping centers. A complete knowledge of the methods of this type of criminal and the ability to recognize them come only from long years of experience in performing patient surveillance and trailing of them. This knowledge is essential for the effective control and apprehension of this type of thief.

34. According to this paragraph, the pickpocket is *least* likely to operate in a
   (A) baseball park with a full capacity attendance
   (B) subway station in an outlying area late at night
   (C) moderately crowded dance hall
   (D) over-crowded department store.

35. According to this paragraph, the one of the following factors which is *not* necessary for the successful operation of the pickpocket is that
   (A) he be proficient in the operations required to pick pockets
   (B) the "right" potential victims be those who have been the subject of such a theft previously
   (C) his operations be hidden from the view of others
   (D) the potential victim be unaware of the actions of the pickpocket.

36. According to this paragraph, it would be most correct to conclude that police officers who are successful in apprehending pickpockets
   (A) are generally those who have had lengthy experience in recognizing all types of criminals
   (B) must, by intuition, be able to recognize potential "right" victims
   (C) must follow the pickpockets in their southward movement
   (D) must have acquired specific knowledge skills in this field.

Answer Questions 37 and 38 solely on the basis of the following paragraph:

The medical examiner may contribute valuable

data to the investigator of fires which cause fatalities. By careful examination of the bodies of any victims, he not only establishes cause of death, but may also furnish, in many instances, answers to questions relating to the identity of the victim and the source and origin of the fire. The medical examiner is of greatest value to law enforcement agencies because he is able to determine the exact cause of death through an examination of tissue of apparent arson victims. Thorough study of a burned body or even of parts of a burned body will frequently yield information which illuminates the problems confronting the arson investigator and the police.

37. According to the above paragraph, the most important task of the medical examiner in the investigation of arson is to obtain information concerning the
    (A) identity of arsonists
    (B) cause of death
    (C) identity of victims
    (D) source and origin of fires.

38. The central thought of the above paragraph is that the medical examiner aids in the solution of crimes of arson when
    (A) a person is burnt to death
    (B) identity of the arsonist is unknown
    (C) the cause of the fire is known
    (D) trained investigators are not available.

Answer Questions 39 to 42 solely on the basis of the following paragraph:

It is not always understood that the term "physical evidence" embraces any and all objects, living or inanimate. A knife, gun, signature or burglar tool is immediately recognized as physical evidence. Less often is it considered that dust, microscopic fragments of all types, even an odor, may equally be physical evidence and often the most important of all. It is well established that the most useful types of physical evidence are generally microscopic in dimensions, that is, not noticeable by the eye and therefore most likely to be overlooked by the criminal and by the investigator. For this reason microscopic evidence persists for months or years after all other evidence has been removed and found inconclusive. Naturally, there are limitations to the time of collecting miscroscopic evidence as it may be lost or decayed. The exercise of judgment as to the possibility or profit of delayed action in collecting the evidence is a field in which the expert investigator should judge.

39. The one of the following which the above paragraph does *not* consider to be physical evidence is a
    (A) criminal thought
    (B) minute speck of dust
    (C) raw onion smell
    (D) typewritten note.

40. According to the above paragraph, the rechecking of the scene of a crime
    (A) is useless when performed years after the occurrence of the crime
    (B) is advisable chiefly in crimes involving physical violence
    (C) may turn up microscopic evidence of value
    (D) should be delayed if the microscopic evidence is not subject to decay or loss.

41. According to the above paragraph, the criminal investigator should
    (A) give most of his attention to weapons used in the commission of the crime
    (B) ignore microscopic evidence until a request is received from the laboratory
    (C) immediately search for microscopic evidence and ignore the more visible objects
    (D) realize that microscopic evidence can be easily overlooked.

42. According to the above paragraph,
    (A) a delay in collecting evidence must definitely diminish its value to the investigator
    (B) microscopic evidence exists for longer periods of time than other physical evidence
    (C) microscopic evidence is generally the most useful type of physical evidence
    (D) physical evidence is likely to be overlooked by the criminal and by the investigator.

Answer Questions 43 to 45 solely on the basis of the following paragraph:

In addition to making the preliminary investigation of crimes, patrolmen should serve as eyes, ears and legs for the detective division. The patrol division may be used for surveillance, to serve warrants and bring in suspects and witnesses, and to perform a number of routine tasks for the detectives which will increase the time available for tasks that require their special skills and facilities. It is to the advantage of individual detectives, as well as of the detective division, to have patrolmen working in this manner; more cases are cleared by arrest and a greater proportion of stolen property is recovered when, in addition to the detective regularly assigned, a number of patrolmen also work on the case. Detectives may stimulate the interest and participation of patrolmen by keeping them currently informed of the presence, identity or description, hangouts, associates, vehicles and method of operation of each criminal known to be in the community.

43. According to this paragraph, a patrolman should
(A) assist the detective in certain of his routine functions
(B) be considered for assignment as a detective on the basis of his patrol performance
(C) leave the scene once a detective arrives
(D) perform as much of the detective's duties as time permits.

44. According to this paragraph, patrolmen should aid detectives by
(A) accepting assignments from detectives which give promise of recovering stolen property
(B) making arrests of witnesses for the detective's interrogation
(C) performing all special investigative work for detectives
(D) producing for questioning individuals who may aid the detective in his investigation.

45. According to this paragraph, detectives can keep patrolmen interested by
(A) ascertaining that patrolmen are doing investigative work properly
(B) having patrolmen directly under his supervision during an investigation
(C) informing patrolmen of the value of their efforts in crime prevention
(D) supplying the patrolmen with information regarding known criminals in the community. (2621)

Answer Questions 46 to 48 solely on the basis of the following paragraph:

"Foot patrol has some advantages over all other methods of patrol. Maximum opportunity is provided for observation within range of the senses and for close contact with people and things that enable the patrolman to provide a maximum service as an information source and counselor to the public and as the eyes and ears of the police department. A foot patrolman loses no time in alighting from a vehicle, and the performance of police tasks is not hampered by responsibility for his vehicle while afoot. Foot patrol, however, does not have many of the advantages of a patrol car. Lack of both mobility and immediate communication with headquarters lessens the officer's value in an emergency. The area that he can cover effectively is limited and, therefore, this method of patrol is costly."

46. According to this paragraph, the foot patrolman is the eyes and ears of the police department because he is
(A) in direct contact with the station house
(B) not responsible for a patrol vehicle
(C) able to observe closely conditions on his patrol post
(D) a readily available information source to the public.

47. The most accurate of the following statements concerning the various methods of patrol, according to this paragraph, is that
(A) foot patrol should sometimes be combined with motor patrol
(B) foot patrol is better than motor patrol
(C) helicopter patrol has the same advantages as motor patrol
(D) motor patrol is more readily able to communicate with superior officers in an emergency.

48. According to this paragraph, it is correct to state that foot patrol is
(A) economical since increased mobility makes more rapid action possible
(B) expensive since the area that can be patrolled is relatively small
(C) economical since vehicle costs need not be considered
(D) expensive since giving information to the public is time consuming.

Answer questions 49 to 51 solely on the basis of the following paragraph:

"The police laboratory performs a valuable service in crime investigation by assisting in the reconstruction of criminal action and by aiding in the identification of persons and things. When studied by a technician, physical things found at crime scenes often reveal facts useful in identifying the criminal and in determining what has occurred. The nature of substances to be examined and the character of the examinations to be made vary so widely that the services of a large variety of skilled scientific persons are needed in crime investigations. To employ such a complete staff and to provide them with equipment and standards needed for all possible analyses and comparisons is beyond the means and the needs of any but the largest police departments. The search of crime scenes for physical evidence also calls for the services of specialists supplied with essential equipment and assigned to each tour of duty so as to provide service at any hour."

49. If a police department employs a large staff of various types in its laboratory, it will affect crime investigation to the extent that
(A) most crimes will be speedily solved
(B) identification of criminals will be aided
(C) search of crime scenes for physical evi-

dence will become of less importance
(D) investigation by police officers will not usually be required.

50. According to this paragraph, the most complete study of objects found at the scenes of crimes is
(A) always done in all large police departments
(B) based on assigning one technician to each tour of duty
(C) probably done only in large police departments
(D) probably done in police departments of communities with low crime rates.

51. According to this paragraph, a large variety of skilled technicians is useful in criminal investigations because
(A) crimes cannot be solved without their assistance as part of the police team
(B) large police departments need large staffs
(C) many different kinds of tests on various substances can be made
(D) the police cannot predict what methods may be tried by wily criminals.

Correct Answers For The Foregoing Questions

(Please make every effort to answer the questions on your own before looking at these answers. You'll make faster progress by following this rule.)

1. C	10. C	19. C	28. B	37. B	46. C
2. C	11. D	20. D	29. D	38. A	47. D
3. B	12. A	21. C	30. A	39. A	48. B
4. D	13. B	22. D	31. B	40. C	49. B
5. A	14. D	23. D	32. C	41. D	50. C
6. D	15. C	24. C	33. E	42. C	51. C
7. C	16. B	25. C	34. C	43. A	
8. D	17. D	26. C	35. B	44. D	
9. A	18. C	27. A	36. D	45. D	

Practice Using Answer Sheets

Alter numbers to match the practice and drill questions in each part of the book.
Make only ONE mark for each answer. Additional and stray marks may be counted as mistakes.
In making corrections, erase errors COMPLETELY. Make glossy black marks.

1 A B C D E	1 A B C D E	1 A B C D E	1 A B C D E	1 A B C D E
2 A B C D E	2 A B C D E	2 A B C D E	2 A B C D E	2 A B C D E
3 A B C D E	3 A B C D E	3 A B C D E	3 A B C D E	3 A B C D E
4 A B C D E	4 A B C D E	4 A B C D E	4 A B C D E	4 A B C D E
5 A B C D E	5 A B C D E	5 A B C D E	5 A B C D E	5 A B C D E
6 A B C D E	6 A B C D E	6 A B C D E	6 A B C D E	6 A B C D E
7 A B C D E	7 A B C D E	7 A B C D E	7 A B C D E	7 A B C D E
8 A B C D E	8 A B C D E	8 A B C D E	8 A B C D E	8 A B C D E
9 A B C D E	9 A B C D E	9 A B C D E	9 A B C D E	9 A B C D E
0 A B C D E	0 A B C D E	0 A B C D E	0 A B C D E	0 A B C D E

1 A B C D E	1 A B C D E	1 A B C D E	1 A B C D E	1 A B C D E
2 A B C D E	2 A B C D E	2 A B C D E	2 A B C D E	2 A B C D E
3 A B C D E	3 A B C D E	3 A B C D E	3 A B C D E	3 A B C D E
4 A B C D E	4 A B C D E	4 A B C D E	4 A B C D E	4 A B C D E
5 A B C D E	5 A B C D E	5 A B C D E	5 A B C D E	5 A B C D E
6 A B C D E	6 A B C D E	6 A B C D E	6 A B C D E	6 A B C D E
7 A B C D E	7 A B C D E	7 A B C D E	7 A B C D E	7 A B C D E
8 A B C D E	8 A B C D E	8 A B C D E	8 A B C D E	8 A B C D E
9 A B C D E	9 A B C D E	9 A B C D E	9 A B C D E	9 A B C D E
0 A B C D E	0 A B C D E	0 A B C D E	0 A B C D E	0 A B C D E

1 A B C D E	7 A B C D E	13 A B C D E	19 A B C D E	25 A B C D E
2 A B C D E	8 A B C D E	14 A B C D E	20 A B C D E	26 A B C D E
3 A B C D E	9 A B C D E	15 A B C D E	21 A B C D E	27 A B C D E
4 A B C D E	10 A B C D E	16 A B C D E	22 A B C D E	28 A B C D E
5 A B C D E	11 A B C D E	17 A B C D E	23 A B C D E	29 A B C D E
6 A B C D E	12 A B C D E	18 A B C D E	24 A B C D E	30 A B C D E

TEAR OUT ALONG THIS LINE AND MARK YOUR ANSWERS AS INSTRUCTED IN THE TEXT

READING QUESTIONS ON ROUTINES

DIRECTIONS: Below each of the following passages you will find one or more incomplete statements about the passage. Select the words or expressions that most satisfactorily complete each statement in accordance with the meaning of the paragraph.

Questions 1 to 10 relate to the report of an accident. Under "A" you are given the regulations governing filling out the report form. Under "B" you are given the completed report upon the basis of which you are to answer the questions.

"A"—1. A report form will be filled out for each person injured.

2. Be brief, but do not omit any information which can help the Department reduce number of accidents. If it is necessary, use more than one card.

3. Under "Details" enter all important facts not reported elsewhere on the card, which may be pertinent to the completeness of the report as: the specific traffic violation, if any; whether the injured person was crossing not at crossing; crossing against lights; the direction the vehicle was proceeding and if making right or left turn; attending surgeon; etc. If the officer is an eye witness he should be able to determine the cause.

"B"—Report:

INJURED PERSON: John C. Witherspoon; SEX: Male; AGE: 52
ADDRESS: 2110 Fairwell Road, N.Y.C.
PLACE OF OCCURRENCE: 72nd Street and Broadway; DATE: 3:12.65
ACCIDENT: Yes; NO. OF PERSONS INVOLVED: 12; TIME: 10 a.m.
NATURE OF INJURY: Right forearm, fractured
STRUCK BY: Auto No. 3
DRIVER INVOLVED:

Auto 1. Helmut Baldman 11 Far Street—Lic. 2831 owner

Auto 2. John Dunn 106 Near Ave.—Lic. 1072 owner

Auto 3. Robert Payne 32 Open Road—Lic. 666 owner

DETAILS: (1) Vehicle 1 came out of 72nd Street just as the lights along 72nd Street were changing to green going west. (2) Vehicle 2 proceding north north along Broadway continuied across the intersection as the lights in his direction turned red. (3) Vehicle 1 colliding with Vehicle 2 turning said vehicle over and throwing it into the path of Vehicle 3 going east along 72nd Street. (4) This had manifold results: other vehicles were struck; a hydrant was obliterated; several pedestrians were injured; there was considerible property damage; and three riders in the cars involved were killed. (5) This was a very tragic accident.

1. In the report, the one of the following words which was misspelled is
(A) fractured
(B) owner
(C) vehicle
(D) proceding
(E) none of the foregoing.

2. In the report, the one of the following words which was misspelled is
(A) continuied
(B) across
(C) intersection
(D) colliding
(E) none of the foregoing.

3. In the report, the one of the following words which was misspelled is
(A) manifold
(B) obliterated
(C) pedestrians
(D) considerible
(E) none of the foregoing.

4. In the report, the one of the following words which was used incorrectly is
   (A) manifold
   (B) obliterated
   (C) intersection
   (D) fractured
   (E) colliding.

5. In the report, under "Details" there are several errors in grammar. Of the changes listed below, a change which will correct an existing error in grammar is
   (A) Change sentence (1) to, "Vehicle 1, going west, came out of 72nd Street just as the lights along 72nd Street were changing to green."
   (B) Change sentence (2) to, "Vehicle 2 proceded north along Broadway continuied across the intersection as the lights in his direction turned red."
   (C) Change sentence (3) to, "Vehicle 1 colliding with vehicle 2 turns said vehicle over and throwing it into the path of vehicle 3 going east along 72nd St."
   (D) Change sentence (4) to, "This has had manifold results: there was considerible property damage; a hydrant was obliterated; and several pedestrians were injured."
   (E) None of the foregoing changes.

6. A change which will correct an existing error in grammar is
   (A) Change sentence (1) to, "Vehicle 1 came out of 72nd St. just as the lights along 72nd Street changed to green going west."
   (B) Change sentence (2) to, "Vehicle 2 proceding north along Broadway continuied across the intersection when the light in his direction turned red."
   (C) Change sentence (3) to, "Vehicle 1 collided with vehicle 2 turning said vehicle over and throwing it into the path of vehicle 3 going east along 72nd Street."
   (D) Change all semicolons in sentence (4) to commas
   (E) None of the foregoing changes.

7. Of the following critical evaluations of the report, the most correct is that it is a
   (A) Good report; it gives a graphic description of the accident
   (B) Bad report; the damage to the car is not given in detail
   (C) Bad report; it does not indicate, in detail, the cause of Witherspoon's injury
   (D) Bad report; there is no indication of what happened to the 11 persons other than Witherspoon who were involved
   (E) Good report; it is very brief.

8. Of the following, the report indicates most clearly
   (A) The driver at fault
   (B) That Witherspoon was a pedestrian
   (C) That the reporting officer was an eye witness
   (D) The names of all the drivers involved
   (E) That some city property was damaged.

9. Of the following, the report indicates least clearly
   (A) The time of the accident
   (B) The direction in which Baldman was driving
   (C) How the accident might have been avoided
   (D) The number of persons involved
   (E) The injury to Witherspoon.

10. From the report, as submitted, it is most reasonable to infer that
   (A) Baldman was at fault
   (B) The information is too hazy to determine the guilty person
   (C) Dunn was at fault
   (D) Something was wrong with the light system
   (E) The accident was the fault of no one person.

Answer questions 11 to 13 solely on the basis of the following paragraph:

"All members of the police force must recognize that the people, through their representatives, hire and pay the police and that, as in any other employment, there must exist a proper employer-employee relationship. The police officer must understand that the essence of a correct police attitude is a willingness to serve, but at the same time he should distinguish between service and servility, and between courtesy and softness. He must be firm but also courteous, avoiding even an appearance of rudeness. He should develop a position that is friendly and unbiased, pleasant and sympathetic, in his relations with the general public, but firm and impersonal on occasions calling for regulation and control. A police officer should understand that his primary purpose is to prevent violations, not to arrest people. He should recognize the line of demarcation between a police function and passing judgment which is a court function. On the other side, a public that cooperates with the police, that supports them in their efforts and that observes laws and regulations may be said to have a desirable attitude."

11. In accordance with this paragraph, the proper attitude for a police officer to take is
    (A) to be pleasant and sympathetic at all times
    (C) to be stern and severe in meting out justice
    (B) to be friendly, firm and impartial to all
    (D) to avoid being rude, except in those cases where the public is uncooperative.

12. Assume that an officer is assigned by his superior officer to a busy traffic intersection and is warned to be on the lookout for motorists who skip the light or who are speeding. According to this paragraph, it would be proper for the officer in this assignment to
    (A) give a summons to every motorist whose car was crossing when the light changed
    (B) hide behind a truck and wait for drivers who violate traffic laws
    (C) select at random motorists who seem to be impatient and lecture them sternly on traffic safety
    (D) stand on post in order to deter violations and give offenders a summons or a warning as required.

13. According to this paragraph, a police officer must realize that the primary purpose of police work is to
    (A) provide proper police service in a courteous manner
    (B) decide whether those who violate the law should be punished
    (C) arrest those who violate laws
    (D) establish a proper employer-employee relationship.

Answer questions 14 to 17 solely on the basis of the following paragraph:

"When a vehicle has been disabled in the tunnel, the officer on patrol in this zone shall press the *emergency truck* light button. In the fast lane, red lights will go on throughout the tunnel; in the slow lane, amber lights will go on throughout the tunnel. The yellow zone light will go on at each signal control station throughout the tunnel and will flash the number of the zone in which the stoppage has occurred. A red flashing pilot light will appear only at the signal control station at which the *emergency truck* button was pressed. The emergency garage will receive an audible and visual signal indicating the signal control station at which the *emergency truck* button was pressed. The garage officer shall acknowledge receipt of the signal by pressing the acknowledgement button. This will cause the pilot light at the operated signal control station in the tunnel to cease flashing and to remain steady. It is an answer to the officer at the operated signal control station that the emergency truck is responding to the call."

14. According to this paragraph, when the *emergency truck* light button is pressed
    (A) amber lights will go on in every lane throughout the tunnel
    (B) emergency signal lights will go on only in the lane in which the disabled vehicle happens to be
    (C) red lights will go on in the fast lane throughout the tunnel
    (D) pilot lights at all signal control stations will turn amber.

15. According to this paragraph, the number of the zone in which the stoppage has occurred is flashed
    (A) immediately after all the lights in the tunnel turn red
    (B) by the yellow zone light at each signal control station
    (C) by the emergency truck at the point of stoppage
    (D) by the emergency garage.

16. According to this paragraph an officer near the disabled vehicle will know that the emergency tow truck is coming when
    (A) the pilot light at the operated signal control station appears and flashes red
    (B) an audible signal is heard in the tunnel
    (C) the zone light at the operated signal control station turns red
    (D) the pilot light at the operated signal control station becomes steady.

17. Under the system described in the above paragraph, it would be correct to come to the conclusion that
    (A) officers at all signal control stations are expected to acknowledge that they have received the stoppage signal
    (B) officers at all signal control stations will know where the stoppage has occurred
    (C) all traffic in both lanes of that side of the tunnel in which the stoppage has occurred must stop until the emergency truck has arrived
    (D) there are two emergency garages, each able to respond to stoppages in traffic going in one particular direction.

Answer questions 18 to 20 solely on the basis of the following quotation:

"In cases of accident it is most important for an officer to obtain the name, age, residence, occupation and a full description of the person injured, names and addresses of witnesses. He shall also obtain a statement of the attendant circumstances. He shall carefully note contributory conditions, if any, such as broken pavement, excavation, lights not burning, snow and ice on the roadway, etc. He shall enter all the facts in his memorandum book and on Form NY-17 or Form NY-18, and promptly transmit the original of the form to his superior officer and the duplicate to headquarters.

"An officer shall render reasonable assistance to sick or injured persons. If the circumstances appear to require the services of a physician, he shall summon a physician by telephoning the superior officer on duty and notifying him of the apparent nature of the illness or accident and the location where the physician will be required. He may summon other officers to assist if circumstances warrant.

"In case of an accident or where a person is sick on City property, an officer shall obtain the information necessary to fill out card Form NY-18 and record this in his memorandum book and promptly telephone the facts to his superior officer. He shall deliver the original card at the expiration of his tour to his superior officer and transmit the duplicate to headquarters."

18. According to this quotation, the most important consideration in any report on a case of accident or injury is to
   (A) obtain all the facts
   (B) telephone his superior officer at once
   (C) obtain a statement of the attendant circumstances
   (D) determine ownership of the property on which the accident occurred.

19. According to this quotation, in the case of an accident on City property, the officer should always
   (A) summon a physician before filling out any forms or making any entries in his memorandum book
   (B) give his superior officer on duty a prompt report by telephone
   (C) immediately bring the original of Form NY-18 to his superior officer on duty
   (D) call at least one other officer to the scene to witness conditions.

20. If the procedures stated in this quotation were followed for all accidents in New York City, an impartial survey of accidents occurring during any period of time in this city may be most easily made by
   (A) asking a typical officer to show you his memorandum book
   (B) having a superior officer investigate whether contributory conditions mentioned by witnesses actually exist
   (C) checking all the records of all superior officers
   (D) checking the duplicate card files at headquarters.

Answer Questions 21 to 23 on the basis of the following paragraph:

"The use of a roadblock is simply an adaptation to police practices of the military concept of encirclement. Successful operation of a roadblock plan depends almost entirely on the amount of advance study and planning given to such operations. A thorough and detailed examination of the roads and terrain under the jurisdiction of a given police agency should be made with the locations of the roadblocks pinpointed in advance. The first principle to be borne in mind in the location of each roadblock is the time element. Its location must be at a point beyond which the fugitive could not have possibly traveled in the time elapsed from the commission of the crime to the arrival of the officers at the roadblock."

21. According to the above paragraph
   (A) military operations have made extensive use of roadblocks
   (B) the military concept of encirclement is an adaptation of police use of roadblocks
   (C) the technique of encirclement has been widely used by military forces
   (D) a roadblock is generally more effective than encirclement
   (E) police use of roadblocks is based on the idea of military encirclement.

22. According to the above paragraph
   (A) advance study and planning are of minor importance in the success of roadblock operations
   (B) a thorough and detailed examination of all roads within a radius of fifty miles should precede the determination of a roadblock location
   (C) consideration of terrain features are important in planning the location of roadblocks
   (D) the pinpointing of roadblocks should be performed before any advance study is made
   (E) a roadblock operation can seldom be successfully undertaken by a single police agency.

23. According to the above paragraph
    (A) the factor of time is the sole consideration in the location of a roadblock
    (B) the maximum speed possible in the method of escape is of major importance in roadblock location
    (C) the time of arrival of officers at the site of a proposed roadblock is of little importance
    (D) if the method of escape is not known it should be assumed that the escape is by automobile
    (E) a roadblock should be sited as close to the scene of the crime as the terrain will permit.

Answer Questions 24 to 26 on the basis of the following paragraph:

"A number of crimes, such as robbery, assault, rape, certain forms of theft and burglary, are high visibility crimes in that it is apparent to all concerned that they are criminal acts prior to or at the time they are committed. In contrast to these, check forgeries, especially those committed by first offenders, have low visibility. There is little in the criminal act or in the interaction between the check passer and the person cashing the check to identify it as a crime. Closely related to this special quality of the forgery crime is the fact that, while it is formally defined and treated as a felonious or 'infamous' crime, it is informally held by the legally untrained public to be a relatively harmless form of crime."

24. According to the above paragraph, crimes of "high visibility"
    (A) are immediately recognized as crime by the victims
    (B) take place in public view
    (C) always involve violence or the threat of violence
    (D) usually are committed after dark
    (E) can be observed from a distance.

25. According to the above paragraph,
    (A) the public regards check forgery as a minor crime
    (B) the law regards check forgery as a minor crime
    (C) the law distinguishes between check forgery and other forgery
    (D) it is easier to spot inexperienced check forgers than other criminals
    (E) it is more difficult to identify check forgers than other criminals.

26. As used in this paragraph, an "infamous" crime is
    (A) a crime attracting great attention from the public
    (B) more serious than a felony
    (C) less serious than a felony
    (D) more or less serious than a felony depending upon the surrounding circumstances
    (E) the same as a felony.

Answer Questions 27 and 28 on the basis of the following paragraph:

"The racketeer is primarily concerned with business affairs, legitimate or otherwise, and preferably those which are close to the margin of legitimacy. He gets his best opportunities from business organizations which meet the need of large sections of the public for goods or services which are defined as illegitimate by the same public, such as prostitution, gambling, illicit drugs or liquor. In contrast to the thief, the racketeer and the establishments he controls deliver goods and services for money received."

27. From the above paragraph it can be deduced that suppression of racketeers is difficult because
    (A) victims of racketeers are not guilty of violating the law
    (B) racketeers are generally engaged in fully legitimate enterprises
    (C) many people want services which are not obtainable through legitimate sources
    (D) the racketeers are well organized
    (E) laws prohibiting gambling and prostitution are unenforceable.

28. According to the above paragraph, racketeering, unlike theft, involves
    (A) objects of value
    (B) payment for goods received
    (C) organized gangs
    (D) public approval
    (E) unlawful activities.

Answer Questions 29 through 33 solely on the basis of the following paragraph:

"Lifting consists of transferring a print that has been dusted with powder to a transfer medium in order to preserve the print. Chemically developed prints cannot be lifted. Proper lifting of fingerprints is difficult and should be undertaken only when other means of recording the print are neither available nor suitable. Lifting should not be attempted from a porous surface. There are two types of commercial lifting tape which are good transfer mediums: rubber adhesive lift, one side of which is gummed and covered with thin, transparent celluloid; and transparent lifting tape, made of cellophane, one side of which is gummed. A package of acetate covers, frosted on one side and used to cover and protect the lifted print, accompanies each roll. If commercial tape is not available, transparent scotch tape may be used. The investigator should remove the celluloid or acetate cover from the lifting tape; smooth the tape, gummy side down, firmly and evenly over the entire print; gently peel the tape off the surface; replace the cover; and attach pertinent identifying data to the tape. All parts of the print should come in contact with the tape; air pockets should be avoided. The print will adhere to the lifting tape. The cover permits the print to be viewed and protects it from damage. Transparent lifting tape does not reverse the print. If a rubber adhesive lift is utilized, the print is reversed. Before a direct comparison can be made, the lifted print must be photographed. the negative reversed, and a positive made."

29. An investigator wishing to preserve a record of fingerprints on a highly porous surface should
    (A) develop them chemically before attempting to lift them
    (B) lift them with scotch tape only when no other means of recording the print are available
    (C) employ some method other than lifting
    (D) dust them with powder before attempting to lift them with rubber adhesive lift.

30. Disregarding all other considerations, the simplest process to use in *lifting a fingerprint* from a window pane is that involving the use of
    (A) rubber adhesive lift, because it gives a positive print in one step
    (B) dusting powder and a camera, because the photograph is less likely to break than the window pane
    (C) a chemical process, because it both develops and preserves the print at the same time
    (D) transparent lifting tape, because it does not reverse the print.

31. When a piece of commercial lifting tape is being used by an investigator wishing to lift a clear fingerprint from a smoothly-finished metal safe-door, he should
    (A) prevent the ends of the tape from getting stuck to the metal surface because of the danger of forming air-pockets and thus damaging the print
    (B) make certain that the tape covers all parts of the print and no air-pockets are formed
    (C) carefully roll the tape over the most significant parts of the print only to avoid forming air-pockets
    (D) be especially cautious not to destroy the air-pockets since this would tend to blur the print.

32. When fingerprints lifted from an object found at the scene of a crime are to be compared with the fingerprints of a suspect, the lifted print
    (A) can be compared directly only if a rubber adhesive lift was used
    (B) cannot be compared directly if transparent scotch tape was used
    (C) can be compared directly if transparent scotch tape was used
    (D) must be photographed first and a positive made if any commercial lifting tape was used.

33. When a rubber adhesive lift is to be used to lift a fingerprint, the one of the following which must be gently peeled off first is the
    (A) acetate cover
    (B) celluloid strip
    (C) dusted surface
    (D) tape off the print surface.

34. "In examining the scene of a homicide one should not only look for the usual, standard traces — fingerprints, footprints, etc. — but should also have eyes open for details which at first glance may not seem to have any connection with the crime." The most logical inference to be drawn from this statement is that
    (A) in general, standard traces are not important
    (B) sometimes one should not look for footprints
    (C) usually only the usual, standard traces are important
    (D) one cannot tell in advance what will be important.

35. "Pistols with the same number of barrel grooves may be differentiated by the direction of the twist of the rifling, which may be either to the left or to the right." Of the following statements, the one which can most accurately be inferred from the quotation is that
    (A) most pistols have the same number of grooves
    (B) some pistols have rifling twisted both left and right
    (C) the direction of the twist in any pistol can be either left or right
    (D) pistols with different numbers of grooves are rifled differently
    (E) all pistols have grooves.

Answer questions 36 to 42 on the basis of the

information appearing in the paragraph below.

"The first consideration in shooting a revolver is how to stand in a steady position. You may almost face the target in assuming a comfortable shooting stance, or you may face away from the target as much as ninety degrees, and still find it possible to stand easily and quietly. The principal point to observe is to spread the feet apart at least eight inches. This varies with the individual according to the length of his legs. Stand firmly on both feet. Do not bend either leg at the knee and be careful to develop a stance which does not allow the body to lean backward or forward. Ease and naturalness in posture with body muscles relaxed is the secret of good shooting form. The shooting arm should be straight, with the weight of the pistol supported not so much by the arm as by the muscles of the shoulder. Do not tense any muscle of the arm or hand while holding the revolver; especially avoid locking the elbow. The grip of the gun should be seated in the hand so that an imaginary line drawn along the forearm would pass through the bore of the gun. The heel of the hand should reach around the stock far enough to go past the center line of the gun. The thumb can be either alongside the hammer, on top of the frame, or it can be pointed downward toward the tip of the trigger finger. The high position is preferable, because when you are shooting rapid fire the thumb will have a shorter distance to move to reach the hammer spur."

36. The one of the following subjects discussed in the above paragraph is the proper method of
(A) leading a moving target
(B) squeezing the trigger
(C) gripping the revolver
(D) using revolver sights.

37. According to the above paragraph, the secret of good shooting form is
(A) proper sighting of the target
(B) a relaxed and natural position
(C) firing slowly and carefully
(D) keeping the thumb alongside the hammer.

38. For proper shooting stance, it is recommended that the weight of the pistol be supported by
(A) the muscles of the shoulder
(B) locking the elbow
(C) the muscles of the forearm
(D) tensing the wrist muscles.

39. The chief advantage of employing a high thumb position in firing a revolver is to
(A) maintain a more uniform grip
(B) achieve greater accuracy
(C) achieve better recoil control
(D) facilitate more rapid shooting.

40. When firing a revolver at a target, the angle at which you should face the target
(A) is 45 degrees
(B) is 90 degrees
(C) is greater for taller persons
(D) varies naturally from person to person.

41. According to the above paragraph, the revolver should be held in such a manner that the
(A) bore of the revolver is slightly below the heel of the hand
(B) revolver, horizontally, is level with the shoulder
(C) center line of the revolver is a continuation of the forearm
(D) revolver is at a 45 degree angle with the target.

42. Of the following, the most accurate statement concerning proper shooting position is that the
(A) left knee should be bent slightly
(B) feet should be spread at least eight inches apart
(C) you should lean slightly forward as you fire each shot
(D) weight of the body should be on the right foot.

The paragraph below is selected from a typical uniformed force manual. Read the paragraph carefully and then answer questions 43 to 48 solely on the basis of the information appearing in the paragraph.

"The revolvers issued by this Department are of two makes: the .38 Colt Official Police and the .38 Smith and Wesson Special. The same ammunition, .38 Colt Special or .38 Smith and Wesson Special, is used in both guns. The principal difference between these revolvers is that the cylinder-releasing bolt knob on the Colt revolver is moved to the rear to release the cylinder releasing bolt, while on the Smith and Wesson this knob is moved to the front. The Colt can be cocked with the cylinder open, while with the Smith and Wesson the cylinder releasing bolt knob must be moved to the rear in order to do this. The Colt is heavier; 2 lbs. 1 oz. unloaded, 2 lbs. 4 oz. loaded; while the Smith and Wesson weighs 1 lb. 14 oz. unloaded and 2 lbs. 1 oz. loaded. These revolvers are unquestionably among the best made. No other revolver, with the possible exception of the English Wembly, approaches their quality. The muzzle velocity of these revolvers, using standard ammunition, is 879 feet per second. The chamber pressure is 12,000 lbs. per square inch. The fixed sights are set for approximately 25 yards."

43. On the basis of the paragraph on the preceding page, the revolvers which have the same weight are the
(A) Smith and Wesson, loaded, and the Colt, loaded
(B) Colt, unloaded, and the Smith and Wesson unloaded
(C) Smith and Wesson, loaded, and the Colt, unloaded
(D) Colt, loaded, and the Smith and Wesson, unloaded.

44. Of the following, the most accurate statement of a difference between the .38 Colt Official Police and the .38 Smith and Wesson Special is that the Colt, unlike the Smith and Wesson,
(A) has a muzzle velocity of 879 feet
(B) has a cylinder-releasing bolt
(C) uses .38 Smith and Wesson ammunition
(D) can be cocked with the cylinder open.

45. Of the following, the most accurate statement that can be made concerning the English Wembly, solely on the basis of the above paragraph, is that it
(A) weighs more than 2 lbs. unloaded
(B) compares favorably with the best revolvers made
(C) uses .38 Colt or Smith and Wesson ammunition
(D) has a chamber pressure exceeding 12,000 lbs. per square inch.

46. In the above paragraph, the number .38 refers most accurately to the
(A) diameter of the bore
(B) length of the bullet
(C) circumference of the cartridge
(D) thickness of the cylinder.

47. As used in the above paragraph, the term muzzle velocity refers most accurately to the
(A) acceleration of the projectile in flight
(B) average speed of the bullet in flight
(C) rate of expansion of the gases in the muzzle
(D) speed at which the bullet leaves the revolver.

48. Of the following, the least accurate statement concerning the two revolvers issued by the Department, on the basis of the above paragraph, is that both
(A) can use the same ammunition
(B) have a cylinder-releasing bolt knob
(C) have adjustable sights
(D) have a chamber pressure of 12,000 lbs. per square inch.

Correct Answers

(You'll learn more by writing your own answers before comparing them with these.)

1. D	11. B	21. C	31. B	41. C
2. A	12. D	22. C	32. C	42. B
3. D	13. A	23. B	33. B	43. C
4. B	14. C	24. A	34. D	44. D
5. A	15. B	25. A	35. C	45. B
6. C	16. D	26. C	36. C	46. A
7. C	17. B	27. C	37. B	47. D
8. E	18. A	28. B	38. A	48. C
9. C	19. B	29. C	39. D	
10. B	20. D	30. D	40. D	

JUDGMENT AND REASONING QUESTIONS

"Blest are those whose blood and judgment are so well commingled that they are not a pipe for fortune's finger to sound what stop she please." With practice you may be blessed, not only in Shakespeare's phrase, but also with high scores on a kind of question that is rapidly gaining favor with examiners. You can learn to judge of particulars and to distinguish between better and best.

JUDGMENT questions are usually multiple-choice questions. Each question consists of a partial statement followed by five choices, *one* and *only one* of which will *best* complete the original statement. In some cases, *several* of the choices will make a true or correct statement. In all cases, however, there is *one* choice which is *more* correct and *less* open to exceptions than any other choice that could be made. In answering sample questions, eliminate immediately from consideration those choices which are least correct, far-fetched, or which otherwise are extraneous to the original statement.

A SAMPLE QUESTION ANALYZED

The following sample test question, which has been analyzed, will help the candidate establish a methodology for answering judgment questions.

Example: The one of the following which is the best source of current business information is the

(A) almanac
(B) dictionary
(C) city directory
(D) telephone directory
(E) newspaper.

First, it is important to analyze the question. Notice the adjectives: *best, current* and *business*. Of the five possible choices, the correct one must have the three qualities. It must be the *best* source of *current business* information.

Ask yourself the following questions regarding the choices: (1) Is it a source of information? (2) Is it a source of *business* information? (3) Is it a source of *current* information? (4) Is it the *best* source of *current business* information?

Let us analyze the five choices:

(A) almanac: (a) The almanac *is* a source of information. (b) The almanac could be called a source of *current* information since an almanac is generally issued annually, and for a time has *current* information. (c) However, an almanac is generally *not* a source of *business* information. An almanac is defined as "a book containing a calendar of days, weeks, and months with the times of the rising and setting of the sun, moon, etc. Therefore, "almanac" is not the proper choice.

(B) dictionary: (a) The dictionary *is* a source of information. (b) The dictionary is a source of *business* information because it gives us the meaning of words, including business terms. (c) Some dictionaries *may* be a source of *current* information right after they come off the press, but any dictionary is not *always* a source of *current* information. Therefore, the dictionary is not the proper answer.

(C) city directory: (a) The city directory *is* a source of information. (b) The city directory is a source of *business* information, because it gives us the names, addresses and business occupations of city inhabitants. (c) The city directory is a source of *current* information because it gives the present or *current* addresses and occupations of people living in the city. So far in our analysis, we see that the city directory *is* a source of *current business* information. (d) Now the question is: Is it the *best* source of current business information? Let us examine the *other* choices before we decide.

(D) telephone directory: (a) The telephone directory *is* a source of information. (b) The telephone directory is a source of *business* information because it gives us the names, addresses, *business* and phone numbers of city inhabitants. (c) The telephone directory is a source of *current* information because like the city directory, it indicates the present or *current* addresses, etc. of city inhabitants, since copies are issued twice a year. (d) Again the question remains: Is it the *best* source of current business information? Let us examine the last choice.

(E) newspaper: (a) The newspaper *is* a source of information. (b) The newspaper is a source of *business* information, since almost all newspapers have a *business section*. (c) The newspaper is a source of *current* information, since it is issued in many cases several times daily.

At this point, it is clear that of the five choices, three of them, the city directory, telephone directory and the newspaper, are all sources of current business information.

We must now decide which is the *best*. Compared to the city directory and the telephone directory, it becomes very apparent that the *newspaper* is the *best* source of *current, business* information. This method should be used in answering the sample test questions which follow.

PREVIOUS TEST QUESTIONS FOR PRACTICE

Read the following questions carefully. From the five suggestions for an answer, select the one choice which best completes the statement. Indicate the letter preceding your choice for the best answer.

1. The average span of life has increased chiefly because
   (A) modern civilization exerts less pressure on the individual
   (B) the individual does not have to work as hard as formerly
   (C) modern inventions conserve the individual's energy
   (D) advances in the field of medicine have made possible control of many formerly fatal diseases
   (E) the human body over a period of centuries has built up greater resistance to disease.

2. Zoning has been introduced for residential districts in order to
   (A) keep the district residential, thereby preventing confusion and unnecessary movement
   (B) maintain real estate values
   (C) fix the growth of the city in definite patterns
   (D) keep unwanted populations out of exclusive districts
   (E) reduce friction between communities.

3. The rate of increase of the farm population in the United States has been greater than that of cultivated farm land. We may conclude from this that
   (A) there will be more farmers than city dwellers in a short time
   (B) the rural population will shortly become too many for the available land
   (C) we may soon expect a movement from the farms to the cities
   (D) there will be more people to cultivate the same land
   (E) too many people are cultivating too little land.

4. An automobile can pick up speed more quickly than a locomotive train chiefly because it
   (A) has a less complicated mechanism than the locomotive
   (B) runs on rubber tires instead of on tracks
   (C) the automobile uses gasoline instead of steam as fuel
   (D) the automobile is lighter in weight than the locomotive
   (E) the automobile is capable of operating at a higher speed than the locomotive.

5. Replacement of obsolete machinery by modern equipment is often a benefit to the manufacturer in that it
   (A) relieves the strain on the workers
   (B) lowers the selling price of his product
   (C) lowers his overhead
   (D) produces a better product at a lower unit cost
   (E) reduces taxes.

6. Which of the following would be the surest indication that a druggist may have violated the legal requirement that narcotic drugs be dispensed only on a physician's prescription?
   (A) a number of people known to have purchased other drugs from him are believed to possess narcotics, but no prescriptions issued to these persons are in the druggist's file
   (B) he is himself an addict
   (C) his wholesaler refuses to sell him narcotics

(D) the total of his present narcotics stock and the amount legally accounted for is much less than his purchases
(E) the supply of narcotics in stock is less than the amount he recently reported.

7. Stars are invisible in the daytime principally because
(A) the distance between the earth and the stars increases during the night
(B) the relative brightness of the sun is greater than that of the stars during the day
(C) the earth's rotation places them on the opposite side of the earth
(D) they do not reflect the light of the sun during the day
(E) they are really still visible as they can be seen from the bottom of a deep well.

8. Sculpture predated painting as an art because
(A) it is more important than painting
(B) it is simpler than painting
(C) it was used as an adjunct in construction
(D) it is more interesting to the primitive mind
(E) it requires primitive strength.

9. Custom regulations concerning the importation of fruit trees exist primarily in order to
(A) prevent the smuggling of fruit trees into the country
(B) aid farmers in maintaining high prices for their fruits
(C) prevent the introduction into the United States of foreign destructive fruit insects
(D) prevent foreign products from flooding the American market
(E) aid in the introduction of new varieties of fruit trees into the United States.

10. In starting a load, a horse has to pull harder than he does to keep it moving because
(A) the load weighs less when it is moving
(B) there is nó friction after the load is moving
(C) the horse becomes accustomed to pulling the load
(D) the wheels stick to the axles
(E) the horse has to overcome the tendency of the wagon to remain at rest.

11. The best reason for the rule in criminal cases requiring that the defendant's guilt be established beyond a reasonable doubt is
(A) in a civil case the plaintiff must prove his claim in the same way
(B) a fair preponderance of the credible evidence is necessary in a civil suit
(C) the District Attorney has his own investigators, the Police Department and other official assistance in preparing his case whereas the defendant has to rely mainly on his own lawyer
(D) it is so provided in the State or Federal Constitutions
(E) because it is one of the strongest safeguards under our system of law against unjust convictions.

12. From 1930 to 1940 there was a 7% rise in the population of the United States. During the same period there was a rise of 60% in the numbers of married people. The increase in the number of married people may be attributed to
(A) an increased birth rate
(B) a natural increase in the population of the country
(C) a large number of marriages from 1930 to 1940
(D) unrest in the world
(E) previous population increases.

13. The price of a two-pound can is less than double that of a one-pound can because
(A) packaging costs are not proportional to the quantity of material in a package
(B) a cheaper grade of merchandise is always included in larger packages
(C) the manufacturer would rather sell small packages
(D) more expensive merchandise is usually in smaller packages
(E) large packages are a good advertisement.

14. Men work chiefly because they must
(A) support the state
(B) support themselves
(C) enjoy themselves
(D) utilize leisure time
(E) broaden their viewpoint on life.

15. Mass production results in lower prices chiefly because
(A) the cost of making each unit is lowered
(B) a larger amount of material is used
(C) competition becomes keener
(D) demand for the product increases

(E) the articles produced are of an inferior quality.

16. Your superior directs you to find certain papers. You know the purpose for which the papers are to be used. In the course of your search for the papers, you come across certain material which would be very useful for the purpose to be served by the papers. You should
(A) bring the papers to your superior and ask whether he wishes the other materials
(B) go to your superior immediately and ask whether he wishes both the papers and the materials
(C) bring to your superior the other materials together with the papers
(D) bring only the other materials and point out to your superior how these materials are of greater value than the papers
(E) bring only the papers and say nothing about the other materials.

17. The purpose of new regulations requiring that the use of any excessive flavoring or coloring matter in whiskey be noted on the label is to
(A) keep people from buying such whiskey
(B) make the taste of whiskey less pleasant
(C) let the buyer know the exact quality of his purchases
(D) decrease the number of different blends of whiskey
(E) keep distillers from using any such matters.

18. The fact that ships leaving shore seem to drop below the horizon proves chiefly that
(A) the ocean and the horizon merge at a certain point
(B) the farther from shore, the lower the ship
(C) the earth is round
(D) the distance between the ship and the shore is increased
(E) the ship gradually fades out.

19. The individual distinguishes differences in colors primarily because colors
(A) have different chemical compositions
(B) have different wave-lengths
(C) are all part of the color spectrum
(D) reflect light
(E) are visible except to those who are color blind.

20. The various forms of social insurance are aimed at
(A) eradicating unhappiness
(B) effecting a radical change in our social system
(C) eliminating the causes of dependency
(D) spreading the cost of maintaining those in need over as many people and as wide a period of time as possible
(E) getting the most good to the greatest number.

21. The fact that fossil fish are found on a mountain indicates that
(A) fishes once lived on land
(B) the mountain-top was once below sea-level
(C) fish were one of the first organisms existent upon the earth
(D) the level of the sea and the mountain was once equal
(E) fossil fish are valuable as relics of prehistoric life.

22. The Government does not allow pictures to be made of its paper money because in that way
(A) it preserves the bills
(B) discourages counterfeiting
(C) it stabilizes the currency
(D) it prevents paper money from being used in preference to coins
(E) it conceals the infinite detail in the currency.

23. "All minors everywhere are highly emotional, for they are adolescents." This statement assumes most nearly that
(A) all adolescents who are highly emotional are minors
(B) all adolescents are minors
(C) few minors are not emotional
(D) any person who is an adolescent is highly emotional
(E) some adolescents are not highly emotional.

24 Rare manuscripts are reproduced on photographic film
(A) to reduce the possibility of loss by fire
(B) so that the text may be available without any disturbance to the original manuscript
(C) so that they may be stored in smaller space

(D) to facilitate ready reference
(E) to aid scholars in research.

25. The chief reason why a bank can extend its loans beyond the volume of the cash in its possession is that.
(A) it takes a long time for checks drawn upon it to be cashed
(B) checks drawn upon it are likely to be deposited with it instead of being cashed
(C) checks drawn upon it are likely to be deposited in another bank
(D) the bank does not have to supply the required loan immediately
(E) the bank can extend its loan thirty per cent beyond cash at hand by federal law.

26. Water from a spring in the woods should generally be boiled before being used for drinking purposes chiefly because
(A) it may contain dirt
(B) boiling will remove any taste of clay
(C) any sediment contained in the water will settle to the bottom after boiling
(D) it may contain harmful bacteria
(E) the minerals in it will be eliminated by boiling.

27. The air is cool at the bottom of an unused chimney because it is
(A) undisturbed
(B) under pressure
(C) farther from the outside air
(D) heavier and cool air settled there
(E) away from the sun's rays.

28. If the earth were made of lead, objects would
(A) weigh more
(B) weigh less
(C) retain their present weight
(D) tend to decrease in dimension
(E) corrode.

29. The relative position of stars in the sky is continually changing because
(A) of the stellar "drift"
(B) the earth moves eastward around the sun once a year
(C) of the semi-annual increase in the earth's velocity
(D) of changes in the relative distance between the earth and the stars
(E) of phenomena as yet unexplained.

30. Leverage is most useful in
(A) multiplying energy
(B) decreasing work
(C) reducing friction
(D) gaining mechanical advantage
(E) bending heavy bars.

31. Water power is one of the most natural and at the same time most truly economical sources of energy chiefly because
(A) water has a relatively high velocity
(B) water power can be easily harnessed
(C) water is readily available and can be cheaply and easily converted into power
(D) water power readily lends itself to the operation of many machines
(E) water power contains the greatest amount of energy known to man.

32. Winds result from
(A) the effects on the air of the difference in heat of the tropics and the polar regions
(B) the erratic movements of the sea
(C) the movements of the moon
(D) earthquakes
(E) changes in the atmosphere about the equator.

33. It becomes profitable to import a commodity chiefly whenever labor and capital engaged in its domestic productions yield
(A) a profit which is less than the same agents would yield in other fields
(B) a lesser number of products than would be normally expected
(C) a profit similar to that which they would yield in other fields
(D) a very small profit
(E) less profits than a competitive firm.

34. The Government arbitrarily assigns frequencies to radio broadcasting stations
(A) to facilitate licensing procedures
(B) to prevent more than one station broadcasting on the same frequency
(C) to reduce static and interference
(D) to reserve the air for amateur operators
(E) to avoid the necessity of further restrictions.

35. The apparent motion of the sun across the sky is caused by
(A) the earth's speed
(B) the rotation of the earth on its axis
(C) the earth's centrifugal force

(D) the relative variation in so-called "sun-spots"
(E) a spectrum phenomenon.

36. Water tanks are maintained on the top of tall buildings chiefly in order to
(A) maintain a reserve supply of water if the normal water supply should fail
(B) prevent lightning from striking the building by acting as an arrester
(C) have water available in the event of a fire
(D) supply the upper floors with water by a process of first pumping it into the tanks
(E) convert the water into electric power by a turbine process.

37. The fact that the sun seems to rise in the east and set in the west is proof that
(A) only the sun is in motion
(B) only the earth is in motion
(C) either the sun or the earth is in motion
(D) the east and the west are merely abstract concepts
(E) there are 12 hours in the average day.

38. "Because telephone directories contain printed pages, they are called books." This statement assumes most nearly that
(A) some books do not contain printed pages
(B) not all telephone directories are books which contain printed pages
(C) material which contains printed pages is called a book
(D) all books which contain printed pages are called telephone directories
(E) all telephone directories must have printed pages.

39. Leather is considered the best material for shoes chiefly because
(A) it is waterproof
(B) it is durable
(C) it is easily procurable
(D) it is flexible and durable
(E) it can be easily manufactured in various styles.

40. Skyscrapers are a development of city life because
(A) land is limited and expensive
(B) engineers have the knowledge wherewith to build them
(C) people like to live in the upper stories where the air is pure
(D) they are in conformity with zoning regulations
(E) they add to a city's beauty.

41. Automobile accident insurance rates vary from city to city chiefly because
(A) it is difficult for automobile accident insurance companies to arrive at a standard rate applicable to all cities
(B) the accident rate varies from city to city
(C) people in some cities are better educated in safety rules and regulations than in others
(D) safety laws vary from one city to another
(E) the number of automobile drivers varies from city to city.

42. An insulating process is currently being used in modern house construction chiefly because
(A) it makes houses sound-proof
(B) it makes houses less costly to construct
(C) insulation makes a house waterproof
(D) the insulation tends to reduce house fueling costs
(E) it saves time in construction.

43. The ability of elements to produce heat while they are uniting proves chiefly that
(A) all elements unite at extreme heat
(B) heat is a purifying agent
(C) heat is a by-product of every chemical flux
(D) elements contain heat energy
(E) when elements unite a compound is formed.

44. Electricity is used as the chief agent in flashing messages from place to place mainly because
(A) it is less costly in the long run
(B) aerial wiring is eliminated
(C) maximum speed is obtainable
(D) it is applicable to telegrams
(E) the element of space is reduced.

45. The sound which issues from a violin when a bow is drawn across one of the strings is due chiefly to
(A) air waves set in motion by the bow
(B) ether waves set in motion by the bow
(C) a partial vacuum in the vicinity of the sound chamber which is caused by the vibrating motion of the bow

(D) vibration of the string
(E) the tenseness of the string.

46. A clay pitcher of water will crack if the water freezes chiefly because
(A) during the process of freezing the water expands
(B) during the process of freezing the water contracts
(C) the crystallization process of ice formation causes the ice to solidify
(D) the tension strength of clay decreases as the temperature decreases
(E) the rate of expansion of water has the same ratio as that of contraction of the pitcher.

Correct Answers For The Foregoing Questions

(Please try to answer the questions on your own before looking at our answers. You'll do much better on your test if you follow this rule.)

1. D	7. B	13. A	19. B	25. B	31. C	37. C	43. D
2. A	8. C	14. B	20. D	26. D	32. A	38. C	44. C
3. D	9. C	15. A	21. D-B	27. D	33. A	39. D	45. D
4. D	10. E	16. A	22. B	28. A	34. B	40. A	46. A
5. D	11. E	17. C	23. D	29. B	35. B	41. B	
6. D	12. C	18. C	24. B	30. D	36. D	42. D	

SCORE	.... %
	NO. CORRECT ÷
	NO. OF QUESTIONS ON THIS TEST

Practice Using Answer Sheets

Alter numbers to match the practice and drill questions in each part of the book.
Make only ONE mark for each answer. Additional and stray marks may be counted as mistakes.
In making corrections, erase errors COMPLETELY. Make glossy black marks.

1	A B C D E	1	A B C D E	1	A B C D E	1	A B C D E	1	A B C D E
2	A B C D E	2	A B C D E	2	A B C D E	2	A B C D E	2	A B C D E
3	A B C D E	3	A B C D E	3	A B C D E	3	A B C D E	3	A B C D E
4	A B C D E	4	A B C D E	4	A B C D E	4	A B C D E	4	A B C D E
5	A B C D E	5	A B C D E	5	A B C D E	5	A B C D E	5	A B C D E
6	A B C D E	6	A B C D E	6	A B C D E	6	A B C D E	6	A B C D E
7	A B C D E	7	A B C D E	7	A B C D E	7	A B C D E	7	A B C D E
8	A B C D E	8	A B C D E	8	A B C D E	8	A B C D E	8	A B C D E
9	A B C D E	9	A B C D E	9	A B C D E	9	A B C D E	9	A B C D E
0	A B C D E	0	A B C D E	0	A B C D E	0	A B C D E	0	A B C D E

1	A B C D E	1	A B C D E	1	A B C D E	1	A B C D E	1	A B C D E
2	A B C D E	2	A B C D E	2	A B C D E	2	A B C D E	2	A B C D E
3	A B C D E	3	A B C D E	3	A B C D E	3	A B C D E	3	A B C D E
4	A B C D E	4	A B C D E	4	A B C D E	4	A B C D E	4	A B C D E
5	A B C D E	5	A B C D E	5	A B C D E	5	A B C D E	5	A B C D E
6	A B C D E	6	A B C D E	6	A B C D E	6	A B C D E	6	A B C D E
7	A B C D E	7	A B C D E	7	A B C D E	7	A B C D E	7	A B C D E
8	A B C D E	8	A B C D E	8	A B C D E	8	A B C D E	8	A B C D E
9	A B C D E	9	A B C D E	9	A B C D E	9	A B C D E	9	A B C D E
0	A B C D E	0	A B C D E	0	A B C D E	0	A B C D E	0	A B C D E

1	A B C D E	7	A B C D E	13	A B C D E	19	A B C D E	25	A B C D E
2	A B C D E	8	A B C D E	14	A B C D E	20	A B C D E	26	A B C D E
3	A B C D E	9	A B C D E	15	A B C D E	21	A B C D E	27	A B C D E
4	A B C D E	10	A B C D E	16	A B C D E	22	A B C D E	28	A B C D E
5	A B C D E	11	A B C D E	17	A B C D E	23	A B C D E	29	A B C D E
6	A B C D E	12	A B C D E	18	A B C D E	24	A B C D E	30	A B C D E

TEAR OUT ALONG THIS LINE AND MARK YOUR ANSWERS AS INSTRUCTED IN THE TEXT

PATROL INSPECTOR

JUDGMENT FOR LAW ENFORCEMENT OFFICERS

The following questions test your judgment as a law enforcement officer in fundamental problems of police protection and law enforcement. In each question, a certain amount of data is supplied, or it is assumed that you already possess sufficient police knowledge to answer the question. Read each question twice; the first time for overall meaning, the second to be sure you have missed no detail. Beware of trick questions.

1. "One can only see what one observes and one observes only things which are already in the mind." Of the following, the chief implication of this statement is that
   (A) observation, to be most effective, should be directed and conscious
   (B) all aspects of a situation, unless the law enforcement officer exercises caution, are likely to strike him with equal forcefulness
   (C) observation should be essentially indirect if it is to be accurate
   (D) memory is essentially perception one step removed from observation.

2. "The number of arrests made is not always the best indication of a successful policeman." The statement most consistent with the above quotation is that
   (A) a number of factors should be considered in properly evaluating the performance of a policeman
   (B) there is a negative correlation between the number of arrests made and the success of a policeman
   (C) policemen should avoid making arrests whenever possible
   (D) the success of a policeman cannot be precisely and objectively measured.

3. A law enforcement officer is in the habit in his free time of occasionally inventing imaginary law enforcement problems on his post and attempting to provide appropriate solutions to these happenings. This sort of behavior is best characterized as
   (A) undesirable, since it may lead to insanity
   (B) desirable, since it exercises his mind
   (C) useful, because it is conclusive evidence of his competence
   (D) undesirable, in that his attention is less readily given to what is actually happening on his post
   (E) desirable, since he may, as a result, be better prepared for emergencies.

4. "Training produces co-operation and brings about lower unit costs of operation." According to this statement, it is most logical to assume that
   (A) a program of personnel training is a major feature of every large business organization
   (B) training is a factor in improving morale and efficiency
   (C) training is of more value to new workers than to old employees
   (D) unless personnel costs can be lowered, training is of little value.

5. As an intelligent law enforcement officer, you should know that, of the following, the one which is least likely to be followed by an increase in crime is
   (A) war
   (C) poor housing
   (B) depression
   (D) prosperity.

6. In lecturing on the law of arrest an instructor remarked: "To go beyond is as bad as to fall short." The one of the following which most nearly expresses his meaning is
   (A) never undertake the impossible
   (B) extremes are not desirable
   (C) look before you leap
   (D) too much success is dangerous.

of the following that most nearly expresses his meaning is
(A) negligence seldom accompanies success
(B) incomplete work is careless work
(C) conscientious work is never attended by failure
(D) a conscientious person never makes mistakes.

8. The cardinal function of a police department is
(A) the prevention of crime
(B) the efficiency and discipline of its members
(C) to preserve property values
(D) to minimize conflicts.

9. Law enforcement officials receive badges with numbers on them so that
(A) their personalities may be submerged
(B) they may be more easily identified
(C) they may be spied upon
(D) their movements may be kept under constant control.

10. If you were asked what you thought of a person you didn't know, what should you say?
(A) I will go and get acquainted
(B) I think he is all right
(C) I don't know him and can't say
(D) I think he is worthless.

11. The best attitude for an officer to take is to
(A) be constantly on the alert
(B) be hostile
(C) vary his watchfulness with the apparent necessity for it
(D) regard tact as his most effective weapon for handling any degree of disorder.

12. An officer who has been assigned to work with you has a receding chin. It is most probable that he will
(A) be much like the other men in your group
(B) lack will power to a marked degree
(C) be a very timid person
(D) constantly carry tales to you about the other officers.

13. The annual number of arrests recorded in City A is 1,000. The annual number of arrests recorded in city B is 1,200. It is safe to infer from this information
(A) that there are more criminals in City A than in city B
(B) that more persons are imprisoned in city A than in City B
(C) there is more disrespect for law in city A than in City B
(D) none of the foregoing.

14. 10 percent of the inmates released from a certain prison are arrested as parole violators. It follows that
(A) 90 percent have reformed
(B) 10 percent have reformed
(C) none has reformed
(D) none of the foregoing is necessarily true.

15. It has been stated that arrests are made in only 44 percent of the crimes committed, while only 40 percent of those arrested are convicted. The most reasonable inference from these data is that
(A) most criminal acts are not immediately followed by the arrest of the criminal
(B) a small number of persons is arrested
(C) most of those persons who are arrested are also convicted
(D) people without influence are most likely to be convicted after arrest.

16. An insane person who has a wife and two children is arrested on a charge of burglary. It follows from these data that
(A) we have here insufficient information from which to draw any conclusions with reference to the relation between crime and insanity
(B) burglary is a crime which attracts lunatics
(C) this proves that not all lunatics are burglars
(D) a burgler is one type of lunatic.

17. A certain committee found that over 90 percent of the murders in the United States are committed by use of pistols. It follows that
(A) almost all murders are caused by the possession of pistols
(B) 90 percent of murders can be eliminated by eliminating the sale and use of pistols
(C) the pistol is a mechanical aid to crime
(D) no information is available with regard to the way murders happen.

18. The causes of crime
(A) are exactly the same today as in the past
(B) have been accurately and completely determined
(C) are an unimportant matter
(D) are an extremely complicated problem.

19. A criminal is typically one who

(A) has a peculiarly shaped head
(B) exhibits a most degenerate kind of behavior
(C) is an intelligent, well educated person
(D) looks like other people.

20. There would be no crime if there were no
(A) weapons
(B) criminals
(C) stupid laws
(D) private property.

21. An officer receives instructions from his supervisor which he does not fully understand. For the officer to ask for a further explanation would be
(A) good; chiefly because his supervisor will be impressed with his interest in his work
(B) poor; chiefly because the time of the supervisor will be needlessly wasted
(C) good; chiefly because proper performance depends on full understanding of the work to be done
(D) poor; chiefly because officers should be able to think for themselves.

22. The FBI reports that the crime rate in New Jersey last year was 10.6 percent higher than in the previous year, while the average increase in crime throughout the United States was 7.6 percent. It may logically be concluded from these facts that
(A) most New Jersey residents have lost their respect for the law
(B) New Jersey police officials are more conscientious than those of other states
(C) New Jersey's laws are more severe than those of other states
(D) New Jersey's increased crime rate may be due to a combination of reasons not listed above.

23. The one of the following statements concerning the behavior of law enforcement officers which is most accurate is
(A) a show of confident assurance on the part of a law enforcement officer will make it possible to cover a shortage of knowledge in any given duty
(B) in ordinary cases, when a newly appointed officer does not know what to do, it is always better to do too much than to do too little
(C) it is not advisable that officers recommend the employment of certain attorneys for individuals taken into custody
(D) a prisoner who is morose and refuses to talk will bear less watching by an officer than one who threatens to kill himself.

24. A law enforcement officer should know that character can be influenced only when and in so far as
(A) the desire for ideals has been aroused
(B) a knowledge of principles of conduct has been acquired
(C) problems of behavior have been clearly defined
(D) plans for meeting specific situations are carried into conduct.

25. In dealing with children a law enforcement officer should always
(A) treat them the same as adults
(B) instill in them a fear of the law
(C) secure their confidence
(D) impress them with the right of the law to punish them for wrong-doing.

26. Of the following, the greatest danger in arming a policeman detailed to guard prisoners in hospitals is that
(A) the gun may accidentally go off, wounding prisoners and others within gunshot
(B) the policeman may use the gun without adequate cause
(C) the prisoners may disarm the policeman
(D) it is hazardous to permit too many people to possess firearms.

27. Charging a fee for fortune-telling is not permitted under the laws of this State. In spite of this, fortune-telling in various forms remains popular. Of the following, the *least* likely reason for this popularity is that many people
(A) fear to make their own decisions in important matters
(B) have such drab lives that they must search for a hope of change
(C) wish to use fortune-tellers for entertainment at their social gatherings
(D) wish to make contacts with loved ones who have died
(E) wish to place blame on some supernatural power for their failures.

28. The one of the following which is the most probable reason for the considerably increasing proportion of serious crimes committed by women is

(A) that the proportion of women in the population is increasing
(B) that greater supervision of women results in a greater number of arrests
(C) the success of women in achieving social equality with men
(D) the increasing number of crime stories in the movies and on television
(E) the increasing number of crime gangs in operation.

29. Of the following types of crimes, increased police vigilance would probably be *least* successful in preventing
(A) murder
(B) burglary
(C) prostitution
(D) automobile thefts
(E) robbery.

30. In most hotels, couples who wish to rent a hotel room are required to carry a suitcase in order to be allowed to register. Of the following, the most valid reason for this regulation is that
(A) the hotel wishes to be protected against possible non-payment of the bill
(B) couples who carry a suitcase are surely married
(C) couples will be discouraged from entering into illicit relations on the impulse of the moment
(D) couples who carry a suitcase are likely to be strangers in town and therefore have a legitimate claim to a hotel room.
(E) the hotel will thus be able to maintain complete respectability.

31. "Undoubtedly the most important influence upon the growing youngster is that wielded by the adults whom he observes day after day." Accordingly, the type of adult behavior that generally would be *least* likely to adversely affect youngsters is
(A) dishonesty by public officials
(B) lack of courtesy in the home
(C) intolerance in the school
(D) racial discrimination in the neighborhood youth club
(E) hypocrisy in religious practices.

32. It frequently happens that a major crime of an unusual nature is followed almost immediately by an "epidemic" of several crimes, in widely scattered locations, which have elements similar to the first one. Of the following, the most likely explanation for this situation is that
(A) the same criminal is likely to commit the same type of a crime
(B) a gang of criminals will operate in several areas simultaneously
(C) newspaper publicity on a major crime is apt to influence other would-be criminals
(D) the same causes which are responsible for the first crime are also responsible for the others
(E) crimes are committed simultaneously to divert the efforts of the police.

33. "In studying juvenile delinquency in an area, it can be noted that the recorded activities of courts dealing with children's cases do not always give a true picture of the extent of juvenile delinquency in the area, especially if the police are so ineffective that many cases of delinquency do not reach the courts." On this basis, it can be stated most accurately that
(A) a population which has many delinquents will necessarily result in high delinquency figures
(B) low delinquency figures are possible only in a population of relatively well-adjusted children
(C) delinquency figures bear no relationship to the number of well-adjusted children in the population
(D) low delinquency figures may mean lax law enforcement or they may mean a population of relatively well-adjusted children
(E) low delinquency figures can result only from lax law enforcement.

34. "Many well meaning people have proposed that officers in uniform not be permitted to arrest juveniles." This proposal is
(A) good; the police are not equipped to handle juvenile offenders
(B) bad; juvenile offenders would lose respect for all law enforcement agencies
(C) good; offending juveniles should be segregated from hardened criminals
(D) bad; frequently it is the uniformed officer who first comes upon the youthful offender
(E) good; contact with the police would prevent any rehabilitative measures from being taken.

35. "A member of the department shall not indulge in intoxicants while in uniform. A member of the department not required to wear a uniform and a uniformed member while out of uniform shall not indulge in intoxicants to an extent unfitting him or her for duty." It follows that a

(A) member off duty, not in uniform, may drink intoxicants to any degree desired
(B) member not on duty, in uniform, may drink intoxicants
(C) member on duty, in uniform, may drink intoxicants
(D) uniformed member, in civilian clothes, may not drink intoxicants
(E) member on duty, not in uniform, may drink intoxicants.

36. The reason police officers have greater authority than private citizens in making arrests is
(A) to protect citizens against needless arrest
(B) to insure a fair trial
(C) that they have greater knowledge of the law
(D) that they are in better physical shape.

37. "The treatment to be given the offender cannot after the fact of his offense; but we can take measures to reduce the chances of similar acts in the future. We should banish the criminal, not in order to exact revenge nor directly to encourage reform, but to deter him and others from further illegal attacks on society." According to this paragraph the principal reason for punishing criminals is to
(A) prevent the commission of future crimes
(B) remove them safely from society
(C) avenge society
(D) teach them that crime does not pay.

38. "The law enforcement officer's art consists in applying and enforcing a multitude of laws and ordinances in such degree or proportion and in such manner that the greatest degree of social protection will be secured. The degree of enforcement and the method of application will vary with each neighborhood and community." According to the foregoing paragraph
(A) each neighborhood or community must judge for itself to what extent the law is to be enforced
(B) a law enforcement officer should only enforce those laws which are designed to give the greatest degree of social protection
(C) the manner and intensity of law enforcement is not necessarily the same in all
(D) all laws and ordinances must be enforced in a community with the same degree of intensity.

39. It is well known that most criminals in the city
(A) belong to subversive organizations
(B) work at respectable jobs during the day
(C) are professionally trained
(D) come from crowded localities.

40. When arrested, boys under 16 are not brought to the same place of detention as older ones. The reason for this separation is most likely to
(A) keep them with others of their own age
(B) protect them from rough police methods
(C) help them get sound legal aid
(D) keep them from contact with hardened criminals.

41. Many criminals dress well and look like gentlemen, but have no regard for a human life if it stands in their way. A reasonable conclusion from this statement is that
(A) it is almost certain death to combat a criminal
(B) criminals are frequently gentlemen
(C) even some gentlemen have no regard for human lives
(D) a well-dressed man may be a criminal.

Correct Answers

(You'll learn more by writing your own answers before comparing them with these.)

1. A	9. B	17. C	25. C	33. D
2. A	10. C	18. D	26. C	34. D
3. E	11. A	19. D	27. C	35. E
4. B	12. A	20. B	28. C	36. A
5. D	13. D	21. C	29. A	37. A
6. B	14. D	22. D	30. C	38. C
7. A	15. A	23. C	31. A	39. D
8. A	16. A	24. A	32. C	40. D
				41. D

PATROL INSPECTOR

JUDGMENT ON THE JOB

(WHAT WOULD YOU DO IF?)

1. A patrolman stationed along the route of a parade has been ordered by his superior to allow no cars to cross the route while the parade is in progress. An ambulance driver on an emergency run attempts to drive his ambulance across the route while the parade is passing. Under these circumstances, the patrolman should
   (A) ask the driver to wait while the patrolman contacts his superior and obtains a decision
   (B) stop the parade long enough to permit the ambulance to cross the street
   (C) direct the ambulance driver to the shortest detour available which will add at least ten minutes to the run
   (D) hold up the ambulance in accordance with the superior's order
   (E) advise the driver to telephone the hospital and notify his superior that he is being delayed by the parade.

2. An off-duty patrolman in civilian clothes is riding in the rear of a bus. He notices two teen-age boys tampering with the rear emergency door. The most appropriate action for him to take is to
   (A) watch the boys closely but take no action unless they actually open the emergency door
   (B) report the boys' actions to the bus operator and let the bus operator take whatever action he deems best
   (C) signal the bus operator to stop, show the boys his badge and then order them off the bus
   (D) show the boys his badge, order them to stop their actions and take down their names and addresses
   (E) tell the boys to discontinue their tampering, pointing out the dangers to life that their actions may create.

3. You find that traffic has become congested on a main highway. When you investigate, you find that an automobile has struck and killed a six year old girl. The patrolman at the scene reports that the girl has been removed by an ambulance. The automobile, however, has not been moved since the accident and is blocking traffic. Of the following, the best action to take prior to removing the car from the roadway is to
   (A) make a quick sketch of the scene in your memorandum book for future reference
   (B) indicate by means of chalk marks the position of the car and skid marks
   (C) secure the testimony of competent witnesses who will be able to corroborate the position of the car and the cause of the accident
   (D) test the automobile's brakes to detect possible mechanical defects.

4. Assume that you are on your way home late at night. You notice smoke pouring out of one of the windows of a house in which several families reside. Your first consideration under these circumstances should be to
   (A) determine the cause of the smoke
   (B) arouse all the residents in the house
   (C) carry out to safety any persons overcome by smoke
   (D) summon fire apparatus to the scene.

5. A woman, bleeding profusely from the mouth and nose, comes to you and insists you arrest her husband, whom she accuses of beating her with a hammer. After you have apprehended him, the woman informs you that she does not wish to prefer any charges against him and requests that you release him. The *best* reason for refusing this request is that
   (A) a crime is a wrong done to society as a whole
   (B) the victim of a crime is seldom afraid to prefer charges
   (C) the police department is anxious to have every complaint brought to trial
   (D) an arrest should be made only on a complaint
   (E) the fact that a complainant wishes to with-

draw a charge indicates that the damage done was trivial.

6. While present at a performance in a theatre, you, a law enforcement official, are notified that there is a fire under the stage. Under these circumstances, you would least expect
   (A) to transmit the alarm from the nearest box
   (B) to remove fire appliances from their places
   (C) to ascertain whether there was a fire
   (D) to announce to the audience that there was a fire in the theatre, and would everybody please pass out quietly.

7. A prisoner under your care is epileptic. You should
   (A) make fun of him in the expectation that he will become ashamed of his behavior and stop having fits
   (B) pay no attention to him
   (C) take especial care that he does not escape
   (D) be sure that he does not hurt himself.

8. You notice something unusual on your post. You should immediately
   (A) report the matter in writing to your superior officer
   (B) look up the rules on the matter
   (C) investigate the matter
   (D) wait for a time to see whether anything will happen.

9. A prisoner asks you to recommend a good lawyer to him. You should
   (A) comply with his request
   (B) tell him you wish to consult your superior officer before making your suggestion
   (C) tell him it would be undesirable for you to do as he asks
   (D) suggest that he study the law himself, since he has plenty of time.

10. A policeman is required to familiarize himself with the location of fire boxes on his post. Of the following, the best reason for this requirement is that
    (A) alertness is a very important qualification of a good policeman
    (B) defective equipment will be discovered
    (C) in case of emergency, time will not be lost in looking for a fire box
    (D) senders of false alarms will be quickly detected.

11. A woman finds a four-year-old boy on a crowded subway platform at Times Square. After unsuccessfully trying to locate the boy's mother, with whom the child says he was traveling, she brings him to the nearest police precinct. After taking the necessary preliminary measures, the policeman on duty at the precinct requires that the woman remain until contact is made with the boy's mother. This action is
    (A) justifiable; the woman may have established rapport with the child and separation may be threatening to him
    (B) unjustifiable; the boy may be a rejected child
    (C) unjustifiable; such policy generally applied may discourage the public from taking any action in connection with lost children
    (D) justifiable; further questioning may be required.

12. Suppose that a policeman is detailed to transport a prisoner to a courthouse. While thus engaged, he is stopped by an influential friend of the prisoner who asks him to release the prisoner. Of the following, the most desirable procedure for the policeman to follow is to
    (A) explain his errand and then proceed to the courthouse
    (B) let the prisoner go, for an officer should not antagonize men of influence
    (C) ask the friend if he will be personally responsible for the future conduct of the prisoner, and if so, let the prisoner go
    (D) release the prisoner after giving him a serious lecture.

13. A policeman is summoned into a subway station where a man has collapsed and is lying unconscious on the floor. His breath smells strongly of alcohol. For the policeman to summon medical aid immediately is
    (A) undesirable; the man is merely intoxicated and can be handled by the policeman alone
    (B) desirable; the man's unconsciousness may have a medical cause
    (C) undesirable; the commotion caused by the incident will be aggravated by the appearance of an ambulance
    (D) desirable; medical aid is necessary to help him regain consciousness in any event
    (E) undesirable; the man in his intoxicated condition will, upon coming to, probably react violently to a doctor.

14. "A policeman should know the occupations and habits of the people in the area to which she is assigned. In heavily populated districts, however, it is too much to ask that the policeman know all the people in his district " If this statement is correct, the one of the following which

would be the most practical course for a policeman to follow is to
(A) concentrate on becoming acquainted with the oldest residents of the district
(B) limit his attention to people who work as well as live in the district
(C) limit his attention to people with criminal records
(D) concentrate on becoming acquainted with key people such as janitors, bartenders and local merchants
(E) concentrate on becoming acquainted with the newest residents of the district.

15. A policeman notices a two year old child standing by himself in front of a supermarket and crying. The one of the following actions which the policeman should take *first* is to
(A) feed the child
(B) look for possible identification on the child's clothing
(C) take the child to the police precinct until he is claimed
(D) inquire in the supermarket in an attempt to find the mother
(E) call the precinct to find out if the child has been reported missing.

16. A policeman notices in a crowded subway station that a child of about seven has been pushed out of the train involuntarily. The crowd piling into the car is so thick that the child is unable to get back into the train. After the train has gone, the policeman learns from the child that her mother was also on the train, but was probably unable to get out because of the crowd pushing in. The child knows her own address, a considerable distance away and in an opposite direction from the one in which she was traveling. Of the following, the best action for the policeman to take *first* is to
(A) take the child home
(B) explain to the child how to go home and let her go alone
(C) leave the child with instructions to wait until her mother returns
(D) wait at the station with the child long enough to give a chance for the mother to return from the next station
(E) find a passenger traveling towards the child's home who is willing to take her there.

17. The one of the following which is the most accurate statement concerning the proper attitude of a policeman toward men in his custody is that he should
(A) ignore any serious problems of the prisoner if they have no bearing on the charges against him
(B) not inform a man he has arrested of the reason for his arrest
(C) feel no restraint in divulging all the information he has about a particular case to reporters
(D) watch a brooding and silent prisoner more carefully than one who noisily threatens suicide
(E) not permit a prisoner to give vent to his feelings at any time.

18. Two rival youth gangs have been involved in several minor clashes. The youth patrolman working in their area believes that a serious clash will occur if steps are not taken to prevent it. Of the following, the *least* desirable action for the patrolman to take in his effort to head off trouble is to
(A) arrest the leaders of both groups as a warning
(B) warn the parents of the dangerous situation
(C) obtain the cooperation of religious and civic leaders in the community
(D) alert all social agencies working in that neighborhood
(E) report the situation to his superior.

19. If, while you are on traffic duty at a busy intersection, a pedestrian asks you for directions to a particular place, the best course of conduct is to
(A) ignore the question and continue directing traffic
(B) tell the pedestrian to ask a patrolman on foot patrol
(C) answer the question in a brief, courteous manner
(D) leave your traffic post only long enough to give clear and adequate directions.

20. A police officer hears two shots fired and proceeds in the direction of the shots. He comes upon an intoxicated man who is angrily scream-

ing at a woman. The officer notices that the handle of a pistol is protruding from the man's pocket, and orders him to surrender the pistol. The man apparently ignores the order and continues screaming at the woman. For the officer now to fire a warning shot over the man's head would be

(A) bad; it is quite possible that the man is so intoxicated that he did not clearly hear or understand the officer's order
(B) bad; the officer should realize that an intoxicated person is not entirely responsible for his actions
(C) good; the warning shot will impress the man with the seriousness of the situation
(D) good; since the man had already fired twice, the officer should take no further chances.

21. A gas-main explosion has caused some property damage. Examination by an emergency repair crew clearly indicates that no further explosions will occur. Nevertheless, rumors are circulating that more explosions and greater damage are going to occur. This situation has resulted in a high degree of fear among local residents. The best of the following actions for a police officer on duty at the scene to take *first* would be to
(A) ignore the rumors since they are false and no real danger exists
(B) inform the people of the true circumstances of the emergency
(C) question several people at the scene in an attempt to determine the source of the rumors
(D) order everyone to leave the area quickly and in an orderly fashion.

22. Probationary Patrolmen A and B are given a special assignment by the sergeant. Patrolman B does not fully understand some of the instructions given by the sergeant concerning the carrying out of the assignment. Of the following, it would be best for Patrolman B to
(A) proceed with those parts of the assignment which he understands and ask for an explanation from the sergeant when he can go no further
(B) observe Patrolman A's work carefully in order to determine how the assignment is to be carried out
(C) ask the sergeant to explain that portion of the instructions which he does not fully understand before starting the assignment
(D) suggest to Patrolman A that he supervise the operation since he probably better understands the sergeant's instructions.

23. Which of the following situations, if observed by you while on patrol, should you consider most suspicious and deserving of further investigation?
(A) A shabbily dressed youth is driving a new Buick.
(B) An old car has been parked without lights outside an apartment house for several hours.
(C) A light is on in the rear of a one-family, luxurious residence.
(D) Two well-dressed men are standing at a bus stop at 2 A.M. and arguing heatedly.

24. Suppose that, while you are patrolling your post, a middle-aged woman informs you that three men are holding up a nearby express office. You rush immediately to the scene of the holdup. While you are still about 75 feet away, you see the three men, revolvers in their hands, emerge from the office and make for what is apparently their getaway car, which is pointed in the opposite direction. Of the following, your first consideration in this situation should be to
(A) enter the express office in order to find out what the men have taken
(B) maneuver quickly so as to get the getaway car between you and the express office
(C) make a mental note of the descriptions of the escaping men for immediate alarm
(D) attempt to disable the car in which the holdup men seek to escape.

25. While you are on patrol you notice that the lone occupant of a car parked at the top of a long, steep hill is a boy about 7 years old. The boy is playing with the steering wheel and other controls. The first action for you to take is to
(A) make sure that the car is safely parked
(B) test the car's emergency brake to make sure it will hold
(C) drive the car to the bottom of the hill and park it there
(D) test the car's controls to make sure that the boy has not changed anything
(E) order the boy to leave the car for his own safety.

26. A storekeeper has complained to you that every day at noon several peddlers congregate outside his store in order to sell their merchandise. You should
(A) inform him that such complaints must be made directly to the Police Commissioner
(B) inform him that peddlers have a right to earn their living too

(C) make it your business to patrol that part of your post around noon
(D) pay no attention to him as this storekeeper is probably a crank inasmuch as nobody else has complained.

27. A patrolman is frequently advised to lie down before returning fire, if a person is shooting at him. This is primarily because
(A) a smaller target will thus be presented to the assailant
(B) he can return fire more quickly while in the prone position
(C) the assailant will think he has struck the patrolman and cease firing
(D) it will indicate that the patrolman is not the aggressor.

28. "Policemen should call for ambulances to transport injured people to the hospital rather than use patrol cars for this purpose." Of the following, the most valid reason for this policy is that
(A) there is less danger of aggravating injuries
(B) patrol cars cannot be spared from police duty
(C) patrol cars are usually not equipped for giving emergency first aid
(D) medical assistance reaches the injured person sooner
(E) responsibility for treating injured people lies with the Department of Hospitals.

29. A patrolman is approached by an obviously upset woman who reports that her husband is missing. The first thing the patrolman should do is to
(A) check with the hospitals and the police station
(B) tell the woman to wait a few hours and call the police station if her husband has not returned by then
(C) obtain a description of the missing man so that an alarm can be broadcast
(D) ask the woman why she thinks her husband is missing
(E) make certain that the woman lives in his precinct.

30. A patrolman seeing a person writing indecent matter on an advertising poster should arrest him, and take along the section of the poster that was written on to
(A) remove the temptation for others to add to it
(B) call it to the attention of the poster man
(C) present it as evidence
(D) prevent its being seen by children.

31. When approaching a suspect to make an arrest, it is *least* important for the patrolman to guard against the possibility that the suspect may
(A) be diseased
(B) have a gun
(C) use physical force
(D) run away.

32. An acceptable proof of the present address of the person to whom a patrolman is issuing a summons would logically be
(A) a recent photograph
(B) society membership cards
(C) recently postmarked letters addressed to him
(D) the deed to the house.

Correct Answers

(You'll learn more by writing your own answers before comparing them with these.)

1. B	9. C	17. D	25. A
2. E	10. C	18. A	26. C
3. B	11. C	19. C	27. A
4. D	12. A	20. A	28. A
5. A	13. B	21. B	29. D
6. D	14. D	22. C	30. C
7. D	15. D	23. A	31. A
8. C	16. D	24. C or D	32. C

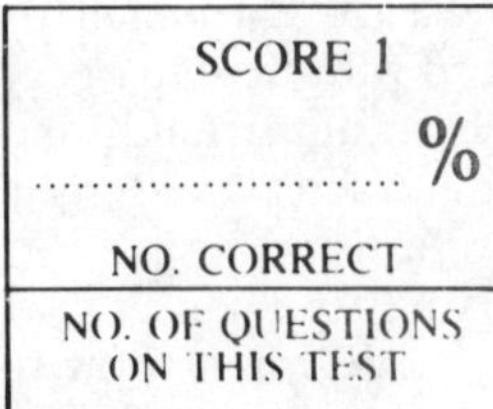

PATROL INSPECTOR

PREDICTIVE PRACTICE EXAMINATION

Based on all the information available before going to press we have constructed this examination to give you a comprehensive and authoritative view of what's in store for you. To avoid any misunderstanding, we must emphasize that this test has never been given before. We devised it specially to provide a final opportunity of employing all you've learned in a situation that closely simulates the real thing.

The time allowed for the entire examination is 3½ hours. In order to create the climate of the test to come, that's precisely what you should allow yourself . . . no more, no less. Use a watch and keep a record of your time, especially since you may find it convenient to take the test in several sittings.

TEST QUESTIONS FOR PRACTICE

SOURCES OF INFORMATION: RECORDS AND REPORTS

(Records, Federal and local, public and private, are the supreme ordinary sources of investigative information. Some of the following questions are from the City and State of New York. The location of records may vary from state to state, but the same types of records may be found in every state, and the investigator must know where to find them.)

1. In checking a person's employment record, the investigator may encounter a refusal on the part of a former employer to furnish any information. In such a case, the investigator should
   (A) advise the person concerned that he must secure the necessary data from the employer himself
   (B) note such refusal and call attention to it in his final report
   (C) report only those employments which can be checked
   (D) visit this employer several times at intervals several weeks apart until he obtains his co-operation.

2. Of the following, the most probable reason why personal references given by an applicant for a job may not be reliable is that these references
   (A) do not know the applicant thoroughly
   (B) may have been bribed by the applicant
   (C) often are friends of the applicant
   (D) will over-emphasize the undesirable aspects of the applicant's character.

3. In deciding whether to make use of a source of information in connection with an investigation, the investigator should be influenced mainly by the
   (A) expense entailed in the use of the source
   (B) relative availability of the source
   (C) relative proximity of the source
   (D) reliability of the information offered by the source.

4. In the business world, title companies are generally concerned with matters relating to the
   (A) investment in securities
   (B) laws of copyright
   (C) ownership of real property
   (D) registration of patents.

Questions 5 to 11 consist of matters about which you might have to consult records or secure information in the course of your work. In Column I are listed various government agencies, county, city, state and federal. For each question, select from Column I the government agency where you are most likely to be able to consult the records or secure the information you desire. Write the capital letter preceding that government agency in the properly numbered space on your answer sheet.

5. Births and deaths

6. Certificates of incorporation

7. Estates of deceased persons

8. Instruments affecting titles to real property in the City

9. Naturalization proceedings

10. Old age and survivor's insurance

11. Settlement and adjustment of claims against the City

COLUMN I

(A) Board of Estimate
(B) City Register
(C) Comptroller's Office
(D) Department of Commerce
(E) Department of Health
(F) Department of Health, Education and Welfare
(G) Department of Justice
(H) Department of Labor
(J) Department of State
(K) District Attorney's Office
(L) Municipal Court
(M) Surrogates' Courts.

12. Among the following, the present home and business address of a member of the board of directors of a New York City bank may most readily be obtained from
(A) Moody's Banks and Finance Directory
(B) Poor's Register
(C) Trow's New York City Directory
(D) Dau's New York Blue Book.

13. Among the following, a list of the names and addresses of various professional associations and societies in the United States would be found in the
(A) World Almanac
(B) Encyclopedia Brittanica
(C) Congressional Record
(D) Poor's Register.

14. In an action against the City of New York personal service of the summons is made by delivering a copy thereof to the mayor,
(A) treasurer or city clerk
(B) comptroller or city clerk
(C) treasurer or corporation counsel
(D) comptroller or corporation counsel.

15. When dictating a report to a stenographer, it is *least* important to
(A) be brief and say only what is essential
(B) be emphatic and speak with expression
(C) spell out all involved words
(D) work from an outline previously prepared.

16. An investigator's report always includes his personal judgment of the credibility of witnesses mentioned in his report. This practice is
(A) desirable mainly because it can be used to support the position that the investigator wants to take with respect to the case
(B) undesirable mainly because it is of no value to the reader of the report
(C) desirable mainly because it is part of the investigative function to evaluate the credibility of witnesses
(D) undesirable mainly because judgments should be formed on the basis of facts, not opinions.

17. Before you submit the written report of an investigation which you conducted, you become aware of some previously unknown information relating to the case. Your decision as to whether to re-write your report to include this additional information should be influenced mainly by the
(A) amount of time remaining in which to submit the report
(B) bearing this additional information will have on the findings and recommendations of the report
(C) extent of the revision that will be required in the original report in order to include this additional information
(D) feasibility of submitting a supplementary report at a later date.

18. "The most thorough investigation is of no value if the report written by the investigator does not enable the reader to readily decide the correct action to be taken." Of the following, the *least* direct implication of the preceding quotation is that the
(A) investigation conducted must be very thorough to be of value

(B) investigation report is generally written by the person who made the investigation

(C) purpose of the investigation report is to give superiors a basis for action

(D) worth of the investigation is affected by the report submitted.

19. "Even if no one else is interested in the case you are investigating, it is still recommended that you keep a record of the progress of the case by means of regular reports for the file." Of the following, the one which is *not* a good reason for this recommendation is that

(A) it is difficult for the memory to retain all the information gathered on every case during the course of daily investigations

(B) it may become necessary to review the case while the person assigned to it is temporarily away from the office because of illness or other reason

(C) the final report on the investigation will be briefer if it includes only the important material from the daily reports

(D) the person investigating the case may resign or transfer to another job.

20. A form relating to possible insurance coverage of accident victims has a space headed "Name of Carrier." The word "Carrier" in this case most probably refers to the

(A) accident victim

(B) insurance company

(C) policy beneficiary

(D) policy holder.

21. "The first 3 numerals in a social security number indicate the state where the employee resided when the number was assigned." According to the preceding quotation, if your investigation indicates that the first 3 numerals of a New York resident's Social Security number do not correspond to the numbers for the state, it is most reasonable to conclude that

(A) the numbers assigned to New York have been revised

(B) there is an error in the social security number

(C) this person at one time did not live in New York

(D) this person is not a bona fide New York resident.

22. Mary Hartley, age 40, wife of William Hartley, had stated in an application that she was a graduate of a certain high school and had completed 2 years of college in another city. A written inquiry to these two schools brought the reply that they had no record of Mary Hartley ever having attended their respective schools. Of the following, it is most probable that the

(A) records in question, being rather old, had been destroyed

(B) records in question had been lost or misplaced

(C) woman exaggerated her education in her application

(D) woman was listed on the school records under another name.

23. Suppose you are checking an alphabetical card reference file to locate information about "George Dyerly." After checking all the "D's" you can find a card only for a "George Dyrely." Of the following the best action for you to take is to

(A) check the balance of the file to see if the card you are interested in has been misfiled

(B) check the data on the card to see if it relates to the same person in whom you are interested

(C) correct the spelling of the name on your records and reports to conform to the spelling on the card

(D) reject this reference file as a source of information regarding this person.

24. A satisfaction piece is an instrument

(A) which purports to discharge land from the lien of a mortgage

(B) by which pending litigation is settled out of court

(C) acknowledging payment of a money judgment

(D) by which a lien on personal property is discharged.

25. A book in which deeds are recorded in the City Register's Office is referred to as a

(A) text (B) folio

(C) volume (D) liber.

EVIDENCE IN INVESTIGATION

26. The investigator has seized several silver coins which have similar characteristics. He reports that they are counterfeit coins, because he has made several tests. Which of the following

tests least proves that the coins are spurious?
(A) the bad coins have more resilience than known good coins
(B) the reeding is worn off, but microscopic examination shows the spacing to be uneven
(C) a test shows the silver on the coins is only plating
(D) the spurious coins have a greasy feel.

27. The investigator is seeking a connecting clue to the identification of a gang of illicit whiskey manufacturers. Which of the following is the most valuable clue?
(A) a tip from an employee in a hotel that a mysterious looking group of persons have met in the lobby several times in one week
(B) a peculiar brand of whiskey has been discovered by an expert investigator
(C) a piece of equipment essential in the production of the liquor
(D) a bill of sale indicating purchase of ingredients.

28. An effort is made to establish the authorship of a piece of written material which has been found. Four types of suspects are tested to compare their handwriting with that on the piece of paper found. Which of these types is likely to show the least systematization in handwriting?
(A) a girl in a finishing school
(B) a man who had only a few years of elementary schooling and has not had much opportunity to write since his early training
(C) a high school teacher
(D) a woman employed in a secretarial capacity.

29. The investigator decides to preserve some material because of its possible evidential value. Which of the following steps in his procedure is wrong?
(A) he takes it directly from the person
(B) he handles it with his fingers
(C) he folds it to fit the envelope to be used as a container
(D) he labels the envelope with the date and name of the person.

30. The investigator wants to make a note of the spot where a person stood when he fired an automatic pistol. He finds an empty shell in the vicinity and he should conclude that the shell will be found in relation to the shooter
(A) to the right
(B) to the right and a few feet to the rear of that point
(C) to the right and a few feet to the front of that point
(D) a few feet to the front.

31. The investigator finds several footprints near the scene of the crime. He examines them carefully and finds that the line along the inner sides of both heel-prints is straight and parallel to the line of direction in which the person was going, but there is evidence of a changing step length. The investigator concludes that the person who made the footprints
(A) limps
(B) was drunk
(C) was wounded
(D) suffered from Parkinson's disease.

32. An investigator has found a suit of a suspect who worked in a brickyard, and wants to have the dust that might be found in the suit analyzed for possible evidence. Which of the following procedures is best in order to obtain the evidence desired
(A) empty the pockets of the coat and send their contents to the laboratory
(B) place the suit in a paper bag and beat the bag with the suit in it
(C) send the suit to the dry cleaner and then send it to the laboratory.

33. A latent fingerprint has been discovered on a door-knob. The easiest method of preserving it is by
(A) "lifting" it with an adhesive tape
(B) "fixing" it with iodine vapor
(C) developing it by immersion in equal parts of milk and water.

34. An investigator reports his findings of the use of Marihuana by the "X" Laboratory. He examines the records which show on the fifteenth of the current month the Laboratory had 40 ounces. The records up to that time account for the disposal of 30 ounces since the first of the month when the total amount owned by the Laboratory was 100 ounces. This investigator also reports that 10 days before the investigation, which was made on the thirtieth of the month, the Laboratory sent a formal report to the government which gave the amount of Marihuana in stock at that time as 30 ounces, and the receipt from the wholesaler of 15 ounces. The investigator

reports an illegal use of Marihuana by the "X" Laboratory because

(A) the total of the narcotic used and the amount on hand fifteen days before the date of the investigation is less than the total amount recorded on the first of the month

(B) the amount in stock at the time of the Laboratory's Report plus the new acquisition of Marihuana from the wholesaler during the month is less than the total at the beginning of the month

(C) the totals of the amount disposed of and on hand on the fifteenth of the month, plus the new amount purchased during the month are less than the quantity in stock on the first of the month

(D) the totals of Narcotics in stock in the middle of the month, at the time of the Laboratory's report, the amount used on the fifteenth of the month and the amount of additional Marihuana acquired after that time are more than 100 ounces.

Your answers to questions 35 and 36 must be based only on the information given in the following quotation and not upon any other information you may have.

"An assumption commonly made in regard to the reliability of testimony is that when a number of persons report upon the same matter,those details upon which there is an agreement may in general be considered as substantiated. Experiments have shown, however, that there is a tendency for the same errors to appear in the testimony of different individuals, and that, quite apart from any collusion, agreement of testimony is no proof of dependability."

35. According to the above quotation, it is commonly assumed that details of an event are substantiated when
(A) a number of persons report upon them
(B) a reliable person testifies to them
(C) no errors are apparent in the testimony of different individuals
(D) several witnesses are in agreement about them.

36. According to the above quotation, agreement in the testimony of different witnesses to the same event is
(A) evaluated more reliably when considered apart from collusion
(B) not the result of chance
(C) not a guarantee of the accuracy of the facts
(D) the result of a mass reaction of the witnesses.

37. "The investigator should never rely entirely on the data given him by a witness." Of the following, the chief justification for this statement is the fact that
(A) human perceptions are often incomplete and frequently affected by distortions
(B) recall and recognition are apt to be more accurate when the passage of time has caused momentary passions and prejudices to cool
(C) a witness to an occurrence cannot always be found
(D) witnesses usually contradict each other.

38. In fidelity bond investigations the employer applying for the bond is investigated in addition to the employee to be bonded. The most likely reason for this is that
(A) employers can be depended upon to be reliable but fraud by an employer involves greater sums of money
(B) the employer's auditing methods and his methods of handling valuables affect his risk status
(C) there are as many dishonest employers as there are dishonest employees
(D) there is such a great number of cases where the employer and the employee conspire to defraud the insurance company.

39. Upon passing the ward of a patient whose investigation has indicated apparent inability to pay for city hospital care, the investigator notes a private duty nurse attending the patient at the bedside. What he has observed is of importance to the investigator primarily as an indication that the
(A) doctors probably ordered this additional nursing care
(B) patient's condition may have become critical
(C) patient may have other potential financial resources
(D) private duty nurse is probably a member of the patient's family.

40. A copy, accompanied by a certificate of the proceedings necessary to be taken in order to authorize the same to be entered of record, is called
(A) an exemplified copy
(B) a certified copy

(C) a true copy
(D) a verified copy.

41. "Prima facie" evidence is evidence which
(A) suffiices to establish a fact unless rebutted or until overcome by other evidence
(B) has not been tested or measured as to its validity
(C) shows the existence of one fact by proof of the existence of other facts from which the first may be inferred
(D) results from certain presumptions of law, which may not have a basis in fact.

42. Even when an investigator is convinced of the honesty and truthfulness of a witness thorough checking of all reported information with physical facts is imperative because, among the following
(A) mere parol testimony is not accepted as legal evidence
(B) the observation of the witness may have been imperfect due to some factors which distort normal sensory perception
(C) the physical facts may have changed since they were observed by the witness
(D) an interview with a witness is merely an informal questioning conducted to learn facts.

43. In the course of an investigation of a claim for damages for personal injuries sustained by an individual, an anonymous letter is received by the investigator, accusing this individual of mistreating his wife and children. The most advisable of the following courses of action for the investigator to pursue is
(A) as a law enforcement officer, to report the matter to the proper authorities
(B) to place less credence in the testimony given by the individual, in view of this impeachment of his character
(C) to attempt to trace the letter and inquire further into the allegations made therein before submitting his report
(D) to disregard the letter, since it has no direct bearing on the matter under investigation.

44. The best reason, among the following, for obtaining a written and signed statement of the testimony of a witness is that
(A) unless reduced to writing it cannot ultimately be placed in evidence in court
(B) the witness may be unavailable at the time of a subsequent trial or may attempt to change his testimony
(C) the investigator's notes of the interview may be defective or incomplete
(D) such a written statement becomes "best evidence" whereas the investigator's report is mere hearsay.

45. When an investigator hears an important statement made by a witness and the witness is not willing to reduce the statement to writing, the most advisable of the following procedures for the investigator to follow is to
(A) write it himself and have the witness sign it, if he is willing to do so
(B) write it himself and insist that the witness sign it
(C) write it himself, making sure the witness does not see it
(D) threaten to write it himself, if the witness will not do so.

THE INTERVIEW

46. The investigator is convinced that establishing the presence of a gun at the scene of crime is important to his case. His witness causes him to decide that this crucial question must be framed so that it will contain a minimum of suggestiveness. For this reason which one of the following questions should be asked?
(A) Did you see the gun?
(B) Didn't you see the gun?
(C) Did you see a gun?
(D) Didn't you see a gun?

47. In questioning a suspect, it is probably true that the best place for the interview is
(A) in suspect's home in the presence of his family
(B) in the office of the investigator where other suspects are present during the interview
(C) in the suspect's home where the suspect and the investigator are the only persons present
(D) in the investigator's office with friends of the suspect present.

48. In the investigation of a crime, the investigator has found evidence in the neighborhood pointing to "W" as the suspect. A person named "x" is known to have been near the scene of the crime and is considered by the witness investigator a principal witness. Tools were found at the scene of the crime and have been traced to "Y," who sold them to the suspect.

The investigator has reason to believe that "z" while not the principal witness, is the most trustworthy one. Which one should the investigator interrogate last?
(A) W (B) X
(C) Y (D) Z.

49. In establishing the best relationship for a successful interview with a person who can give information, the investigator should proceed in an attitude of
(A) firm and official demeanor because he is an authorized representative of the Federal Government
(B) acting in a nonchalant manner so as to disarm suspicion of the interviewee
(C) gaining and deserving the confidence of the interviewee
(D) plainly implying trouble as a consequence of not giving information.

50. During the interview the most desirable impression the informant should get is that the investigator is
(A) full of righteous indignation because the law has been violated and a crime was committed
(B) shrewd, astute, clever
(C) stupid and gullible
(D) straight-forward and frank.

The statements in questions 51-53 were made by a foreman about a worker under his supervision. In Column II you will find a list of characterizations of the statements. Distribute the statements according to locations in Column II.

51. He was a good worker, as may be seen from the record of his production.

52. He must have been sick on the day in question because he did not report for work.

53. He had a strong character and iron will which one could see from his firm square jaw.

COLUMN II

(A) Inference
(B) Fallacy
(C) Fact.

54. To combine accuracy and completeness to a maximum degree, the investigator should adopt one of the following methods of interviewing
(A) question and answer form through the interview
(B) combination of free narrative in letting the interviewee talk and questions and answers, using the former method first
(C) allowing the interviewee to talk freely so as to tell his story in the form of a statement
(D) questions and answers, followed by free narrative.

55. The investigator is interviewing a loquacious and garrulous type of person. The most desirable procedure for the investigator is to
(A) let him ramble on no matter how irrelevant his subject matter may be at times because it may bear on the topic
(B) stop him just as soon as he strays from the subject under discussion by letting him know the irrelevant facts have nothing to do with the case
(C) interpose questions directly to get the desired information
(D) make a relevant statement to guide the conversation.

56. An investigator reports the following statements of a witness who described a fugitive suspect
(A) he used "hifalutin" language and long words
(B) he dressed in a queer style and wore a high stiff collar
(C) he must have been a foreigner because he had an accent in his speech
(D) he wore a handle-bar mustache.
Which of the above statements should the investigator report as opinion rather than fact?

The following statement is made by a suspect: "On June 16, 1940 I was employed by the "X" company in Albany, N.Y. where I had been working for about six months. I worked on the night shift from 9 p.m. to 6 a.m. with one hour off for lunch. The foreman of the shop and the men working near me saw me nearly all the time, either at my work or in the company lunch room. I could not have been in New York City during the night of June 16."

The investigator writes a report of his work. In Column I you will find the statements of the investigator. In Column II is a list of comments or characterizations of those statements. Distribute the items in Column II according to the appropriate allocations in Column I.

COLUMN I

57. I checked with the company at Albany and found the suspect worked there six months.

58. He lived at the Y.M.C.A. in Albany.

59. Because the machinery of the plant broke down on June 15, he worked on June 16 on the day shift from 8 a.m. to 5 p.m. so as to finish a job that had to be shipped out.

60. I examined his clothing and found some dust in his pockets which might be valuable as evidence because particles of dust have been found at the scene of law violation in New York City, but the dust has not yet been examined in the Laboratory.

61. The task of finding this suspect has been difficult because I had to interview his family, minister of his church and about a dozen friends and relatives in several cities.

62. His physical appearance, like the shape of his head, shifty eyes and his features in general, give indication that he is of the criminal type.

63. In spite of the fact that he lived in the Y.M.C.A. and went to church occasionally, his character is questionable, judging from what the preacher said he heard of the suspects behavior at various times.

COLUMN II

(A) Inconsistent with statement of suspect.
(B) Statement of opinion.
(C) Irrelevant statement.
(D) Consistent with suspect's statement.
(E) Hearsay statement.
(F) Value of statement is contingent on further investigation.
(G) Omitted in suspect's statement.

64. The investigator has before him a timid and self-conscious witness who could give information on a smuggler. The law enforcement agent wants to ask the witness the following questions
(A) do you know how sumgglers go about their work
(B) what do you know of the character of the accused person
(C) are you related to the accused person
(D) where were you at the time when the merchandise was brought on shore.

Which of the above questions should the investigator ask the timid man first?

65. The "oldest inhabitant" of the community is brought before the investigator for information. He is a dogged character who knows "right is right" and no matter what anyone says about him, he has witnessed more changes in the town than anybody in the vicinity many miles around. The investigator realizes he must win him over and make an appeal to him so he will co-operate in giving information. Which of the following appeals will be least helpful in attaining his objective?
(A) his independence of spirit
(B) his shrewdness and cunning
(C) his wonderful memory
(D) his love of justice.

66. If an investigator questions a nervous witness, whose answers sometimes tumble out, "Yes," "No," "I don't know" in rapid succession, the best attitude for the investigator to adopt is
(A) impatience (B) severity
(C) contempt (D) sympathy.

Which of the following questions should an investigator refrain from asking because it implies an answer of opinion rather than a fact
(A) did you see the umbrella
(B) was there a clock in the room
(C) did you hear a sound outside the room
(D) did you notice the arm-chair in the room?

In Column I you will find a list of questions describing a picture, and in Column II you will find characterizations of their types. Distribute the items in Column II according to the appropriate allocation in Column I.

COLUMN I

67. Was there not a dog in the picture?

68. Is there a dog in the picture?

69. Is the dog white or black?

70. What color is the dog?

COLUMN II

(A) Assumes or implies the presence of a feature that was not present.
(B) Has two alternatives and does not entirely preclude a third possibility.
(C) Induces moderate suggestion.
(D) Has two specified alternatives.

71. The investigator is questioning a witness whom he suspects to be mentally retarded. As soon as he is aware of this suspicion, the investigator should
(A) let him alone because his statements would have little if any value
(B) proceed with the questions to see what possible information could be obtained
(C) give him an elementary intelligence test, such as repetition of few numbers or a simple statement that involves reasoning in finding an absurdity
(D) arrange at once to take him to a psychiatric institution for examination.

The investigator is required to make decisions on questions to be used in an interview. In Column I you will find the three decisions he might make about each question. Mark on your answer sheet the letter of the appropriate decision found in Column I.

72. Did you see Smith give Jones the opium?

73. Did you not see Smith handle the opium?

74. Why did Smith act so nervously when he let Jones into the house?

COLUMN I

(A) Unsatisfactory because it is a leading question.
(B) A satisfactory question under the circumstances.
(C) An unsatisfactory question because it calls for opinion.

Questions 75-77 refer to the following information: An investigator writes a report on statements he has received from a man suspected of forgery and from a witness and must decide whether the facts given by the suspect are (A) consistent (B) inconsistent (C) omitted when compared with the statement of the witness. The following is the statement of the suspect:

"I worked for the X Bank for 10 years and worked my way up from a clerical job to the head of the investment department. Last year I left the Bank to join a Wall Street firm as the director of the sales department handling endowment securities exclusively."

Mark on your answer sheet the letter corresponding to the decision of the investigator as to the extent of agreement.

The statements from the witness who is the President of the X Bank are:

75. He was ambitious and finally became the chief of one of our important departments in the Bank.

76. His ambition led him to make unwarranted statements to our clients in order to get their business which meant more commissions for him.

77. He finally "pulled a fast one" in one deal hoping to cover up before he was discovered, but that act amounted to fraud and we told him to leave our organization.

Questions 78-80 are statements received by an investigator on the character of a suspect. Each of the statements may be
(A) favorable to the suspect on the question of character
(B) unfavorable
(C) irrelevant from the standpoint of character.

Mark on your answer sheet the letter denoting the investigator's decision as to the appropriateness of each statement.

78. His hobbies have been motor boating and baseball.

79. He has lived in the same house for 8 years and was never more than a month in arrears in paying his rent.

80. Although he had ability, he could not get along well with his fellow employees or with his superiors in his place of work.

81. When signed statements of witnesses are forwarded with the report of an investigation, it is generally best to
(A) merely highlight the main points of the statements in the report, commenting on any contradictions
(B) repeat the statements verbatim in the body of the report and call attention to the original statements attached

(C) re-type in the report those parts of the statements that are not significant and of doubtful validity, thus calling the reader's attention to them and avoiding misinterpretation

(D) save space by not taking up the statements in the report since they are attached and available to the reader of the report.

Your answers to questions 82 and 83 must be based only on the information given in the following quotation and not upon any other information you may have.

"The accuracy of the information about past occurrence obtainable in an interview is so low that one must take the stand that the best use to be made ot the interview in this connection is as a means of finding clues and avenues of access to more reliable sources of information. On the other hand, feelings and attitudes have been found to be clearly and correctly revealed in a properly conducted personal interview."

82. According to the above quotation, information obtained in a personal interview
   (A) can be corroborated by other clues and more reliable sources of information revealed at the interview
   (B) can be used to develop leads to other sources of information about past events
   (C) is not reliable
   (D) is reliable if it relates to recent occurrences

83. According to the above quotation, the personal interview is suitable for obtaining
   (A) emotonal reactions to a given situation
   (B) fresh information on factors which may be forgotten
   (C) revived recollection of previous' events for later use as testimony
   (D) specific information on material already reduced to writing.

84. "Carefully planned interviews tend to impose restrictions which leave little room for spontaneity." A flaw in this criticism of the planned interview is that it does not take into account that
   (A) a planned interview obviates the need for spontaneity.
   (B) even the planned interview may be flexible
   (C) not all planned interviews impose restrictions
   (D) restrictions that result from planning are undesirable.

85. "The investigator must always bear in mind that he has no power to force the interviewee to give him information." Of the following, the chief implication of this statement for the investigator in his work is that
   (A) he may nevertheless utilize forceful persuasion as a tool since the interviewee is not aware of his lack of power to apply pressure
   (B) he should develop techniques for leading the interviewee into making certain admissions without the latter being aware of it
   (C) he should place considerable emphasis on developing the voluntary co-operation of the interviewee
   (D) information that he obtains by force is of doubtful validity.

86. An investigator who wanted to interview the head of a business firm introduced himself by saying: "I am James Smith of the State Legal Department and I would like to check with you certain information given us by Herbert Brown, a former employee of yours." The approach used by the investigator was
   (A) good because by giving so little information he has lost nothing if the employer should refuse to co-operate
   (B) poor because he should first try to establish a friendly relationship with the employer before stating the purpose of his visit
   (C) good because he came directly to the point by stating who he was and what he wanted
   (D) poor because he should have stressed with the employer the importance of cooperating with government agencies in all investigative matters.

87. When a statement which may be submitted as evidence in court has been secured from a person after questioning, it is often typed with intentional errors and given to the person to read. Such action is usually based on a
   (A) desire to be able to counteract any later denial by the person that he was aware of the contents; if the person corrects and initials the errors and then signs the statement, it is evidence that he was aware of the contents
   (B) desire to distinguish the truthful from the untruthful person; an error which

makes for inconsistency within the statement will be noticed much more readily by the truthful person
(C) need for careful proofreading; when the person discovers several mistakes, he will be alerted to watch for other possible mistakes
(D) need for testing the mental functioning of the person at the time of making the statement; if he does not detect the errors, he is functioning abnormally.

88. Continuous taking of notes during an interview is generally
(A) desirable because no important facts will be forgotten
(B) undesirable because it gives the person being interviewed a clue to the importance of the information being obtained from him
(C) desirable because the interviewer cannot write as fast as the person being interviewed can speak
(D) undesirable because it may put the person being interviewed ill at ease.

89. The person being interviewed was quite nervous and often strayed from the subject. As the time available for the interview was drawing to a close, the interviewer glanced at his watch and interrupted abruptly, saying: "We really don't have much time left you know, so suppose I just ask you a series of questions and you answer them quickly and truthfully." The interviewer's action would generally be considered
(A) in conflict with the principles of interviewing which suggest that prospects for gaining or maintaining rapport with the interviewee should not be jeopardized
(B) in harmony with the principles of interviewing which endorse the directness, efficiency and respect-inspiring effect of this approach
(C) in conflict with the principles of interviewing which suggest that techniques for conduct of the interview should not be altered once they are put into use
(D) in harmony with the principles of interviewing which suggest that this approach would extract more reliable information than any other in the remaining time.

90. A certain investigator usually avoids any expression of his personal opinions on morals, politics or family relations when he is interviewing anyone in connection with an investigation. Such a policy is generally
(A) bad mainly because the investigator misses opportunities for finding things in common with the person being interviewed
(B) good mainly because the investigator's expressed opinions may influence the information offered by the person being interviewed
(C) bad mainly because the investigator's approach should be informal and frank rather than restrained
(D) good mainly because the interview will be speeded up.

91. Interviewing witnesses by the question and answer method, rather than allowing the witness to tell his story without interruption, will generally
(A) increase the range but decrease the accuracy of the report
(B) decrease the range but increase the accuracy of the report
(C) decrease both the range and accuracy of the report
(D) increase both the range and the accuracy of the report.

92. Experiments have shown that the most satisfactory method, among the following, for obtaining dependable data in an interview is by employment of
(A) the free narrative method, in which the person interviewed is permitted to talk without interruption
(B) the question and answer method, in which the person interviewed gives information only in response to questions
(C) a combination of the question and answer and free narrative methods, with the free narrative given first
(D) a combination of the question and answer and free narrative methods, with the question and answer interview given first.

93. The personal interview as a means of obtaining information about past occurrences is
(A) the most reliable and accurate method
(B) useful principally as a means of finding clues to more reliable sources of information
(C) generally as reliable as recourse to documentary sources
(D) qualitatively inferior but quantitatively superior to all other methods.

94. If a person interviewed seems hesitant to talk while the investigator is taking notes, the most advisable of the following procedures for the investigator is to
(A) adjourn the interview until a time when it can be conducted in a place with a hidden microphone to record it
(B) secure his co-operation by explaining to the witness the importance of full and complete notes for good investigation reports
(C) complete the interview without note-taking, and, at the first opportunity after the interview, reduce it to writing
(D) administer an oath to the person so that he will commit perjury by failing to tell the whole truth.

95. If the memory of a witness fails him about the time of an occurrence concerning which he is being questioned, the most advisable of the following procedures for the investigator to follow is to
(A) supply the data for him in his report
(B) assume the presence of a motive for concealing the information
(C) request him to make an affidavit to that effect
(D) try to give him some associated ideas to refresh his memory.

96. Among the following it is generally desirable to interview a person outside his home or office because
(A) the presence of relatives and friends may prevent him from speaking freely
(B) a person's surroundings tend to color his testimony
(C) the person will find less distraction outside his home or office
(D) a person tends to dominate the interview when in familiar surroundings.

97. In interviewing a person "suggestive questions" should be avoided because, among the following
(A) the answers to leading questions are not admissible in evidence
(B) an investigator must be fair and impartial
(C) the interrogation of a witness must be formulated according to his mentality
(D) they are less apt to lead to the truth.

98. Information obtained by an investigator from a very small child should be carefully evaluated because of the following reasons: children
(A) are less observing than adults
(B) have less retentive memories
(C) easily confuse their own experiences with those of others
(D) are apt to have been coached by adults.

99. In the course of a routine investigation of sales tax payments, the examination of a firm's books discloses to the investigator evidence that the firm's bookkeeper may be appropriating large sums of the firm's funds to his own use. The investigator's best course of action, among the following, would be to
(A) warn the bookkeeper of his discovery but take no further action, since his obligations are toward the City not the firm
(B) advise the firm of his suspicions, suggesting an audit of the books
(C) immediately report his findings to the District Attorney
(D) take no action other than to include the evidence among the findings in his report.

100. If a person you are interviewing in connection with a character investigation obviously is not telling the truth, the most advisable of the following procedures is to
(A) let him talk as much as he likes, so that he may eventually contradict himself and tell the truth
(B) threaten him with criminal prosecution if he does not tell the truth
(C) administer an oath to him before he is questioned
(D) disregard his testimony entirely and question him no further.

THE INVESTIGATOR'S LEGAL VOCABULARY

101. "Where the language of an *instrument* has a settled legal meaning, its construction is not open to evidence." The word "instrument" as used in this sentence means most nearly
(A) the formal expression of a legal agreement
(B) a court decision
(C) any legal act
(D) any means of accomplishment
(E) an implement.

102. *Arraignment* is most nearly
(A) the statement of pleading on the part

of the people of the state regarding an offense in question
(B) directing the arrest of an offender against whom an indictment has been found
(C) preparation of a prisoner to appear before a court for sentence
(D) the assembling of all the charges and evidence supporting the charges
(E) the reading under the jurisdiction of a court of an indictment or information to a defendant and delivering a copy to him.

103. A *statute of limitations* is a law
(A) limiting the time within which a criminal prosecution or civil action must be commenced
(B) prohibiting a second prosecution for a crime for which a person has once been tried
(C) regulating the descent and distribution of the property of a person dying intestate
(D) limiting the sentence that may be imposed upon conviction for a particular crime.

104. A writ directed to the person detaining a prisoner, commanding him to produce that prisoner in court at a designated time is called a writ of
(A) prohibition (B) habeas corpus
(C) mandamus (D) extradition.

105. An instrument in writing, signed by a magistrate, commanding a person to appear at a designated time and place to answer a complaint is called a
(A) subpoena (B) summons
(C) presentment (D) warrant.

106. A child who, through no neglect on the part of his parents, is homeless is called
(A) a rejected child
(B) a destitute child
(C) a delinquent child
(D) an abandoned child.

107. A contract that allows individuals or corporations to use public property is known as a
(A) license (B) indenture
(C) patent (D) franchise.

108. The delivery of an arrested person to his sureties, upon their giving security for his appearance at the time and place designated to submit to the jurisdiction and judgment of the court, is known as
(A) bail (B) habeas corpus
(C) parole (D) probation.

109. A written accusation of a crime presented by a grand jury is called
(A) a commitment (B) an arraignment
(C) an indictment (D) a demurrer.

110. The one of the following statements made by a prisoner that is corectly called an *alibi* is
(A) "He struck me first."
(B) "I didn't intend to hurt him."
(C) "I was miles away from there at the time."
(D) "I don't remember what happened."

111. A person who, after the commission of a crime, conceals the offender with the intent that the latter may escape from arrest and trial, is called
(A) an accessory (B) an accomplice
(C) a confederate (D) an associate.

112. A sworn statement of fact is called
(A) an affidavit
(B) an oath
(C) an acknowledgment
(D) a subponea.

113. The word *knowingly,* when included in the definition of a crime, means with
(A) malice aforethought
(B) deliberation and premeditation
(C) knowledge that the facts exist which constitute the act or omission
(D) knowledge of the unlawfulness of the act or omission which constitutes a crime.

114. A person who dies without leaving a will is called
(A) deceased (B) intestate
(C) testator (D) ancestor.

115. An instrument commanding a person to appear in court, bringing with him certain documents and records is called
(A) subpoena
(B) warrant
(C) summons
(D) subpoena duces tecum.

116. An exact copy of a document is called
(A) facsimile (B) exordium
(C) execution (D) habendum.

117. Evidence, such as will prevail, if not rebutted is
(A) corraborative (B) cumulative
(C) prima facie (D) direct.

118. Evidence from which a fact not directly proved is to be inferred as a necessary or probable consequence is called
(A) circumstantial (B) cumulative
(C) inferential (D) collateral.

119. The subscription to a written instrument, signed by the witnesses to its execution, stating that they have witnessed it is called
(A) novation (B) acknowledgment
(C) consummation (D) attestation.

120. A person who has *derivative* United States citizenship is one who has citizenship through
(A) birth in the United States
(B) his own naturalization proceedings
(C) marriage with a naturalized citizen
(D) the naturalization of a parent.

121. If a deceased person left a will and nominated in it someone to manage and distribute his estate, such person, when duly appointed is called
(A) manager (B) executor
(C) administrator (D) guardian.

122. The act of going before a competent officer and declaring the execution of an instrument is called
(A) oath (B) affidavit
(C) acquitance (D) acknowledgment.

123. The part of an instrument which reads: "Sworn to before me this eighteenth day of December, 1948. Joseph Smith, Notary Public, State of New York" is known as the
(A) jurat (B) authentication
(C) certification (D) attestation.

124. A sworn statement made by the person who served a summons, setting forth the place and manner of service, is called
(A) an admission of service
(B) an affidavit of service
(C) a certificate of service
(D) an acknowledgment of service.

125. An investigation manual directs that all investigator's reports contain a precis. The term "precis" is synonymous with
(A) extract (B) paraphrase
(C) synopsis (D) conclusion.

Correct Answers For The Foregoing Questions

(Please make every effort to answer the questions on your own before looking at these answers. You'll make faster progress by following this rule.)

1. B	17. B	33. A	49. C	65. B	81. A	97. D	113. C
2. C	18. A	34. A	50. D	66. D	82. B	98. C	114. B
3. D	19. C	35. D	51. C	67. C	83. A	99. B	115. D
4. C	20. B	36. C	52. A	68. D	84. B	100. A	116. A
5. E	21. C	37. A	53. B	69. B	85. C	101. A	117. C
6. J	22. D	38. B	54. B	70. A	86. C	102. E	118. A
7. M	23. B	39. C	55. D	71. C	87. A	103. A	119. D
8. B	24. A-C	40. A	56. C	72. B	88. D	104. B	120. D
9. G	25. D	41. A	57. D	73. A	89. A	105. B	121. B
10. F	26. A	42. B	58. G	74. C	90. B	106. B	122. D
11. C	27. D	43. D	59. A	75. A	91. A	107. D	123. A
12. B	28. C	44. B	60. F	76. C	92. C	108. A	124. B
13. A	29. C	45. A	61. C	77. B	93. B	109. C	125. C
14. D	30. B	46. C	62. B	78. C	94. C	110. C	
15. B	31. A	47. C	63. E	79. B	95. D	111. A	
16. C	32. B	48. A	64. C	80. A	96. A	112. A	

PART THREE

Practice and Preparation-
General Test Subjects
of the Examination

Practice Using Answer Sheets

Alter numbers to match the practice and drill questions in each part of the book.
Make only ONE mark for each answer. Additional and stray marks may be counted as mistakes.
In making corrections, erase errors COMPLETELY. Make glossy black marks.

1 A B C D E	1 A B C D E	1 A B C D E	1 A B C D E	1 A B C D E
2 A B C D E	2 A B C D E	2 A B C D E	2 A B C D E	2 A B C D E
3 A B C D E	3 A B C D E	3 A B C D E	3 A B C D E	3 A B C D E
4 A B C D E	4 A B C D E	4 A B C D E	4 A B C D E	4 A B C D E
5 A B C D E	5 A B C D E	5 A B C D E	5 A B C D E	5 A B C D E
6 A B C D E	6 A B C D E	6 A B C D E	6 A B C D E	6 A B C D E
7 A B C D E	7 A B C D E	7 A B C D E	7 A B C D E	7 A B C D E
8 A B C D E	8 A B C D E	8 A B C D E	8 A B C D E	8 A B C D E
9 A B C D E	9 A B C D E	9 A B C D E	9 A B C D E	9 A B C D E
0 A B C D E	0 A B C D E	0 A B C D E	0 A B C D E	0 A B C D E

1 A B C D E	1 A B C D E	1 A B C D E	1 A B C D E	1 A B C D E
2 A B C D E	2 A B C D E	2 A B C D E	2 A B C D E	2 A B C D E
3 A B C D E	3 A B C D E	3 A B C D E	3 A B C D E	3 A B C D E
4 A B C D E	4 A B C D E	4 A B C D E	4 A B C D E	4 A B C D E
5 A B C D E	5 A B C D E	5 A B C D E	5 A B C D E	5 A B C D E
6 A B C D E	6 A B C D E	6 A B C D E	6 A B C D E	6 A B C D E
7 A B C D E	7 A B C D E	7 A B C D E	7 A B C D E	7 A B C D E
8 A B C D E	8 A B C D E	8 A B C D E	8 A B C D E	8 A B C D E
9 A B C D E	9 A B C D E	9 A B C D E	9 A B C D E	9 A B C D E
0 A B C D E	0 A B C D E	0 A B C D E	0 A B C D E	0 A B C D E

1 A B C D E	7 A B C D E	13 A B C D E	19 A B C D E	25 A B C D E
2 A B C D E	8 A B C D E	14 A B C D E	20 A B C D E	26 A B C D E
3 A B C D E	9 A B C D E	15 A B C D E	21 A B C D E	27 A B C D E
4 A B C D E	10 A B C D E	16 A B C D E	22 A B C D E	28 A B C D E
5 A B C D E	11 A B C D E	17 A B C D E	23 A B C D E	29 A B C D E
6 A B C D E	12 A B C D E	18 A B C D E	24 A B C D E	30 A B C D E

TEAR OUT ALONG THIS LINE AND MARK YOUR ANSWERS AS INSTRUCTED IN THE TEXT

ARRANGING PARAGRAPHS IN LOGICAL ORDER

DIRECTIONS: In these questions, four given sentences may or may not be arranged in the order in which they would logically appear in a paragraph. Following the four given sentences are five suggested sequences, lettered A, B, C, D, and E, from which you are to select the sequence that indicates the best arrangement of the sentences. For example: If, in the first question, you find that the fourth sentence should come first, the first sentence should be second, the second sentence should be third, and the third sentence should be fourth, you would look among the five choices for the answer 4-1-3-2, and designate the letter which precedes that sequence as your answer.

1. 1. There is also good reason for careful attention to internal communication.
   2. Effective communication with those inside the organization makes for fewer misunderstandings, and fewer disgruntled employees.
   3. Harmony within the business carries over into public relations with outsiders.
   4. In the area of office communication, primary attention is usually centered upon relations with outsiders - customers, suppliers, and others.

   (A) 2-3-1-4 (B) 4-1-2-3
   (C) 3-2-1-4 (D) 1-3-2-4
   (E) 4-2-3-1

2. 1. The underlying theory of dictation is that it enables the executive to pass on to others his mature judgment on important matters in a minimum of time, leaving him free to exercise executive direction in other phases of management.
   2. What are the characteristics of an efficient dictator, an inefficient dictator?
   3. How does one go about dictating?
   4. Research studies and personal experiences tell us that sometimes only time and effort in practicing good dictation procedure can turn a poor dictator into a good one.

   (A) 2-1-4-3 (B) 4-2-1-3
   (C) 1-3-4-2 (D) 2-4-3-1
   (E) 3-2-1-4

3. 1. A systematic plan for handling the mail will speed up the performance of office work.
   2. Regardless of the volume of mail, competent supervision and control are necessary.
   3. The provision of facilities for handling mail will depend largely upon the volume to be handled.
   4. The number of persons forming the mailroom staff, in turn, varies with the volume of correspondence to be handled and the degree to which mechanical equipment is used.

   (A) 1-3-4-2 (B) 2-1-3-4
   (C) 3-1-4-2 (D) 4-3-2-1
   (E) 2-4-1-3

4. 1. A budget is a plan of financial requirements during a given time period.
   2. It necessarily is based upon analysis of the situation which faces the enterprise.
   3. It develops a course of action to be followed.

4. The general uses of any budget are those of planning financial needs in advance and providing a basis for controlling current expenditures.

(A) 3-2-4-1 (B) 4-2-3-1
(C) 2-4-3-1 (D) 1-2-3-4
(E) 4-1-3-2

5. 1. The employee has little control over any of them.

2. The cost of the training period and its effectiveness will depend upon the degree to which these conditions are properly controlled by the employer.

3. The conditions under which the employee must learn will materially affect the length of the training period.

4. These conditions can be controlled by the employer.

(A) 1-2-4-3 (B) 4-2-1-3
(C) 3-4-2-1 (D) 2-4-3-1
(E) 1-4-3-2

6. 1. But once that point is reached, reappraisal and modification should be made in light of the skill and experience of the work force and the cost of perfectionism.

2. The second caution is that the development effort should be aimed at creating a simple, workable procedure as distinct from a perfect precedure.

3. As one speaker put it, "Hire a few workers to mop the floor so that you don't have to develop a perfect system that will keep 400 people from dropping things on the floor."

4. To be sure, the initial effort should be directed toward developing the ideal.

(A) 4-1-3-2 (B) 3-1-4-2
(C) 2-1-3-4 (D) 2-4-1-3
(E) 1-2-4-3

7. 1. They include computation and rate tables, codes, charts, price lists, wiring diagrams, account titles and definitions, and the like.

2. The use and usefulness of these devices should be fully explored during the survey of work methods.

3. In general, the analyst's objective should be to find out if all special data required to perform any part of the routine are readily available, conveniently arranged, and kept up to date.

4. Work aids are the nonmechanical devices of many kinds used to facilitate repetitive clerical operations.

(A) 1-2-3-4 (B) 4-1-2-3
(C) 3-1-4-2 (D) 2-1-4-3
(E) 3-2-4-1

8. 1. This is just another way of stating the important principle that duplication is not always avoidable or wasteful.

2. On this whole matter of combining forms, one point of caution needs to be stressed: The analyst must be careful not to go beyond the point of diminishing returns.

3. In some situations it may be the simplest way of meeting the requirements.

4. He must not fall into the error of seeking combination for its own sake.

(A) 2-4-1-3 (B) 3-4-1-2
(C) 4-1-2-3 (D) 1-3-4-2
(E) 3-1-2-4

9. 1. The big risk, of course, in funneling all proposed procedure instructions through a single point is that the adoption of worthwhile changes will be unnecessarily delayed.

2. The approvals required must be clearly specified and held to a minimum, and the procedures staff must be geared to process recommended changes quickly.

3. Unless this is done, operating personnel will soon become discouraged from submitting recommendations through the prescribed channels and will revert to making its own changes as the need arises.

4. To avoid this danger, the path of revision must be short, easy to follow, and well understood by everyone.

(A) 4-1-3-2 (B) 3-1-2-4
(C) 1-4-2-3 (D) 2-4-1-3
(E) 4-3-2-1

10. 1. For one man, everything he does falls under the heading of administration.
    2. To a large extent, what the administrative functions of your job are depend on what you say they are.
    3. You can talk to a dozen executives without getting two to agree.
    4. Another executive will tell you only planning and decision making belong there.

    (A) 1-2-4-3 (B) 2-1-3-4
    (C) 3-2-4-1 (D) 4-1-2-3
    (E) 3-1-4-2

11. 1. The importance of communications is axiomatic.
    2. When the phrase "two-way" precedes the word "communications," there is the feeling in some quarters that we have said everything there is to say on the subject.
    3. But communications may proceed in two directions and still not be inclusive enough to make it possible for you to do a thorough communications job.
    4. The fact is, the communications load of many executives tends to be decidedly uneven.

    (A) 4-3-1-2 (B) 2-3-4-1
    (C) 3-4-1-2 (D) 1-2-3-4
    (E) 4-1-2-3

12. 1. In actuality, this isn't the case at all.
    2. The trouble with many approaches to problem solving is the mistaken idea that problems come to you spelled out in clear and simple terms.
    3. For example, a problem may grow so imperceptibly that it may actually have been around for years before it begins to take on the aspects of a problem.
    4. Or the facts of a case may be indistinguishable from the fancies.

    (A) 3-4-1-2 (B) 2-1-3-4
    (C) 1-3-2-4 (D) 4-2-1-3
    (E) 2-3-4-1

13. 1. Regardless of the reason, the effects of the vacuum range from the disheartening to the deadly.
    2. Men in management, more often than you might think, find themselves "in solitary."
    3. It's seldom calculated, but the fact remains, they have no one to talk to.
    4. Lack of direct channels to colleagues may reflect anything from poor personal relationships to faulty organizational setup.

    (A) 4-1-3-2 (B) 2-4-1-3
    (C) 2-3-4-1 (D) 3-1-4-2
    (E) 1-4-3-2

14. 1. They must operate to accomplish any one of the primary tasks.
    2. These processes are planning, doing, and controlling.
    3. They cause the organization to function.
    4. Three processes are at work in an organization.

    (A) 4-3-2-1 (B) 1-2-3-4
    (C) 3-1-4-2 (D) 2-4-1-3
    (E) 4-1-3-2

15. 1. Difficulty in the application of the principle of unity of command arises principally from its blind application to a static organization structure to meet a need that fluctuates with conditions and situations.
    2. The relationships shown on an organization chart seem as inflexible and static as the structure of the organization itself.
    3. If the organization is to serve its purpose, however, it cannot be entirely static because it is dealing with moving and changing situations.
    4. The relationships between the component units of the organization enable it to become a flexible, living organism.

    (A) 2-4-3-1 (B) 4-1-3-2
    (C) 3-4-1-2 (D) 2-1-3-4
    (E) 1-2-3-4

16. 1. These may help, but good communications are possible only when there is mutual understanding—and trust—over a two-way circuit.
    2. Poor communication is basically the result of a lack of mutual confidence between management and labor.
    3. It can and does exist almost regardless of the number of memoranda, house organs, bulletin boards, and conferences.

4. This occurs on all levels, between sections, departments, divisions, foremen, managers, executives.
(A) 4-1-3-2 (B) 2-4-3-1
(C) 3-1-2-4 (D) 1-4-3-2
(E) 4-3-1-2

17. 1. It cannot be answered by listing "qualities an executive should have" and then trying to assess executives accordingly.
2. Quite simply, it is the lack of any precise means of judging executive ability.
3. Of all the weaknesses in these development methods, however, only one is fundamental.
4. Appraising performance is not difficult, but appraising qualities and potentialities involves the basic problem of the nature of leadership.
(A) 4-3-2-1 (B) 2-1-3-4
(C) 1-3-2-4 (D) 4-3-1-2
(E) 3-1-4-2

18. 1. As both labor and management are slowly learning, good relations are not learned from books or made by laws, but grow out of individual attitudes and understanding.
2. For there are too many psychological and sociological pressures working against industrial harmony that are beyond the control of any individuals or groups.
3. If they are broad, the *chances* of achieving good relations are greatly increased but, unfortunately, not assured.
4. If either of these is narrow, friction is inevitable.
(A) 3-2-1-4 (B) 2-4-3-1
(C) 4-1-2-3 (D) 2-1-3-4
(E) 1-4-3-2

Correct Answers

(You'll learn more by writing your own answers before comparing them with these.)

1. B	6. D	10. E	14. A
2. E	7. B	11. D	15. E
3. A	8. A	12. B	16. B
4. D	9. C	13. C	17. A
5. C			18. E

SCORE

.... %

NO. CORRECT

NO. OF QUESTIONS ON THIS TEST

PATROL INSPECTOR

READING COMPREHENSION AND INTERPRETATION

We have good reason to believe that this kind of question will appear on your test. We want you to practice now and profit later. Guide and schedule your practice.

THE READING INTERPRETATION TEST

The questions on reading interpretation given below are all in the form of a multiple choice. Read each statement or paragraph, and the five statements based on it that follow. From each group, choose the ONE that will best complete the original statement, or interpret the essential idea of the paragraph. In some cases, SEVERAL of the statements will make a TRUE or CORRECT statement, but only ONE will interpret the sense of the paragraph exactly, and be least open to exceptions.

You may want to answer on facsimiles of the kind of answer sheets provided on machine-scored examinations. For practice purposes we have provided several such facsimiles at the back of the book. Tear one out if you wish, and mark your answers on it . . . just as you would do on an actual exam.

In machine-scored examinations you should record all your answers on the answer sheet provided. Don't make the mistake of putting answers on the test booklet itself.

In some examinations you may be instructed to mark your answers in the test booklet. In such cases you should be careful that no other marks interfere with the legibility of your answers.

It is most important that you learn to mark your answers clearly and in the right place.

You will find the correct answers to these questions on page 226.However, you oughtn't to peek until you have answered them all by yourself.

A good paragraph generally has one central thought or topic sentence. Your main task is to locate and absorb that thought while reading the paragraph. The correct interpretation of the paragraph is based upon that thought, and not upon personal opinions, prejudices or preferences. The ability to *grasp* the central idea of a passage can be acquired by practice—practice that will also increase the speed with which you read.

In making your choice of the correct statement, the following suggestions will prove helpful:

1. Read the paragraph through quickly to get the general sense.
2. Reread the paragraph, concentrating on the central idea, and try to picture it as a unit.
3. Examine the five choices carefully, but rapidly, eliminating immediately those which are far-fetched or irrelevant.
4. Be sure to consider *only the facts given in the paragraph to which the choice refers!*
5. Be especially careful of trick expressions or "catch-words" which sometimes destroy the validity of a seemingly true statement. These include the expressions: "under all circumstances," "at all times," "never," "always," "under no conditions," "absolutely," "completely," and "entirely."

Certain physical factors affect your reading. You should always read sitting in a comfortable position, erect, with head slightly inclined. The light should be excellent, with both an indirect and a direct source available; direct light should come from behind and slightly above your shoulder, in such a way that the type is evenly illumined. Hold the reading matter at your own best reading distance and at a convenient height, so you don't stoop or squint. It goes without saying that, if you need glasses, you should certainly use them when reading.

To prepare for a test in Reading Comprehension, then, you should keep the above ideas firmly in mind. Practice reading, for practice will improve your skill. Never retreat to your older, easier method of reading once you have grasped the way we have indicated here. In a very short time, you will find the new method of reading easier than the old. You will read faster. You will understand more of what you read. You will enjoy reading more. You will accomplish more reading in less time. It will no longer be a chore, but a pleasant and profitable relaxation.

Questions

(Reading) "Radio has just about reached in 20 years the goal toward which print has been working for 500: to extend its audience to include the entire population. In 1966, in the United States, nine out of ten families had radios—45 million sets going an average of five hours a day."

1. According to the above paragraph:
   (A) the entire nation has radio sets
   (B) nine out of ten individuals listen an average of five hours a day to the radio
   (C) The radio-listening public grew much more rapidly than did the reading public.
   (D) there are more radios in the United States than in other countries
   (E) the total possible radio audience is larger than the reading public.

(Reading) "What gave this country the isolation it enjoyed in the 19th century was the statesmanship of Jefferson, Adams, Madison, and Monroe on this side of the Atlantic and of men like Canning on the other side. American independence of the European system did not exist in the two centuries before the Monroe Doctrine of 1823, and it has not existed in the century which began in 1914."

2. According to the above paragraph:
   (A) America enjoyed greater isolation from European affairs from 1823 to 1914 than before or after
   (B) the isolation of this country from European affairs was, prior to 1914, the result of our geographic position
   (C) canning was a statesman living in the 20th century
   (D) America is less isolated today than it has ever been
   (E) the statesmanship of Washington helped to keep America free from foreign entanglements.

(Reading) "It may be said that the problem in adult education seems to be not the piling up of facts but practice in thinking."

3. According to the above paragraph:
   (A) educational methods for adults and young people should differ
   (B) adults do not seem to retain new facts
   (C) adults seem to think more than young people
   (D) a well-educated adult is one who thinks but does not have a store of information
   (E) adult education should stress ability to think.

(Reading) "Approximately 19,000 fatal accidents in 1965 were sustained in industry. There were approximately 130 non-fatal injuries to each fatal injury."

4. According to the above paragraph, the number of non-fatal accidents during 1965 was approximately:
   (A) 146,000 (B) 190,000
   (C) 1,150,000 (D) 2,500,000
   (E) 3,200,000.

(Reading) "In a lightning-like military advance, similar to that used by the Germans, the use of persistent chemicals is unnecessary and might be of considerable detriment to a force advancing over a broad front."

5. According to the above paragraph:
   (A) chemicals should not be used by a defending army
   (B) the Germans advanced in a narrow area
   (C) an advancing army may harm itself through the use of chemicals
   (D) chemicals are unnecessary if warfare is well-organized
   (E) chemical warfare is only effective if used by an advancing army.

(Reading) "The X-ray has gone into business. Developed primarily to aid in diagnosing human ills, the machine now works in packing plants, in foundries, in service stations, and in a dozen ways contributes to precision and accuracy in industry."

6. According to the above paragraph, the X-ray:
   (A) was first developed to aid business

(B) is more of a help to business than to medicine
(C) is being used to improve the functioning of business
(D) is more accurate for packing plants than for foundries
(E) increases the output of such industries as service stations.

(Reading) "For the United States, Canada has become the most important country in the world yet there are few countries about which Americans know less. Canada is the third largest country in the world; only Russia and China are larger. The area of Canada is more than a quarter of the whole British Empire."

7. According to the above paragraph:
(A) the British Empire is smaller than Russia or China
(B) the territory of China is greater than that of Canada
(C) Americans know more about Canada than about China or Russia
(D) the United States is the most important nation in the world as far as Canada is concerned
(E) the Canadian population is more than one quarter the population of the British Empire.

(Reading) "Although the rural crime reporting area is much less developed than that for cities and towns, current data are collected in sufficient volume to justify the generalization that rural crime rates are lower than those of urban communities."

8. According to the above paragraph:
(A) better reporting of crime occurs in rural areas than in cities
(B) there appears to be a lower proportion of crime in rural areas than in cities
(C) cities have more crime than towns
(D) crime depends on the amount of reporting
(E) no conclusions can be drawn regarding crime in rural areas because of inadequate reporting.

(Reading) "A hundred years ago, the steamboat was the center of life in the thriving Mississippi towns. Came the railroads; river traffic dwindled and the white-painted vessels rotted at the wharves. During the World War, the government decided to relieve rail congestion by reviving the long-forgotten waterways."

9. According to the above paragraph:
(A) the railroads were once the center of thriving river towns on the Mississippi River
(B) the volume of river transportation was greater than the volume of rail transportation during the World War
(C) growth of river transportation greatly increased the congestion on the railroads
(D) business found river transportation more profitable than railroad transportation during the World War
(E) in the past century the volume of transportation on the Mississippi has varied.

(Reading) "I consider that a man's brain originally is like a little empty attic, and you have to stock it with such furniture as you choose. A fool takes in all the lumber of every sort that he comes across, so that the knowledge which might be useful to him gets crowded out, or at best is jumbled up with a lot of other things, so that he has a difficulty in laying his hands upon it. It is a mistake to think that that little room has elastic walls and can distend to any extent. Depend upon it there comes a time when for every addition of knowledge you forget something that you knew before."

10. According to the preceding paragraph, knowledge
(A) should be sought for its own sake
(B) is always valuable
(C) should be avoided
(D) should be acquired only if it is necessary
(E) may be acquired without limitation.

(Reading) "In a recent questionnaire circulated among the students of a certain college, there was a general agreement among the students questioned that the greatest single influence of the movies has been to give them a better understanding of the people and customs of other parts of the world. The degree of approval given this statement was a third greater than that accorded to the second most important influence, that of a desire for greater freedom in social relations."

11. Judging from the data derived from the above-mentioned questionnaire, the chief single influence of the movies
(A) is an emphasis upon crime and crime prevention
(B) reveals the astounding information that the larger majority of college students attend the movies regularly
(C) is a tendency to create a desire for greater freedom of social relations among college students
(D) is the dissemination of the broad cultural aspects of lands other than our own
(E) is the graphic presentation of foreign folklore.

(Reading) "Specialization is made possible by the process of exchange. The farmer specializes in the raising of certain food products and raw materials. He produces in the course of a year's time many more bushels of corn than he and his family can possibly consume. On the other hand, being a specialist, he has no time to make for himself the wide variety of other products such as food, clothing, shelter, newspapers, machinery and many other goods which he needs. What he does is to exchange his corn for those products. So it is with all other producers."

12. Which of the following does the above paragraph indicate is one of the principal results of specialization?
    (A) the process of exchange has been greatly accelerated
    (B) the farmer produces more corn than he and his family can possibly consume.
    (C) the farmer can no longer make his own clothes
    (D) the farmer's produce must be sent to the open market for distribution
    (E) food products become the specialized field of the farmer.

(Reading) "When from a sufficient although partial classification of facts a simple principle has been discovered which describes the relationship and sequences of any group, then this principle or law itself generally leads to the discovery of a still wider range of hitherto unregarded phenomena in the same or associated fields."

13. Which of the following phrases most adequately describes the preceding quotation?
    (A) relationship between group classifications
    (B) establishment of principles derived from group relationships and sequences
    (C) association of phenomena in a wide range of varied fields
    (D) establishment of general laws in hitherto undiscovered fields
    (E) discovery of hitherto unregarded phenomena in their relationships and sequences to varied groups.

(Reading) "The capacity of the banks to grant loans depends, in the long run, on the amount of money deposited with them by the public. In the short run, however, it is a well known fact that the banks not only can but do lend more than is deposited with them. If such lending is carried to excess, it leads to inflation."

14. On the basis of the preceding paragraph it is most reasonable to conclude that
    (A) banks often indulge in the vicious practice of lending more than is deposited with them
    (B) in the long run, a sound banking policy operates for the mutual advantage of the bankers and the public.
    (C) inflation is usually the result of excess lending by the banks
    (D) the public must guard against inflation
    (E) bank lending is always in direct ratio with bank deposits.

(Reading) "Even when sheep raising is a principal business and not a farm by-product it is extremely difficult to approach uniformity in the quality of the wool. On one sheep there are at least four qualities. Often, throughout a flock, no two sheep in one season yield exactly the same grade of wool. In addition, since the quality is influenced by the food the sheep eat, the soil over which they graze, and the weather, no two flocks in one year produce the same quality of wool, and the same flock will change from year to year."

15. On the basis of the preceding paragraph one could most reasonably conclude that
    (A) soil is a factor in the quality of sheep-wool
    (B) sheep raising is usually a by-product of the meat-producing industries
    (C) no two sheep in one season yield exactly the same grade of wool
    (D) there is a consistent change in the seasonal quality of wool
    (E) flocks of sheep will change from year to year.

(Reading) "Neither the revolution in manufacture nor that in agriculture could have proceeded without that series of brilliant inventions in transportation and communication which have bound country to city, nation to nation, and continent to continent."

16. Judging from the contents of the preceding paragraph it can most precisely be indicated that
    (A) nations have been brought together more closely by transportation than by manufacture and agriculture
    (B) progress in communication and transportation has been essential to progress in manufacturing and agriculture
    (C) changes in manufacture and agriculture are characterized by a revolutionary process
    (D) industrial changes must be preceded by

brilliant inventions in communication
(E) both industry and transportation serve to bind country to city, nation to nation and continent to continent

(Reading) "Rivers and water courses afford a very convenient and accessible source of supply; and one of the principal reasons for towns in olden times having been established by the banks of rivers is supposed to have been the facility with which, in such a situation, an ample supply of water was secured."

17. According to the preceding paragraph, rivers and water courses are
    (A) valuable
    (B) useful
    (C) convenient sources of water supply for towns
    (D) the main support of ancient towns
    (E) valuable only for ancient towns. (546 1)

(Reading) "In 1895, of the 300 cars owned only four were manufactured in this country. Of the 22 million registered on January 1, 1927, all but an infinitesimal number were manufactured in American plants."

18. The paragraph notes that registered automobiles in this country in 1927
    (A) were far in excess of those manufactured abroad in 1895
    (B) were manufactured in the United States
    (C) increased considerably over the preceding decade
    (D) improved greatly in construction over the 1895 model
    (E) were almost exclusively of domestic construction.

(Reading) "The labor required to produce a bushel of wheat was reduced from three hours in 1830 to ten minutes in 1896; and it has been estimated that fifty men, employing modern farm machinery and the new methods of agriculture, can do the work of five hundred peasants toiling under the conditions of the eighteenth century."

19. On the basis of the facts presented above one could best conclude that
    (A) the increase of efficiency in agriculture is almost as great as that in manufacturing
    (B) peasants in the eighteenth century worked much harder than do our farmers today
    (C) modern farm machinery has resulted in serious unemployment among farmers
    (D) 18 times as much wheat was produced in 1896 as in 1830
    (E) modern farm machinery is labor-saving.

(Reading) "The railroads, building trades, mineral industries, and automotive works normally take two-thirds of our annual production of steel. The remaining third has been around 16 million tons. For this last third of our output the farmers have been the best customers with farm machinery tools and wire constituting their chief demands."

20. Judging from the above facts it would be most reasonable to assume that
    (A) there is an increasing demand for the newer and more efficient farm machinery and tools
    (B) the growth of the steel industry has made possible the growth of all of our basic industries that depend upon steel
    (C) the farmers are our best steel customers
    (D) our normal annual steel output is about 48 million tons
    (E) only one-third of our steel output is exported with the remaining two-thirds consumed by our own industries.

(Reading) "The term 'agent of a foreign principal' means any person who acts or engages or agrees to act as a public-relations counsel, publicity agent, or as agent, servant, representative, or attorney for a foreign principal or for any domestic organization subsidized directly or indirectly in whole or in part by a foreign principal. Such term shall not include a duly accredited diplomatic or consular officer of a foreign government who is so recognized by the Department of State of the United States."

21. According to this paragraph
    (A) no foreign official can be termed an "agent of a foreign principal" unless he is so recognized by the Department of State
    (B) a person who acts as a public-relations counsel for a foreign principal, must be subsidized by that principal before he can be termed its "agent"
    (C) if a foreign publicity agent is subsidized directly by a domestic organization, he may be termed an "agent of a domestic principal"
    (D) outside of accredited and recognized diplomatic officials, persons acting as agents for foreign countries are termed "agents of a foreign principal"
    (E) consular officers and accredited diplomats are exempted from the term "agent of a foreign principal."

(Reading) "It has been at times suggested that it is incongruous for the government to employ one lawyer to prosecute and another to defend the same prisoner. This is a superficial point of view, for it overlooks the principle that the Government should be as anxious to shield the innocent as it is to punish the guilty."

22. According to this quotation
    (A) it is not properly within the scope of the government to provide criminals with both prosecuting and defending lawyers
    (B) a person held for a crime, if he be poor need never fear that he will not be adequately defended, because the government makes provision for competent lawyers to aid him in his defense
    (C) although sometimes criticised, it is governmental policy to provide legal defense for indigent persons accused of crime
    (D) a great government should feel obligated to shield the innocent as well as punish the guilty
    (E) it is an incongruous point of view that the government should concurrently shield the innocent and punish the guilty.

(Reading) "There exists today an unparalleled opportunity for those nations and groups which look forward with clear vision to bring about an early return to sane perspectives and relationships based upon full comprehension that the members of the family of nations must live together amicably and work together in peace or be broken in an utterly destructive misuse of the power and the instruments which, properly used, bear beneficial witness to the amazing constructive capacity of mankind."

23. The above paragraph signifies that
    (A) peace is based upon the rightful use of forces which, if abused, destroy mankind
    (B) world peace is based upon vision
    (C) nations must have vision
    (D) nations, like individuals, look for direction to leaders
    (E) peace is a will-o-the-wisp; the solution is only visionary.

(Reading) "Since the government can spend only what it obtains from the people and this amount is ultimately limited by their capacity and willingness to pay taxes, it is very important that they should be given full information about the work of the government."

24. According to this quotation
    (A) governmental employees should be trained not only in their own work, but also in how to perform the duties of other employees in their agency
    (B) taxation by the government rests upon the consent of the people
    (C) the release of full information on the work of the government will increase the efficiency of governmental operations
    (D) the work of the government, in recent years, has been restricted because of reduced tax collections.

(Reading) "Just as municipal corporations acting in government capacity are free from liability, so also are charitable corporations or associations exempt from liability when carrying on welfare or charitable enterprises, not for profit."

25. According to the above paragraph it follows that
    (A) municipal and charitable corporations are exempt from liability
    (B) a private hospital or clinic which treats indigent patients without making a charge would not be liable for injuries caused
    (C) some charitable organizations operate for profit
    (D) municipal corporations do not operate for profit
    (E) an individual hurt in an automobile accident by a city chauffeur cannot sue a city if the latter is incorporated.

(Reading) "A hundred years ago the ownership of real estate was a fairly reliable index of 'ability to pay' and was therefore an equitable basis for the levying of taxes. But, with the rise of the present complex economic order with its far-reaching associations and subtle relationships, property has assumed many novel and intangible forms which fall quite outside the incidence of the tax on real estate."

26. According to the import of the foregoing paragraph one can conclude most accurately that
    (A) the best basis for the levying of taxes is 'ability to pay'
    (B) since property is not always easily recognizable as such, the government is faced with the problem of tax evasion
    (C) in our present complex economic order, ownership of property can no longer be considered a reliable index of 'ability to pay'
    (D) a tax based on 'ability to pay' would result in greater equality in the distribution of wealth
    (E) real estate today is only one kind of property.

(Reading) "Old age insurance, under which benefits are paid as a right and not on the basis of need to upwards of thirty millions of workers, is the one feature of the Social Security Act that is wholly administered by the Federal Government."

27. This paragraph indicates most nearly that
    (A) under the Social Security Act, the Federal Government administers old age insurance to any who deserve it
    (B) the States have no part in administering Social Security old age insurance
    (C) thirty million workers are eligible for old age insurance
    (D) the Social Security Act is administered by the Federal Government
    (E) every year thirty million workers receive old age insurance.

(Reading) "Statutes to prevent and penalize adulteration of foods and to provide for sanitation of them are in force in every state. Such legislation has been upheld as proper under the police power of the state, as it is obviously designed to promote the health and general welfare of the people."

28. It is reasonable to conclude from the above paragraph that
    (A) the state provides for drastic measures to deal with offenders of the pure food laws
    (B) to make laws for the purpose of promoting the general health and general welfare of the people, is a proper function of the state
    (C) adulterated food is an outstanding menace to public health
    (D) every state has adequately provided for the prevention of adulteration of foods, by enforcement of suitable legislation
    (E) the right of the state to penalize adulteration of foods has never been questioned.

(Reading) "Many industrial processes are dangerous to the health of the worker and may give rise to occupational disease. The state, as the guardian of public health and welfare, has a legitimate interest in conserving the vitality of industrial workers and may, to this end, make appropriate laws, and give to boards or departments authority to make regulations to carry out the law. Such laws and rules may prohibit dangerous conditions, regulate the plant or the person, or compensate for injuries received."

29. It can best be inferred from the preceding paragraph that
    (A) workmen's compensation laws are in force in practically all the states
    (B) the state makes laws that prohibit industrial processes that it considers dangerous to the health of the worker
    (C) Government regulation of industry is highly desirable
    (D) the state is interested in lessening the occurrence of occupational disease
    (E) the state compensates the worker for injuries received while carrying out the duties of his occupation.

Answer questions 30 to 36 on the basis of the information appearing in the paragraph below.

(Reading) "The first consideration in shooting a revolver is how to stand in a steady position. You may almost face the target in assuming a comfortable shooting stance, or you may face away from the target as much as ninety degrees, and still find it possible to stand easily and quietly. The principal point to observe is to spread the feet apart at least eight inches. This varies with the individual according to the length of his legs. Stand firmly on both feet. Do not bend either leg at the knee and be careful to develop a stance which does not allow the body to lean backward or forward. Ease and naturalness in posture with body muscles relaxed is the secret of good shooting form. The shooting arm should be straight, with the weight of the pistol supported not so much by the arm as by the muscles of the shoulder. Do not tense any muscle of the arm or hand while holding the revolver; especially avoid locking the elbow. The grip of the gun should be seated in the hand so that an imaginary line drawn along the forearm would pass through the bore of the gun. The heel of the hand should reach around the stock far enough to go past the center line of the gun. The thumb can be either alongside the hammer, on top of the frame, or it can be pointed downward toward the tip of the trigger finger. The high position is preferable, because when you are shooting rapid fire the thumb will have a shorter distance to move to reach the hammer spur."

30. The one of the following subjects discussed in the above paragraph is the proper method of
    (A) leading a moving target
    (B) squeezing the trigger
    (C) gripping the revolver
    (D) using revolver sights

31. According to the above paragraph, the secret of good shooting form is
(A) proper sighting of the target
(B) a relaxed and natural position
(C) firing slowly and carefully
(D) keeping the thumb alongside the hammer.

32. For proper shooting stance, it is recommended that the weight of the pistol be supported by
(A) the muscles of the shoulder
(B) locking the elbow
(C) the muscles of the forearm
(D) tensing the wrist muscles.

33. The chief advantage of employing a high thumb position in firing a revolver is to
(A) maintain a more uniform grip
(B) achieve greater accuracy
(C) achieve better recoil control
(D) facilitate more rapid shooting.

34. When firing a revolver at a target, the angle at which you should face the target
(A) is 45 degrees
(B) is 90 degrees
(C) is greater for taller persons
(D) varies naturally from person to person.

35. According to the above paragraph, the revolver should be held in such a manner that the
(A) bore of the revolver is slightly below the heel of the hand
(B) revolver, horizontally, is level with the shoulder
(C) center line of the revolver is a continuation of the forearm
(D) revolver is at a 45 degree angle with the target.

36. Of the following, the most accurate statement concerning proper shooting position is that the
(A) left knee should be bent slightly
(B) feet should be spread at least eight inches apart
(C) you should lean slightly forward as you fire each shot
(D) weight of the body should be on the right foot.

SOME QUESTIONS ON BUSINESS PROBLEMS AND PROCEDURES

(Reading) "One effect of specialization in industry is the loss of versatility which it has brought to the individual worker. Often, each laborer is trained to do a particular task and no other. The result is that he is almost entirely dependent for employment upon the demand for labor of his particular type. If anything happens to interrupt that demand he is deprived of employment."

37. This paragraph indicates that
(A) the unemployment problem is a direct result of specialization in industry
(B) the demand for labor of a particular type is constantly changing
(C) the average laborer is not capable of learning more than one particular task at a time
(D) some cases of unemployment may be due to the lack of versatility of the worker
(E) too much specialization is as dangerous as too little.

(Reading) "Never was management needed more than now. The most essential characteristic of management is organization, and the organization must be such that management can distribute enough responsibility and authority upon it to maintain the balance and perspective necessary to make such weighty decisions as are thrust upon it today."

38. The above paragraph is a plea for
(A) better business
(B) adequately controlled responsibility
(C) well regulated authority
(D) better management through organization
(E) less perspective and more balance.

(Reading) "One of the results of the increasing size of business organizations has been to make less and less practical any great amount of personal contact between superior and subordinate. Consequently, one finds in business today a greater dependence upon records and reports as a means whereby the executive may secure information and exercise control over the operations of the various departments."

39. According to this paragraph, the increasing size of business organizations
(A) has caused a complete cleavage between employer and employee
(B) makes for impracticality in relationships between the employer and employee

(C) has tended toward class distinctions in large organizations
(D) has resulted in a more indirect means of controlling the operations of various departments
(E) has made evaluation of the work of the employee more objective.

(Reading) "For mediocre executives who do not have a flair for positive administration, the implantation in subordinates of anxiety about job retention is a safe, if somewhat unimaginative, method of insuring a modicum of efficiency in the working organization."

40. Of the following, the most accurate statement according to this quotation is that
(A) implanting anxiety about job retention is a method usually employed by the mediocre executive to improve the efficiency of his organization
(B) an organization will operate with at least some efficiency if employees realize that unsatisfactory work performance may subject them to dismissal
(C) successful executives with a flair for positive administration relieve their subordinates of any concern for their job security
(D) the implantation of anxiety about job security in subordinates should not be used as a method of improving efficiency
(E) anxiety in executives tends to make them think that it is present in employees also.

(Reading) "In large organizations some standardized and yet simple and inexpensive method of giving employees information regarding company policies and rules, as well as specific instructions regarding their actual duties, is practically essential. This is the purpose of all office manuals of whatever type."

41. The above quotation notes that office manuals
(A) are all about the same
(B) should be simple enough for the average employee to understand
(C) are necessary to large organizations
(D) act as constant reminders to the employee of his duties
(E) are the only means by which the executive of a large organization can reach his subordinates.

Items 42 to 44 are to be answered solely on the basis of the information contained in the following passage:

(Reading) "It is common knowledge that ability to do a particular job and performance on the job do not always go hand in hand. Persons with great potential abilities sometimes fall down on the job because of laziness or lack of interest in the job, while persons with mediocre talents have often achieved excellent results through their industry and their loyalty to the interests of their employers. It is clear, therefore, that the final test of any employee is his performance on the job."

42. The most accurate of the following statements, on the basis of the above paragraph, is that
(A) employees who lack ability are usually not industrious
(B) an employee's attitudes are more important than his abilities
(C) mediocre employees who are interested in their work are preferable to employees who possess great ability
(D) superior capacity for performance should be supplemented with proper attitudes.

43. On the basis of the above paragraph, the employee of most value to his employer is *not* necessarily the one who
(A) best understands the significance of his duties
(B) achieves excellent results
(C) possesses the greatest talents
(D) produces the greatest amount of work.

44. According to the above paragraph, an employee's efficiency is best determined by an
(A) appraisal of his interest in his work
(B) evaluation of the work performed by him
(C) appraisal of his loyalty to his employer
(D) evaluation of his potential ability to perform his work.

(Reading) "Interest is essentially an attitude of continuing attentiveness, found where activity is satisfactorily self-expressive. Whenever work is so circumscribed that the chance for self-expression or development is denied, monotony is present."

45. On the basis of this quotation, it is most accurate to state that

(A) tasks which are repetitive in nature do not permit self-expression and therefore create monotony
(B) interest in one's work is increased by financial and non-financial incentives
(C) jobs which are monotonous can be made self-expressive by substituting satisfactory working conditions
(D) workers whose tasks afford them no opportunity for self-expression find such tasks to be monotonous
(E) work is monotonous unless there is activity which satisfies the worker.

(Reading) "During the past few years business has made rapid strides in applying to the field of office management the same fundamental principles of procedure and method that have been in successful use for years in production work. Indeed, present-day competition, resulting as it has in smaller margins of profit, has made it essential to give the most careful attention to the efficient organization and management of internal administrative affairs in order that individual productivity may be increased and unit costs reduced."

46. According to the above paragraph
(A) office management always lags behind production work
(B) present day competition has increased individual productivity
(C) efficient office management seeks to reduce gross costs
(D) the margin of profits widens as individual productivity is increased
(E) similar principles have met with equal success in the fields of office management and production work.

(Reading) "The direct lighting arrangement is exemplified by the individual desk light or the ceiling light with the ordinary reflector which diffuses all of the rays downward. Such lighting arrangements are considered the least satisfactory of any, due principally to the fact that there is almost sure to be a glare of some sort on the working surface."

47. The above paragraph indicates that direct lighting is least satisfactory as a method of lighting chiefly because
(A) the light is diffused causing eye strain
(B) the shade on the individual desk lamp is not constructed along scientific lines
(C) the working surface is usually obscured by the glare
(D) the ordinary reflector causes the rays to fall perpendicularly
(E) direct lighting is injurious to the eyes.

(Reading) "The principal advantage of wood over steel office equipment is the fact that, in the case of files in a burning building, for example, while the wooden exterior of the cabinet may burn somewhat, the papers will not be charred so quickly as when they are in a steel cabinet. This is due to the fact that wood burns slowly and does not transmit heat, while steel, although it does not burn, is a conductor of heat, with the result that, under similar circumstances, papers would be charred more quickly in a steel cabinet."

48. Judging from this information alone, the principal advantage of wood over steel office equipment is
(A) in case of fire, papers will not be destroyed in a wooden cabinet
(B) wooden equipment is cheaper to replace
(C) steel does not resist fire as well as wood
(D) steel equipment is heavy and cannot be moved about very easily
(E) wood is a poor conductor of heat.

Questions 49 and 50 are to be answered solely on the basis of the information contained in the following quotation:

(Reading) "Forms are printed sheets of paper on which information is to be entered. While what is printed on the form is most important, the kind of paper used in making the form is also important. The kind of paper should be selected with regard to the use to which the form will be subjected. Printing a form on an unnecessarily expensive grade of paper is wasteful. On the other hand, using too cheap or flimsy a form can materially interfere with satisfactory performance of the work the form is being planned to do. Thus a form printed on both sides normally requires a heavier paper than a form printed only on one side. Forms to be used as permanent records, or which are expected to have a very long life in files, require a quality of paper which will not disintegrate or discolor with age. A form which will go through a great deal of handling requires a strong tough paper, while thinness is a necessary qualification where the making of several carbon copies of a form will be required."

49. According to this quotation, the type of paper used for making forms
(A) should be chosen in accordance with the use to which the form will be put
(B) should be chosen before the type of printing to be used has been decided upon
(C) is as important as the information which is printed on it

(D) should be strong enough to be used for any purpose.

50. According to this quotation, forms that are
   (A) printed on both sides are usually economical and desirable.
   (B) to be filed permanently should not deteriorate as time goes on
   (C) expected to last for a long time should be handled carefully
   (D) to be filed should not be printed on inexpensive paper.

Questions 51 to 53 are to be answered solely on the information contained in the following quotation:

(Reading) "The equipment in a mail room may include a mail metering machine. This machine simultaneously stamps, postmarks, seals, and counts letters as fast as the operator can feed them. It can also print the proper postage directly on a gummed strip to be affixed to bulky items. It is equipped with a meter which is removed from the machine and sent to the post office to be set for a given number of stampings of any denomination. The setting of the meter must be paid for in advance. One of the advantages of metered mail is that it by-passes the cancellation operation and thereby facilitates handling by the post office. Mail metering also makes the pilfering of stamps impossible, but does not prevent the passage of personal mail in company envelopes through the meters unless there is established a rigid control or censorship over outgoing mail."

51. According to this quotation, the post office
   (A) is responsible for training new clerks in the use of mail metering machines
   (B) usually recommends that both large and small firms adopt the use of mail metering machines
   (C) is responsible for setting the meter to print a fixed number of stampings
   (D) examines the mail metering machines to see that they are properly installed in the mail room.

52. According to this quotation, the use of mail metering machines
   (A) requires the employment of more clerks in a mail room than does the use of postage stamps
   (B) interferes with the handling of large quantities of outgoing mail
   (C) does not prevent employees from sending their personal letters at company expense
   (D) usually involves smaller expenditures for mail room equipment than does the use of postage stamps.

53. On the basis of this quotation, it is most accurate to state that
   (A) mail metering machines are often used for opening envelopes
   (B) postage stamps are generally used when bulky packages are to be mailed
   (C) the use of metered mail tends to interfere with rapid mail handling by the post office
   (D) mail metering machines can seal and count letters at the same time.

SOME QUESTIONS ON SCIENCE AND MECHANICS

(Reading) "During the last century and a half the economic life of the western world has been transformed by a series of remarkable inventions and the general application of science to the productive process. A revolution, more profound in its effects than any armed revolt that ever shook the foundations of a political state, has been achieved in the three realms of manufacture, agriculture, and communication."

54. The paragraph notes that science
   (A) has revolutionized the productive process
   (B) has shaken the foundations of manufacturing, agriculture and communication
   (C) is the tool of the inventor
   (D) has been an important factor in the founding of the agricultural process
   (E) is becoming more and more the determining factor in modern civilization.

(Reading) "The judgments of science are distinguished from the judgments of opinion by being more impartial, more objective, more precise, more subject to verification by any competent observer, and by being made by those who by their nature and training should be better judges."

55. Which of the following does the quotation note is a distinguishing feature of the judgments of science?

(A) they can be verified by all observers
(B) they can be tested by advanced laboratory methods
(C) no opinion is accepted until validated
(D) no truth is accepted a priori
(E) they are usually propounded by experts in their fields.

(Reading) "A scientific law is related to the perceptions and conceptions formed by the perceptive and reasoning faculties in man; it is meaningless except in its associations with these; it is the resume or brief expression of the relationships and sequences of certain groups of these perceptions and conceptions, and exists only when formulated by man."

56. An assumption that is most in accord with this paragraph is that a scientific law
(A) may have meaning apart from the human mind if it is a summation of related scientific facts
(B) is essentially a product of the human mind
(C) may be related to man's reasoning faculties and yet not be based on experience
(D) is as variable as the human mind
(E) may exist without the human mind, but has no meaning until perceived.

(Reading) "We find many instances in early science of the use of the 'a priori' method of scientific investigation. Scientists thought it proper to carry over the generalizations from one field to another. It was assumed that the planets revolved in circles on account of the geometrical simplicity of the circle. Even Newton assumed that there must be seven primary colors corresponding to the seven tones of the musical scale."

57. According to the paragraph one might best conclude that
(A) Newton sometimes used the 'a priori' method of investigation
(B) scientists no longer consider it proper to carry over generalizations from one field to another
(C) the planets revolve about the earth in ellipses rather than in circles
(D) even great men like Newton sometimes make mistakes
(E) the number of notes in the musical scale has no connection with the number of primary colors.

(Reading) "Knowledge of the composition of food materials has been greatly enlarged as the result of the determination of fuel value per unit weight, the discovery of vitamins and an approach to their quantitative estimation and detailed analytical studies of individual constituents."

58. The one of the following statements which best characterizes the above quotation is
(A) the composition of food materials has been greatly enlarged
(B) food value per unit weight has added greatly to our knowledge of vitamins
(C) quantitative estimation of fuel value in individual foods has added to our knowledge of their individual constituents
(D) investigation into the composition of food materials has been aided by detailed analytical studies of their individual constituents
(E) the determination of the unit weight in individual foods has increased our knowledge of the nature of their fuel contents.

(Reading) "Formerly it was thought that whole wheat and graham breads were far superior to white bread made from highly refined wheat flour. However, it is now believed that the general use of milk solids in white bread has significantly narrowed the nutritional gap between the two types of bread. About the only dietary advantages that can now be claimed for whole wheat bread are its higher content of iron and of vitamin B, both of which are also easily obtainable from many other common foods."

59. The paragraph notes that
(A) white bread is fattening because of its milk content
(B) whole wheat bread is not much more nutritious than white bread
(C) whole wheat bread contains roughage
(D) white bread has the dietary disadvantage that it contains neither iron nor vitamin B
(E) contrary to popular misconception, white bread is not inferior in quality to bread made from graham or whole wheat flour.

(Reading) "The view is widely held that butter is more digestible and better absorbed than other fats because of its low melting point. There is little scientific authority for such a view. As margarine is made today, its melting point is close to that of butter, and tests show only the slightest degree of difference in digestibility of fats of equally low melting points."

60. According to the paragraph one could most reasonably conclude that

(A) butter is more easily digested than margarine
(B) the concept that butter has a lower melting point than other fats is a common misconception, disproved by scientists
(C) there is not much difference in the digestibility of butter and margarine
(D) most people prefer butter to margarine
(E) it sometimes becomes necessary to use a substitute for butter.

(Reading) "More produce is artificially ripened by treatment with ethylene gas, which makes possible shipment in 'the firm green condition,' and the sale of fruit and vegetables before they would naturally be in season. This method of ripening is prohibited only when it is applied to oranges so unripe as to contain less than 8 parts of sugar to 1 of acid."

61. It can be reasonably concluded from the preceding paragraph that
(A) artificial ripening is not harmful unless applied to oranges containing less than 8 parts of sugar to 1 of acid
(B) fruits and vegetables are usually shipped in the firm green condition
(C) oranges are ripe when they contain more than 8 parts of sugar to 1 of acid
(D) the law does not prohibit the use of ethylene ripening in most cases
(E) it is dangerous to eat fruit and vegetables out of season, since they are often artificially ripened.

(Reading) "Salt has always been important in our diet as a flavoring for food, but it is only recently that doctors have come to recognize it as an absolute necessity. Most living things contain salt and it is almost impossible to eat a normal diet without getting some. However, that 'some' may not be enough, and now doctors recommend that those who normally use little salt step up their salt consumption in hot weather, when more than the usual salt intake is required by the body."

62. According to the preceding paragraph one could assume most correctly that
(A) salt is necessary if life is to be maintained
(B) people living on a normal diet have an intake of salt which is sufficient to maintain good health
(C) salt is more essential to the body in summer than in winter
(D) all organic life contains salt in one form or another
(E) up to very recently, the most important function of salt has been its use in the flavoring of foods.

(Reading) "In a general way, the size and form of the brain is determined by the size and form of the cranial cavity. Some skulls are relatively long and narrow, others short and broad, and these variations correspond to general variations in the shape of the brain. But conformation of the skull, as seen from the outside is not an accurate indication of the conformation of the brain within."

63. The paragraph notes that
(A) intelligence in humans is, in a general way, correlated with the volume of the cranial cavity
(B) the size and form of the external skull is not an accurate indication of the conformation of the cranial cavity
(C) as we go up the rungs of the ladder of evolution, we note a gradual increase in the size of the brain
(D) there is no connection between the size of the skull and the size of the brain
(E) the size and form of the brain is an inherited trait, just as is the conformation of the cranial cavity.

(Reading) "Whether or not the nerve impulses in various nerve fibers differ in kind is a question of great interest in physiology. The usually accepted view is that they are identical in character in all fibers and vary only in intensity"

64. Judging from the information contained in the foregoing paragraph it could be most correctly assumed that
(A) nerve fibers are the product of neural impulses
(B) nerve fibers are usually accepted as differing in kind
(C) the nature of neural impulses is still a moot question
(D) the student of physiology accepts the view that nerve impulses sometimes differ in intensity
(E) the character of nerve fibers is accepted as being constant.

(Reading) "For the most part, in humid climates, a thick growth of vegetation protects the moist soil from the wind with a cover of leaves and stems and a mattress of interlacing roots. But in arid regions either vegetation is wholly lacking, or scant growths are found huddled in detached clumps, leaving inter-space of unprotected ground.

Little or no moisture is present to cause the particles to cohere, and they are therefore readily lifted and drifted by the wind."

65. According to the quotation
    (A) vegetation is always present in humid climates
    (B) lack of moisture decreases cohesion of earth particles in arid regions
    (C) moisture is an important element in soil and rock erosion
    (D) the wind is the chief agent in the dispersal of the top-soil layer
    (E) tree roots are closely associated with the thick growth of vegetation in moist climates.

(Reading) "A hurricane acts as a syphon on a grand scale, drawing water and air to its center. It raises water in the same way that liquid rises in a straw used in sipping a drink. It is not just the central core of the hurricane that produces this effect, but the whole hurricane area, more than 100 miles in diameter. The hurricane is a low-pressure area and the pressure gets lower as the center is approached. The lower the pressure gets the higher it raises the level of the ocean."

66. The above paragraph intimates that
    (A) hurricanes can be controlled
    (B) all low-pressure areas result in hurricanes for that area
    (C) the pressure is inversely proportional to the height the water level of the ocean rises
    (D) hurricanes are comparatively few in this section of the country
    (E) the physical principles governing a hurricane are not adequately known.

(Reading) "Certain occult chemical changes, such as fermentation, have been somewhat lately found to be due to the action of innumerable living micro-organisms, known under the general name of bacteria; and the decomposition of sewage has been recently discovered to result from a similar cause."

67. According to the preceding paragraph certain occult chemical changes are due to
    (A) oxidation
    (B) fermentation
    (C) decomposition
    (D) bacteria
    (E) sewage

(Reading) "The dangers of the ancient triple menace of the operating room—shock, hemorrhage and infection—have been virtually eliminated. Transfusion of blood is employed to combat shock and hemorrhage. It also is used to build up a patient so weakened by disease that operation otherwise would be impossible."

68. The principle idea expressed in the preceding paragraph is
    (A) asepsis has removed the danger from infection
    (B) operations are no longer as dangerous as formerly
    (C) a blood transfusion usually precedes a serious operation
    (D) operating technique has greatly improved due to the rise in standards of medical schools
    (E) hemorrhages are very rare.

(Reading) "The indiscriminate or continual use of any drug, without the supervision of a capable physician, is very dangerous. Even those drugs not usually considered harmful, if taken for a period of years, may result in a form of chronic poisoning. One should not have a prescription refilled unless the physician prescribes a given amount because he wishes use of a drug to be discontinued after a certain time. One should never use the prescription which a physician has prescribed for another patient because although the symptoms may seem to be the same, there may be differences apparent to the expert, but which the layman does not see, and which imply an entirely different ailment and different medication."

69. The paragraph notes that
    (A) the use of drugs is very dangerous
    (B) if a physician prescribes a drug, it is safe to refill the prescription
    (C) the people with similar symptoms are usually suffering from the same ailment
    (D) a drug which is not harmful when taken for a limited time, may be dangerous when taken over a longer period of time
    (E) a good physician will never prescribe a dangerous drug.

(Reading) "The rates of vibration that can be perceived by the ear as musical tones lies between fairly well-defined limits, although in this organ, as in the case of the eye, there are individual variations, which are more marked in the case of the ear, since its range of appreciation is larger."

70. The quotation points out that the ear
    (A) is limited in its sense for vibration by the nature of its variations
    (B) is the most sensitive of the auditory organs
    (C) differs from the visual sense in its broader range of appreciation
    (D) is sensitive to a great range of musical tones
    (E) depends for its sense on the rate of vibration of a limited range of sound waves.

(Reading) "It is probably safe to assume that the majority of individuals reach the limits set by nature to mental growth, somewhere between the ages of fourteen and a half and sixteen years. From this time on they cease to show increased capacity to meet those novel situations which, for their solution, make demands on native ability rather than mere experience. Growth in intellectual effectiveness after 16 is ascribed to wider experience and more information, rather than an increase in general mental capacity."

71. According to the import of the preceding paragraph, one can assume with greater accuracy that the majority of individuals between the ages of fourteen and a half and sixteen years
    (A) make demands on mere experience rather than on native ability
    (B) are still in the adolescent state
    (C) show an increase rather than a decrease in general mental capacity
    (D) reach the capacity of their mental growth as set by nature
    (E) cease to show increased capacity to meet novel situations.

Correct Answers For The Foregoing Questions

(Please make every effort to answer the questions on your own before looking at these answers. You'll make faster progress by following this rule.)

1. C	10. D	19. E	28. B	37. D	46. D	55. E	64. C
2. A	11. D	20. D	29. D	38. D	47. D	56. B	65. B
3. E	12. B	21. D	30. C	39. D	48. E	57. A	66. C
4. D	13. B	22. C	31. B	40. B	49. A	58. D	67. D
5. C	14. C	23. A	32. A	41. C	50. B	59. B	68. B
6. C	15. A	24. B	33. D	42. D	51. C	60. C	69. D
7. B	16. B	25. B	34. D	43. C	52. C	61. D	70. C
8. B	17. C	26. E	35. C	44. B	53. D	62. C	71. D
9. E	18. E	27. B	36. B	45. D	54. A	63. B	

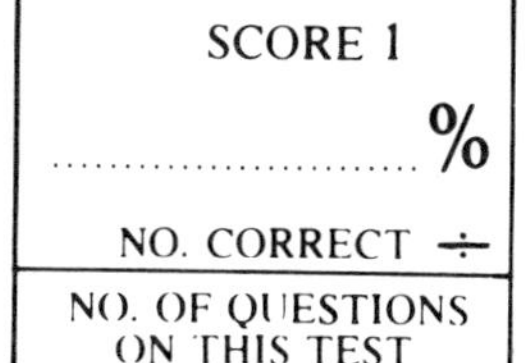

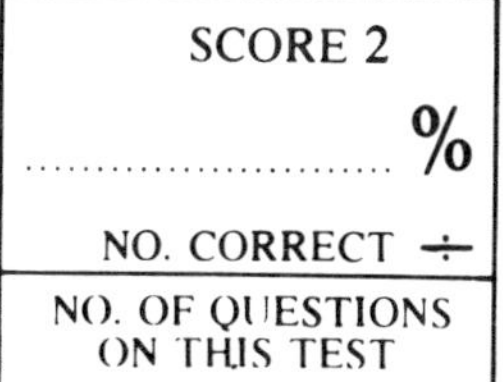

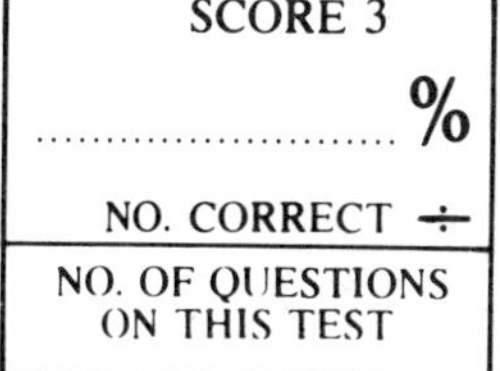

Practice Using Answer Sheets

Alter numbers to match the practice and drill questions in each part of the book.
Make only ONE mark for each answer. Additional and stray marks may be counted as mistakes.
In making corrections, erase errors COMPLETELY. Make glossy black marks.

1 A B C D E	1 A B C D E	1 A B C D E	1 A B C D E	1 A B C D E
2 A B C D E	2 A B C D E	2 A B C D E	2 A B C D E	2 A B C D E
3 A B C D E	3 A B C D E	3 A B C D E	3 A B C D E	3 A B C D E
4 A B C D E	4 A B C D E	4 A B C D E	4 A B C D E	4 A B C D E
5 A B C D E	5 A B C D E	5 A B C D E	5 A B C D E	5 A B C D E
6 A B C D E	6 A B C D E	6 A B C D E	6 A B C D E	6 A B C D E
7 A B C D E	7 A B C D E	7 A B C D E	7 A B C D E	7 A B C D E
8 A B C D E	8 A B C D E	8 A B C D E	8 A B C D E	8 A B C D E
9 A B C D E	9 A B C D E	9 A B C D E	9 A B C D E	9 A B C D E
0 A B C D E	0 A B C D E	0 A B C D E	0 A B C D E	0 A B C D E

1 A B C D E	1 A B C D E	1 A B C D E	1 A B C D E	1 A B C D E
2 A B C D E	2 A B C D E	2 A B C D E	2 A B C D E	2 A B C D E
3 A B C D E	3 A B C D E	3 A B C D E	3 A B C D E	3 A B C D E
4 A B C D E	4 A B C D E	4 A B C D E	4 A B C D E	4 A B C D E
5 A B C D E	5 A B C D E	5 A B C D E	5 A B C D E	5 A B C D E
6 A B C D E	6 A B C D E	6 A B C D E	6 A B C D E	6 A B C D E
7 A B C D E	7 A B C D E	7 A B C D E	7 A B C D E	7 A B C D E
8 A B C D E	8 A B C D E	8 A B C D E	8 A B C D E	8 A B C D E
9 A B C D E	9 A B C D E	9 A B C D E	9 A B C D E	9 A B C D E
0 A B C D E	0 A B C D E	0 A B C D E	0 A B C D E	0 A B C D E

1 A B C D E	7 A B C D E	13 A B C D E	19 A B C D E	25 A B C D E
2 A B C D E	8 A B C D E	14 A B C D E	20 A B C D E	26 A B C D E
3 A B C D E	9 A B C D E	15 A B C D E	21 A B C D E	27 A B C D E
4 A B C D E	10 A B C D E	16 A B C D E	22 A B C D E	28 A B C D E
5 A B C D E	11 A B C D E	17 A B C D E	23 A B C D E	29 A B C D E
6 A B C D E	12 A B C D E	18 A B C D E	24 A B C D E	30 A B C D E

TEAR OUT ALONG THIS LINE AND MARK YOUR ANSWERS AS INSTRUCTED IN THE TEXT

AN ARTIFICIAL LANGUAGE

The language you are about to study was created ex nihilo, *out of nothing. It has no past and will have no future except as the principles upon which it is based are common to all languages, living or dead.*

The material on the following pages is planned to help you prepare for the Language Aptitude portion of your test.

The study material and practice exercises are based on the construction of an artificial language. Go over these lessons carefully, and then, when you face the actual examination, the exact syllables you are confronted with may be unfamiliar, but you will have had practice in the same principles of language formation.

Don't try all this section at one sitting. If possible, take one exercise daily. Keep in mind that you do not have to memorize the new vocabulary, that you can refer to it as often as necessary. The test is designed to test your knowledge of general language construction and grammatical principles.

ARTIFICIAL LANGUAGE RULES

There are the following parts of speech: Noun, Pronoun, Adjective, Verb, Participle, Adverb, Preposition, Conjunction, Interjection. Their uses are the same as in English.

There are no articles.

The grammatical distinctions are: Number, Gender, Case, Person, Degree, Tense, Mood, Voice.

These distinctions are marked by adding a sound or syllable at the beginning or end of the simple root-form. EXAMPLE—The one word PULOGOMS stands for five words, *they will have been seen.* They is indicated by the ending OMS; will have been by the syllable PU at the beginning; LOG is the root, meaning, as a verb, to see. PU and OMS may be analyzed thus: *u* as a verb-prefix indicates the future-perfect; *p* is the sign of the passive voice. In OMS, *s* denotes the plural, *m* denotes the masculine third person, *o* is characteristic of all person endings and unites them to the verb.

When no such distinctive syllables are added it is understood that the number is singular, gender masculine, nominative case, third person, positive degree, present tense, indicative mood, active voice.

Nouns have number, gender and case.

Pronouns have number, gender, case and person.

Verbs have number, gender, case and person.

Adjectives and adverbs have degree. Adjectives may also have the inflection of the noun.

NUMBER AND NUMBERS

The simple form is the singular number.

The plural always ends in *s*.

Man, a man. Plural, Mans, *Vom,* a woman, *Voms,* women. *Ob,* I, *Obs,* we. *Ol,* you (singular), *Ols,* you (plural).

Numerals are always placed after the things numbered. *Man bal,* one man; *Mans Tel,* two men; *Voms kil,* three women.

The first nine numerals end in l, and are as follows:

1........bal	4........fol	7........vel
2........tel	5........lul	8........jol
3........kil	6........mal	9........zul

The tens are formed by adding s

10........bals	40........fols	70........vels
20........tels	50........luls	80........jols
30........kils	60........mals	90........zuls

Numbers composed of tens and units unite the two parts by "e". For example: *balsebal,* 11; *balsetel,* 12; *telsebal,* 21; *lulsevel,* 57; *zulsezul,* 99.

Tum, hundred; *mil,* thousand; *balion;* million; these are preceded by one of the digits. Example:—*baltum,* 100; *teltum,* 200; *kilmil,* 3000; *folmil foltum,* 4400; *lulmil lultum lulselul,* 5555.

FIRST EXERCISE AND VOCABULARY

BUK ....book	JIP ....sheep
DEL ....day	MAN ......man
DOAB ....dollar	MUG ......mouse
DOG ....dog	MUL ....month
DOM ......house	PUL ....boy
E ....and	VIG ....week
GAN ....goose	YEL ....year

Questions

1. Put all of the above nouns into the plural, giving the English meaning of each.
2. Express in the artificial language: books, days, men, houses, mice, months, geese, boys, weeks, dollars.
3. Would you use *ol* or *ols* in the following sentences:

   "Are you an American?"
   "Will you take your seats?"
4. Give the translation of the following numbers: 2, 5, 33, 42, 3, 41, 6, 25, 50, 75, 100, 7, 77, 777, 7777, 8, 18, 6, 99, 15, 13, 64, 51, 84, 77, 333, 1887, 12.
5. Express: 5 men; 3 boys; 12 years; $20; 10 years; 3 months; 6 mice; $50; 16 houses; 3,000 books; 100 sheep; 55 boys; 32 years and ten months; 7 days; one week; 30 days; one month; 365 days; 12 months; 52 weeks; one year; $2,769.
6. Give the English for the following:

MANS BALS ____________

GAN BAL ____________

OBS ____________

MULS KIL ____________

DOMS FOL ____________

YELS BALTUM ____________

JIPS TEL ____________

MUGS ZUL ____________

DOABS BALSETEL ____________

BUKS TELTUM ____________

MULS BALSETEL ____________

YEL BAL ____________

OLS ____________

OBS TEL ____________

CASES

The case endings are the first three vowels. For example:

Kim .... who?
Kima .... whose?
Kime .... to whom?
Kimi .... whom?

The names of the cases are: Kimfal, Kimafal, Kimifal, taken from the word "kim" with the word "fal" meaning case.

EXERCISE TWO AND VOCABULARY

GIVOM	gives	**LOGOM**	sees
BLINOM	brings	LABOM	has
NAM	hand	FUT	foot
DUP	hour	MON	money
O	Interjection used in addressing a person.	FAT	father
		LOG	eye

TRANSLATE INTO ENGLISH: Man labom dogi. Man labom dogis tel. Pul labom dogis tel e jipi bal. Dog logum gani. Pul logom dogi. Man givom dogi pule. Pul givom gani mane. Man givom doabis kil pule. Man labom futis tel e namis tel. Dog mana labom futis fol. Fat mana givom doabis fol pule. O fat! man givom doab bal pule. Kim blinom dogis mane? Pul blinom dogis mane. Kim labom moni? Fat labom moni.

Answer in the artificial language the following questions: Kim labom dogi? Kim logom gani? Kim givom dogi pule? Kime pul blinom dogis ?

Caution—In translating into this language do not overlook the difference between the subject and the object of the sentence. Put the subject in the kimfal and the object in the Kimifal. In the above exercises there is one error in this respect, purposely left uncorrected. Did you notice it?

Translate the following sentences from English.

Who has the dog? The boy has two dogs. The man has three dogs. The dog has four feet. The man gives money. The man gives money to the boy. The boy's father gives a dollar to the man. The year has twelve months. The month has thirty days. The week has seven days. The day has 24 hours. Who brings the goose? Who sees the dog? Who sees the two sheep? To whom does the man give money? To whom does the boy bring money. The boy brings five dollars to the father.

PERSONS

The pronoun of the first person is *ob,* I; plural *obs,* we.

When the verb is in the first person the pronoun is united with it as a person ending, forming one word. *Binob,* I am; *pukob,* I speak; *komobs,* we come; *golobs,* we go.

The pronoun of the second person is ol (you sing., or ols, you, plural).

These syllables *ol* and *ols* are likewise suffixed to the verb, forming one word. *Binol* You (sing.) are; *Golols,* you (pl.) are going.

In the third person, there are four pronouns: *om* for masculine and neuters; *of* for feminines; *os,* impersonal or abstract; *on,* collective.

These pronouns are also affixed to the verb, *binom,* he is or it is. Examples: *Pukof,* she speaks; *golofs* they (women) go; *nifros,* it shows; *sagon,* they say.

Even when the subject of a verb is a noun the *om* or *of* must be added: *of* for a feminine subject, *om* for others.

For example, the conjugation of a verb:

Singular	Plural
binob, I am	*binobs,* we are
binol, you are	*binols,* you are
binom, he is, it is	*binoms,* they are
binof, she is	*binofs,* they are
binos, it is	
binon, one is	

EXERCISE THREE AND VOCABULARY

Buk, book	*Komob,* I come	*Golob,* I go
Lilob, I hear	*Binob,* I am	*Pukob,* I speak

Translate into English: Binob. Givob. Blinob. Pukob. Golob. Komob. Labob buki. Givobs moni. Labobs bukis tel. Givob moni mane. Blinobs bukis pula.

Translate from English: I speak. I go. I have the goose. We have the books. I have five books. We give money to the man. I bring the books. I bring the boys' books. I bring books to the boys. We give books to the boys.

EXERCISE FOUR

Translate into English: Labol buki. Pukol. Golol. Labols fati. Blinol buki obe. Blinob bukis ole. Givols moni pules. Pukobs e lilols.

Translate from English: You have the book. You have books. You speak and we hear. You see the man. We come and you go. You come and I go. You have books. You give books to the boys. You speak to me. I give money to you. You give money to me. He comes. She goes. He gives money to the man. She has the book. He brings a dog to the boy. She speaks. He sees the man and the boy. He gives me money.

EXERCISE FIVE AND VOCABULARY

Tid, instruction	*Selob,* I sell	*Bod,* bread
Tidob, I teach	*Lamob,* I buy	*Mit,* meat
Fidob, I eat	*Tedel,* merchant	*Yeb,* grass
Dlinob, I drink	*Vin,* wine	*Vom,* woman
Liladob, I read	*Vat,* water	*Kis,* what?
	Mot, mother	*Kat,* cat

Translate into English: Tidom. Kim tidom? Man tidom. Selom buke. Kim selom bukis? Ob selob bukis. Givom moni. Kim givom mòni? Fat givom moni. Man tidom puli. Tedel selom bukis. Man dlinom vati. Vom dlinof vini. Kat fidom mugi. Pul fidom bodi.

Kisi givom pule? Givom moni e bodi pule. Kisi blinof mane. Blinof vati. Kisi vom fidof. Fidof bodi e dlinof vati. Kisi man fidom? Fidom bodi e dlinom vini. Jip fidom yebi.

Supply the proper endings in the following sentences:

Man dlin ____________ vin ________________

Vom dlin __________ vat __________________

Fat pul_____ giv _____ mon ____ vom _______

Mot blin________ bod _______ pul ___________

Translate from English: He comes. Who comes? The man comes. He eats bread. He gives a dollar. Who gives a dollar? The father gives a dollar. The man has a dog. The boy buys a book. The father drinks wine. The mother drinks water. The dog sees the cat. The boy eats bread. What does he eat? He eats bread. Who eats bread? What does she give to the boy? She gives the boy money. What does the woman eat? She eats bread and meat. The dog sees three sheep.

I eat meat, you eat bread; he drinks water, she drinks wine. We have books. You (pl.) have eyes. They have ears.

EXERCISE SIX AND VOCABULARY

Penob, I write
Pened, a letter (correspondence)
Tonab, letter (of alphabet)

Translate into English: Tidoms. Kims tidoms? Mans tidoms. Seloms bukis. Tedels seloms bukis pules. Laboms moni. Kims laboms moni? Tedels laboms moni. Mans fidoms bedi e miti. Voms dlinofs vini e vati. Man penom penedi. Tedels penoms penedis. Puls penoms tonabis. Voms penofs penedis manes.

Translate from English: The dogs see the sheep. The sheep see the dog. The sheep sees the dog. The men write letters. The boys see the letters (a, b). The women drink water. The men drink wine. The sheep eats grass.

EXERCISE SEVEN AND VOCABULARY

Nim, animal	*Nif,* snow	*Tot,* thunder
Julel, scholar	*Das,* that	*Dil,* part
Dlin, a drink	*Fid,* food	*Sag,* Say

Translate into English: Man binom tedel. Vig binom dels vel. Del binom dil viga. Dup binom dil dela. Mul binom dil yela. Vat e vin binoms dlins. Nifos. Totos. Logon nimis. Dlinom vati. Fidons bodi. Liladon bukis.

Translate from English: The boy is a scholar. Dogs and sheep are animals. The day is a part of the year. Bread is food. Wine is a drink. Water is a drink. I am a merchant. You are a scholar. You are scholars. It thunders. One eats meat. It snows. They say that you are a scholar.

Supply the proper endings:

Dog fid ______bod ______________

Dogs e jips bin______nim __________

Sagon das tot ________________

Logon das nif ________________

RULES FOR GENDERS

Om, he (it) *Of,* she *Os,* it *ji,* female

All nouns are considered as masculine unless expressly denoting females. Thus, *of* is used for female persons or animals; *om* is used for males, and, for living things whose sex is disregarded, and for lifeless things (it). *Os* is used as "it," speaking abstractly, where no noun is referred to, as "It is fair weather."

Words, if relating to men, are masculine without any prefix; if relating to animals, the unprefixed word is common gender. The name of the male animal has the prefix *om;* the name of the female, the prefix *ji.*

For example:

Omjeval, stallion *Jeval,* horse *Jijeval,* mare.

EXERCISE EIGHT AND VOCABUULARY

Flen, friend	*Sanel,* physician
Lautel, author	*Matel,* husband
Nelijel, Englishman	*Jeval,* horse
Vomul, Miss	*Viudel,* widower
Tidel, teacher	*Blod,* brother
Lanel, angel	*Maria,* Mary

Translate: Lady-friend. Doctor's wife. Widow. Authoress. Miss Mary is an angel. Doctress. Mare. Sister. Englishwoman. Wife.

FORMATION OF ADJECTIVES

The ordinal numerals, first, second, third, etc., end in *id.* First, *balid;* second, *telid;* tenth, *balsid;* eleventh, *balsebalid;* 377th, *kiltumvelsevelid.* There is also an interrogative form, *kimid?,* meaning "which or how man-many-th". Example: *"Del kimid mula binom?"* What day of the month is it?

EXERCISE NINE AND VOCABULARY

Balul, January *Telul,* February

In the same manner form the months to

Zulzul, September	*Batul,* December
Balsul, October	*Baludel,* Sunday
Babul, November	*Teludel,* Monday, etc.

Exercises for Translation:

Balul binom mul balid. Velul binom mul velid. Kiludel binom del kilid velid viga. Batul binom mul balsetelid yela. Dup kilid. Dup kimid binom? Binom dup balsid.

Saturday is the seventh day of the week. November is the eleventh month. It is four o'clock.

RULES FOR POSSESSIVE PRONOUNS

The possessives may be rendered in two ways.

1. By the kimafal of the pronoun; *fat oba,* my father; *fat obas,* our father.

2. By the suffix—*ik* forming a possessive adjective; *buk obik,* my book; *buks omsik,* their books; *buk at binom olik;* this book is yours.

EXERCISE TEN AND VOCABULARY

Nelijapuk,	English language
Nelijel,	Englishman
Flentapuk,	French language
Flentel,	Frenchman
Sikod,	therefore
Son,	son
Cil,	child
Lofob,	I love

Tidel obik tidom pulis lul. Kim binom tidel ola? Tidel obsik labom julelis telsefol. Puk obas binom nelijapuk. Fat obik labom sonis kil e jisonis tel; sikid, labob blodis tel e jiblodis tel. Binobs cils lul. Fat obsik lofom cilis omik. Mot obsik lofof cilis ofa. Fat e mot obsik lofoms cilis omsik.

My teacher reads a book. Your father has four dogs. Who is your (pl.) teacher? Our teacher is a Frenchman. Our father and mother love their children. Who is our father? Our father is the husband of our mother. Your father and my mother are friends. My teacher's language is French. Your teacher reads my books.

RULES FOR DEMONSTRATIVES

The demonstrative pronouns, which are used as adjectives, and also by themselves are the following:

at, et, it, ot, ut, som

Examples:

At, this; *man at,* this man.
Et, that; *pul et,* that boy.
It, self; *man it,* the man himself. *Ob it;* I myself.
Ot, same; *tidel ot;* the same teacher.
Ut, that (one who); *man ut,* the man who.
Som, such. *vom som,* such a woman.

EXERCISE ELEVEN AND VOCABULARY

Laned, country (not city)
Dom, house
Sevob, know, be acquainted with
Zif, town
Lodob, I live, dwell
Lan, country (nations, etc.)
Lodop, dwelling
Ab, but
No, not or no.
Men, human being, person
In, in (followed by kimfal)

Translation exercise:

Dom at binom lodop obsik. Man et labom cilis kil; sevob cilis ab no mani it. Zif at labom domis tum e menis veltum. Mans, voms e cils binoms mens. Sevol tideli e tedeli e ob sevob manis ot. Man ut kel lodom in dom et binom lautel e penom bukis.

This country is mine. I live in that house. The men who live in that town know us. We live in the same town. These animals are horses.

RELATIVE PRONOUN

The relative pronoun is *kel,* who, which, what. It has the force of a conjunction and a pronoun. It is used independently or as an adjective.

INTERROGATIVE PRONOUN

The interrogative pronoun is *kim? kif? kis?* when used independently and *kiom? kiof?* and *kios?* when used as an adjective.

ADJECTIVES END IN "IK"

Adjectives are formed from nouns by adding the suffix "*ik.*" Examples, *Gud,* goodness; *gudik,* good. *Lof,* love; *lofik,* dear, *loflik,* lovely. *Yel,* year; *yelik,* pertaining to the year; *yelsik,* yearly.

EXERCISE TWELVE AND VOCABULARY

Sevob, I know	*Din,* thing
Lad, lady	*Lautob,* compose (a book).

Translate: **Sevob mani kel penom bukis ats. Man keli sevob penom bukis ats. Kim penom bukis? Lautel. Kis binom lautel? Lautel binom man ut kel lautom bukis. Kif binof lad at kel labof dogi? Lad at binof jisanel B——; matel ofa binom sanel obsik.**

I see the man who gives money to the boys. Who knows the author of this book? The doctor's wife knows the man who is the author of the book. What is a merchant? A merchant is a man who buys and sells things. Who is that woman? That woman is a teacher who teaches boys and girls.

ARTIFICIAL LANGUAGE ANSWERS

EXERCISE ONE

1. **Buks, Dels. Doabs. Dogs. Doms. Gans. Jips. Mans. Mugs. Muls. Puls. Vigs. Yels.**

2. Buks, dels, mans, doms, mugs, muls, gans, puls, vigs, doabs.

3. Ol in first sentence; ols in second.

4. **Tel, lul, kilsekol, folsetel, kil, folsebal, mal, telselul, luls, velselul, baltum, vel, velsevel, veltum velsevel, velmil veltum velsevel, jol, balsejol, mal, zulsezul, balselul, balsekil, malsefol, lulsebal, jolsefol, velsevel, kiltum kilsekil, balmil joltum jolsevel, balsetel.**

5. Mans lul; puls kil; yels balsetel; doabs tels; yels bals; muls kil; mugs mal; doabs luls; doms balsemal; buks kilmil; jips baltum; puls lulselul; yels kilsetel e muls bals; dels vel; vig bal; dels kils; mul bal; dels kiltum malselul, muls balsetel, vigs lulsetel, yel bal; doabs telmil veltum malsezul.

6. 10 men; one goose; we; three months; four houses; 100 years; two sheep; nine mice; twelve dollars; 200 books; twelve months; you; we two.

EXERCISE TWO

The man has a dog. The man has two dogs. The boy has two dogs and one sheep. The dog sees the goose. The boy sees the dog. The man gives the dog to the boy.

The boy gives the goose to the man. The man gives the boy three dollars. The man has two feet and two hands. The man's dog has four feet. The man's father gives four dollars to the boy. (the next sentence is incorrect;) *doab* should be *doabi*, then it will read "Father! The man gives one dollar to the boy." Who brings the dogs to the man? The boy brings the dogs to the man. Who has money? The father has money.

Pul labom dogi, (or) Man labom dogi.
Dog logom gani.
Man givom dogi pule.
Pul blinom dogis mane.

Kim labom dogi? Pul labom dogis tel. Man labom dogis kil. Dog labom futis fol. Kim labom namis tel? Man givom moni. Man givom moni pule. Fat pula givom doabi mane. Yel labom mulis balsetel. Mul labom delis kils. Vig labom delis vel. Del labom dupis telsefol. Kim blinom gani: Kim logom dogi? Kim logom jipis tel? Kime man givom moni? Kime pul blinom moni. Pul blinom doabis lul fate.

EXERCISE THREE

I am. I give. I bring. I speak. I go. I come. I have a book. We give money. We have two books. I give money to the man. We bring the boy's books.

Pukob. Golob. Labob gani. Labobs bukis. Labob bukis lul. Givobs moni mane. Blinob bukis. Blinob bukis pulas. Blinob bukis pules. Givobs bukis pules.

EXERCISE FOUR

You have the book. You speak. You go. You have a father. You bring me a book. I bring you books. You give money to the boys. We speak and you hear.

Labol buki. Labols bukis. Pukols e lilobs. Logol mani. Komob e golols. Komol e golob. Lobol bukis. Givol bukis pules. Pukol obe. Givob moni ole. Givol moni obe.

Komon. Golof. Givom moni mane. Labof buki. Blinom dogi pule. Pukof. Logom mani e puli. Givom moni obe.

EXERCISE FIVE

He teaches. Who teaches? The man teaches. He sells books. Who sells books? I sell books. He gives money. Who gives money? The father gives money. The man teaches the boy. The merchant sells books. The man drinks water. The woman drinks wine. The cat eats the mouse. The boy eats bread.

What does he give the boy? He gives the boy money and bread. What does she bring to the man? She brings water. What does the woman eat? She eats bread and drinks water. What does the man eat? He eats bread and drinks wine. The sheep eats grass.

Man dlinom vini.
Vom dlinof vati.
Fat pula givom moni vome.
Mot blinof bodi pule.

Komom. Kim komom? Man komom. Fidom bodi. Givom doabi. Kim givom doabi? Fat givom doabi. Man labom dogi. Pul lamom buki. Fat dlinom vini. Mot dlinof vati. Dog logom kati. Pul fidom bodi. Kisi fidom? Fidom bodi. Kim fidom bodi? Kisi givof pule? Givof moni pule. Kisi vom fidof? Fidof bodi e miti. Dog logom jipis kil.

Fidob miti, fidol bodi; dlinom vati, dlinof vini. Labobs bukis. Labols logis. Laboms lilis.

EXERCISE SIX

They teach. Who teaches? The men teach. They sell books. The merchants sell books to the boys. They have money. Who has money? The merhants have money. The men eat bread and meat. The women drink wine and water. The man writes a letter. The merchants write letters. The boys write letters. The women write letters to the men.

Dogs logoms jipis. Jips logoms dogi. Jip logom dogi. Jip logom dogi. Mans penoms penedis. Puls logoms tonabis. Voms dlinofs vati. Mans dlinoms vini. Jip fidom yebi.

EXERCISE SEVEN

The man is a merchant. The week is seven days. The day is a part of the week. The hour is a part of the day. The month is a part of the year. Water and wine are drinks. It snows. It thunders. One sees animals. One drinks water. Bread is eaten. Books are read.

Pul binom julel. Dogs e jips binoms nims. Del binom dil yela. Bod binom fid. Vin binom dlin. Vat binom dlin. Binob tedel. Binol julel. Binols julels. Totos. Fidon miti. Nifos. Sagon das binol julel.

Dog fidom bodi. Dogs e jips binoms nims. Sagon das totos. Logon das nifos.

EXERCISE EIGHT

Jiflen. Jimatel sanela. Jiviudel. Jilautel. Vomul Maria binof jilanel. Jisanel. Jijeval. Jiblod. Jinelijel. Jimatel.

EXERCISE NINE

January is the first month. July is the seventh month. Tuesday is the third day of the week. December is the twelfth month of the year. Three o'clock. What (O'clock) time is it? It is ten o'clock.

Veludel binom del velid viga. Babul binom mul balsebalid. Binom dup folid.

EXERCISE TEN

My teacher teaches five boys. Who is your teacher? Our teacher has twenty-four scholars. Our language is English. My father has three sons and two daughters; so I have two brothers and two sisters. There are five of us children. Our father loves his children. Our mother loves her children. Our father and mother love their children.

Tidel obik liladom buki. Fat olik labom dogis fol. Kim binom tidel olsik? Tidel obsik binom flentel. Fat e mot obsik lofoms cifis omsik. Kim binom fat obsik? Fat obsik binom matel mota obsik. Fat olik e mot obik binoms flens. Puk tidal obik binom flentapuk. Tidel olik liladom bukis obik.

EXERCISE ELEVEN

This house is our home. That man has three children; I know the children, but not the man himself. This town has a hundred houses and seven hundred persons. Man, women and children are human beings. You know the teacher and the merchant and I know the same man. The man who lives in that house is an author and writes books.

Lan at binom obik. Lodob in dom et. Mans ut kels lodom in zif et sevoms obis. Lodobs in zif ot. Nims ats binoms jevals.

EXERCISE TWELVE

I know the man who writes these books. The man, whom I know, writes these books. Who writes books? The author. What is an author? An author is the man who writes books. Who is that lady who has the dog? That lady is doctoress B; her husband is our physician.

Logob mani ut kel givom moni pules. Kim sevom luateli buka at? Jimatel sanela sevof mani ut kel binom lautel buka. Kis binom tedel? Tedel binom man kel lamom e selom dinis. Kim binof vom et? Vom et binof jitidel kel tidof pulis e jipulis.

SCORE 1
.... %
NO. CORRECT
NO. OF QUESTIONS ON THIS TEST

SCORE 2
.... %
NO. CORRECT
NO. OF QUESTIONS ON THIS TEST

SCORE 3
.... %
NO. CORRECT
NO. OF QUESTIONS ON THIS TEST

SCORE 4
.... %
NO. CORRECT
NO. OF QUESTIONS ON THIS TEST

SCORE 5
.... %
NO. CORRECT
NO. OF QUESTIONS ON THIS TEST

Practice Using Answer Sheets

Alter numbers to match the practice and drill questions in each part of the book.
Make only ONE mark for each answer. Additional and stray marks may be counted as mistakes.
In making corrections, erase errors COMPLETELY. Make glossy black marks.

TEAR OUT ALONG THIS LINE AND MARK YOUR ANSWERS AS INSTRUCTED IN THE TEXT

1 A B C D E
2 A B C D E
3 A B C D E
4 A B C D E
5 A B C D E
6 A B C D E
7 A B C D E
8 A B C D E
9 A B C D E
0 A B C D E

1 A B C D E
2 A B C D E
3 A B C D E
4 A B C D E
5 A B C D E
6 A B C D E
7 A B C D E
8 A B C D E
9 A B C D E
0 A B C D E

1 A B C D E
2 A B C D E
3 A B C D E
4 A B C D E
5 A B C D E
6 A B C D E
7 A B C D E
8 A B C D E
9 A B C D E
0 A B C D E

1 A B C D E
2 A B C D E
3 A B C D E
4 A B C D E
5 A B C D E
6 A B C D E
7 A B C D E
8 A B C D E
9 A B C D E
0 A B C D E

1 A B C D E
2 A B C D E
3 A B C D E
4 A B C D E
5 A B C D E
6 A B C D E
7 A B C D E
8 A B C D E
9 A B C D E
0 A B C D E

1 A B C D E
2 A B C D E
3 A B C D E
4 A B C D E
5 A B C D E
6 A B C D E
7 A B C D E
8 A B C D E
9 A B C D E
0 A B C D E

1 A B C D E
2 A B C D E
3 A B C D E
4 A B C D E
5 A B C D E
6 A B C D E
7 A B C D E
8 A B C D E
9 A B C D E
0 A B C D E

1 A B C D E
2 A B C D E
3 A B C D E
4 A B C D E
5 A B C D E
6 A B C D E
7 A B C D E
8 A B C D E
9 A B C D E
0 A B C D E

1 A B C D E
2 A B C D E
3 A B C D E
4 A B C D E
5 A B C D E
6 A B C D E
7 A B C D E
8 A B C D E
9 A B C D E
0 A B C D E

1 A B C D E
2 A B C D E
3 A B C D E
4 A B C D E
5 A B C D E
6 A B C D E
7 A B C D E
8 A B C D E
9 A B C D E
0 A B C D E

1 A B C D E
2 A B C D E
3 A B C D E
4 A B C D E
5 A B C D E
6 A B C D E

7 A B C D E
8 A B C D E
9 A B C D E
10 A B C D E
11 A B C D E
12 A B C D E

13 A B C D E
14 A B C D E
15 A B C D E
16 A B C D E
17 A B C D E
18 A B C D E

19 A B C D E
20 A B C D E
21 A B C D E
22 A B C D E
23 A B C D E
24 A B C D E

25 A B C D E
26 A B C D E
27 A B C D E
28 A B C D E
29 A B C D E
30 A B C D E

TOP SCORES ON VOCABULARY TESTS

Although questions on vocabulary may not actually appear on your test, it is advisable to practice with the kind of material you have in this chapter. Words and their meanings are quite important in pushing up your score on tests of reading, comprehension, effective writing and correct usage. By broadening your vocabulary, you will definitely improve your marks in these and similar subjects.

INCREASE YOUR VOCABULARY

How is your vocabulary? Do you know the meanings of just about every word you come upon in your reading—or do you find several words that stump you? You must increase your vocabulary if you want to read with understanding. Following are six steps that you can take in order to build up your word power:

(a) Read as much as you have the time for. Don't confine yourself to one type of reading either. Read all kinds of things—newspaper, magazines, books. Seek variety in what you read—different newspapers, several types of magazines, all types of books (novels, poetry, essays, plays, etc.). If you get into the habit of reading widely, your vocabulary will grow by leaps and bounds. You'll learn the meanings of words *by context.* That means that, very often, even though you may not know the meaning of a certain word in a sentence, the other words that you are familiar with will help you get the meaning of the hard word.

(b) Take vocabulary tests. There are many practice books which have word tests. We suggest one of these: *2300 Steps to Word Power*—$1.45 (Arco Publishing Co.). These tests are fun to take—and they will build up your vocabulary fast.

(c) Listen to lectures, discussions, and talks by people who speak well. There are some worthwhile TV programs that have excellent speakers. Listen to such people—you'll learn a great many words from them simply by listening to them.

(d) Use a dictionary. Whenever you don't know the meaning of a word, make a note of it. Then, when you get to a dictionary, look up the meaning of the word. Keep your own little notebook—call it "New Words." In a month or two, you will have added a great many words to your vocabulary. If you do not have a dictionary at home, you should buy one. It is just as important in your life as pots and pans, furniture, or a television set. A good dictionary is not expensive. Any one of the following is highly recommended—and costs about five or six dollars:

Standard College Dictionary (Funk and Wagnalls)

Seventh New Collegiate Dictionary (Merriam-Webster)

American College Dictionary (Random House)

You'll never regret buying a good dictionary for your home.

(e) Play word games. Have you ever played Anagrams or Scrabble? They're really interesting. Buy one of these at a stationery store. They are quite inexpensive but effective in building up your vocabulary. Crossword puzzles will teach you new words also. Practically every daily newspaper has a crossword puzzle.

(f) Learn stems, prefixes, and suffixes. It is very important that you know these.

BASIC LETTER COMBINATIONS

One of the most efficient ways in which you can build up your vocabulary is by a systematic study of the basic word and letter combinations which make up the greater part of the English language.

Etymology is the science of the formation of words, and this somewhat frightening-sounding science can be of great help to you in learning new words and identifying words which may be unfamiliar to you. You will also find that the progress you make in studying the following pages will help to improve your spelling.

A great many of the words which we use every day have come into our language from the Latin and Greek. In the process of being absorbed into English, they appear as parts of words, many of which are related in meaning to each other.

For your convenience, this material is presented in easy-to-study form. Latin and Greek syllables and letter-combinations have been categorized into three groups:

1. *Prefixes:* letter combinations which appear at the beginning of a word.
2. *Suffixes:* letter combinations which appear at the end of a word.
3. *Roots or stems:* which carry the basic meaning and are combined with each other and with prefixes and suffixes to create other words with related meanings.

With the prefixes and suffixes, which you should study first, we have given examples of word formation with meanings, and additional examples. If you find any unfamiliar words among the samples, consult your dictionary to look up their meanings.

The list of roots or stems is accompanied by words in which the letter combinations appear. Here again, use the dictionary to look up any words which are not clear in your mind.

Remember that this section is not meant for easy reading. It is a guide to a program of study that will prove invaluable if you do your part. Do not try to swallow too much at one time. If you can put in a half-hour every day, your study will yield better results.

After you have done your preliminary work and have gotten a better idea of how words are formed in English, schedule the various vocabulary tests and quizzes we have provided in this chapter. They cover a wide variety of the vocabulary questions commonly encountered on examinations. They are short quizzes, not meant to be taken all at one time. Space them out. Adhere closely to the directions which differ for the different test types. Keep an honest record of your scores. Study your mistakes. Look them up in your dictionary. Concentrate closely on each quiz . . . and watch your scores improve.

ETYMOLOGY - A KEY TO WORD RECOGNITION

PREFIXES

PREFIX	MEANING	EXAMPLE
ab, a	away from	absent, amoral
ad, ac, ag, at	to	advent, accrue, aggressive, attract
an	without	anarchy
ante	before	antedate
anti	against	antipathy
bene	well	beneficent
bi	two	bicameral
circum	around	circumspect
com, con, col	together	commit confound, collate
contra	against	contraband
de	from, down	descend
dis, di	apart	distract, divert
ex, e	out	exit, emit
extra	beyond	extracurricular
in, im, il, ir, un	not	inept, impossible, illicit
inter	between	interpose
intra, intro, in	within	intramural, introspective

PREFIX	MEANING	EXAMPLE
mal	bad	malcontent
mis	wrong	misnomer
non	not	nonentity
ob	against	obstacle
per	through	permeate
peri	around	periscope
poly	many	polytheism
post	after	post-mortem
pre	before	premonition
pro	forward	propose
re	again	review
se	apart	seduce
semi	half	semicircle
sub	under	subvert
super	above	superimpose
sui	self	suicide
trans	across	transpose
vice	instead of	vice-president

SUFFIXES

SUFFIX	MEANING	EXAMPLE
able, ible	capable of being	capable, reversible
age	state of	storage
ance	relating to	reliance
ary	relating to	dictionary
ate	act	confiscate
ation	action	radiation
cy	quality	democracy

SUFFIX	MEANING	EXAMPLE
ence	relating to	confidence
er	one who	adviser
ic	pertaining to	democratic
ious	full of	rebellious
ize	to make like	harmonize
ment	result	filament
ty	condition	sanity

LATIN AND GREEK STEMS

STEM	MEANING	EXAMPLE
ag, ac	do	agenda, action
agr	farm	agriculture
aqua	water	aqueous
cad, cas	fall	cadence, casual
cant	sing	chant
cap, cep	take	captive, accept
capit	head	capital
cede	go	precede
celer	speed	celerity
cide, cis	kill, cut	suicide, incision
clud, clus	close	include, inclusion
cur, curs	run	incur, incursion
dict	say	diction
duct	lead	induce
fact, fect	make	factory, perfect
fer, lat	carry	refer, dilate
fring, fract	break	infringe, fracture
frater	brother	fraternal
fund, fus	pour	refund, confuse
greg	group	gregarious
gress, grad	move forward	progress, degrade
homo	man	homicide
ject	throw	reject
jud	right	judicial
junct	join	conjunction
lect, leg	read, choose	collect, legend
loq, loc	speak	loquacious, interlocutory
manu	hand	manuscript
mand	order	remand
mar	sea	maritime
mater	mother	maternal
med	middle	intermediary
min	lessen	diminution
mis, mit	send	remit, dismiss
mort	death	mortician
mote, mov	move	remote, remove
naut	sailor	astronaut
nom	name	nomenclature
pater	father	paternity
ped, pod	foot	pedal, podiatrist
pend	hang	depend
plic	fold	implicate
port	carry	portable
pos, pon	put	depose, component
reg, rect	rule	regicide, direct
rupt	break	eruption
scrib, scrip	write	inscribe, conscription
anthrop	man	anthropology

STEM	MEANING	EXAMPLE
arch	chief, rule	archbishop
astron	star	astronomy
auto	self	automatic
biblio	book	bibliophile
bio	life	biology
chrome	color	chromosome
chron	time	chronology
cosmo	world	cosmic
crat	rule	autocrat
dent, dont	tooth	dental, indent
eu	well, happy	eugenics
gamos	marriage	monogamous
ge	earth	geology
gen	origin, people	progenitor
graph	write	graphic
gyn	women	gynecologist
homo	same	homogeneous
hydr	water	dehydrate
logy	study of	psychology
meter	measure	thermometer
micro	small	microscope
mono	one	monotony
onomy	science	astronomy
onym	name	synonym
pathos	feeling	pathology
philo	love	philosophy
phobia	fear	hydrophobia
phone	sound	telephone
pseudo	false	pseudonym
psych	mind	psychic
scope	see	telescope
soph	wisdom	sophomore
tele	far off	telepathic
theo	god	theology
thermo	heat	thermostat
sec	cut	dissect
sed	remain	sedentary
sequ	follow	sequential
spect	look	inspect
spir	breathe	conspire
stat	stand	status
tact, tang	touch	tactile, tangible
ten	hold	retentive
term	end	terminal
vent	come	prevent
vict	conquer	evict
vid, vis	see	video, revise
voc	call	convocation
volv	roll	devolve

PATROL INSPECTOR

VOCABULARY TEST QUESTIONS FOR PRACTICE

The following questions have been selected to give you as broad a sampling as possible of words which have appeared on previous tests. The ease or difficulty with which you answer these questions will indicate whether or not your word power is adequate for the test you are about to take.

YOU will find these questions divided into separate sub-tests of ten questions each. This division has been made for two reasons: (1) the average number of vocabulary questions on tests of this grade is ten: (2) by doing each sub-test separately, you are enabled to see your progress as you proceed from one test to the next.

You will note that following each test, space is provided for recording the time you took to do the test, and for recording the number of correct answers. By comparing the second test with the first, the third with the second, etc., you will be able to see whether or not you are improving your word power as you study. Successful study should result in speedier time on each successive test, accompanied by increasing accuracy. If this is not the case when you have completed all the tests, then you had better begin again until the desired results are obtained.

These tests, as you will see, take several forms. In general, they are multiple-choice type asking for a word's definition or its opposite. Some questions ask whether a word is used correctly or not, and require you to answer "True" if it is, and "False" if it isn't. You will find, however, that a majority of questions are of the former type. The number of questions in any one form reflects its frequency on actual exams.

Use a watch or clock to keep an accurate record of the time consumed by each test. Read the instructions which precede each test carefully. You may check your accuracy by referring to the answers at the end of the chapter. Do not refer to these answers until you have completed each test.

Sample Test Question Analyzed

The questions may appear in one of several forms, but one of the most numerous is that of choosing a word which is most nearly the same in meaning as the question word. The example below has been chosen because it will help to illustrate the way in which vocabulary questions are answered.

Blacken the appropriate space for the letter preceding the word which is most nearly the same in meaning as the *italicized* word in the sentence.

Sample Question. One who is *garrulous* in his relations with others is, most nearly:

(A) complaining
(B) careless
(C) overly talkative
(D) defensive (E) dishonest.

Notice that the instructions ask for the selection of the choice which is *most nearly* the same in meaning as the italicized word.

First, examine the italicized word. If you know its meaning, your task is fairly simple. But suppose you do not know what *garrulous* means. Perhaps we can eliminate some of the choices by analyzing them.

(A) Complaining: Does *complaining* have anything to do with *garrulous*? It might. However, a synonym for *complaining* is querulous. In this case, it is best to avoid *complaining* as a possibility, since it is probably there to confuse you.

(B) Careless: Most people know what careless means. Here again is a word which only sounds like the question word. You would not use *garrulous* to describe a neglectful person.

(C) Overly Talkative: There is nothing to indicate that this phrase is not a synonym for *garrulous*. Do not eliminate it as a possibility.

(D) Defensive: You can think of synonyms for this one, like protective, safe-guarding, and maybe even fortress and garrison may come to mind. In general, any word that sounds like the question word should be avoided. You would do well to eliminate *defensive* as a possibility.

(E) Dishonest: There is not much to indicate that this is not a synonym for *garrulous*, and none of the synonyms for *dishonest* sounds like the question word. It cannot be eliminated entirely.

The choice is now between (C) and (E); *overly talkative* and *dishonest*. If you have no idea at all regarding the meaning of *garrulous*, then you must guess. Since three of the choices have already been eliminated, you have a much better chance to guess correctly.

Garrulous: The dictionary defines *garrulous* as: "given to continual and tedious talking," "habitually loquacious," "chattering," "verbose." Therefore, (C) "overly talkative" is the correct answer.

NINE TEST-TYPE QUIZZES FOR PRACTICE

DIRECTIONS: For each question read all the choices carefully. Then select that answer which you consider correct or most nearly correct. Write the letter preceding your best choice next to the question. Should you want to answer on the kind of answer sheet used on machine-scored examinations, we have provided several such facsimiles. On some machine-scored exams you are instructed to "place no marks whatever on the test booklet." In other examinations you may be instructed to mark your answers in the test booklet. In such cases you should be careful that no other marks interfere with the legibility of your answers. It is always best NOT to mark your booklet unless you are sure that it is permitted. It is most important that you learn to mark your answers clearly and in the right place.

FOR THE SAMPLE QUESTION that follows, select the appropriate letter preceding the word which is most nearly the same in meaning as the capitalized word:

1. DISSENT: (A) approve (B) depart (C) disagree (D) enjoy

DISSENT is most nearly the same as (C), disagree, so that the acceptable answer is shown thus on your answer sheet:

A B C D

ANSWER SHEETS AND CORRECT ANSWERS APPEAR AFTER EACH TEST

SYNONYMS TEST ONE

DIRECTIONS: For each of the following questions, select the choice which best answers the question or completes the statement.

Correct key answers to all these test questions will be found at the end of the test.

1. An amendment is a
   (A) civic center (B) charter
   (C) penalty (D) change.

2. A quorum is a
   (A) minority (B) committee
   (C) majority (D) bicameral system.

3. Clearance refers to a
   (A) weight (B) hoistway
   (C) distance (D) cleaning process.

4. Pasteurized milk is milk that has been
   (A) watered (B) condemned
   (C) embargoed (D) purified.

5. Antitoxin is used in cases of
   (A) corrupt governmental officials
   (B) sanitary inspection
   (C) disease
   (D) elevator construction.

6. Libel refers to the
   (A) process of incurring financial liability
   (B) publication of a false statement which injures others
   (C) deportation of aliens
   (D) necessity for compulsory schooling.

7. Naturalization refers to the process of
   (A) becoming a civil service employee
   (B) being summoned to court
   (C) becoming a citizen
   (D) pledging allegiance to the American flag.

8. To comply with a rule means to
   (A) abide by a rule (B) abrogate a rule
   (C) dislike a rule (D) ignore a rule.

9. A budget is a
   (A) financial statement
   (B) method for training operators
   (C) device for insuring courtesy
   (D) means for selecting judges

10. A fulcrum is part of a
    (A) typewriter (B) lever
    (C) radio (D) lamp.

Correct Answers

Answer Sheet

	A	B	C	D	E
1					
2					
3					
4					
5					
6					
7					
8					
9					
10					

SCORE

.................%

NO. CORRECT ÷ NO. OF QUESTIONS ON THIS TEST

Correct Answers

	A	B	C	D	E
1				■	
2			■		
3			■		
4				■	
5			■		
6		■			
7			■		
8	■				
9	■				
10		■			

SYNONYMS TEST TWO

DIRECTIONS: Each of the questions in this test is numbered and consists of pairs of words. Each pair of words is preceded by a letter. For each question, select the one pair of words wherein both words are synonymous. Mark the letter, A, B, C, D, or E, preceding that pair on your answer sheet.

Correct key answers to all these test questions will be found at the end of the test.

1. (A) transitory-permanent (B) prohibit-allow (C) beautiful-ugly (D) broken-disunited (E) ferocious-mild.
2. (A) elucidate-clarify (B) recent-ancient (C) enthusiasm-apathy (D) equivocal-indubitable (E) evade-acknowledge.
3. (A) extricate-imprison (B) concur-endorse (C) intimidate-assure (D) lucid-obscure (E) molest-comfort.
4. (A) abandon-hold (B) awkward-skillful (C) consistent-varying (D) constrain-beseech (E) tedious-tiresome.
5. (A) deficient-ample (B) waste-conserve (C) compromise-quarrel (D) sanguine-optimistic (E) desist-persevere.
6. (A) monotony-variety (B) remote-near (C) propitiate-appease (D) many-few (E) veracity-deception.
7. (A) fraud-honesty (B) important-significant (C) mollify-vex (D) abate-maintain (E) authorize-forbid.
8. (A) eradicate-destroy (B) barbarous-humane (C) compulsion-freedom (D) concur-differ (E) incite-quell.
9. (A) morose-cheerful (B) munificent-penurious (C) censorious-fault-finding (D) predominate-subordinate (E) extricate-bind.
10. (A) gratify-displease (B) grudge-good will (C) interpose-withdraw (D) irresponsible-accountable (E) augment-increase.

Correct Answers For The Foregoing Questions

To assist you in scoring yourself we have provided Correct Answers alongside your Answer Sheet. May we therefore suggest that while you are doing the test you cover the Correct Answers with a sheet of white paper.....to avoid temptation and to arrive at an accurate estimate of your ability and progress.

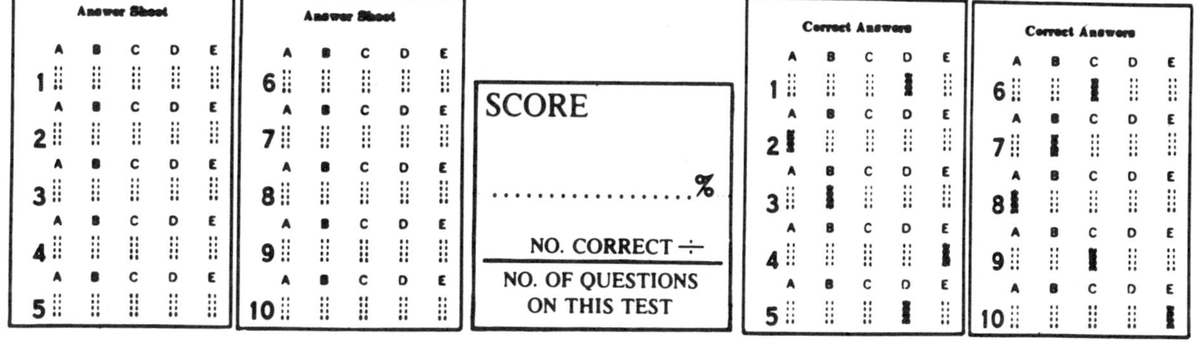

Question	Correct Answer
1	D
2	A
3	B
4	E
5	D
6	C
7	B
8	A
9	C
10	E

SYNONYMS TEST THREE

Although vocabulary questions may not actually appear on your test. it is advisable to try to improve your vocabulary. Words and their meanings are quite important on reading, writing and correct usage tests. By broadening your vocabulary, you will definitely improve your marks in these and similar subjects.

DIRECTIONS: For each of the following statements, mark T if the statement is True, and F if it is False.

1. A *competent* employee is one who is slow and inefficient. T F
2. A person who commits *perjury* does not tell the truth. T F
3. The *prosecutor* in a criminal case is the lawyer who presents evidence against the defendant. T F
4. A *destitute* person has a large amount of money. T F
5. A person with a *florid* complexion has a pale face. T F
6. A noise that is *audible* is capable of being heard. T F
7. Anyone who is *agile* is quick and nimble. T F
8. An employee who gives information in a *curt* manner is sympathetic and courteous. T F
9. A person who is *prudent* is careless in his attention to duty. T F
10. If a person pays an *exorbitant* amount of money for an article, he is paying a fair price. T F

Now, push forward! Test yourself and practice for your test with the carefully constructed quizzes that follow. Each one presents the kind of question you may expect on your test. And each question is at just the level of difficulty that may be expected. Don't try to take all the tests at one time. Rather, schedule yourself so that you take a few at each session, and spend approximately the same time on them at each session. Score yourself honestly, and date each test. You should be able to detect improvement in your performance on successive sessions.

A portion of the standard answer sheet is provided after each test for marking your answers in the way you'll be required to do on the actual exam. At the right of this answer sheet, to make the scoring job simpler (after you have derived your own answers), you'll find our correct answers.

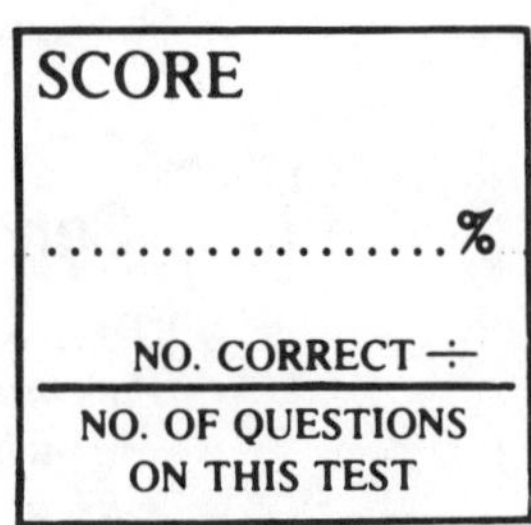

Correct Answers

(You'll learn more by writing your own answers before comparing them with these.)

1. F	6. T
2. T	7. T
3. T	8. F
4. F	9. F
5. F	10. F

SYNONYMS TEST FOUR

DIRECTIONS: This test contains a list of numbered words, and other words divided into five groups—Group A, Group B, Group C, Group D and Group E. For each of the numbered words, select that word in one of the five groups which is most nearly the same in meaning. The letter of that group is the answer for that item. Your answer sheet and our correct answers follow the last question.

Correct key answers to all these test questions will be found at the end of the test.

Group A

indication ambiguous excruciating thin

Group B

confirmation financial phobia erasure

Group C

fiduciary similar yellowish skill

Group D

theft winding receive procrastination

Group E

franchise heir hardy preference

1. fiscal
2. deletion
3. equivocal
4. corroboration
5. tortuous
6. predilection
7. sallow
8. virtuosity
9. scion
10. tenuous

Correct Answers For The Foregoing Questions

To assist you in scoring yourself we have provided Correct Answers alongside your Answer Sheet. May we therefore suggest that while you are doing the test you cover the Correct Answers with a sheet of white paper.....to avoid temptation and to arrive at an accurate estimate of your ability and progress.

Answer Sheet

	A	B	C	D	E
1					
2					
3					
4					
5					
6					
7					
8					
9					
10					

SCORE

..................%

NO. CORRECT ÷
NO. OF QUESTIONS ON THIS TEST

Correct Answers

	A	B	C	D	E
1		■			
2		■			
3	■				
4		■			
5				■	
6					■
7			■		
8			■		
9					■
10	■				

SYNONYMS TEST FIVE

DIRECTIONS: This test contains a list of numbered words, and other words divided into five groups—Group A, Group B, Group C, Group D and Group E. For each of the numbered words, select that word in one of the five groups which is most nearly the same in meaning. The letter of that group is the answer for that item. Your answer sheet and our correct answers follow the last question.

Correct key answers to all these test questions will be found at the end of the test.

1. prophylactic
2. palliation
3. redolent
4. indictment
5. misfeasance
6. holograph
7. ancillary
8. hectic
9. obsolescence
10. holocaust

Group A

ruddy retribution mitigation decadence

Group B

dental fragrant accusation symptom

Group C

preventive destruction aggravation testimony

Group D

intimidation subsidiary feverish trespass

Group E

consecration excited corpulence handwritten

Correct Answers For The Foregoing Questions

To assist you in scoring yourself we have provided Correct Answers alongside your Answer Sheet. May we therefore suggest that while you are doing the test you cover the Correct Answers with a sheet of white paper.....to avoid temptation and to arrive at an accurate estimate of your ability and progress.

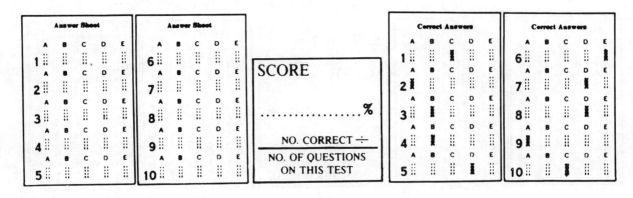

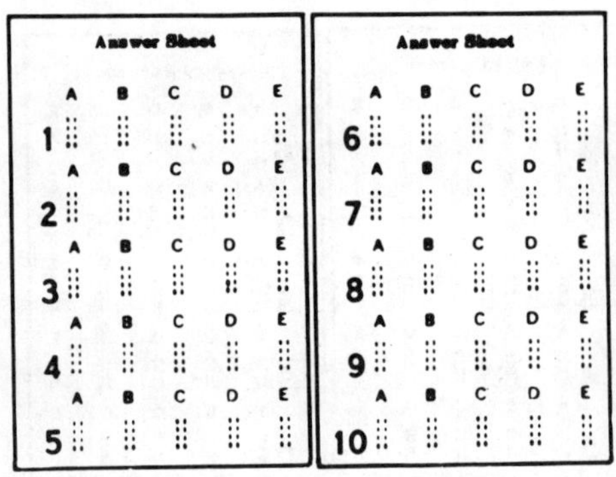

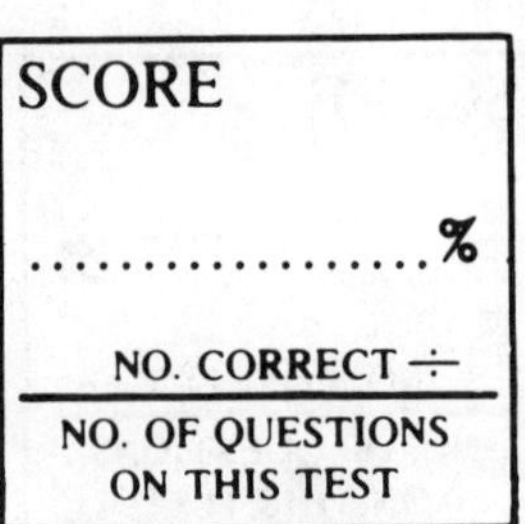

Correct Answers

1	C
2	A
3	B
4	B
5	D
6	E
7	D
8	D
9	A
10	C

SYNONYMS TEST SIX

DIRECTIONS: For each question in this test, select the appropriate letter preceding the word which is most nearly the same in meaning as the italicized word in each sentence.

Correct key answers to all these test questions will be found at the end of the test.

1. The person who is *diplomatic* in his relations with others is, most nearly
   (A) well dressed (B) very tactful
   (C) somewhat domineering (D) deceitful and tricky
   (E) verbose.

2. Action at this time would be *inopportune*. The word "inopportune" means most nearly
   (A) untimely (B) premeditated
   (C) sporadic (D) commendable
   (E) fortunate.

3. The word *appraise* means most nearly
   (A) consult (B) attribute
   (C) manage (D) honor
   (E) judge.

4. The word *cognizant* means most nearly
   (A) rare (B) reluctant
   (C) aware (D) haphazard
   (E) correlated.

5. *Probity* is an important requirement of many positions. The word "probity" means most nearly
   (A) analytical ability (B) vision
   (C) tried integrity (D) clear insight
   (E) perseverence.

6. The word *denote* means most nearly
   (A) encumber (B) evade
   (C) furnish (D) indicate
   (E) reduce in rank.

7. The competent employee should know that a method of procedure which is *expedient* is most nearly
   (A) unchangeable (B) based upon a false assumption
   (C) unduly harmful (D) difficult to work out
   (E) suitable to the end in view.

8. An incentive which is *potent* is most nearly
   (A) impossible (B) highly effective
   (C) not immediately practicable (D) a remote possibility
   (E) universally applicable.

9. An employer who is *judicious* is most nearly
   (A) domineering (B) argumentative
   (C) sincere (D) arbitrary
   (E) wise.

10. He presented a *controversial* plan. The word "controversial" means most nearly
   (A) subject to debate (B) unreasonable
   (C) complex (D) comparable
   (E) well formulated.

Answer Sheet

	A	B	C	D	E
1					
2					
3					
4					
5					
6					
7					
8					
9					
10					

SCORE

.... %

NO. CORRECT ÷ NO. OF QUESTIONS ON THIS TEST

Correct Answers

	A	B	C	D	E
1		▮			
2	▮				
3					▮
4			▮		
5			▮		
6				▮	
7					▮
8		▮			
9					▮
10	▮				

SYNONYMS TEST SEVEN

DIRECTIONS: For each question in this test, select the appropriate letter preceding the word which is most nearly the same in meaning as the italicized word in each sentence.

Correct key answers to all these test questions will be found at the end of the test.

1. "He sent the irate employee to the personnel manager." The word *irate* means most nearly
   (A) irresponsible (B) untidy
   (C) insubordinate (D) angry.
2. An *ambiguous* statement is one which is
   (A) forceful and convincing
   (B) capable of being understood in more than one sense
   (C) based upon good judgment and sound reasoning processes
   (D) uninteresting and too lengthy.
3. To *extol* means most nearly to
   (A) summon (B) praise
   (C) reject (D) withdraw.
4. The word *proximity* means most nearly
   (A) similarity (B) exactness
   (C) harmony (D) nearness.
5. "His friends had a detrimental influence on him." The word *detrimental* means most nearly
   (A) favorable (B) lasting
   (C) harmful (D) short-lived.
6. "The chief inspector relied upon the veracity of his inspectors." The word *veracity* means most nearly
   (A) speed (B) assistance
   (C) shrewdness (D) truthfulness.
7. "There was much diversity in the suggestions submitted." The word *diversity* means most nearly
   (A) similarity (B) value
   (C) triviality (D) variety.
8. "The survey was concerned with the problem of indigence." The word *indigence* means most nearly
   (A) poverty (B) corruption
   (C) intolerance (D) morale.
9. "The investigator considered this evidence to be extraneous." The word *extraneous* means most nearly
   (A) significant (B) pertinent but unobtainable
   (C) not essential (D) inadeqluate.
10. "He was surprised at the temerity of the new employee." The word *temerity* means most nearly
    (A) shyness (B) enthusiasm
    (C) rashness (D) self-control.

Correct Answers

Answer Sheet

	A	B	C	D	E
1					
2					
3					
4					
5					
6					
7					
8					
9					
10					

SCORE

................%

NO. CORRECT ÷ NO. OF QUESTIONS ON THIS TEST

Correct Answers

	A	B	C	D	E
1				▮	
2		▮			
3		▮			
4				▮	
5			▮		
6				▮	
7				▮	
8	▮				
9			▮		
10			▮		

SYNONYMS TEST EIGHT

DIRECTIONS: In each of the sentences below, one word is in italics. Following each sentence are four or five lettered words or phrases. For each sentence, choose the letter preceding the word or phrase which most nearly corresponds in meaning with the italicized word.

Correct key answers to all these test questions will be found at the end of the test.

1. The change in procedure *stimulated* the men
   (A) rewarded (B) antagonized
   (C) gave an incentive to
   (D) restricted the activities of
   (E) lowered the efficiency of.
2. Courage is a trait difficult to *instill.* The word "instill" means most nearly
   (A) measure exactly (B) impart gradually
   (C) predict accurately (D) restrain effectively
   (E) discuss meaningfully.
3. The vehicle was left *intact.* The word "intact" means most nearly
   (A) a total loss (B) unattended
   (C) where it could be noticed (D) undamaged
   (E) repaired.
4. The witness was *recalcitrant.* The word "recalcitrant" means most nearly
   (A) cooperative (B) delirious
   (C) highly excited
   (D) accustomed to hard work
   (E) stubbornly resistant.
5. A *conscientious* person is one who
   (A) feels obligated to do what he believes right
   (B) rarely makes errors
   (C) frequently makes suggestions for procedural improvements
   (D) has good personal relationships with others
   (E) is consistent in his behavior.
6. It was reported that *noxious* fumes were escaping. The word "noxious" means most nearly
   (A) concentrated (B) gaseous
   (C) greenish colored (D) heavy
   (E) harmful.
7. A person with a *sallow* complexion was seen near the scene. The word "sallow" means most nearly
   (A) ruddy (B) dark
   (C) pale and yellowish (D) highly freckled
   (E) red and florid.
8. The word *cogent* means most nearly
   (A) confused (B) opposite
   (C) unintentional (D) convincing
   (E) irrelevant.
9. The word *divergent* means most nearly
   (A) simultaneous (B) differing
   (C) approaching (D) parallel
   (E) twisting.
10. The word *ostensibly* means most nearly
    (A) undoubtedly (B) infrequently
    (C) powerfully (D) apparently
    (E) slowly.

Answer Sheet

	A	B	C	D	E
1					
2					
3					
4					
5					
6					
7					
8					
9					
10					

SCORE

..................%

NO. CORRECT ÷

NO. OF QUESTIONS ON THIS TEST

Correct Answers

	A	B	C	D	E
1			■		
2		■			
3				■	
4					■
5	■				
6					■
7			■		
8				■	
9		■			
10				■	

SYNONYMS TEST NINE

DIRECTIONS: In each of the sentences below, one word is in italics. Following each sentence are four or five lettered words or phrases. For each sentence, choose the letter preceding the word or phrase which most nearly corresponds in meaning with the italicized word.

Correct key answers to all these test questions will be found at the end of the test.

1. To say that the work is *tedious* means, most nearly, that it is
   (A) technical (B) interesting
   (C) tiresome (D) confidential.

2. A *vivacious* person is one who is
   (A) kind (B) talkative
   (C) lively (D) well-dressed.

3. An *innocuous* statement is one which is
   (A) forceful (B) harmless
   (C) offensive (D) brief.

4. To say that the order was *rescinded* means, most nearly, that the order was
   (A) revised (B) canceled
   (C) misinterpreted (D) confirmed.

5. To say that the administrator *amplified* his remarks means, most nearly, that the remarks were
   (A) shouted (B) expanded
   (C) carefully analyzed (D) summarized briefly.

6. "Peremptory commands will be resented in any organization." The word *peremptory* means most nearly
   (A) unexpected (B) unreasonable
   (C) military (D) dictatorial.

7. A person should know the word *sporadic* means, most nearly
   (A) occurring regularly (B) sudden
   (C) scattered (D) disturbing.

8. To *oscillate* means, most nearly, to
   (A) lubricate (B) waver
   (C) decide (D) investigate.

9. A *homogeneous* group of persons is characterized by its
   (A) similarity (B) teamwork
   (C) discontent (D) differences.

10. A *vindictive* person is one who is
    (A) prejudiced (B) unpopular
    (C) petty (D) revengeful.

Correct Answers

Answer Sheet

	A	B	C	D	E
1					
2					
3					
4					
5					
6					
7					
8					
9					
10					

SCORE

..................%

NO. CORRECT ÷ NO. OF QUESTIONS ON THIS TEST

Correct Answers

	A	B	C	D	E
1			C		
2			C		
3		B			
4		B			
5		B			
6				D	
7			C		
8		B			
9	A				
10				D	

VERBAL ANALOGIES

The verbal analogy is a variation of the vocabulary question, and a form of question often met with on intelligence tests. The questions presented below test your understanding of the meanings of words, and also your ability to grasp the relationships between words and the ideas they represent. The aim of this section is to give you experience.

IN addition to their simple meanings, words carry subtle shades of implication that depend in some degree upon the relationship they bear to other words. There are various classifications of relationship, such as similarity (synonyms) and opposition (antonyms). The careful student will examine each word in these analogy questions for the exact shade of meaning indicated.

The ability to detect the exact nature of the relationship between words is a function of your intelligence. In a sense, the verbal analogy test is a vocabulary test. But it is also a test of your ability to analyze meanings, think things out and to see the relationships between ideas and words, and avoid confusion of ideas. In mathematics, this type of situation is expressed as a ratio and proportion problem: $3:5 = 6:X$. Sometimes verbal analogies are written in this mathematical form:

CLOCK: TIME—THERMOMETER: (A) hour (B) degrees (C) temperature (D) climate (E) weather.

Or the question may be put:

CLOCK is to TIME as THERMOMETER is to (A) hour (B) degrees (C) temperature (D) climate (E) weather.

The problem is to determine which of the lettered words has the same relationship to thermometér as time has to clock.

The best way of determining the correct answer is to provide the word or phrase which shows the relationship between these words. In the example above, the word is measures. However, this may not be enough. The analogy must be correct in exact meaning. Climate or weather would not be exact enough. Temperature, of course, is the correct answer.

You will find that many of the choices you have to select from have some relationship to the third word. You must select the one with a relationship most closely approximating the relationship between the first two words.

In analogy questions, the relationship between the first two words may not always be expressed in the form of a single verb. Sometimes, the relationship may be one of:

(1) Purpose or function
Example:
SHIP is to RUDDER as HORSE is to REIN; BLADE is to KNIFE as BIT is to DRILL.

(2) Class, or part of a thing
Example:
WATER is to LIQUID as AIR is to GAS; CRAB is to CRUSTACEAN as MAN is to MAMMAL.

(3) Synonyms or Antonyms
Example:
BAD is to GOOD as GUILTY is to INNOCENT; CHARITABLE is to ELEEMOSYNARY as PROXIMATE is to PROPINQUITY

(4) Other relationships—family, sex, position, etc.
Example:
UNCLE is to NEPHEW as AUNT is to NIECE; SOW is to PIG as GANDER is to GOOSE; HORIZONTAL is to VERTICAL as LYING is to STANDING.

(5) Grammatical Form
Example:
IS is to WAS as DO is to DID; I is to MY as HE is to HIS; DATUM is to DATA as MAN is to MEN; GOOD it to WELL as SUPERB is to SUPERBLY.

There are numerous types of analogy relationships that cannot be classified. If you follow the methods analyzed above, however, you will be able to determine the various relationships in a similar manner and arrive at the correct conclusions.

Practice for Verbal Analogies

In each of the following questions the FIRST TWO words in capital letters go together in some way. Find how they are related. Then write the correct letter to show which one of the last five words goes with the THIRD word in capital letters in the same way that the second word in capital letters goes with the first.

The important rule to remember in answering an analogy question is to determine the specific relationship of the first two words of the analogy, and then choose the word given in the alternatives bearing a similar relationship to the third member of the analogy.

It is also important to point out some of the more important pitfalls involved in answering this type of question. Let us take some sample questions:

I. FOOD is to HUNGER as SLEEP is to
   (A) night (B) dream
   (C) weariness (D) health
   (E) rest

Obviously, all of the words are related to sleep in some way. None of them except weariness bears the same relationship to sleep as hunger does to food. Before answering one of these questions, then, we must fix in our minds the relationship that the first two words of the analogy bear to each other.

(A) although one sleeps at night, it is not the night that is relieved by sleep.
(B) sleep is certainly related to dream because people dream when they sleep. But again, it is not dreams that are relieved by sleep.
(C) food relieves hunger and sleep relieves weariness. Therefore weariness is correct.
(D) sleep is productive, in part, of health, but this is not the relationship that we are seeking.
(E) sleep results in rest but food does not result in hunger.

II. CUP is to DRINK as PLATE is to
   (A) supper (B) fork
   (C) dine (D) earthenware
   (E) silver

What is the relationship between cup (noun) and drink (verb)?

It is obvious that one DRINKS from a cup.

What does one do from a plate in the same manner that one drinks from a cup?

It becomes apparent that of the five choices offered, (C) dine, is the only one which bears a similar relationship, since one dines from a plate. A closer analogy would have been one EATS from a plate, but since this word is not offered, the best of the five choices is DINE.

Notice that all of the remaining choices bear some relationship to the word PLATE but not the same that CUP bears to DRINK.

(A) supper is related to plate since one's supper may be eaten from a plate. Supper, however, is a noun, and the part of speech required is a verb.
(B) fork is related to plate since both are eating utensils, but this is not the relationship required, so it must be eliminated.
(D) earthenware is related to plate since many plates are made of earthenware, but this also is not the relationship called for.
(E) silver is related to plate since in one sense they are synonyms. There is also a relationship established in the word "silver-plated," but neither of these is the relationship required.

III. GUILLOTINE is to DECAPITATE as RAZOR is to
   (A) beard (B) hair
   (C) shave (D) cut
   (E) steel

This is the type of analogy which deals with the use, purpose or function of an object or instrument.

The purpose of a guillotine is to decapitate.

What is a razor used for?

It is obvious that the most important use of the razor is to shave, so (C) is the correct answer.

Notice the relationships of the remaining choices:

(A) razor is related to beard, since it is used to cut beards, but it is not the relationship required. Also, the sense of the analogy calls for a verb, not a noun.
(B) razor is related to hair, since it cuts hair, but hair is not the purpose of razor.
(D) cut is one of the uses of a razor, but it is not its primary function. Relatively it is not as important as shave.
(E) steel is related to razor in the sense that some razors are made of steel, but since steel is not the function of a razor, it must be eliminated as incorrect.

IV. ADDER is to SNAKE as CROCODILE is to

(A) ruminant (B) marsh
(C) reptile (D) carnivore
(E) rapacious

This is a type of analogy question frequently met on examinations. The candidate must learn to distinguish between a specific and a general. In many cases it is a question of comparing a specie of an animal, plant, tree, bird, etc., to its broader classification.

An adder is a kind or type of snake.

Snake is a general term including many different species, of which adder is only one. In the same way, which of the five choices is the general classification under which the specie crocodile can be classified?

(A) a ruminant is an animal that chews the cud, as a goat or a sheep. A crocodile is not a ruminant.

(B) a marsh is a tract of low, miry land. It has no connection with types of crocodiles.

(C) reptile is a broad classification of animals including the crocodile. It has the same relation to crocodile as adder has to snake, and is therefore the correct choice.

(D) a carnivore is a mammalian animal which lives on flesh for food. The crocodile is not of this type.

(E) rapacious is an adjective meaning "subsisting on prey or animals seized by violence." Since rapacious is not a type of crocodile, it could not possibly be the correct choice.

V. BREAKABLE is to FRANGIBLE as GULLIBLE is to

(A) credulous (B) deceptive
(C) capable (D) lurid
(E) marine

This is an analogy formed by comparing two adjectives.

They are synonymous since they have the same meanings.

Inasmuch as the first words of the analogy are adjectives the second pair must also be adjectives.

Gullible is an exact synonym of credulous and is therefore the most correct choice.

None of the other choices bears any resemblance in meaning to gullible.

Sample Test Questions

In each of the following, the first two words in capital letters go together in some way. Find how they are related. Then choose the letter showing which of the remaining words goes with the third word in capital letters in the same way that the second word in capital letters goes with the first.

1. GUN: SHOTS—KNIFE:
(A) run (B) cuts
(C) hat (D) bird

2. EAR: HEAR—EYE:
(A) table (B) hand
(C) see (D) foot

3. DRESS: WOMAN—FEATHERS:
(A) bird (B) neck
(C) feet (D) bill

4. HANDLE: HAMMER—KNOB:
(A) key (B) room
(C) shut (D) door

5. SHOE: FOOT—HAT:
(A) coat (B) nose
(C) head (D) collar

6. WATER: DRINK—BREAD:
(A) cake (B) coffee
(C) eat (D) pie

7. FOOD: MAN—GASOLINE:
(A) gas (B) oil
(C) automobile (D) spark

8. EAT: FAT—STARVE:
(A) thin (B) food
(C) bread (D) thirsty

9. MAN: HOME—BIRD:
(A) fly (B) insect
(C) worm (D) nest

10. GO: COME—SELL:
(A) leave (B) buy
(C) money (D) papers

11. PENINSULA: LAND—BAY:
(A) boats (B) pay
(C) ocean (D) Massachusetts

12. HOUR: MINUTE—MINUTE:
(A) man (B) week
(C) second (D) short

13. ABIDE: DEPART—STAY:
(A) over (B) home
(C) play (D) leave

14. JANUARY: FEBRUARY—JUNE:
(A) July (B) May
(C) month (D) year

15. BOLD: TIMID—ADVANCE:
(A) proceed (B) retreat
(C) campaign (D) soldiers

16. ABOVE: BELOW—TOP:
(A) spin (B) bottom
(C) surface (D) side

17. LION: ANIMAL—ROSE:
(A) smell (B) leaf
(C) plant (D) thorn

18. TIGER: CARNIVOROUS—HORSE:
(A) cow (B) pony
(C) buggy (D) herbivorous

19. SAILOR: NAVY—SOLDIER:
(A) gun (B) cap
(C) hill (D) army

20. PICTURE: SEE—SOUND:
(A) noise (B) music
(C) hear (D) bark

21. SUCCESS: JOY—FAILURE:
(A) sadness (B) success
(C) fail (D) work

22. HOPE: DESPAIR—HAPPINESS:
(A) frolic (B) fun
(C) joy (D) sadness

23. PRETTY: UGLY—ATTRACT:
(A) fine (B) repel
(C) nice (D) draw

24. PUPIL: TEACHER—CHILD:
(A) parent (B) dolly
(C) youngster (D) obey

25. CITY: MAYOR—ARMY:
(A) navy (B) soldier
(C) general (D) private

26. ESTABLISH: BEGIN—ABOLISH:
(A) slavery (B) wrong
(C) abolition (D) end

27. DECEMBER: JANUARY—LAST:
(A) least (B) worst
(C) month (D) first

28. GIANT: DWARF—LARGE:
(A) big (B) monster
(C) queer (D) small

29. ENGINE: CABOOSE—BEGINNING:
(A) commence (B) cabin
(C) end (D) train

30. DISMAL: CHEERFUL—DARK:
(A) sad (B) stars
(C) night (D) bright

31. QUARREL: ENEMY—AGREE:
(A) friend (B) disagree
(C) agreeable (D) foe

32. RAZOR: SHARP—HOE:
(A) bury (B) dull
(C) cuts (D) tree

33. WINTER: SUMMER—COLD:
(A) freeze (B) warm
(C) wet (D) January

34. RUDDER: SHIP—TAIL:
(A) sail (B) bird
(C) dog (D) cat

35. GRANARY: WHEAT—LIBRARY:
(A) desk (B) books
(C) paper (D) librarian

36. DOOR is to HINGE as LEG is to
(A) knee (B) ulna
(C) sock (D) toe

37. SAND: GLASS—CLAY:
(A) stone (B) hay
(C) bricks (D) dirt

38. MOON: EARTH—EARTH:
(A) ground (B) Mars
(C) sun (D) sky

39. TEARS: SORROW—LAUGHTER:
(A) joy (B) smile
(C) girls (D) grain

40. COLD: ICE—HEAT:
(A) lightning (B) warm
(C) steam (D) coat

In each of the following, the first two words in capital letters go together in some way. Find how they are related. Then choose the letter showing which of the remaining words goes with the third word in capital letters in the same way that the second word in capital letters goes with the first.

41. REMUNERATIVE is to PROFITABLE as FRAUDULENT is to
(A) lying (B) slander
(C) fallacious (D) plausible
(E) reward

42. AX is to WOODSMAN as AWL is to
(A) cut (B) hew
(C) plumber (D) pierce
(E) cobbler

43. SURGEON is to SCALPEL as BUTCHER is to
(A) mallet (B) cleaver
(C) chisel (D) wrench
(E) medicine

44. CAT is to FELINE as HORSE is to
(A) equine (B) tiger
(C) quadruped (D) carnivorous
(E) vulpine

45. ADVERSITY is to HAPPINESS as VEHEMENCE is to
(A) misfortune (B) gayety
(C) troublesome (D) petulance
(E) serenity

46. NECKLACE is to ADORNMENT as MEDAL is to
(A) jewel (B) metal
(C) bravery (D) bronze
(E) decoration

47. GUN is to HOLSTER as SWORD is to
(A) pistol (B) scabbard
(C) warrior (D) slay
(E) plunder

48. ARCHAEOLOGIST is to ANTIQUITY as ICHTHYOLOGIST is to
(A) theology (B) ruins
(C) horticulture (D) marine life
(E) mystic

49. SHOE is to LEATHER as HIGHWAY is to
(A) passage (B) road
(C) asphalt (D) trail
(E) journey

50. SERFDOM is to FEUDALISM as ENTREPRENEUR is to
(A) laissez faire (B) captain
(C) radical (D) agriculture
(E) capitalism

51. FIN is to FISH as PROPELLER is to
(A) auto (B) airplane
(C) grain elevator (D) water

52. PULP is to PAPER as HEMP is to
(A) rope (B) baskets
(C) yarn (D) cotton

53. SKIN is to MAN as HIDE is to
(A) scales (B) fur
(C) animal (D) hair
(E) fish

54. RAIN is to DROP as SNOW is to
(A) ice (B) cold
(C) zero (D) flake

55. WING is to BIRD as HOOF is to
(A) dog (B) foot
(C) horse (D) girl
(E) horseshoe

56. CONSTELLATION is to STAR as ARCHIPELAGO is to
(A) continent (B) peninsula
(C) country (D) island
(E) mono

57. ACCOUNTANCY is to BOOKKEEPING as COURT REPORTING is to
(A) law (B) judgment
(C) stenography (D) lawyer
(E) judge

58. RUBBER is FLEXIBILITY as PIPE is to
(A) iron (B) copper
(C) pliability (D) elasticity
(E) rigidity

59. ABSENCE is to PRESENCE as STABLE is to
(A) steady (B) secure
(C) safe (D) changeable
(E) influential

60. SAFETY VALVE is to BOILER as FUSE is to
(A) motor (B) house
(C) wire (D) city
(E) factory

61. SCHOLARLY is to UNSCHOLARLY as LEARNED is to
(A) ignorant (B) wise
(C) skilled (D) scholarly
(E) literary

62. IMMIGRANT is to ARRIVAL as EMIGRATION is to
(A) leaving (B) alien
(C) native (D) Italian
(E) emigrant

63. GOVERNOR is to STATE as GENERAL is to
(A) lieutenant (B) navy
(C) army (D) captain
(E) admiral

64. LETTER CARRIER is to MAIL MESSENGER is to
(A) value (B) dispatches
(C) easy (D) complicated
(E) fast

65. CLOTH is to COAT as GINGHAM is to
(A) doll (B) cover
(C) washable (D) dress
(E) dressmaker

66. BOAT is to DOCK as AIRPLANE is to
(A) wing (B) strut
(C) engine (D) wind
(E) hangar

67. OAT is to BUSHEL as DIAMOND is to
(A) gram (B) hardness
(C) usefulness (D) carat
(E) ornament

68. PHYSIOLOGY is to SCIENCE as LAW is to
(A) jurist (B) court
(C) profession (D) contract
(E) suit

69. LACONIC is to BRIEF as PROLIX is to
(A) terse (B) wearisome
(C) curt (D) epigrammatic
(E) concise

70. CAPTAIN is to VESSEL as DIRECTOR is to
(A) touring party (B) board
(C) travel (D) orchestra
(E) musician

71. FATHER is to DAUGHTER as UNCLE is to
(A) son (B) daughter
(C) son-in-law (D) niece
(E) aunt

72. PISTOL is to TRIGGER as MOTOR is to
(A) wire (B) dynamo
(C) amperes (D) barrel
(E) switch

73. CUBE is to PYRAMID as SQUARE is to
(A) box (B) Egypt
(C) pentagon (D) triangle
(E) cylinder

74. PROFIT is to SELLING as FAME is to
(A) buying (B) cheating
(C) bravery (D) praying
(E) loving

75. BINDING is to BOOK as WELDING is to
(A) box (B) tank
(C) chair (D) wire
(E) pencil

76. GYMNASIUM is to HEALTH as LIBRARY is to
(A) sick (B) study
(C) books (D) knowledge
(E) school

77. RIGHT is to WRONG as SUCCEED is to
(A) aid (B) profit
(C) fail (D) error
(E) gain

78. INDIAN is to AMERICA as HINDU is to
(A) Hindustan (B) Mexico
(C) soil (D) magic
(E) India

79. WEALTH is to MERCENARY as GOLD is to
(A) Midas (B) miner
(C) fame (D) eleemosynary
(E) South Africa

80. BOTTLE is to BRITTLE as TIRE is to
(A) elastic (B) scarce
(C) rubber (D) spheroid
(E) automobile

81. SOPRANO is to HIGH as BASS is to
(A) violin (B) good
(C) low (D) fish
(E) soft

82. OLFACTORY is to NOSE as TACTILE is to
(A) tacit (B) bloody
(C) finger (D) handkerchief
(E) stomach

83. STREET is to HORIZONTAL as BUILDING is to
(A) tall (B) brick
(C) broad (D) vertical
(E) large

84. ALLEGIANCE is to LOYALTY as TREASON is to
(A) obedience (B) rebellion
(C) murder (D) felony
(E) homage

85. CANVAS is to PAINT as CLAY is to
(A) mold (B) cloth
(C) statue (D) art
(E) aesthetic

86. FISH is to FIN as BIRD is to
(A) wing (B) five
(C) feet (D) beak
(E) feathers

87. CONQUEST is to ASCENDANCY as SUBJUGATION is to
(A) omission (B) frustration
(C) censure (D) vilify
(E) mastery

88. SOLUTION is to MYSTERY as LEARNING is to
(A) study (B) books
(C) college (D) school
(E) detective

89. ALUMNUS is to ALUMNA as PRINCE is to
(A) castle (B) king
(C) knight (D) country
(E) princess

90. OCCULT is to OVERT as SECRET is to
(A) abstract (B) outward
(C) science (D) tarry
(E) concealed

91. CAT is to DOG as TIGER is to
(A) wild (B) fur
(C) wolf (D) bovine
(E) zebra

92. SALINE is to SALT as FRESH is to
(A) sweet (B) stale
(C) sour (D) insipid
(5) lukewarm

93. FLANNEL is to WOOL as LINEN is to
(A) cotton (B) flax
(C) silk (D) rayon
(E) chamois

94. CONTEMPORARY is to PRESENT as POSTERITY is to
(A) past (B) present
(C) modern (D) ancient
(E) future

95. MOON is to EARTH as EARTH is to
(A) Mars (B) moon
(C) sky (D) sun
(E) orbit

96. ACUTE is to CHRONIC as INTENSE is to
(A) sardonic (B) tonic
(C) persistent (D) pretty
(E) sick

97. VALLEY is to GORGE as MOUNTAIN is to
(A) hill (B) cliff
(C) pinnacle (D) high
(E) altitude

98. EAST is to WEST as NORTHWEST is to
(A) Southeast (B) Southwest
(C) North (D) South
(E) Northeast

99. GASOLINE is to PETROLEUM as SUGAR is to
(A) oil (B) cane
(C) plant (D) molasses
(E) sweet

100. AGGRAVATE is to TEASE as FONDLE is to
(A) vex (B) wound
(C) embrace (D) pursuit
(E) untidy
(E) congress

101. LATITUDE is to LONGITUDE as WARP is to
(A) weave (B) woof
(C) thread (D) line
(E) straight

102. EDGE is to CENTER as EFFUSIVE is to
(A) unemotional (B) exuberant
(C) eclectic (D) eccentricity

103. DISCIPLE is to MENTOR as PROSELYTE is to
(A) opinion (B) expedition
(C) leader (D) football

104. ARTIFICE is to FINESSE as INEPT is to
(A) inefficient (B) artistic
(C) tricky (D) insatiable

105. CAPTAIN is to STEAMSHIP as PRINCIPAL is to
(A) interest (B) school
(C) agent (D) concern

106. DIME is to SILVER as PENNY is to
(A) mint (B) copper
(C) currency (D) value

107. REVERT is to REVERSION as SYMPATHIZE is to
(A) sympathic (B) symposium
(C) sympathy (D) sympathizer

108. REGRESSIVE is to REGRESS as STERILE is to
(A) sterilization (B) sterilize
(C) sterility (D) sterilizer

109. DOWN is to DOWNY as AGE is to
(A) aging (B) old
(C) ancient (D) historic

110. I is to MINE as MAN is to
(A) men (B) his
(C) man's (D) mine

111. DISLOYAL is to FAITHLESS as IMPERFECTION is to
(A) contamination (B) depression
(C) foible (D) decrepitude
(E) praise

112. NECKLACE is to PEARLS as CHAIN is to
(A) metal (B) prisoner
(C) locket (D) silver
(E) links

113. DRIFT is to SNOW as DUNE is to
(A) hill (B) rain
(C) sand (D) hail
(E) desert

114. DILIGENT is to UNREMITTING as DIAMETRIC is to
(A) pretentious (B) geographical
(C) adamant (D) contrary
(E) opposite

115. GALLEY is to VESSEL as PERSIMMON is to
(A) machine (B) fruit
(C) engine (D) vehicle
(E) communication

116. PERSPIRATION is to PORES as HAIR is to
(A) endoderm (B) head
(C) diathermy (D) electrolysis
(E) filament

117. LIQUID is to SYPHON as SMOKE is to
(A) chimney (B) fire
(C) flame (D) flue
(E) tobacco

118. EXTORT is to WREST as CONSPIRE is to
(A) entice (B) plot
(C) deduce (D) respire
(E) convey

119. WIDOW is to DOWAGER as CONSORT is to
(A) enemy (B) constable
(C) companion (D) distaff
(E) curette

120. EMINENT is to LOWLY as FREQUENT is to
(A) often (B) frivolous
(C) enhance (D) soon
(E) rare

121. GAUDY is to OSTENTATIOUS as DEJECTED is to
(A) oppressed (B) inform
(C) rejected (D) depressed
(E) determined

122. SALT is to MINE as MARBLE is to
(A) palace (B) engraving
(C) stone (D) quarry
(E) sapphire

123. BRICK is to BUILDING as LEATHER is to
(A) steer (B) hide
(C) belt (D) horse
(E) calf

124. BASS is to LOW as SOPRANO is to
(A) intermediate (B) feminine
(C) alto (D) eerie
(E) high

125. SHOE is to FOOT as HELMET is to
(A) steel (B) head
(C) combat (D) duel
(E) football

126. FINGER is to TACTILE as NOSE is to
(A) proboscis (B) smell
(C) olfactory (D) redolent
(E) perfume

127. WATER is to FLUID as IRON is to
(A) metal (B) rusty
(C) solid (D) rails
(E) mines

Correct Answers For The Foregoing Questions

1. B	17. C	33. B	49. C	65. D	81. C	97. B	113. C
2. C	18. D	34. B	50. E	66. E	82. C	98. A	114. E
3. A	19. D	35. B	51. B	67. D	83. D	99. D	115. B
4. D	20. C	36. A	52. A	68. C	84. B	100. C	116. A
5. C	21. A	37. C	53. C	69. B	85. A	101. B	117. D
6. C	22. D	38. C	54. D	70. D	86. A	102. A	118. B
7. C	23. B	39. A	55. C	71. D	87. B	103. C	119. C
8. A	24. A	40. C	56. D	72. E	88. A	104. A	120. E
9. D	25. C	41. C	57. C	73. D	89. E	105. B	121. D
10. B	26. D	42. E	58. E	74. C	90. B	106. B	122. D
11. C	27. D	43. B	59. D	75. B	91. C	107. C	123. C
12. C	28. D	44. A	60. A	76. D	92. A	108. B	124. E
13. D	29. C	45. E	61. A	77. C	93. B	109. B	125. B
14. A	30. D	46. E	62. A	78. E	94. E	110. C	126. C
15. B	31. A	47. B	63. C	79. A	95. D	111. C	127. C
16. B	32. B	48. D	64. B	80. A	96. C	112. E	

TOP SCORES IN SPELLING

The material in this chapter has appeared repeatedly on past examinations. It's all quite relevant, and well worth every minute of your valuable study time. Beginning with basic rules and a concise text, it proceeds to an illuminating presentation of a wide variety of questions and answers that exemplify the basic text while they strengthen your ability to answer actual test questions quickly and accurately.

THE importance of spelling cannot be overestimated. Bad spelling is a principal cause of failure among examinees.

It is impossible in this brief resume to supply a set of easy rules for all cases and all exceptions. However, we can give you some guidance that will almost certainly raise your test score.

We offer here a set of rules and a word list based on our study of many tests. After working through the sample test questions with these rules in mind, we suggest that you make a list of any words which you have misspelled. Further study of this list should then give you a big boost.

We also suggest that you find in your local library such books as "Words Frequently Misspelled," and "Spelling Word Lists," for supplementary work.

A FEW RULES THAT REALLY HELP

1. EI or IE

I COMES BEFORE *E*

Examples: friend, belief, niece, grieve

EXCEPT AFTER *C*

Examples: deceit, ceiling, conceive, receipt

OR WHEN SOUNDED LIKE *AY*

Examples: vein, neighbor, feign, heinous

Exceptions: either, neither, height, foreign, sovereign, forfeit, seize, counterfeit, financier

2. S or ES

ADD *ES*

TO WORDS ENDING IN *S, SH, X* OR *Z*

Examples: rush, rushes; success, successes; bench, benches; fox, foxes

AND TO WORDS ENDING IN *Y* AFTER A CONSONANT, BUT FIRST CHANGE *Y* TO *I*

Examples: try, tries; artery, arteries; community, communities

ADD *S* ALONE

TO ANY OTHER WORDS WHERE *S* IS NEEDED

Examples: boy, boys; chair, chairs; friend, friends; want, wants; decide, decides

3. L or LL

FINAL *L* IS DOUBLED

FOLLOWING A SINGLE VOWEL IN WORDS OF ONE SYLLABLE

Examples: fall, bell, sill, doll, hull

FOLLOWING A SINGLE VOWEL IN WORDS OF MORE THAN ONE SYLLABLE, WHEN THE STRESS FALLS ON THE LAST SYLLABLE

Examples: recall, fortell, distill

FINAL *L* IS SINGLE

FOLLOWING MORE THAN ONE VOWEL IN WORDS OF ONE SYLLABLE

Examples: bail, real, soul, feel

FOLLOWING MORE THAN ONE VOWEL IN WORDS OF MORE THAN ONE SYLLABLE WHEN THE STRESS FALLS ON THE LAST SYLLABLE

Examples: conceal, ideal, detail

FOLLOWING A SINGLE VOWEL IN WORDS OF MORE THAN ONE SYLLABLE, WHEN THE STRESS FALLS *BEFORE* THE LAST SYLLABLE

Examples: marginal, alcohol, dismal

4. SUFFIXES

These are syllables that are added to a base word to make a new word.

Some common suffixes:

able	less
ed	ly
er	ment
ful	ness
ing	ous

You can add these suffixes to some base words without changing the spelling of either the base word or the suffix.

Base Word	*Suffix*	*New Word*
expend	able	expendable
roar	ed	roared
read	er	reader
use	ful	useful
sink	ing	sinking
count	less	countless
love	ly	lovely
arrange	ment	arrangement
glad	ness	gladness
peril	ous	perilous

However, some base words must be changed slightly before you can add the suffix. Here are some rules for these changes.

IN WORDS ENDING IN *E*

DROP THE *E* WHEN THE SUFFIX BEGINS WITH A VOWEL

Examples: like, likable; love, loved; trace, tracer

OR AFTER *DG*

Examples: judge, judgment; acknowledge, acknowledging

IN WORDS ENDING IN *Y*

CHANGE *Y* TO *I* AFTER A CONSONANT IN WORDS OF MORE THAN ONE SYLLABLE

Examples: lovely, lovelier; accompany, accompaniment; tardy, tardiness; levy, levied

BUT KEEP THE *Y* WHEN YOU ADD *ING*

Examples: rally, rallying; fry, frying; reply, replying; destroy, destroying

AND WHEN YOU ADD *LY* OR *NESS* TO WORDS OF ONE SYLLABLE

Examples: sly, slyly, slyness; shy, shyly, shyness; dry, dryly, dryness

Exceptions: day, daily; lay, laid; say, said; slay, slain; pay, paid

IN WORDS ENDING IN A CONSONANT

DOUBLE THE FINAL CONSONANT IF IT FOLLOWS A SINGLE VOWEL IN WORDS OF ONE SYLLABLE, AND IF THE SUFFIX BEGINS WITH A VOWEL

Examples: fat, fatter; hop, hopping; wed, wedding

OR IF IT FOLLOWS A SINGLE VOWEL IN WORDS OF MORE THAN ONE SYLLABLE AND THE STRESS REMAINS ON THE SAME SYLLABLE

Examples: refer, referred; control, controlled

5. PREFIXES

These are syllables that go in front of a base word to make a new word.

Some common prefixes:

ab	com	en	ir	per
ac	con	il	mal	pro
ad	de	im	mis	re
bi	dis	in	over	under

You can add any prefix to a base word without changing the spelling of either the prefix or the base word.

Examples:

Prefix	*Base Word*	*New Word*
ab	normal	abnormal
ac	company	accompany
ad	join	adjoin
bi	lateral	bilateral
com	mission	commission
con	dense	condense
de	centralize	decentralize
dis	organize	disorganize
en	lace	enlace
il	legible	illegible
im	possible	impossible
in	sincere	insincere
ir	rational	irrational
mis	spell	misspell
mal	formed	malformed
over	do	overdo
per	form	perform
pre	text	pretext
pro	noun	pronoun
re	flex	reflex
under	go	undergo

We listed the foregoing rules in the order of their importance for you. Should they seem more than you can handle, we suggest that you memorize *at least* the following: all three points of (1); the first two points of (2) (the third point is practically self-evident); and the first two points of (3) (because if you know when to double the final *l*, you can leave it single for all the words that do not fit into these rules).

If you memorize these eight short statements, you will have taken a big step towards success in any spelling examination. Then study (4) carefully, and try to think of additional words you can make by using a base word and a suffix. Check your result, and if you have made mistakes, study it again until getting the right answer comes naturally. Go over (5), too, but you needn't put so much effort into it. The important thing here is to be able to recognize a prefix when you see it.

WORDS FREQUENTLY MISSPELLED

aberration
abeyance
abscess
abundance
accessible
accumulation
acquaint
across
actually
adage
addressee
adjunct
adoption
advise
aggravate
allege
amendment
amplify
ancient
anecdote
anemia
angle
annoyance
antipathy
apologetic
apparatus
appellate
appetite
aquatic
arouse
arraignment
ascertain
assessment
aversion

baccalaureate
bankruptcy
beatitude
beleaguered
belligerent
biased
biscuit
blamable
bookkeeping
bounteous
bureau

capitol
carburetor
category
cemetery
chamois
character
chauffeur
circumstantial
citation
clamorous
clique
colossal
column
commandant
commemorate
committal
community
compel
complacency
conciliatory
confectionery
connoisseur
consummation
controller
conversant
coroner
corporal
correlation
correspondence
corrugated
criticism
crucial
crystallized
currency

dearth
deceive
deferred
deliberate
demurrage
denunciatory
derogatory
description
desecration
detrimental
dilapidated
diocese
diphtheria
disappearance
dissatisfied
distinguished

ecstasy
eczema
effects
elaborate
electrolysis
embarrass
eminently
emolument
emphasis
emphatically
ephemeral
equilibrium
equinoctial
equipped
essential
exaggerate
exceed
exercise
exhortation
existence
extraordinary

facilitation
fallibility
fascinated
feudal
financier
foreign
forfeit
function

gelatin
grandeur

harass
hearth
heinous
heritage
hindrance
histrionic
hygienic

illegitimate
imminent
impartiality
impeccable
impromptu
incongruity
indictment
individual
ingenuous
inimitable
innocuous
integrity
intelligence
intercede
interruption
irreparably

jeopardy
journal
judgment
judiciary

laboratory
labyrinth
lacquer
liquidate
loose
lucrative

mackerel
maintenance
maneuver
marital
masquerade
matinee
mechanical
medallion
medieval
mediocrity
memoir
midget
mischievous
moribund
murmuring
myriad
negligible
nevertheless

nickel
ninth
occur
official
ordinance

pacifist
pamphlet
panicky
parliament
patient
patronize
peculiar
permissible
picnicking
piquancy
plagiarism
pneumonia
policy
possession
prairie
preceding
precious
predatory
predilection
preferably
preparation
presumptuous
previous
principal
proletarian
promissory
propaganda
psychology
publicity
punctilious

queue

realize
reasonable
recognizable
regrettable
rehearsal
relevant
renascence
repetitious

resilience
resonance
responsibility
rheostat
rhetorical
rhythm
routine

sacrilegious
salable
salient
sandwich
scissors
scripture
secretary
senior
similar
sobriquet
sophomore
source
sovereign
specialized
specifically
staunch
stretch
subversive
succeed
summarize
surfeit
surgeon
symmetrical
tariff
temperament
thorough
transaction
transient
tremendous

vacillate
vacuum
vengeance

warrant
whether
wholly
wield

yacht

PREVIOUS QUESTIONS IN SPELLING

SEVEN TEST-TYPE QUIZZES FOR PRACTICE

Test 1 — How Do You Spell It?

DIRECTIONS: This test gives four suggested spellings for each word listed. Choose the spelling you know to be correct and mark your answer accordingly.

1. (A) transeint (B) transient (C) trancient (D) transent
2. (A) heratage (B) heritage (C) heiritage (D) heretage
3. (A) exibition (B) exhibition (C) exabition (D) exhebition
4. (A) intiative (B) enitiative (C) initative (D) initiative
5. (A) similiar (B) simmilar (C) similar (D) simuler
6. (A) sufficiantly (B) sufisiently (C) sufficiently (D) suficeintly
7. (A) anticipate (B) antisipate (C) anticapate (D) antisapate
8. (A) intelligence (B) inteligence (C) intellegence (D) intelegence
9. (A) referance (B) referrence (C) referense (D) reference
10. (A) conscious (B) consious (C) conscius (D) consceous
11. (A) paralell (B) parellel (C) parellell (D) parallel
12. (A) abundence (B) abundance (C) abundants (D) abundents
13. (A) spesifically (B) specificaly (C) specifically (D) specefically
14. (A) elemanate (B) elimenate (C) elliminate (D) eliminate
15. (A) resonance (B) resonnance (C) resonence (D) reasonance
16. (A) benaficial (B) beneficial (C) benefitial (D) bennaficial
17. (A) retrievable (B) retreivable (C) retrievible (D) retreavable
18. (A) collosal (B) colossal (C) colosal (D) collossal
19. (A) inflameable (B) inflamable (C) enflamabel (D) inflammable
20. (A) auxillary (B) auxilliary (C) auxilary (D) auxiliary
21. (A) corregated (B) corrigated (C) corrugated (D) coregated
22. (A) accumalation (B) accumulation (C) acumulation (D) accumullation
23. (A) consumation (B) consummation (C) consumeation (D) consomation
24. (A) retorical (B) rhetorical (C) rhetorrical (D) retorrical
25. (A) inimitable (B) iminitable (C) innimitable (D) inimitible
26. (A) proletarian (B) prolletarian (C) prolatarian (D) proleterian

27. (A) appelate (B) apellate (C) appellate (D) apelate

28. (A) esential (B) essencial (C) essential (D) essantial

29. (A) assessment (B) assesment (C) asessment (D) assesmant

30. (A) ordinence (B) ordinnance (C) ordinanse (D) ordinance

31. (A) disapearance (B) disappearance (C) disappearense (D) disappearence

32. (A) attendence (B) attendanse (C) attendance (D) atendance

33. (A) acertain (B) assertain (C) ascertain (D) asertain

34. (A) specimen (B) speciman (C) spesimen (D) speceman

35. (A) relevant (B) relevent (C) rellevent (D) relavant

36. (A) anesthetic (B) aenesthetic (C) anestitic (D) annesthetic

37. (A) foriegn (B) foreign (C) forriegn (D) forreign

38. (A) interuption (B) interruption (C) interrupsion (D) interrupcion

39. (A) acquiesence (B) acquiescence (C) aquiescense (D) acquiesance

40. (A) exceed (B) exsede (C) exseed (D) excede

41. (A) maneuver (B) manuver (C) maneuvere (D) manneuver

42. (A) correlation (B) corrolation (C) corellation (D) corralation

43. (A) hinderence (B) hindranse (C) hindrance (D) hindrencė

44. (A) existence (B) existance (C) existense (D) existince

45. (A) bankrupcy (B) bankruptcy (C) bankruptsy (D) bankrupsy

46. (A) receipts (B) receits (C) reciepts (D) recieps

47. (A) impromtu (B) inpromtu (C) impromptu (D) impromptue

48. (A) pronounciation (B) pronunciatun (C) pronunciation (D) pronounciatun

49. (A) entirly (B) entirely (C) entirley (D) entireley

50. (A) complecation (B) complicasion (C) complication (D) complacation

51. (A) condem (B) condemn (C) condemm (D) condenm

52. (A) ocassion (B) occassion (C) ocasion (D) occasion

53. (A) contagious (B) contageous (C) contagous (D) contagiose

54. (A) perminent (B) permenant (C) permanent (D) permanant

55. (A) proceed (B) procede (C) prosede (D) proseed

56. (A) embarassment (B) embarrasment (C) embarasment (D) embarrassment

57. (A) cematery (B) cemetary (C) cemitery (D) cemetery

58. (A) believable (B) believeable (C) believeble (D) believible

59. (A) council (B) counsil (C) counsle (D) councel

60. (A) achievement (B) acheivment (C) achievment (D) acheivement

61. (A) Wendesday (B) Wensday (C) Wednesday (D) Wendnesday

62. (A) classify (B) classafy (C) classefy (D) classifey

63. (A) concensus (B) concencus (C) consencus (D) consensus

64. (A) suffiscent (B) sufficient (C) sufficiant (D) suffiscient

65. (A) responsable (B) responseable (C) responsibil (D) responsible

66. (A) remittence (B) remmittence (C) remmittance (D) remittance

67. (A) probible (B) probable (C) probbable (D) probabil

68. (A) weigt (B) wieght (C) weight (D) waight

69. (A) argument (B) argumint (C) argumant (D) arguement

70. (A) priceing (B) prising (C) priseing (D) pricing

71. (A) ballanced (B) balanced (C) balansed (D) balanct

72. (A) operateing (B) oparating (C) oparrating (D) operating

73. (A) privelege (B) privilege (C) privelige (D) privilige

74. (A) expenses (B) expences (C) expensses (D) expensces

75. (A) mispell (B) misspell (C) misspel (D) mispel

76. (A) occurrance (B) occurence (C) occurrence (D) ocurrence

77. (A) receit (B) receipt (C) reciept (D) reciet

78. (A) conscience (B) conscence (C) consciense (D) conscense

79. (A) deterent (B) deterrant (C) deterant (D) deterrent

80. (A) responsable (B) responsceable (C) responsible (D) responcible

81. (A) noticable (B) noticible (C) noticeable (D) noticeble

82. (A) passable (B) passible (C) passeble (D) passeable

83. (A) dissplaid (B) displayed (C) dissplayed (D) displaid

84. (A) tryeing (B) trieing (C) trying (D) triing

85. (A) imaterial (B) immaterial (C) imaterrial (D) imatterial

86. (A) balancing (B) balanceing (C) balansing (D) balanseing

87. (A) conceed (B) consede (C) concede (D) conseed

88. (A) innumerible (B) innumerable (C) inumerable (D) inumerible

89. (A) maintainance (B) maintenance (C) maintenence (D) maintanance

Correct Answers For The Foregoing Questions

1. B	9. D	17. A	25. A	32. C	39. B	46. A	53. A	60. A	67. B	74. A	82. A
2. B	10. A	18. B	26. A	33. C	40. A	47. C	54. C	61. C	68. C	75. B	83. B
3. B	11. D	19. D	27. C	34. A	41. A	48. C	55. A	62. A	69. A	76. C	84. C
4. D	12. B	20. D	28. C	35. A	42. A	49. B	56. D	63. D	70. D	77. B	85. B
5. C	13. C	21. C	29. A	36. A	43. C	50. C	57. D	64. B	71. B	78. A	86. A
6. C	14. D	22. B	30. D	37. B	44. A	51. B	58. A	65. D	72. D	79. D	87. C
7. A	15. A	23. B	31. B	38. B	45. B	52. D	59. A	66. D	73. B	80. C	88. B
8. A	16. B	24. B								81. C	89. B

SCORE

%

NO. CORRECT ÷

NO. OF QUESTIONS ON THIS TEST

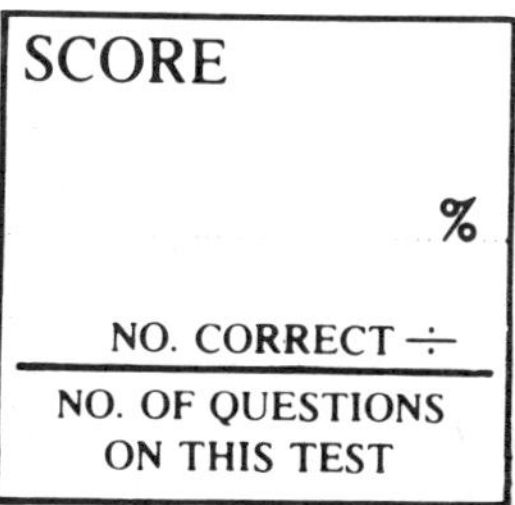

Test 2 — One Out of Four

DIRECTIONS: Each of the following four word groups contains one word that is spelled correctly. Choose the correctly-spelled word.

1. (A) authority (B) similiar (C) refering (D) preferebly
2. (A) suficient (B) wheather (C) actueally (D) minimum
3. (A) volentary (B) syllabus (C) embodyeing (D) pertanent
4. (A) simplified (B) comunity (C) emfasis (D) advant
5. (A) approppriate (B) expedient (C) adopshun (D) satisfactarily
6. (A) unconsiously (B) pamflet (C) asess (D) adjacent
7. (A) mortgages (B) infalible (C) eradecated (D) sourse
8. (A) predescessor (B) obsolete (C) unimpared (D) sporadicaly
9. (A) impenitrable (B) recognisable (C) paresite (D) vigilance
10. (A) emfatically (B) manefold (C) anxieties (D) expence
11. (A) emfatically (B) inculcate (C) skilfel (D) indigense
12. (A) indespensable (B) incumbrance (C) intolerible (D) desicration
13. (A) exibit (B) critisism (C) recieved (D) conspicuous
14. (A) biennial (B) monatary (C) beninant (D) complacensy
15. (A) propriaty (B) legalety (C) acquiesce (D) conversent
16. (A) ajusted (B) porportionate (C) inaugurated (D) dubeous
17. (A) responsability (B) soceity (C) individuel (D) increments
18. (A) subordonate (B) transaction (C) buisness (D) effitiency
19. (A) condemnation (B) exsees (C) ordinerily (D) capasity
20. (A) discuscion (B) statistics (C) producktion (D) disguissed
21. (A) constrictive (B) proposel (C) partisipated (D) desision
22. (A) comtroller (B) inadequasy (C) resolusion (D) promotion
23. (A) progresive (B) reciepts (C) dependent (D) secsion
24. (A) seperate (B) speciallized (C) funshions (D) publicity
25. (A) instrament (B) vicinity (C) offical (D) journale
26. (A) unecessary (B) responsebility (C) suprintendent (D) recommendation
27. (A) resonable (B) curency (C) occur (D) critisise
28. (A) apetite (B) preliminary (C) concilatory (D) cruseal
29. (A) afilliation (B) amendement (C) ansient (D) patient
30. (A) recipeint (B) pretious (C) uncertainty (D) maritial
31. (A) illigetimate (B) peciular (C) addressee (D) consintrated
32. (A) convalescent (B) detramental (C) elaberate (D) accessable

33. (A) accomodate (B) prejudise
 (C) preveous (D) exaggerate

34. (A) corroner (B) inditment
 (C) seized (D) scissers

35. (A) araignment (B) emolument
 (C) faciletation (D) ordanence

Correct Answers

(You'll learn more by writing your own answers before comparing them with these.)

Answer Sheet

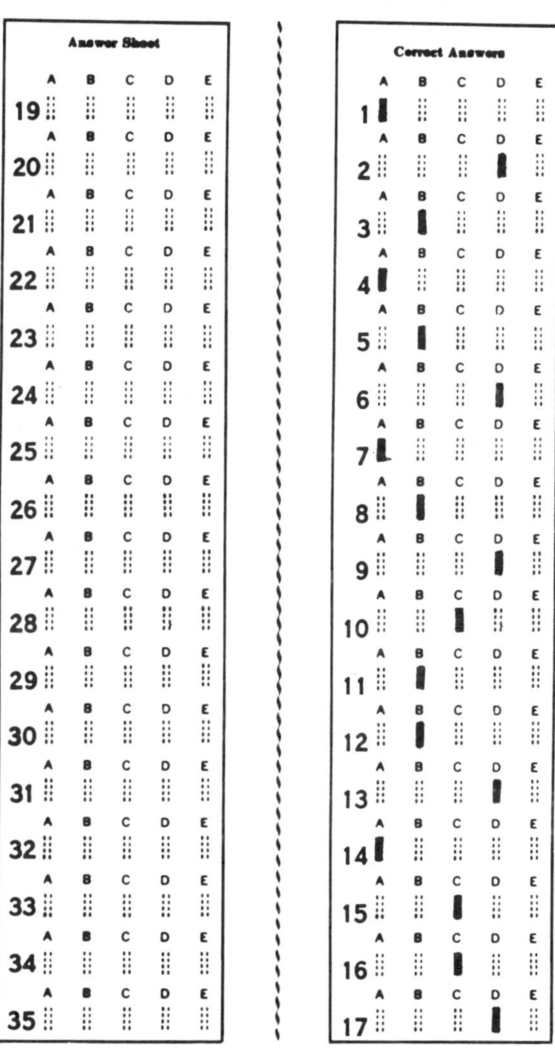

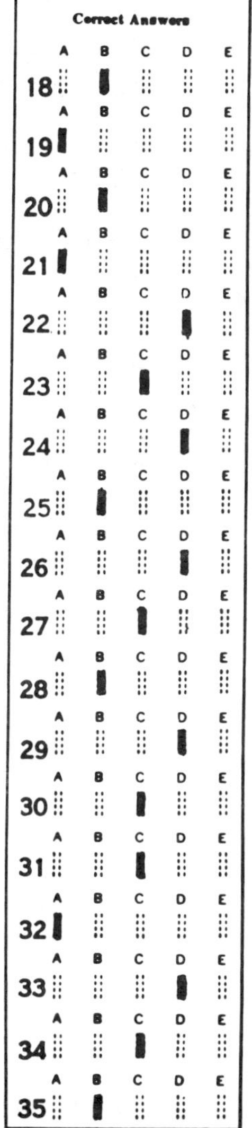

SCORE

%

NO. CORRECT ÷

NO. OF QUESTIONS ON THIS TEST

Test 3 — Find the Errors

DIRECTIONS: In this test all words but one of each group are spelled correctly. Indicate the misspelled word in each group.

1. (A) extraordinary (B) statesmen (C) array (D) financeer

2. (A) materialism (B) indefatigible (C) moribund (D) rebellious

3. (A) queue (B) equillibrium (C) contemporary (D) structure

4. (A) acquatic (B) fascinated (C) bogged (D) accommodations

5. (A) embarrassment (B) sosialization (C) imposition (D) incredulous

6. (A) politisians (B) psychology (C) susceptible (D) antipathy

7. (A) convincing (B) vicissetudes (C) negligible (D) foreign

8. (A) characters (B) veracity (C) testimony (D) apolagetic

9. (A) shriek (B) carelogue (C) impeccable (D) ruthless

10. (A) ocassions (B) accomplishment (C) assumed (D) distinguished

11. (A) servicable (B) preparation (C) exceptional (D) initiative

12. (A) primarely (B) available (C) paragraph (D) routine

13. (A) ligament (B) preseding (C) mechanical (D) anecdote

14. (A) judgment (B) conclusion (C) circumlocution (D) breifly

15. (A) censor (B) personel. (C) counterfeit (D) advantageous

16. (A) liquified (B) adage (C) ancient (D) imitation

17. (A) lapse (B) questionnaire (C) concieve (D) staunch

18. (A) calendar (B) typographical (C) inexcusable (D) sallient

19. (A) carreer (B) eminently (C) nevertheless (D) fourth

20. (A) corperal (B) sergeant (C) lieutenant (D) commandant

21. (A) partial (B) business (C) through (D) comission

22. (A) accounts (B) financial (C) reciept (D) answer

23. (A) except (B) conection (C) altogether (D) credentials

24. (A) whose (B) written (C) strenth (D) therefore

25. (A) catalogue (B) familiar (C) formerly (D) secretery

26. (A) debtor (B) shipment (C) fileing (D) correspond

27. (A) courtesy (B) dictionery (C) extremely (D) exactly

28. (A) probaly (B) directory (C) acquired (D) hurriedly

29. (A) hauled (B) freight (C) hankerchief (D) millionaire

30. (A) goverment (B) mileage (C) scene (D) ninety

31. (A) written (B) permenent (C) similar (D) convenient

32. (A) cooperation (B) duplicate (C) negotiable (D) Febuary

33. (A) experience (B) interupt (C) cylinder (D) campaign

34. (A) cordialy (B) completely (C) sandwich (D) respectfully

Test 4 — Playing Word Detective

DIRECTIONS: This probing test measures your ability to detect misspelled words in a text. In each of the following groups of four sentences, there is only one which does not contain a misspelled word. Choose the completely correct sentence in each group.

1. (A) In accordance with their usual custom, the employees presented a gift to the retiring president.
   (B) It is difficult not to critisize them under the circumstances.
   (C) The company has not paid a divedend to the owners of the preferred stock since the beginning of the depression.
   (D) At the time it was thought that any improvement on the invention was impossible.
2. (A) Whether the percentage of profit was as immence as has been charged is doubtful.
   (B) In the early years of the depression, transient and local homeless were sheltered together because of their common lack of funds to pay for domicile.
   (C) It is easier and wiser to suspend judgement until the facts are known.
   (D) The responsability for the situation was put squarely on those to whom it belonged.
3. (A) The recommendations of the committee were adopted by the convention.
   (B) It is usually considered unecessary to analyse the statistics under the present circumstances.
   (C) Hearafter, the company will refuse to sell hinges on credit.
   (D) The lieutenent to whom you referred in your last letter has been transferred to another post.
4. (A) It has been found impossible to adjust the requirements.
   (B) Advancement is slow because opportunities for promotion are infrequent.
   (C) A carrear in the civil service is the ambition of the majority of young entrants.
   (D) Because he has been closly connected with the management of the enterprise for so long, he is well informed on the matter.
5. (A) The indictment supersedes the original document.
   (B) The responsibility of soceity to the individual is a matter of serious moment.
   (C) After the middle of the month, all salary incraments will be adjusted according to the new scheme of proportionate distribution
   (D) He was given explisit directions to limit expenses as far as possible.
6. (A) They were somewhat dubious as to the propriety and quality of the procedure as contemplated.
   (B) It was certain that he would acquiese, once conversant with the full details.
   (C) Although only a biennial publication, its influence was far-reaching and its circulation extensive.
   (D) It was difficult to arouse him to any appreciation of the monatary aspects of the situation.
7. (A) His attitude throughout was one of benignant complacency, in spite of the derision of the multitude.
   (B) The exhibit deserved a more conspicious location and more favorable criticism than it received.
   (C) It should have been considered an incumbrance rather than an advantage, since it was not indespensable, and added greatly to the total load.
   (D) The situation has become intolerable and further desicration of the premises should be discouraged emphatically.
8. (A) To inculcate steadfast principals of economy and skillful administration is the task that confronts us.
   (B) The degree of indigence is relative, fluctuating with the rise and fall of the country's general prosperity.
   (C) The duties of the position are manefold, the anxieties great, and the emoluments scarcely in keeping with the expense of energy demanded.
   (D) Though at first the gloom seemed impenitrable, shadows and, finally, objects became visible and later distinctly recognizable.
9. (A) Investigation into the nature of the parisites, which continually affect the vegetation, demands constant vigilance and unremitting care.

(B) The example set by his predescessor enabled him to embark on his mission secure in the confidence of the majority of the citizens.
(C) Customs which are obsolete in most communities, are found sporadically in all their primitive vigor, unimpaired by the passage of time.
(D) Formerly, guaranteed morgages were considered to be infallible investments, even by the most conservative.

10. (A) The signature of every recipiant must be secured before the list of donations is turned over to the organization.
(B) The tendency to deviate from the proper scientific point of view in these matters should be eradecated at its source.
(C) The authorship of the pamphlet was recently acknowledged, and an explanation of its appearance offered.
(D) Income tax payers provided 46 per cent of all internal revenue reciepts during the last fiscal year.

11. (A) International peace is attainable, dependant only on the acceptance and application of certain principles.
(B) What is expected to become a struggle between the radical and conservative sections was precipitated today.
(C) He said that his action to stop further payments accorded with the request of the comptroler.
(D) He regarded State legislation alone as inadiquate to deal with the issue.

12. (A) The sponsors of the resolution, in a joint statement, defended their proposel as a constructive step toward the promotion of world peace.
(B) A large number of persons participated in the conference.
(C) The most dramatic, and doubtless the most important, ruling was the desision of the court reversing its own previous opinion on the question of State Minimum Wage Laws.
(D) Included in the report to be presented to the delegates as a basis for discuscion are statistics covering production in the various countries.

13. (A) He held fast to his original opinion that much of present research was disguissed promotion material.
(B) The tranquillity in which the session of the House of Representatives was ending was shattered by the bombshell of disagreement.
(C) His decision to assess adjacent property was widely condemmed.
(D) The majority of the approppriation acts and resolutions were special in nature.

14. (A) Is it expedient to amend the constitution by the adoption of the subjoined?
(B) It was the general opinion that this system had not functioned satisfactorily and that it needed to be simplefied.
(C) In the early days, protection against fire was provided by volentary fire departments.
(D) If you would oppose home rule for Illinois cities, draft a provision embodyeing your ideas as to the constitutional relationship which should exist between a state and a municipality.

15. (A) An attempt has been made to give the pertinent facts in sufficient detail so that the student may determine whether the decision actually made was sound.
(B) Should they also have been given authorety to review local bond issues under a plan similar to that adopted in Indiana?
(C) A corperal ranks below either a sergeant or a lieutenant.
(D) A carreer system is eminently desirable for the proper administration of civil service.

16. (A) I believe that I have never seen a typographical error in a calender.
(B) A lapse of memory is not inexcusable.
(C) A questionaire often contains the silliest questions a man can conceive.
(D) I advise you to be staunch and not to yeild, for he is wrong.

17. (A) The duties you will perform are similar to the duties of a patrolman.
(B) Officers must be constantly alert to sieze the initiative.
(C) Officers in this organization are not entitled to special privileges.
(D) Any changes in procedure will be announced publically.

18. (A) It will be to your advantage to keep your firearm in good working condition.
(B) There are approximately fourty men on sick leave.
(C) Your first duty will be to pursuade the person to obey the law.
(D) Fires often begin in flameable material kept in lockers.

Test 5 — Some Right, Some Wrong

DIRECTIONS: In the following list, some words are spelled correctly, some misspelled. On your practice sheet, write CORRECT for those words properly spelled; spell out the word correctly for those misspelled.

1. unparalleled
2. gastliness
3. mediocrity
4. exibition
5. posessing
6. lucritive
7. corresspondence
8. accellerated
9. labirynth
10. duplisity
11. repitious
12. jepardy
13. impartiallity
14. sobriquet
15. accesable
16. incredible
17. connoisseurs
18. fallibility
19. litagation
20. piquansy
21. fuedal
22. predetory
23. desparado
24. incongruity
25. delibarate
26. competetive
27. beleaguered
28. leiutenant
29. equinoxial
30. derogatory
31. denuncietory
32. panickey
33. calendar
34. belligerents
35. abolition
36. predjudice
37. propoganda
38. adolesents
39. irresistible
40. exortation
41. renascence
42. counsil
43. bullitin
44. aberation
45. integraty
46. cristallized
47. irrepairably
48. punctillious
49. catagory
50. parlament
51. medalion
52. bountious
53. aggrevate
54. midgit
55. wierd
56. elliminate
57. murmering
58. hystrionic
59. goverment
60. clamerous
61. garantee
62. presumptious
63. comemmerate
64. indispensible
65. bookeeping
66. disatisfied
67. tremendious
68. interseed
69. inaugerate
70. rehersel
71. nucleous
72. benefiting
73. wholy
74. discription
75. alright
76. representitive
77. mischievious
78. ingenuous
79. accidently
80. exilerate
81. pronounciation
82. fourty
83. mackeral
84. rescind
85. kleptomania
86. summerize
87. resillience
88. regretable
89. questionaire
90. privelege
91. judgment
92. plagiarism
93. vengence
94. subpoena
95. rythm
96. derth
97. impromtue
98. incumbant
99. forfiet
100. maintainance

Test 6 — One Out of Five or None

Either one word is misspelled, or all five words are correctly spelled, in each of the following groups. Next to each question *write* the letter corresponding to the *correction* that should be made.

1. picnicing, remittance, scintilla, niece, wholly
   (A) add a letter
   (B) change a letter
   (C) interchange two adjacent letters
   (D) omit a letter.
2. coolly, eligable, ingenuous, singeing, shoeing
   (A) change "a" to "i"
   (B) change "u" to "i"
   (C) omit an "e"
   (D) add an "e"
3. diphtheria, dichotomy, hypocricy, outrageous, personnel
   (A) change a consonant
   (B) change a vowel
   (C) make no change
   (D) omit a consonant.
4. despoliation, ecstasy, foliage, harrassed, supersede
   (A) add a letter
   (B) change a letter
   (C) interchange two letters
   (D) omit a letter.
5. beneficent, deriliction, feasible, pantomime, sacrilegious
   (A) change wrong letter to a, b, c, d, f, g
   (B) change wrong letter to e, h, j, k, l, m
   (C) change wrong letter to i, n, p, q, r, s, t
   (D) change wrong letter to o, u, v, w, x, y, z.
6. artillery, dispatch, occasionally, potsherd, similiar
   (A) change a letter
   (B) change the placement of a letter
   (C) omit a consonant
   (D) omit a vowel.
7. indispensable, lief, minerology, occurring, seize
   (A) change a vowel to "a"
   (B) change a vowel to "i"
   (C) interchange two adjacent vowels
   (D) omit a letter.
8. existence, gaseous, maintenance, sergeant, vengance
   (A) add "e"
   (B) change "a" to "e"
   (C) change "e" to "a"
   (D) omit "e".
9. changeable, echoes, geneology, mileage, nineteenth
   (A) change "eo" to "ea"
   (B) change "ea" to "i"
   (C) make no change
   (D) omit an "e"
10. apparel, embarrass, erroneous, parallel, quizzes
    (A) change a vowel
    (B) double a consonant
    (C) make no change
    (D) omit a consonant.
11. cemetery, definitely, esculator, medicine, toboggan
    (A) change "e" to "a"
    (B) change "i" to "a"
    (C) change "o" to "a"
    (D) change "u" to "a".
12. innoculate, prejudice, privilege, rarefy, tragedy
    (A) add a consonant
    (B) change a vowel
    (C) make no change
    (D) omit a letter.
13. affiliate, appetite, descendant, gelatin, maneuver
    (A) change a letter
    (B) double a letter
    (C) make no change
    (D) omit a letter.
14. accessible, achievement, acknowledgment, iridescent, questionnaire
    (A) add a letter
    (B) change a letter
    (C) make no change
    (D) omit a letter.
15. accommodate, aplomb, bronichal, surgeon, vacillation
    (A) add a letter
    (B) change the placement of a letter
    (C) make no change
    (D) omit a letter.
16. bankruptcy, correspondance, pinning, impresario, rococo
    (A) add a letter
    (B) change a letter
    (C) make no change
    (D) omit a letter.
17. caffeine, hygiene, lineage. malleable, medeval
    (A) add a vowel
    (B) interchange two adjacent vowels
    (C) omit a consonant
    (D) omit a vowel.

Test 7 — One Out of Four

DIRECTIONS: In this test all words but one of each group are spelled correctly. Indicate the misspelled word in each group.

1. (A) proscenium (B) resilient (C) biennial (D) connoisseur
2. (A) queue (B) equable (C) ecstacy (D) obsequious
3. (A) quizes (B) frolicking (C) maelstrom (D) homonym
4. (A) pseudonym (B) annihilate (C) questionaire (D) irascible
5. (A) diptheria (B) annular (C) acolyte (D) descendant
6. (A) truculant (B) rescind (C) dilettante (D) innuendo
7. (A) prevalence (B) discrete (C) efrontery (D) admissible
8. (A) igneous (B) annullment (C) dissipate (D) abattoir
9. (A) quiescent (B) apologue (C) myrrh (D) inocuous
10. (A) propoganda (B) gaseous (C) iridiscent (D) similar
11. (A) supercede (B) tyranny (C) beauteous (D) victuals
12. (A) geneology (B) tragedy (C) soliloquy (D) prejudice
13. (A) remittance (B) shoeing (C) category (D) gutteral
14. (A) catarrh (B) parlamentary (C) villain (D) omitted
15. (A) vengeance (B) parallel (C) nineth (D) mayoralty
16. (A) changeable (B) therefor (C) incidently (D) dissatisfy
17. (A) orifice (B) deferrment (C) harass (D) accommodate
18. (A) picnicking (B) proceedure (C) hypocrisy (D) seize
19. (A) vilify (B) efflorescence (C) sarcophagus (D) sacreligious
20. (A) paraphenalia (B) apothecaries (C) occurrence (D) plagiarize
21. (A) irreparably (B) comparitively (C) lovable (D) audible
22. (A) nullify (B) siderial (C) salability (D) irrelevant
23. (A) asinine (B) dissonent (C) opossum (D) indispensable
24. (A) discomfit (B) sapient (C) exascerbate (D) sarsaparilla
25. (A) valleys (B) maintainance (C) abridgment (D) reticence
26. (A) tolerance (B) circumferance (C) insurance (D) dominance
27. (A) diameter (B) tangent (C) paralell (D) perimeter
28. (A) providential (B) personal (C) accidental (D) diagonel
29. (A) development (B) retarded (C) homogenious (D) intelligence
30. (A) noticeable (B) forceible (C) practical (D) erasable
31. (A) heroes (B) folios (C) sopranos (D) usuel
32. (A) typical (B) descend (C) summarize (D) continuel
33. (A) courageous (B) recomend (C) omission (D) eliminate
34. (A) compliment (B) illuminate (C) auxilary (D) installation
35. (A) preliminary (B) aquainted (C) syllable (D) analysis
36. (A) accustomed (B) negligible (C) interupted (D) bulletin
37. (A) summoned (B) managment (C) mechanism (D) sequence
38. (A) comittee (B) surprise (C) noticeable (D) emphasize
39. (A) occurrance (B) likely (C) accumulate (D) grievance
40. (A) obstacle (B) particuliar (C) baggage (D) fascinating

Correct Answers For The Foregoing Questions

(Please make every effort to answer the questions on your own before looking at these answers. You'll make faster progress by following this rule.)

TEST 3

1. D
2. B
3. B
4. A
5. B
6. A
7. B
8. D
9. B
10. A
11. A
12. A
13. B
14. D
15. B
16. A
17. C
18. D
19. A
20. A
21. D
22. C
23. B
24. C
25. D
26. C
27. B
28. A
29. C
30. A
31. B
32. D
33. B
34. A

TEST 4

1. A
2. B
3. A
4. A
5. A
6. A
7. A
8. B
9. C
10. C
11. B
12. B
13. B
14. A
15. A
16. B
17. C
18. A

TEST 5

1. correct
2. ghastliness
3. correct
4. exhibition
5. possessing
6. lucrative
7. correspondence
8. accelerated
9. labyrinth
10. duplicity
11. repetitious
12. jeopardy
13. impartiality
14. correct
15. accessible
16. correct
17. correct
18. correct
19. litigation
20. piquancy
21. feudal
22. predatory
23. desperado
24. correct
25. deliberate
26. competitive
27. correct
28. lieutenant
29. equinoctial
30. correct
31. denunciatory
32. panicky
33. correct
34. correct
35. correct
36. prejudice
37. propaganda
38. adolescents
39. correct
40. exhortation
41. correct
42. counsel
43. bulletin
44. aberration
45. integrity
46. crystallized
47. irreparably
48. punctilious
49. category
50. parliament
51. medallion
52. bounteous
53. aggravate
54. midget
55. weird
56. eliminate
57. murmuring
58. histrionic
59. government
60. clamorous
61. guarantee
62. presumptuous
63. commemorate
64. indispensable
65. bookkeeping
66. dissatisfied
67. tremendous
68. intercede
69. inaugurate
70. rehearsal
71. nucleus
72. correct
73. wholly
74. description
75. correct
76. representative
77. mischievous
78. correct
79. accidentally
80. exhilarate
81. pronunciation
82. forty
83. mackerel
84. correct
85. correct
86. summarize
87. resilience
88. regrettable
89. questionnaire
90. privilege
91. correct
92. correct
93. vengeance
94. correct
95. rhythm
96. dearth
97. impromptu
98. incumbent
99. forfeit
100. maintenance

TEST 6

1. A
2. A
3. A
4. D
5. B
6. D
7. A
8. A
9. A
10. C
11. D
12. D
13. C
14. C
15. B
16. B
17. A

TEST 7

1. B
2. C
3. A
4. C
5. A
6. A
7. C
8. B
9. D
10. A
11. A
12. A
13. D
14. B
15. C
16. C
17. B
18. B
19. D
20. A
21. B
22. B
23. B
24. C
25. B
26. B
27. C
28. D
29. C
30. B
31. D
32. D
33. B
34. C
35. B
36. C
37. B
38. A
39. A
40. B

SCORE 1 .... %

NO. CORRECT ÷ NO. OF QUESTIONS

SCORE 2 .... %

NO. CORRECT ÷ NO. OF QUESTIONS

TEST—TAKING MADE SIMPLE

Having gotten this far, you're almost an expert test-taker because you have now mastered the subject matter of the test. Proper preparation is the real secret. The pointers on the next few pages will take you the rest of the way by giving you the strategy employed on tests by those who are most successful in this not-so-mysterious art.

BEFORE THE TEST

T-DAY MINUS SEVEN

You're going to pass this examination because you have received the best possible preparation for it. But, unlike many others, you're going to give the best possible account of yourself by acquiring the rare skill of effectively using your knowledge to answer the examination questions.

First off, get rid of any negative attitudes toward the test. You have a negative attitude when you view the test as a device to "trip you up" rather than an opportunity to show how effectively you have learned.

APPROACH THE TEST WITH SELF-CONFIDENCE. Plugging through this book was no mean job, and now that you've done it you're probably better prepared than 90% of the others. Self-confidence is one of the biggest strategic assets you can bring to the testing room.

Nobody likes tests, but some poor souls permit themselves to get upset or angry when they see what they think is an unfair test. The expert doesn't. He keeps calm and moves right ahead, knowing that everyone is taking the same test. Anger, resentment, fear . . . they all slow you down. "Grin and bear it!"

Besides, every test you take, including this one, is a valuable experience which improves your skill. Since you will undoubtedly be taking other tests in the years to come, it may help you to regard this one as training to perfect your skill.

Keep calm; there's no point in panic. If you've done your work there's no need for it; and if you haven't, a cool head is your very first requirement.

Why be the frightened kind of student who enters the examination chamber in a mental coma? A test taken under mental stress does not provide a fair measure of your ability. At the very least, this book has removed for you some of the fear and mystery that surrounds examinations. A certain amount of concern is normal and good, but excessive worry saps your strength and keenness. In other words, be prepared EMOTIONALLY.

Pre-Test Review

If you know any others who are taking this test, you'll probably find it helpful to review the book and your notes with them. The group should be small, certainly not more than four. Team study at this stage should seek to review the material in a different way than you learned it originally; should strive for an exchange of ideas between you and the other members of the group; should be selective in sticking to important ideas; should stress the vague and the unfamiliar rather than that which you all know well; should be businesslike and devoid of any nonsense; should end as soon as you get tired.

One of the *worst* strategies in test taking is to do *all* your preparation the night before the exam. As a reader of this book, you have scheduled and spaced your study properly so as not to suffer from the fatigue and emotional disturbance that comes from cramming the night before.

Cramming is a very good way to *guarantee poor test results.*

However, you would be wise to prepare yourself factually by *reviewing your notes* in the 48 hours preceding the exam. You shouldn't have to spend more than two or three hours in this way. Stick to salient points. The others will fall into place quickly.

Don't confuse cramming with a final, calm review which helps you focus on the significant areas of this book and further strengthens your confidence in your ability to handle the test questions. In other words, prepare yourself FACTUALLY.

Keep Fit

Mind and body work together. Poor physical condition will lower your mental efficiency. In preparing for an examination, observe the common-sense rules of health. Get sufficient sleep and rest, eat proper foods, plan recreation and exercise. In relation to health and examinations, two cautions are in order. Don't miss your meals prior to an examination in order to get extra time for study. Likewise, don't miss your regular sleep by sitting up late to "cram" for the examination. Cramming is an attempt to learn in a very short period of time what should have been learned through regular and consistent study. Not only are these two habits detrimental to health, but seldom do they pay off in terms of effective learning. It is likely that you will be *more confused* than better prepared on the day of the examination if you have broken into your daily routine by missing your meals or sleep.

On the night before the examination go to bed at your regular time and try to get a good night's sleep. Don't go to the movies. Don't date. In other words, prepare yourself PHYSICALLY.

T-HOUR MINUS ONE

After a very light, leisurely meal, get to the examination room ahead of time, perhaps ten minutes early . . . but not so early that you have time to get into an argument with others about what's going to be asked on the exam, etc. The reason for coming early is to help you get accustomed to the room. It will help you to a better start.

Bring all necessary equipment . . .

. . . pen, two sharpened pencils, watch, paper, eraser, ruler, and any other things you're instructed to bring.

Get settled . . .

. . . by finding your seat and staying in it. If no special seats have been assigned, take one in the front to facilitate the seating of others coming in after you.

The test will be given by a test supervisor who reads the directions and otherwise tells you what to do. The people who walk about passing out the test papers and assisting with the examination are test proctors. If you're not able to see or hear properly notify the supervisor or a proctor. If you have any other difficulties during the examination, like a defective test booklet, scoring pencil, answer sheet; or if it's too hot or cold or dark or drafty, let them know. You're entitled to favorable test conditions, and if you don't have them you won't be able to do your best. Don't be a crank, but don't be shy either. An important function of the proctor is to see to it that you have favorable test conditions.

Relax . . .

. . . and don't bring on unnecessary tenseness by worrying about the difficulty of the examination. If necessary wait a minute before beginning to write. If you're still tense, take a couple of deep breaths, look over your test equipment, or do something which will take your mind away from the examination for a moment.

If your collar or shoes are tight, loosen them.

Put away unnecessary materials so that you have a good, clear space on your desk to write freely.

You Must Have *TO GIVE YOUR* **Best Test** *PERFORMANCE*

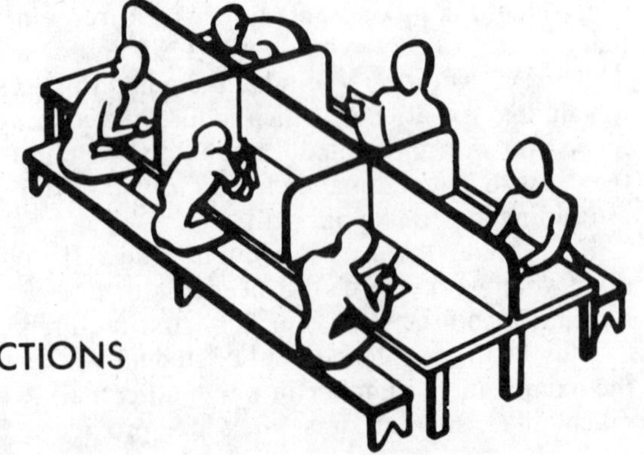

(1) A GOOD TEST ENVIRONMENT

(2) A COMPLETE UNDERSTANDING OF DIRECTIONS

(3) A DESIRE TO DO YOUR BEST

WHEN THEY SAY "GO" — TAKE YOUR TIME!

Listen very carefully to the test supervisor. If you fail to hear something important that he says, you may not be able to read it in the written directions and may suffer accordingly.

If you don't understand the directions you have heard or read, raise your hand and inform the proctor. Read carefully the directions for *each* part of the test before beginning to work on that part. If you skip over such directions too hastily, you may miss a main idea and thus lose credit for an entire section.

Get an Overview of the Examination

After reading the directions carefully, look over the entire examination to get an over-view of the nature and scope of the test. The purpose of this over-view is to give you some idea of the nature, scope, and difficulty of the examination.

It has another advantage. An item might be so phrased that it sets in motion a chain of thought that might be helpful in answering other items on the examination.

Still another benefit to be derived from reading all the items before you answer any is that the few minutes involved in reading the items gives you an opportunity to relax before beginning the examination. This will make for better concentration. As you read over these items the first time, check those whose answers immediately come to you. These will be the ones you will answer first. Read each item carefully before answering. It is a good practice to read each item at least twice to be sure that you understand it.

Plan Ahead

In other words, you should know precisely where you are going before you start. You should know:

1. whether you have to answer all the questions or whether you can choose those that are easiest for you;
2. whether all the questions are easy; (there may be a pattern of difficult, easy, etc.)
3. The length of the test; the number of questions;
4. The kind of scoring method used;
5. Which questions, if any, carry extra weight;
6. What types of questions are on the test;
7. What directions apply to each part of the test;
8. Whether you must answer the questions consecutively.

Budget Your Time Strategically!

Quickly figure out how much of the allotted time you can give to each section and still finish ahead of time. Don't forget to figure on the time you're investing in the overview. Then alter your schedule so that you can spend more time on those parts that count most. Then, if you can, plan to spend less time on the easier questions, so that you can devote the time saved to the harder questions. Figuring roughly, you should finish half the questions when half the allotted time has gone by. If there are 100 questions and you have three hours, you should have finished 50 questions after one and one half hours. So bring along a watch whether the instructions call for one or not. Jot down your "exam budget" and stick to it INTELLIGENTLY.

EXAMINATION STRATEGY

Probably the most important single strategy you can learn is to do the easy questions first. The very hard questions should be read and temporarily postponed. Identify them with a dot and return to them later.

This strategy has several advantages for you:

1. You're sure to get credit for all the questions you're sure of. If time runs out, you'll have all the sure shots, losing out only on those which you might have missed anyway.
2. By reading and laying away the tough ones you give your subconscious a chance to work on them. You may be pleasantly surprised to find the answers to the puzzlers popping up for you as you deal with related questions.
3. You won't risk getting caught by the time limit just as you reach a question you know really well.

A Tested Tactic

It's inadvisable on some examinations to answer each question in the order presented. The reason for this is that some examiners design tests so as to extract as much mental energy from you as possible. They put the most difficult questions at the beginning, the easier questions last. Or they may vary difficult with easy questions in a fairly regular pattern right through the test. Your survey of the test should reveal the pattern and your strategy for dealing with it.

If difficult questions appear at the beginning, answer them until you feel yourself slowing down or getting tired. Then switch to an easier part of the examination. You will return to the difficult portion after you have rebuilt your confidence by answering a batch of easy questions. Knowing that you have a certain number of points "under your belt" will help you when you return to the more difficult questions. You'll answer them with a much clearer mind; and you'll be refreshed by the change of pace.

Time

Use your time wisely. It's an important element in your test and you must use every minute effectively, working as rapidly as you can without sacrificing accuracy. Your exam survey and budget will guide you in dispensing your time. Wherever you can, pick up seconds on the easy ones. Devote your savings to the hard ones. If possible, pick up time on the lower value questions and devote it to those which give you the most points.

Relax Occasionally and Avoid Fatigue

If the exam is long (two or more hours) give yourself short rest periods as you feel you need them. If you're not permitted to leave the room, relax in your seat, look up from your paper, rest your eyes, stretch your legs, shift your body. Break physical and mental tension. Take several deep breaths and get back to the job, refreshed. If you don't do this you run the risk of getting nervous and tightening up. Your thinking may be hampered and you may make a few unnecessary mistakes.

Do not become worried or discouraged if the examination seems difficult to you. The questions in the various fields are purposely made difficult and searching so that the examination will discriminate effectively even among superior students. No one is expected to get a perfect or near-perfect score.

Remember that if the examination seems difficult to you, it may be even more difficult for your neighbor.

Think!

This is not a joke because you're not an IBM machine. Nobody is able to write all the time and also to read and think through each question. You must plan each answer. Don't give hurried answers in an atmosphere of panic. Even though you see a lot of questions, remember that they are objective and not very time-consuming. Don't rush headlong through questions that must be thought through.

Edit, Check, Proofread . . .

. . . after completing all the questions. Invariably, you will find some foolish errors which you needn't have made, and which you can easily correct. Don't just sit back or leave the room ahead of time. Read over your answers and make sure you wrote exactly what you meant to write. And that you wrote the answers in the right place. You might even find that you have omitted some answers inadvertently. You have budgeted time for this job of proofreading. PROOFREAD and pick up points.

One caution, though. Don't count on making major changes. And don't go in for wholesale changing of answers. To arrive at your answers in the first place you have read carefully and thought correctly. Second-guessing at this stage is more likely to result in wrong answers. So don't make changes unless you are quite certain you were wrong in the first place.

FOLLOW DIRECTIONS CAREFULLY

In answering questions on the objective or short-form examination, it is most important to follow all instructions carefully. Unless you have marked the answers properly, you will not receive credit for them. In addition, even in the same examination, the instructions will not be consistent. In one section you may be urged to guess if you are not certain; in another you may be cautioned against guessing. Some questions will call for the best choice among four or five alternatives; others may ask you to select the one incorrect or the least probable answer.

On some tests you will be provided with worked out fore-exercises, complete with correct answers. However, avoid the temptation to skip the directions and begin working just from reading the model questions and answers. Even though you may be familiar with that particular type of question, the directions may be different from those which you had followed previously. If the type of question should be new to you, work through the model until you understand it perfectly. This may save you time, and earn you a higher rating on the examination.

If the directions for the examination are written, read them carefully, at least twice. If the directions are given orally, listen attentively and then follow them precisely. For example, if you are directed to use plus (+) and minus (−) to mark true—false items, then don't use "T" and "F". If you are instructed to "blacken" a space on machine-scored tests, do not use a check (✓) or an "X". Make all symbols legible, and be sure that they have been placed in the proper answer space. It is easy, for example, to place the answer for item 5 in the space reserved for item 6. If this is done, then all of your following answers may be wrong. It is also very important that you understand the method they will use in scoring the examination. Sometimes they tell you in the directions. The method of scoring may affect the amount of time you spend on an item, especially if some items count more than others. Likewise, the directions may indicate whether or not you should guess in case you are not sure of the answer. Some methods of scoring penalize you for guessing.

Cue Words. Pay special attention to qualifying words or phrases in the directions. Such words as *one, best reason, surest, means most nearly the same as, preferable, least correct,* etc., all indicate that *one* response is called for, and that you must select the response which best fits the qualifications in the question.

Time. Sometimes a time limit is set for each section of the examination. If that is the case, follow the time instructions carefully. Your *exam budget* and your watch can help you here. Even if you haven't finished a section when the time limit is up, pass on to the next section. The examination has been planned according to the time schedule.

If the examination paper bears the instruction "Do not turn over page until signal is given," or "Do not start until signal is given," follow the instruction. Otherwise, you may be disqualified.

Pay Close Attention. Be sure you understand what you're doing at all times. Especially in dealing with true-false or multiple-choice questions it's vital that you understand the meaning of every question. It is normal to be working under stress when taking an examination, and it is easy to skip a word or jump to a false conclusion, which may cost you points on the examination. In many multiple-choice and matching questions, the examiners deliberately insert plausible-appearing false answers in order to catch the candidate who is not alert.

Answer clearly. If the examiner who marks your paper cannot understand what you mean, you will not receive credit for your correct answer. On a True-False examination you will not receive any credit for a question which is marked both true and false. If you are asked to underline, be certain that your lines are under and not through the words and that they do not extend beyond them. When using the separate answer sheet it is important *when you decide to change an answer,* you erase the first answer completely. If you leave any graphite from the pencil on the wrong space it will cause the scoring machine to cancel the right answer for that question.

Watch Your "Weights." If the examination is "weighted" it means that some parts of the examination are considered more important than others and rated more highly. For instance, you may find that the instructions will indicate "Part I, Weight 50; Part II, Weight 25, Part III, Weight 25." In such a case, you would devote half of your time to the first part, and divide the second half of your time among Parts II and III.

A Funny Thing . . .

. . . happened to you on your way to the bottom of the totem pole. You *thought* the right answer but you marked the *wrong* one.

1. You *mixed answer symbols*! You decided (rightly) that Baltimore (Choice D) was correct. Then you marked *B* (for Baltimore) instead of *D*.
2. You *misread* a simple instruction! Asked to give the *latest* word in a scrambled sentence, you correctly arranged the sentence, and then marked the letter corresponding to the *earliest* word in that miserable sentence.
3. You *inverted digits!* Instead of the correct number, 96, you wrote (or read) 69.

Funny? Tragic! Stay away from accidents.

Record your answers on the answer sheet one by one as you answer the questions. Care should be taken that these answers are recorded next to the appropriate numbers on your answer sheet. It is poor practice to write your answers first on the test booklet and then to transfer them all at one time to the answer sheet. This procedure causes many errors. And then, how would you feel if you ran out of time before you had a chance to transfer all the answers.

When and How To Guess

Read the directions carefully to determine the scoring method that will be used. In some tests, the directions will indicate that guessing is advisable if you do not know the answer to a question. In such tests, only the right answers are counted in determining your score. If such is the case, don't omit any items. If you do not know the answer, or if you are not sure of your answer, then *guess*.

On the other hand, if the directions state that a scoring formula *will* be used in determining your score or that you are *not to guess,* then *omit* the question if you do not know the answer, or if you are not sure of the answer. When the scoring formula is used, a percentage of the *wrong* answers will be subtracted from the number of *right* answers as a correction for haphazard guessing. It is improbable, therefore, that mere guessing will improve your score significantly. *It may even lower your score.* Another disadvantage in guessing under such circumstances is that it consumes valuable time that you might profitably use in answering the questions you know.

If, however, you are uncertain of the correct answer but have *some* knowledge of the question and are able to eliminate one or more of the answer choices as wrong, your chance of getting the right answer is improved, and it will be to your advantage to *answer* such a question rather than *omit* it.

BEAT THE ANSWER SHEET

Even though you've had plenty of practice with the answer sheet used on machine-scored examinations, we must give you a few more, last-minute pointers.

The present popularity of tests requires the use of electrical test scoring machines. With these machines, scoring which would require the labor of several men for hours can be handled by one man in a fraction of the time.

The scoring machine is an amazingly intricate and helpful device, but the machine is not human. The machine cannot, for example, tell the difference between an intended answer and a stray pencil mark, and will count both indiscriminately. The machine cannot count a pencil mark, if the pencil mark is not brought in contact with the electrodes. For these reasons, specially printed answer sheets with response spaces properly located and properly filled in must be employed. Since not all pencil leads contain the necessary ingredients, a special pencil must be used and a heavy solid mark must be made to indicate answers.

(a) Each pencil mark must be heavy and black. Light marks should be retraced with the special pencil.

(b) Each mark must be in the space between the pair of dotted lines and entirely fill this space.

(c) All stray pencil marks on the paper, clearly not intended as answers, must be completely erased.

(d) Each question must have only one answer indicated. If multiple answers occur, all extraneous marks should be thoroughly erased. Otherwise, the machine will give you *no* credit for your correct answer.

Be sure to use the special electrographic pencil!

HERE'S HOW TO MARK YOUR ANSWERS ON MACHINE-SCORED ANSWER SHEETS:

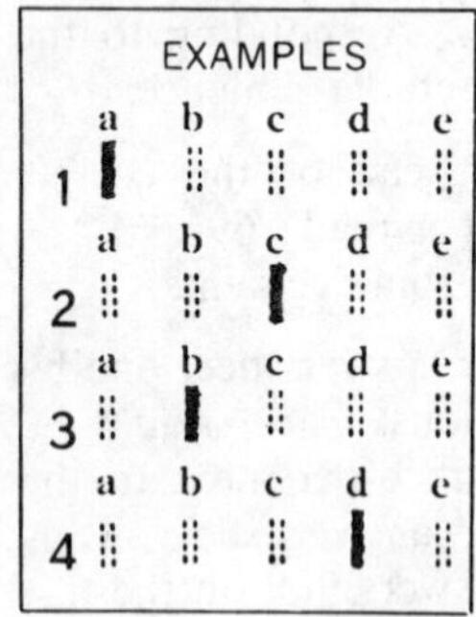

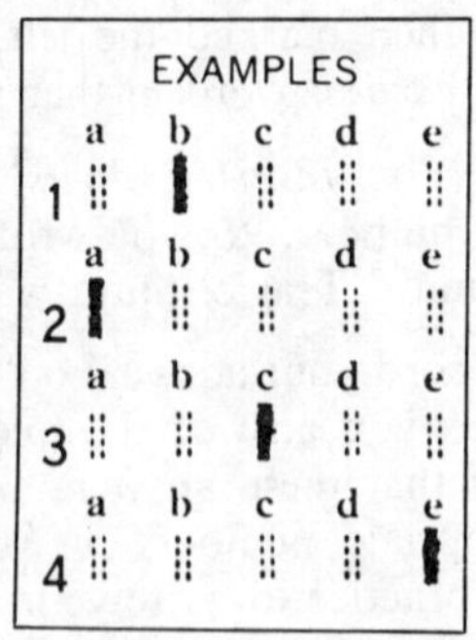

Make only ONE mark for each answer. Additional and stray marks may be counted as mistakes. In making corrections, erase errors COMPLETELY. Make glossy black marks.

Your answer sheet is the only one that reaches the office where papers are scored. For this reason it is important that the blanks at the top be filled in completely and correctly. The proctors will check this, but just in case they slip up, make certain yourself that your paper is complete.

Many exams caution competitors against making any marks on the test booklet itself. Obey that caution even though it goes against your grain to work neatly. If you work neatly and obediently with the test booklet you'll probably do the same with the answer sheet. And that pays off in high scores.

THE GIST OF TEST STRATEGY

- APPROACH THE TEST CONFIDENTLY. TAKE IT CALMLY.

- REMEMBER TO REVIEW, THE WEEK BEFORE THE TEST.

- DON'T "CRAM." BE CAREFUL OF YOUR DIET AND SLEEP ... ESPECIALLY AS THE TEST DRAWS NIGH.

- ARRIVE ON TIME ... AND READY.

- BRING THE COMPLETE KIT OF "TOOLS" YOU'LL NEED.

- CHOOSE A GOOD SEAT. GET COMFORTABLE AND RELAX.

- LISTEN CAREFULLY TO ALL DIRECTIONS.

- APPORTION YOUR TIME INTELLIGENTLY WITH AN "EXAM BUDGET."

- READ ALL DIRECTIONS CAREFULLY. TWICE IF NECESSARY. PAY PARTICULAR ATTENTION TO THE SCORING PLAN.

- LOOK OVER THE WHOLE TEST BEFORE ANSWERING ANY QUESTIONS.

- START RIGHT IN, IF POSSIBLE. STAY WITH IT. USE EVERY SECOND EFFECTIVELY.

- DO THE EASY QUESTIONS FIRST; POSTPONE HARDER QUESTIONS UNTIL LATER.

- DETERMINE THE PATTERN OF THE TEST QUESTIONS. IF IT'S HARD-EASY ETC., ANSWER ACCORDINGLY.

- READ EACH QUESTION CAREFULLY. MAKE SURE YOU UNDERSTAND EACH ONE BEFORE YOU ANSWER. RE-READ, IF NECESSARY.

- THINK! AVOID HURRIED ANSWERS. GUESS INTELLIGENTLY.
- WATCH YOUR WATCH AND "EXAM BUDGET," BUT DO A LITTLE BALANCING OF THE TIME YOU DEVOTE TO EACH QUESTION.
- GET ALL THE HELP YOU CAN FROM "CUE" WORDS.
- REPHRASE DIFFICULT QUESTIONS FOR YOURSELF. WATCH OUT FOR "SPOILERS."
- REFRESH YOURSELF WITH A FEW, WELL-CHOSEN REST PAUSES DURING THE TEST.
- USE CONTROLLED ASSOCIATION TO SEE THE RELATION OF ONE QUESTION TO ANOTHER AND WITH AS MANY IMPORTANT IDEAS AS YOU CAN DEVELOP.
- NOW THAT YOU'RE A "COOL" TEST-TAKER, STAY CALM AND CONFIDENT THROUGHOUT THE TEST. DON'T LET ANYTHING THROW YOU.
- EDIT, CHECK, PROOFREAD YOUR ANSWERS. BE A "BITTER ENDER." STAY WORKING UNTIL THEY MAKE YOU GO.

FOR FURTHER STUDY

ARCO BOOKS FOR MORE HELP

Now what? You've read and studied the whole book, and there's still time before you take the test. You're probably better prepared than most of your competitors, but you may feel insecure about one or more of the probable test subjects. If so, you can still do something about it. Glance over this comprehensive list of books. One of them may be just what you need to assure your success.

Countless attractive careers are open to test takers, as you will see from this selective listing of Arco Books. One or more of them can assure success in the test you are now taking. Perhaps you've discovered that you are weak in language, verbal ability or mathematics. You can brush up in the privacy of your own home with a specialized Arco Book. Why flounder and fail when help is so easily available? Perhaps even more important than doing your best on your present test is to consider other opportunities that are open to you. Look over the lists and make plans for your future. You might get a few ideas for other tests you can start to study for *now*. By taking job tests now you place yourself in the enviable position of picking and choosing the *ideal* job. You'll be able to select from several positions. You won't have to settle for the one (or none).

Each of the following books was created under the same expert editorial supervision that produced the excellent book you are now using.

So even though we only list titles and prices, you can be sure that each book performs a real service . . . saves floundering and failure.

Every Arco Book is guaranteed. Return it for full refund in 10 days if not completely satisfied.

Whatever your goal . . . CIVIL SERVICE . . . TRADE LICENSE . . . TEACHING . . . PROFESSIONAL LICENSE . . . SCHOLARSHIP . . . ENTRANCE TO THE SCHOOL OF *YOUR* CHOICE . . . you can achieve it through the PROVEN QUESTION AND ANSWER METHOD.

START YOUR CAREER BY MAILING THIS COUPON TODAY

ORDER NOW from your bookseller or direct from:

ARCO PUBLISHING COMPANY, INC. 219 Park Avenue South, New York, N.Y. 10003

Please Rush The Following Arco Books
(Order by Number or Title)

. . . .

. . . .

. . . .

. . . .

. . . .

. . . .

☐ I enclose check, cash or money order for $________(price of books, plus 50¢ for first book and 25¢ for each additional book, packing and mailing charge) No C.O.D.'s accepted.

RESIDENTS OF N.Y. AND CALIF. ADD APPROPRIATE SALES TAX.

☐ Please tell me if you have an ARCO COURSE for the position of . . . .

. . . .

☐ Please send me your free COMPLETE CATALOG

NAME________________________________

STREET______________________________

CITY______________STATE______________ZIP # __________

S3420

CIVIL SERVICE AND TEST PREPARATION—GENERAL

Title	No.	Price
Able Seaman, Deckhand, Scowman	01376-1	5.00
Accountant—Auditor	00001-5	6.00
Addiction Specialist, Senior, Supervising, Principal, Turner	03351-7	8.00
Administrative Assistant	00148-8	8.00
Air Traffic Controller, Turner	02088-1	7.00
American Foreign Service Officer	00081-3	5.00
Apprentice, Mechanical Trades	00571-8	5.00
Assistant Accountant—Junior Accountant—Account Clerk	00056-2	6.00
Assistant Station Supervisor, Turner	03736-9	6.00
Associate and Administrative Accountant	03863-2	6.00
Attorney, Assistant—Trainee	01084-3	8.00
Auto Machinist	00513-0	6.00
Auto Mechanic, Autoserviceman	00514-9	6.00
Bank Examiner—Trainee and Assistant	01642-6	5.00
Battalion and Deputy Chief, F.D.	00515-7	6.00
Beginning Office Worker	00173-9	6.00
Beverage Control Investigator	00150-X	4.00
Bookkeeper—Account Clerk, Turner	00035-X	6.00
Bridge and Tunnel Officer—Special Officer	00780-X	5.00
Building Custodian	00013-9	6.00
Bus Maintainer—Bus Mechanic	00111-9	5.00
Bus Operator	01553-5	5.00
Buyer, Assistant Buyer, Purchase Inspector	01366-4	6.00
Captain, Fire Department	00121-6	10.00
Captain, Police Department	00184-4	8.00
Carpenter	00135-6	6.00
Case Worker, Turner	01528-4	8.00
Cashier, Housing Teller	00703-6	4.00
Cement Mason—Mason's Helper, Turner	03745-8	6.00
Chemist—Assistant Chemist	00116-X	5.00
City Planner	01364-8	6.00
Civil Engineer, Senior, Associate, & Administrative, Turner	00146-1	8.00
Civil Service Arithmetic and Vocabulary	00003-1	4.00
Civil Service Course, Gitlin	00702-8	5.00
Teacher's Manual for Civil Service Course, Gitlin	03838-1	2.00
Civil Service Handbook	00040-6	2.00
Claim Examiner—Law Investigator	00149-6	5.00
Clerk New York City	00045-7	4.00
Clerk—Steno Transcriber	00838-5	6.00
College Office Assistant	00181-X	5.00
Complete Guide to U.S. Civil Service Jobs	00537-8	2.00
Construction Foreman—Supervisor—Inspector	01085-1	5.00
Consumer Affairs Inspector	01356-7	6.00
Correction Captain—Deputy Warden	01358-3	8.00
Correction Officer	00186-0	6.00
Court Officer	00519-X	6.00
Criminal Law Quizzer, Salottolo	02399-6	8.00
Criminal Science Quizzer, Salottolo	02407-0	5.00
Detective Investigator, Turner	03738-5	6.00
Draftsman, Civil and Mechanical Engineering (All Grades)	01225-0	6.00
Electrical Engineer	00137-2	5.00
Electrical Inspector	03350-9	8.00
Electrician	00084-8	6.00
Electronic Equipment Maintainer, Turner	01836-4	6.00
Elevator Operator	00051-1	3.00
Employment Interviewer	00008-2	6.00
Employment Security Clerk	00700-1	6.00
Engineering Technician (All Grades), Turner	01226-9	6.00
Exterminator Foreman—Foreman of Housing Exterminators	03740-7	6.00
File Clerk	00962-4	5.00
Fire Administration and Technology	00604-8	6.00
Firefighting Hydraulics, Bonadio	00572-6	7.50
Fireman, F.D.	00010-4	6.00
Food Service Supervisor—School Lunch Manager	01378-8	6.00
Foreman of Auto Mechanics	01360-5	6.00
Foreman	00191-7	5.00
Gardener, Assistant Gardener	01340-0	6.00
General Entrance Series, Arco Editorial Board	01961-1	4.00
General Test Practice for 92 U.S. Jobs	00011-2	5.00
Guard—Patrolman	00122-4	5.00
Heavy Equipment Operator (Portable Engineer)	01372-9	5.00
Homestudy Course for Civil Service Jobs, Turner	01587-X	6.00
Hospital Attendant	00012-0	4.00
Hospital Care Investigator Trainee (Social Case Worker I)	01074-4	5.00
Hospital Clerk	01718-X	3.00
Hospital Security Officer	03866-7	6.00
Housing Assistant	00054-6	5.00
Housing Caretaker	00504-1	4.00
Housing Inspector	00055-4	5.00
Housing Manager—Assistant Housing Manager	00813-X	5.00
Housing Patrolman	00192-5	5.00
How to Pass Employment Tests, Liebers	00715-X	5.00
Internal Revenue Agent	00093-7	5.00
Investigator—Inspector	01670-1	5.00
Junior Administrator Development Examination (JADE)	01643-4	5.00
Junior and Assistant Civil Engineer	01228-5	5.00
Junior Federal Assistant	01729-5	6.00
Laboratory Aide, Arco Editorial Board	01121-1	5.00
Laborer—Federal, State and City Jobs	00566-1	4.00
Landscape Architect	01368-0	5.00
Laundry Worker	01834-8	4.00
Law and Court Stenographer	00783-4	6.00
Law Enforcement Positions	00500-9	6.00
Librarian	00060-0	8.00
Lieutenant, F.D.	00123-2	8.00
Lieutenant, P.D.	00190-9	8.00
Machinist—Machinist's Helper	01123-8	6.00
Mail Handler—U.S. Postal Service	00126-7	5.00
Maintainer's Helper, Group A and C—Transit Electrical Helper	00175-5	6.00
Maintenance Man	00113-5	5.00
Management and Administration Quizzer	01537-3	6.00
Management Analyst, Assistant-Associate	03864-0	8.00
Mathematics, Simplified and Self-Taught	00567-X	4.00
Mechanical Apprentice (Maintainer's Helper B)	00176-3	5.00
Mechanical Aptitude and Spatial Relations Tests	00539-4	6.00
Mechanical Engineer—Junior, Assistant & Senior Grades	03314-2	8.00
Messenger	00017-1	3.00
Mortuary Caretaker	01354-0	6.00
Motor Vehicle License Examiner	00018-X	5.00
Motor Vehicle Operator	00576-9	4.00
Motorman (Subways)	00061-9	6.00
Nurse	00143-7	6.00
Office Assistant GS 1-4 Office Aide	00043-0	5.00
Office Machines Operator	00728-1	4.00
1540 Questions and Answers for Electricians	00754-0	5.00
1340 Questions and Answers for Firefighters, McGannon	00857-1	4.00
Painter	01772-4	5.00
Parking Enforcement Agent	00701-X	4.00
Patrol Inspector	00101-1	4.00
Peace Corps Placement Exams, Turner	01641-8	4.00
Personnel Examiner, Junior Personnel Examiner	00648-X	6.00
Plumber—Plumber's Helper	00517-3	6.00
Police Administration and Criminal Investigation	00565-3	6.00
Police Administrative Aide, Turner	02345-7	5.00
Police Officer—Patrolman P.D, Murray	00019-8	6.00
Police Science Advancement—Police Promotion Course	02636-7	10.00
Policewoman	00062-7	6.00
Post Office Clerk-Carrier	00021-X	5.00
Post Office Motor Vehicle Operator	01162-9	4.00

EDUCATIONAL BOOKS

HIGH SCHOOL AND COLLEGE PREPARATION

Title	Order No.	Price
American College Testing Program Exams	00694-3	5.00
Arco Arithmetic Q & A Review, Turner	02351-1	4.00
Better Business English, Classen	01350-8	3.50
Catholic High School Entrance Examination	00987-X	4.00
The College Board's Examination, McDonough & Hansen	02623-5	4.00
College By Mail, Jensen	02592-1	4.00
College Entrance Tests, Turner	01858-5	5.00
College-Level Examination Program (CLEP), Turner	02574-3	6.00
College Scholarships	00569-6	2.00
The Easy Way to Better Grades, Froe & Froe	03352-5	1.50
Elements of Debate, Klopf & McCroskey	01901-8	4.00
Encyclopedia of English, Zeiger	00655-X	2.50
English Grammar: 1,000 Steps	02012-1	4.00
English Grammar and Usage for Test-Takers, Turner	04014-9	6.00
Good English with Ease, Beckoff	00859-8	2.00
Good English with Ease, Revised edition, Beckoff	03911-6	4.00
Guide to Financial Aids for Students in Arts and Sciences for Graduate and Professional Study, Searles & Scott	02496-8	3.95
Guide to Success in Obtaining Money for College, Lever	03932-9	3.95
High School Entrance and Scholarship Tests, Turner	00666-8	4.00
High School Entrance Examinations—Special Public and Private High Schools	02143-8	5.00
How to Prepare Your College Application, Kussin & Kussin	01310-9	2.00
How to Write Reports, Papers, Theses, Articles, Riebel	02391-0	5.00
Mastering Modern General Mathematics for Secondary School, McDonough	03732-6	5.00
New York State Regents Scholarship	00400-2	4.00
Organization and Outlining, Peirce	02425-9	4.00
Practice for Scholastic Aptitude Tests	01035-5	.95
Scholastic Aptitude Tests	02038-5	5.00
Scoring High on the NMSQT-PSAT, Turner	00413-4	5.00
Scoring High on Reading Tests	00731-1	5.00
Triple Your Reading Speed, Cutler	02083-0	3.00
Typing for Everyone, Levine	02212-4 S	3.95

GED PREPARATION

Title	Order No.	Price
Comprehensive Math Review for the High School Equivalency Diploma Test, McDonough	03420-3	4.00
High School Equivalency Diploma Tests, Turner	00110-0	5.00
Learning to Use Our Language, Pulaski	01518-7	2.50
Preliminary Arithmetic For The High School Equivalency Diploma Test	02165-9	4.00
Preliminary Practice for the High School Equivalency Diploma Test	01441-3	4.00
Preparation for the Spanish High School Equivalency Diploma (Preparacion Para El Exam De Equivalencia De La Escuela Superior—En Espanol)	02618-9	6.00
Step-By-Step Guide to Correct English, Pulaski	03402-5	3.95

General Education Development Series

Title	Order No.	Price
Correctness and Effectiveness of Expression (English HSEDT), Castellano, Guercio & Seitz	03688-5	4.00
General Mathematical Ability (Mathematics HSEDT), Castellano, Guercio & Seitz	03689-3	4.00
Reading Interpretation in Social Sciences, Natural Sciences, and Literature (Reading HSEDT), Castellano, Guercio & Seitz	03690-4	4.00
Teacher's Manual for the GED Series, Castellano, Guercio & Seitz	03692-2	2.50

COLLEGE BOARD ACHIEVEMENT TESTS

Title	Order No.	Price
American History and Social Studies Achievement Test, Altman	01722-8	1.45
Biology Achievement Test, Miller & Weiss	01263-3	.95
Chemistry Achievement Test, Spector & Weiss	01264-1	.95
English Composition Achievement Test	01247-1	.95
French Achievement Test, Biezunski & Boisrond	01668-X	1.45
German Achievement Test, Greiner	01698-1	1.45
Latin Achievement Test	01743-0	1.45
Mathematics: Level I Achievement Test, Bramson	03847-0	3.00
Mathematics: Level II Achievement Test, Bramson	01456-3	.95
Physics Achievement Test, Bruenn	01265-X	1.95
Spanish Achievement Test, Jassey	01741-4	1.45

ARCO COLLEGE CREDIT TEST-TUTORS

Title	Order No.	Price
American History: CLEP and AP Subject Examination, Woloch	03804-7	4.95

PROFESSIONAL CAREER EXAM SERIES

Title	Order No.	Price
Action Guide for Executive Job Seekers and Employers, Uris	01787-2	3.95
Bar Exams	01124-6	5.00
The C.P.A. Exam: Accounting by the "Parallel Point" Method (Two Volumes), Lipscomb	02020-2	15.00
Certificate in Data Processing Examination, Morrison	04032-7	12.00
Certified General Automobile Mechanic, Turner	02900-5	6.00
Computer Programmer, Luftig	01232-3	6.00
Computers and Automation, Brown	01745-7	5.00
Graduate Management Admission Test	03926-4	6.00
Graduate Record Examination Aptitude	00824-5	5.00
Handbook for the Medical College Admission Test, Gladstone, Chazen & Brazil	03500-5	5.00
Health Insurance Agent (Hospital, Accident, Health, Life)	02153-5	5.00
How a Computer System Works, Brown & Workman	03424-6	5.95
How to Become a Successful Model, Krem	03625-7	5.00
The Installation and Servicing of Domestic Oil Burners, Mitchell & Mitchell	00437-1	10.00
Insurance Agent and Broker	02149-7	6.00
Law School Admission Test, Turner	00840-7	5.00
Life Insurance Agents' Examination	02343-0	5.00
A Manual for Certified General Automobile Mechanic (NIASE) Tests, Sharp	03809-8	6.00
Medical College Admission Test, Turner	00996-9	5.00
Miller Analogies Test—1400 Analogy Questions	01114-9	4.00
The 1976-77 Airline Guide to Stewardess and Steward Careers, Morton	02435-6	4.95
Notary Public	00180-1	6.00
Nursing School Entrance Examination, Turner	01202-1	6.00
Oil Burner Installer	00096-1	6.00
The Official 1976-77 Guide to Airline Careers, Morton	03955-8	5.95
Playground and Recreation Director's Handbook	01096-7	6.00
Quizzer for Students of Education, Walton	01447-4	4.00
Real Estate License Examination, Gladstone	03755-5	5.00
Real Estate Salesman and Broker	00098-8	6.00
Refrigeration License Manual, Harfenist	02726-6	10.00
Resumes for Executive Job Hunters, Shykind	02424-0	4.00
Resumes That Get Jobs, Revised edition, Resume Service	03909-4	3.00
Security Representatives' Examinations, Stefano	01934-4	5.00
Simplify Legal Writing, Biskind	03801-2	5.00
Stationary Engineer and Fireman	00070-8	6.00
The Test of English as a Foreign Language (TOEFL), Moreno, Babin & Scallon	02944-7	6.00
Your Resume—Key to a Better Job, Corwen	LR 03734-2	7.00

ADVANCED GRE SERIES

Title	Order No.	Price
Biology: Advanced Test for the G.R.E., Miller	01068-1	3.95
Business: Advanced Test for the G.R.E., Berman, Malea & Yearwood	01599-3	3.95

Title		Code	Price
Postal Inspector	______	00194-1	**5.00**
Postal Promotion Foreman—Supervisor	______	00538-6	**6.00**
Postal Service Officer	______	01658-2	**5.00**
Postmaster	______	01522-5	**5.00**
Practice for Civil Service Promotion	______	00023-6	**6.00**
Practice for Clerical, Typing and Stenographic Tests	______	00005-8	**5.00**
Principal Clerk—Stenographer	______	01523-3	**5.00**
Probation and Parole Officer	______	01542-X	**6.00**
Professional and Administrative Career Examination (PACE)	______	03653-2	**6.00**
Professional Careers Test	______	01543-8	**6.00**
Professional Trainee—Administrative Aide	______	01183-1	**5.00**
Public Health Sanitarian, Coyne	______	00985-3	**8.00**
Railroad Clerk	______	00067-8	**4.00**
Railroad Porter	______	00128-3	**4.00**
Real Estate Assessor—Appraiser—Manager	______	00563-7	**8.00**
Resident Building Superintendent	______	00068-6	**5.00**
Road Car Inspector (T.A.), Turner	______	03743-1	**6.00**
Sanitation Foreman (Foreman & Asst. Foreman)	______	01958-1	**6.00**
Sanitation Man	______	00025-2	**4.00**
School Crossing Guard	______	00611-0	**4.00**
Securing and Protecting Your Rights in Civil Service, Resnicoff	______	02714-2	**4.95**
Senior Clerical Series	______	01173-4	**6.00**
Senior Clerk—Stenographer	______	01797-X	**6.00**
Senior File Clerk, Turner	______	00124-0	**5.00**
Senior and Supervising Parking Enforcement Agent, Turner	______	03737-7	**6.00**
Senior Typist	______	03870-5	**6.00**
Sergeant, P.D.	______	00026-0	**7.00**
Shop Clerk, Turner	______	03684-2	**6.00**
Social Supervisor	______	00028-7	**6.00**
Staff Attendant	______	00828-8	**4.00**
Staff Positions: Senior Administrative Associate and Assistant	______	03490-4	**6.00**
State Trooper	______	00078-3	**6.00**
Statistician—Statistical Clerk	______	00058-9	**5.00**
Stenographer—Typist (Practical Preparation)	______	00147-X	**5.00**
Stenographer—U.S. Government Positions	______	00031-7	**6.00**
Storekeeper—Stockman, Senior Storekeeper	______	01691-4	**6.00**
Structural Apprentice, Turner	______	00177-1	**5.00**
Structure Maintainer Trainee, Groups A to E, Turner	______	03683-4	**6.00**
Supervising Clerk—Income Maintenance	______	02879-3	**6.00**
Supervising Clerk—Stenographer	______	01685-X	**5.00**
Supervision Course	______	01590-X	**5.00**
Surface Line Dispatcher	______	00140-2	**6.00**
Tabulating Machine Operator (IBM)	______	00781-8	**4.00**
Taking Tests and Scoring High, Honig	______	01347-8	**4.00**
Telephone Maintainer: New York City Transit Authority	______	03742-3	**5.00**
Telephone Operator	______	00033-3	**5.00**
Test Your Vocational Aptitude, Asta & Bernbach	______	03606-0	**6.00**
Towerman (Municipal Subway System)	______	00157-7	**5.00**
Trackman (Municipal Subways), Turner	______	00075-9	**5.00**
Track Foreman: New York City Transit Authority	______	03793-3	**6.00**
Traffic Control Agent	______	03421-1	**5.00**
Train Dispatcher	______	00158-5	**5.00**
Transit Patrolman	______	00092-9	**5.00**
Transit Sergeant—Lieutenant	______	00161-5	**4.00**
Treasury Enforcement Agent	______	00131-3	**6.00**
U.S. Professional Mid-Level Positions Grades GS-9 Through GS-12	______	02036-9	**6.00**
U.S. Summer Jobs, Turner	______	02480-1	**4.00**
Ventilation and Drainage Maintainer: New York City Transit Authority, Turner	______	03741-5	**6.00**
Vocabulary Builder and Guide to Verbal Tests	______	00535-1	**4.00**
Vocabulary, Spelling and Grammar	______	00077-5	**4.00**
Welder	______	01374-5	**5.00**
X-Ray Technician	______	01122-X	**4.00**

MILITARY EXAMINATION SERIES

Title		Code	Price
Practice for Army Classification and Placement (ASVAB)	______	03845-4	**6.00**
Practice for the Armed Forces Tests	______	00063-5	**5.00**
Practice for the Navy's Basic Test Battery	______	01300-1	**5.00**
Practice for Air Force Placement Tests	______	01302-8	**6.00**
Practice for Officer Candidate Tests	______	01304-4	**6.00**
Tests for Women the Armed Forces	______	03821-7	**6.00**
U.S. Service Academies	______	01544-6	**6.00**